Foreword

I came of age during the classic phase of the civil rights movement, years when marching and nonviolent direct-action protest took on enormous visibility as powerful and effective weapons for social change. The previous era's legalistic approach, exemplified in the court cases that led to and included *Brown v. Board*, seemed to me and my generation a bit too slow and old-fashioned. The movement in the 1960s was dramatically brought into our own homes through television and other media coverage. We watched the footage of the many events with the same depth of personal emotion and concern that people today watch the videos recorded on phones that catch outrageous acts of brutal injustice. Who can forget the image of James Meredith's entrance into Ole Miss, the firebombed bus of the Freedom Riders, the vicious police attacks on peaceful but unswerving protesters in Birmingham, the eloquent plea of Martin Luther King Jr. at the triumphal March on Washington for the passage of a civil rights act, and the courageous Student Nonviolent Coordinating Committee workers along with the indomitable Fannie Lou Hamer in the Southern voting registration drive of Freedom Summer? Whether witnessed in person or via the media as they occurred, such images were branded on our minds. They will never be forgotten.

Yet we have forgotten, if we ever knew at all, the lawyers who played crucial roles in those events. In the 1960s my generation of activists certainly underemphasized, if not undervalued, Constance Baker Motley of the NAACP Legal Defense and Educational Fund, who argued and won the court battle over Meredith's right to enroll at the University of Mississippi and who walked beside Meredith along the dangerous, heckler-laden path to the school's registrar. Nor did we credit at the time the prowess of the NAACP lobbyist and lawyer Clarence Mitchell in the formulation and successful passage of the congressional legislation that became the Civil Rights Act of 1964. In like manner, my generation of activists boldly voiced our solidarity with the Third World, with the people of color in Asia and Africa who had attained independent nationhood after World War II or found themselves still in the throes of anticolonial struggles in the 1950s and 1960s, and yet we neither recognized nor understood the significant earlier interventions of Walter White and the NAACP in those anticolonial struggles in the late 1940s. This knowledge would come many years later.

Because of the burgeoning scholarship in the past three decades, I have been made keenly aware of my earlier ignorance and have learned as a professor of history to look for continuities over greater periods of time. The "long civil rights movement," according to current studies, encompassed several generations of struggle from the 1930s through the 1970s. Nowhere is this more apparent than in the autobiography of Nathaniel R. Jones, since the vitality of his legal work proved relevant for each generation of activists. Several themes run through the book in this regard. The Northern side of the civil rights movement represents a theme vividly portrayed. Jones's autobiography underscores the emphasis of contemporary historians who call attention to a decades-long protest tradition of blacks in cities outside the South for equal access to public accommodations, for integrated schools and the end to racial disparities in educational resources, and for jobs and housing. Another theme concerns the persistent relevance of the National Association for the Advancement of Colored People. Contrary to images of an elite, top-down organization that grew increasingly out of touch with the

pulse of social activism in the 1960s and 1970s, the NAACP continued during those decades to be at the heart of civil rights challenges. A membership-based organization, the NAACP through its
general counsel Nathaniel Jones took up the legal fight of ordinary
men and women who sought a better life for themselves and their
children.

Jones was hardly out of step with later generations of activists. Of
his years as general counsel for the NAACP between 1969 and 1979,
he writes, "I established my reputation on the steady wave of issues
that emerged involving student protests, military justice, school
desegregation, employment and housing discrimination, and police
excesses." In the late 1960s, when students like myself joined with
other black students both in predominantly white and in historically black colleges and universities to demand Black Studies in
the curriculum, the supportive action of the NAACP saved the day
for the protesting students at San Fernando State College in 1969,
after general counsel Nathaniel Jones arrived to defend them in
court. During the era of black power, Jones had overall responsibility for the historic constitutional cases of public school desegregation (often reduced to the description of mere "school busing cases"
by racist school districts) in Detroit, Cleveland, and Boston. Particularly striking in bridging the 1930s and 1970s is the story of the
last "Scottsboro Boy," Clarence Norris, who while a fugitive from the
law finally won his pardon in 1976 from Governor George Wallace
of Alabama through the NAACP's carefully devised legal strategy.
Answering the Call retrieves from obscurity a valuable but forgotten
chapter in history.

My marriage to A. Leon Higginbotham Jr., an outspoken advocate of racial equality until his death in 1998, also broadened my
understanding of the problem of race in the American legal process and the centrality of lawyers in every phase of the movement.
It was through Leon that I came to know Nathaniel Jones. Leon
met Jones in the 1940s, when both men were in college in Ohio,
and considered him to be a lifelong friend. Their paths followed a
similar trajectory of civil rights lawyering and federal judgeships.
Both remained stalwart in their criticism of the Supreme Court's

retreat from civil rights, which gained momentum during the last decade of the twentieth century. This theme stands out prominently in the critique of Justice Clarence Thomas and his rejection of the constitutionality of the very racial remedies that Thurgood Marshall, his predecessor on the Supreme Court, had formulated during his years as a civil rights lawyer and jurist.

Finally, the international theme of the black freedom struggle comes across in a fascinating way in *Answering the Call*. Given my husband's trips to South Africa both for research and for work with antiapartheid lawyers in the 1980s, I kept abreast of similar activities on the part of Jones. One of the most riveting stories in the autobiography and one that made international news recounts the arrest and imprisonment of Jones, at the time a U.S. federal judge, by the South African police in 1985 for being among those entering a black township deemed threatening to the racist apartheid regime.

Today, as activists march and organize in protest over the killings of unarmed African Americans by the police in cities across this nation, the autobiography of Nathaniel Jones offers a message of inspiration in regard to the continuing struggle for equal justice under the law. I daresay it is a message that speaks compellingly to several generations of struggle. That each generation must have its "rendezvous with destiny," to paraphrase Franklin D. Roosevelt, has been a problem for each generation that does not know or learn from the previous one. And there are lessons to be learned for those who strive in the twenty-first century to dismantle systemic racial inequalities as seen in concentrated poverty, the lack of resources in inner-city schools, disparate sentencing and incarceration, and police brutality. In *Answering the Call*, Jones conveys a profound understanding of the American legal system's historically fraught relationship with black people—be it the slave laws that enshrined the ownership of his great-grandparents and grandparents as human property or the Jim Crow laws that validated racial segregation from the late nineteenth century to the mid-1960; the denial of blacks' right to vote; the racialized penal system of convict leasing in the late nineteenth and early twentieth centuries; or lynching and other forms of mob violence against blacks that led to the founding of the

NAACP in 1909. Yet Nathaniel Jones's life story also conveys experiential knowledge of the importance of civil rights lawyers as well as the judges and elected officials committed to challenging and breaking down racial barriers—to making America live up to its promise of liberty and justice for all. Few persons in the twenty-first century can claim such a long, illustrious, and ongoing role in the struggle for civil rights.

Reminiscent of a religious leader who answers God's call to preach, Jones answered the call of Justice. At a young age in the 1930s, he became conscious of the obligation to fight racial discrimination, which existed not in a distant place but in the separate and unequal realities of jobs, housing, schools, and amusements in his hometown of Youngstown, Ohio. Some eight decades later, this sense of obligation has not faltered. And it is this continuum that *Answering the Call* captures so poignantly and cogently. The civil rights champion and labor leader A. Philip Randolph expressed such a viewpoint in regard to his people's history of struggle when he asserted: "Freedom is never granted; it is won. Justice is never given; it is exacted. Freedom and justice must be struggled for by the oppressed of all lands and races, and the struggle must be continuous, for freedom is never a final fact, but a continuing evolving process to higher and higher levels of human, social, economic, political and religious relationships." *Answering the Call* is ultimately a testament of faith in the black freedom struggle.

Evelyn Brooks Higginbotham
Harvard University

Preface: Why This Book?

Three incidents in the late 1980s and early 1990s combined to focus me on the need to write this book.

The first arose during a meeting of the Good Samaritan Hospital Board of Trustees in Cincinnati. The board was considering a request by the American Hospital Association to sign on to health-care reform policy being developed by the Clinton administration. One of the trustees objected because of the role of "government." I had been on the board for a couple of years and that was not the first time a board member had expressed antigovernment sentiments. After eight years of government bashing by the Reagan administration and its apostles, this, however, was the last straw. I erupted with passion, challenging the notion that "government" is inherently evil. I noted that, as a federal judge, I was part of government, resented the implications of the remark, and was prepared to resign. This drew a chorus of noes from others, including the chairman, Robert Castellini, and the CEO, Sister Myra James Bradley.

I reminded the board that Timothy McVeigh had recently been charged in connection with bombing the Oklahoma City Federal Building. McVeigh was arrested by a deputy sheriff (a government employee), who observed a vehicle on a county road with an expired license tag. The arrest led to the solving of that horrendous crime. As the board debated the balking member's objection and my reaction, Castellini offered a personal testimonial to the positive role that government plays in American life. He said that his family's produce business owed much to the rigorously enforced standards of the U.S. Department of Agriculture, which ensured public confidence in their products. This testimony, coming from a hard-nosed "free-market capitalist," put the antigovernment challengers back on their heels. The motion was approved. Later in the day, both Castellini and Sister Myra James thanked me for the "lesson" taught to the board. The lesson was simply this: too few Americans, including those well-heeled board members, connect their own health and safety to the role that governmental policies and agencies play.

I had been troubled on the Sixth Circuit Court by a number of Reagan-appointed judges who expressed and acted with similar antigovernment sentiments. That goal was to shut down the programs that had enlarged opportunities for the poor and blacks. Having grown up in the Great Depression and benefited from the lifeline that had been tossed to my family and virtually everyone within our acquaintance, I knew firsthand what these programs mean to people. When I was in college (courtesy of the GI Bill) I was socially and politically active in my hometown, Youngstown, Ohio. That activism led to my being appointed to the Mahoning County Welfare Advisory Board, which worked with the director of welfare and the staff to shape the welfare policies of the county. The six other board members included a business leader, a labor-union official, religious leaders, and public officials. The policies included issues of health and welfare for persons of limited or no means, including the aged. This was in the 1950s, before the Great Society, Medicare, and Medicaid. As a result of this experience, and that of my own family during the Depression years, I have a deep appreciation for the role of government in providing a social safety net.

The second incident that convinced me to share my experiences and perspectives took place during a conference of the court in 1994. The Sixth Circuit Court of Appeals, sitting en banc, was considering a challenge to the affirmative action plan of the City of Memphis. The plan was a part of a consent decree that settled a racial discrimination case brought against the Memphis Police and Fire Departments by black applicants and officers. In order to avoid airing its dirty linen regarding the treatment of blacks, the city agreed to adopt an affirmative action plan that would ensure the hiring and promotion of blacks in the police and fire departments. Judge Odell Horton, a distinguished black jurist appointed by President Carter, approved the settlement and entered the consent decree.

The plan operated successfully for years. Blacks joined the ranks and performed well, and the composition of the police and fire departments began to reflect the actual racial composition of the city. However, some disgruntled white officers complained that the plan's two-track feature resulted in hiring and promoting blacks, some of who tested lower (though all had passing grades) than they did, and thus constituted "reverse discrimination." Judge Horton disagreed, holding that the city agreed to the plan that had been carefully tailored to overcome years of systemic discrimination.

White officers appealed Judge Horton's ruling to the Sixth Circuit. When the case was considered by a three-judge panel, the lower-court ruling was upheld. In accordance with court rules, the dissenting judge sought to have the opinion reconsidered by the full fifteen-member court. Upon a majority of the court agreeing to re-hear the case, the panel opinion was vacated and the issue scheduled for re-argument before the full court. Following the argument, the judges went into conference to decide the fate of the affirmative-action plan. There had been a sufficient change in the personnel of the Sixth Circuit since I joined in 1979, with the addition of four conservative judges appointed by President Reagan, to make a difference. I realized, during the conference debate, that a majority of the judges were unsympathetic to affirmative action and were buying the so-called reverse-discrimination argument. Based upon the arguments that appealed to them, I knew that they were totally lacking in their understanding of the role that racial discrimination played in Memphis and throughout the nation. Our treatment of race in this country fuels a perpetuation of what the late Judge A.

Leon Higginbotham described in his classic, *Shades of Freedom*, as "precepts" of white superiority and black inferiority.[1] These precepts help create the phenomenon of "white entitlement," which empowers those who openly disavow racism to engage in massive resistance to legally mandated racial remedies.

I was dismayed by the lack of knowledge about our country's racial history that my judicial colleagues displayed. Most disturbing was the way in which they enthusiastically cited the views of U.S. Supreme Court Justice Clarence Thomas to justify their votes to kill the plan. I was also disturbed by the same historical ignorance manifested by law students I taught at several of the nation's law schools. While those students were otherwise broadly knowledgeable, when it came to the way this nation has treated race and how that treatment continues to shape attitudes, both personal and institutional, they were ill informed at best. It became increasingly clear to me that I had an obligation to offer my perspective based on my life experiences.

Judges appear to provide a detached, objective approach to the resolution of cases that contain elements of race. As I moved into the inner sanctums of the courts, and interacted, close-up, with judges, it became obvious that judges rarely act with detachment and understanding regarding racial matters. They were numb to the fact that the institutions that govern people's lives are shaped by subjective factors tinged with racial and class stereotypes. Even rarer were judges capable of rising above their own prior social and economic conditioning to apply principles of law in a neutral fashion. One of my objectives in this book is to pull back the curtain and to show the public how serious issues are judicially resolved.

The third incident that convinced me to write the book was Dean Joseph Tomain's request that I turn my papers over to the University of Cincinnati College of Law. I was initially skeptical. On further reflection, however, including the instance at the Good Samaritan Board of Trustees meeting when government was scorned as evil incarnate, my mind slowly turned to my pre-lawyer years on the Welfare Advisory Board and the responsibility that government has to the people. This prompted a visit to my mother's attic, which

held what I had come to regard as my clutter: documents and reports that could illuminate this period of my life and serve as an
antidote to the antigovernment virus. By this time I had a positive
resolve to place these materials, along with others accumulated in
other phases of my life, including ten years as general counsel of
the NAACP, in the bosom of the Law School. I was convinced
that a fundamental goal of the Reagan administration was to shrink
government by starving the programs that served as lifelines for
generations of poor people and to render impotent not only the
agencies charged with enforcing the civil rights laws, but also
the federal courts. Most disturbing was the tendency of alumni of
the earlier governmental rescue missions to buy into the Reagan
antigovernment crusade by voting against their own self-interests,
and the interests of those who had yet to ascend the economic ladder out of poverty. Some of the most uncompromising resistance
to the civil rights remedies formulated by the courts and civil rights
agencies came from white groups who themselves remained at
serious risk of being pushed back into a chasm, which, but for
government, they would still be in. The Tea Party movement is a
powerful result of the Reagan antigovernment virus.

Having grown up among whites, been educated with whites,
played with whites, and having also observed the etiquette of racial
and cultural separation, I have insights into the majority world that
allow me to understand much more about them and their insecu-
rities than they understood about me. This is true of most black
Americans. I have what I now recognize are singular perspectives,
and I'd like to share these.

1

The Call

Early one morning in 1985 I stood in a cemetery in Craddock, a township near Port Elizabeth, South Africa, paying my respects to four black antiapartheid activists murdered by that country's security police. We held hands in a circle while the widows and their neighbors sang mournful South African songs as they grieved the loss of their loved ones. None of them had ever seen a black judge. The singing and sobs that pierced the morning silence were suddenly broken by a widow, who with a choking voice spoke up. She fixed her tearful eyes on me and asked if there was something I could do to bring about change, adding, "It is so very hard here."

I walked over to her very slowly, stalling for time to compose myself and come up with an appropriate response. As I took both of her hands, I said that as an American judge, I lacked legal jurisdiction in South Africa, but perhaps she could gain inspiration from what America had done about injustice. I told her of slavery and of murders, kidnappings, disappearances, and the denial of basic human rights, just like what they were experiencing. I emphasized that change came, if at times very slowly, and that change was certain to come to South Africa. I mentioned Frederick Douglass, Abraham Lincoln, the Civil War, and the three constitutional amendments that led to the changed legal status from slaves to citizens. And even this transformation did not ensure equal rights, and thus black and white people in America came together to fight Jim Crow laws, just as they were doing in South Africa against apartheid. Before my appointment to the federal court, I had worked for many years as chief legal counsel for the National Association for the Advancement of Colored People (NAACP), so I was aware of the twentieth-century crusade in the courts to get laws changed and to obtain the right to vote. I assured the widows that black South Africans would win their rights too. That was the message of hope I left with those grieving women at the grave site of their martyred husbands, and it is the message I continue to deliver everywhere. But despite my hope, and this hope is based upon nearly nine decades of living, I am not oblivious to the ups and downs of American history—the struggles, triumphs, setbacks, and travails. My hope is not without frustration. I have attempted to address issues of racial inequality and injustice throughout my life.

In 1909, the centennial of the birth of Abraham Lincoln, the NAACP was founded. The organizers were a noted set of white and black individuals. A select few of the white founders included social reformers William English Walling (New York), Jane Addams (Chicago), Henry Moskowitz (New York), and Mary White Ovington (New York); philanthropist J.G. Phelps Stokes (New York); journalist Lincoln Steffens (Boston); educators John Dewey (New York) and William I. Thomas (Chicago); and newspaper editor Oswald Garrison Villard (New York). Among the most noted black founders were anti-lynching crusader Ida Wells-Barnett (Chicago); scholar W.E.B. Du Bois (Atlanta); and religious leaders Reverend Francis J. Grimké (Washington, D.C.) and Bishop Alexander Walters (New York). On February 12, 1909, these men and women of different races and faith traditions signed and published *The Call*, imploring Americans to discuss and protest the racial problem and to renew the struggle for civil and political rights. Conscious of the irony that the centennial of the Great Emancipator, President Abraham Lincoln, coincided with a time of black voter disfranchisement, newly emergent segregation laws, and racial violence including lynching, they wrote that if Lincoln could come back to life and see America, he would find that "the Supreme Court of the United States, supposedly the bulwark of American liberties, has refused every opportunity to pass squarely upon this disfranchisement of millions by laws avowedly discriminatory and openly enforced in such a manner that the white man may vote and black men may be without a vote in their government."[1]

The founders of the NAACP depicted the poignant image of a disheartened Lincoln who returned to "see the black men and women, for whose freedom a hundred thousand of soldiers gave their lives, set apart on trains, in which they pay first-class fares for third-class service, and segregated in railway stations and in places of entertainment; he would observe that State after State declines to do its elementary duty in preparing the Negro through education for the best exercise of citizenship." The conditions described in *The Call* concluded with this profound truth: "Silence under these conditions means tacit approval. The indifference of the North is already responsible for more than one assault upon democracy, and every such attack reacts as unfavorably upon whites as upon blacks."[2]

I was born in 1926, a mere seventeen years after *The Call* in 1909 and the founding of the NAACP. The short span of time between *The Call* and my birth is a grim reminder of the racial climate in the nation and what my parents faced in their early years and at the time I was born. As a teenager, I was fortunate to have a mentor, Youngstown's NAACP leader J. Maynard Dickerson. One of the many gifts I received from him was knowledge of the NAACP. It was Dickerson who introduced me to the organization's founding documents and motivated me to become a civil rights activist. When I first read *The Call*, the force of its message had an unforgettable impact upon me. I felt summoned to respond and have been striving to do so during the course of my life. Particularly gripping to me were its concluding words: "Hence, we call upon all the believers in democracy to join in a . . . discussion of present evils, the voicing of protests, and the renewal of the struggle for civil and political liberty."[3] I was indeed fortunate to witness legal and legislative efforts that led to the overthrow of legal Jim Crow. Not only was I able to be a witness to much of the change, but I was also fortunate enough to stand on the shoulders of legal giants Charles Hamilton Houston, Thurgood Marshall, William H. Hastie, Robert Carter, and many others, in answering *The Call* of 1909.

Thus, for me, answering calls for racial justice has not been confined to a specific time in the past or the history of a particular organization, but has been defined by the imperatives that guided my life. As I enter the twilight of my life, I offer this chronicle of the steps I have taken in an effort to advance the baton of justice handed to me by forebears who were much more surefooted and fearless than me in answering the Call. With the distance yet to travel to bring justice to all Americans, I implore others to accept the baton and continue the race. Comparing the world of 1909 with the current state of the nation is a measure of the success of those who committed themselves to answering the Call. Yet it is no time for celebration because storm clouds are gathering that threaten to dampen the methods by which significant changes took place. One need only look at what is happening to the gains brought about by *Brown v. Board of Education* and the Voting Rights Act to understand that strong and unrelenting efforts have been unleashed to place the nation once again under what NAACP leader Roy Wilkins once described as the "smothering blanket" of states' rights.

During the decades following *The Call*, the failure to address the denial of equal education and employment opportunities to black Americans, the corruption within the criminal justice system and a jurisprudence distorted by the virus of racism since slavery have created the lingering social alienation we see around us today.

Persons and groups who feel alienated make up the ranks of those who often defy authority. In the violent reaction that erupts in cities, social dynamite—the existence of which the nation has been warned about—ignites.

Disparities between the haves and have-nots, consistent attacks on the programs designed to close the gaps between the advantaged and the disadvantaged, repeated stereotyping of minorities and the poor—all serve to deepen the frustration and anger that permeates many communities.

In reciting these realities I do not mean to disparage the sincere efforts made by many to remove the dry rot that various forms of bigotry have strewn across our country. It is only to urge that a greater effort be put forth to understand what triggers the violent reactions that occur in such places as Ferguson, Missouri, in 2014, when an unarmed Michael Brown was killed by a police officer; or when Eric Garner was strangled to death by New York police during an encounter over selling cigarettes; or the chilling shooting in the back of Walter Scott in North Charleston, South Carolina; or the killing of Eric Courtney Harris by a reserve deputy sheriff in Tulsa, Oklahoma. Add to those tragedies the killing of twelve-year-old Tamir Rice in a park in Cleveland, Ohio, within seconds of the police alighting from their patrol car. To many it seemed as though an epidemic of police killings of black men were taking place with no effective official response. That belief was given credence when grand juries refused to indict police officers, and a judge in Cleveland acquitted an officer of a manslaughter charge that resulted from a chase of two unarmed motorists whose car was riddled with 137 gunshots. However it was the arrest and death of twenty-five-year-old Freddie Gray while in Baltimore police custody that led to the worst civil disorders since the 1960s.

An important lesson learned—though it has taken a long, long time—is that preventative steps are required to reduce the likelihood of violent eruptions; failing that, learning how to positively respond when they do is essential. A model response was crafted in Cincinnati following civil disturbances in 2001, when Susan Dlott, a federal judge, took the lead in consolidating the claims of civil rights violations into a single case and then guided their resolution through a court-approved consent decree. That put the force of federal judicial power behind significant civil rights reforms with respect to police behavior toward citizens.

In the wake of the Baltimore disturbances, the new attorney general, Loretta Lynch, visited several cities to discuss the Cincinnati model. Cleveland and Baltimore invited the Department of

Justice to investigate and review police practices. The Cleveland report called for comprehensive reforms backed up by a consent decree. The mayor welcomed the report and agreed to the consent decree, which will be overseen by the veteran chief judge of the federal court, Solomon Oliver, an African American.

That these corrective responses are built upon the foundations laid by the Kerner Commission of 1967, for which I served as assistant general counsel, gives me hope that there are answers to *The Call* of 1909 in 2015.

My travel to South Africa during the apartheid period was an extension of my lifelong efforts in America to respond to the Call to advance the struggle for "civil and political liberty." Racial and political events during recent years, even with the election of an African American as president of the United States, impel me to record my efforts over nearly seven decades of my life to answer *The Call* of 1909. And to urge, in the commanding words of James Weldon Johnson's historic "Lift Every Voice and Sing," that "we march on 'til victory is won."[4]

2

My Early Life

My parents, Nathaniel Bacon Jones and Lillian Isabelle Brown Jones, moved to Youngstown, Ohio, from the farming communities of Bedford County, Virginia, where they were born and grew up. Bedford County is located along the James River and at the foothills of the Blue Ridge Mountains. The relations between blacks and whites in those communities were non-contentious, largely because the rules governing behavior were clearly understood. The families, black and white, tacitly, and at times humorously, acknowledged their kinship owing to the racial intermixture that resulted from the exploitation by the slave owners whose names we were given. Throughout the Bedford County region one today finds the names Sledd and Brown and Jones.

As is true of nearly all African Americans, slavery was a part of my past. My maternal great-grandfather, Edward Sledd, was born into slavery in Virginia in 1819. He married Ann Rice, who too was born into slavery in 1830. Each was born of a slave parent and an owner. Together they parented seven children, including my maternal grandmother, Ellen Sledd Brown, who was born in 1873. She was the only grandparent I recall ever meeting. Her siblings were: John, born in 1865; William, born in 1867; Marshall, born in 1869; Ephraim, born in 1875; and James, whose birth year was

1878. My great-grandmother Ann Rice Sledd gave birth to her last child at the age of forty-eight.

The 1880 census classified my great-grandparents as mulatto and the 1910 census had a similar classification for my maternal grandmother, Ellen Sledd Brown, whom we affectionately called Gransy. It did not take a reference to the census classification for me and other kin to recognize the intermixture of racial bloodlines. My kin came in all complexions and hues. Gransy had beautiful light-brown skin and a most endearing smile, warm embraces, and a soft and caring voice. I was fourteen years old when Gransy died. I still have vivid memories of her visits to our Rockview Avenue home in Youngstown, after the long ride from Virginia on the Greyhound Bus or on the B&O Railroad.

We had no automobiles with which to meet her at the Greyhound station, so my mother took the streetcar downtown to await her arrival. When they returned to our streetcar stop, we would be gathered at the corner to help carry the suitcases up the hill to our home. Inevitably, in addition to the suitcases would be boxes tied with twine containing hams, bacon, and other items from their farm in Big Island, Virginia. The meats were from hogs my grandfather Joe Brown raised and salted down. The only trip I took to Virginia during my grandfather Joe's lifetime was when I was about a year old. My mother told me he regarded me as underweight and pleaded with her to allow me to stay in order for him to "fatten me up." My grandfather also assured her that he could straighten out my "bow legs." She declined his request. I often wonder what life would have been like for me had I remained in rural Virginia.

My paternal grandparents, Joseph H. Jones and Malinda Jones, were born in Bedford County, Virginia—he in 1852 and she in 1859—and married a few days after Christmas in 1875. They too were former slaves. After their marriage, they produced nineteen offspring, eight of whom were listed in the 1900 U.S. Census: James, born in 1879; Frank A., 1886; Lettie, 1890; Josephine, 1892; Elva, 1894; twins—Etna and Edna—1894; and my father, born in 1899. I set forth this family background in partial rebuttal to a statement a white high school teacher of mine in Youngstown made to a group of black students. His view was that families who came north were unstable—lacked roots, stability, and character. Little did he realize the extent of the insult he was directing at us or of the strength of the bonds that tied those who uprooted and relocated in the North with relatives who remained in the South. I have resented that teacher's remarks all of these years. It was not easy for my parents to pull up stakes, leave their loved ones, and move, with an infant daughter—my older sister, Eleanor—to the city of Youngstown, where they would be strangers. Shortly there-after my mother returned to Virginia to give birth to my brother, Wellington. In the midst of their efforts to adjust in this new environment I was born in Youngstown on May 13, 1926, and two years later, my younger sister, Allie Jean, arrived, increasing our family to six.

My parents migrated north so that their children could have better educational opportunities and my father could seek out better-paying jobs. The schools in Big Island and Bedford County, Virginia, were segregated and in every respect inferior to those white children attended. My mother—who went to the fourth grade in the segregated school of Big Island, and then only a part of the year because of the requirement that they work the farm—often told me of her struggles to get to her one-room school after farm chores and returning to more chores at the end of the day. I have had the opportunity to see the school my mother attended, on a site next to the family church, Rose of Sharon, on Big Island. I was struck by the one-room schoolhouse and the realization that a large number of children were crowded into that small building for instruction at all grade levels. My parents did not expect to find a utopia in Youngstown, but the prospect of jobs made the other risks worthwhile. My parents did not, however, anticipate the pervasiveness of Northern segregation and discrimination that they found. Still, they urged other Virginia relatives to follow us to Youngstown, and several did.

Reflecting on my parents' move from their familiar surroundings in Virginia to Youngstown, Ohio, in 1923, I marvel at their courage. My father was twenty-three years old and my mother was twenty-two. They had no relatives or serious links to that community. They were responding to the recruiting calls from the steel companies and the sense that enhanced educational and quality-of-life opportunities awaited them. My curiosity about the city where my family migrated prompted me to explore Youngstown's history. The early settlers of Youngstown were of New England stock of varying nationalities and creeds. They came west to be a part of the Western Reserve—an area approximately 120 miles long and 78 miles wide, which extended westward from the Pennsylvania border and south of Lake Erie. It had earlier been claimed by Virginia, New York, and Connecticut and was populated primarily by Scotch Irish, English, Irish, Welsh, persons of German extraction, and Scandinavians. African Americans came to the Mahoning Valley and what is now Youngstown shortly after this westward movement got under way. It is believed that John White, whose brother-in-law acquired land in the Western Reserve, was the first black man to reside in Mahoning County. A trickle of blacks arrived by the 1830s, around the time my great-grandmother, Ann Rice Sledd, was born as a slave in Virginia. Blacks found their way to Youngstown in spite of the Ohio legislature's enactment of laws in 1804 to discourage black settlements in Ohio. By 1850 there were ninety African Americans living in the county.

A small number of these early black settlers were born free and had lived in the North before moving to the Youngstown area. Some of the white settlers, perhaps those whose heritage was tied to the earlier abolitionist activity in this area, helped the new black settlers to find housing. The most notable was Jennie Wick of the Wick family. Much about Youngstown continues to bear the Wick name, including the downtown intersection where the Federal courthouse that bears my name is located.

In 1900, there were 648 black residents in Youngstown; the 1910 Census shows the number jumped to 1,936. Between 1910 and 1920 the numbers rose to 6,662. The black population boomed during World War I, when Youngstown area steel mills stepped up recruitment efforts—promising jobs, better wages, and improved living conditions to Southern workers. The black population doubled from 6,662 to 14,552 between 1920 and 1930, when my parents moved to Youngstown. During the Great Depression of the 1930s, the black population stagnated, but then surged again after the advent of World War II as war production stepped up. Census figures from 1950 show an increase in population from 14,615 to 21,540. To gain a sense of the significance of the black presence in the community, these numbers should be compared to the overall population for the corresponding periods: 1900—44,885; 1910—79,000; 1920—132,000; 1930—170,000; 1940—167,629; 1950—168,237.

Although the local white majority comprised many who descended from the early settlers of northern Europe, the bulk were first-generation immigrants from southern and eastern Europe, from such countries as Italy, Greece, Ukraine, Poland, and Russia. They were targets of the nation's first Quota Law, enacted on May 19, 1921. This Emergency Quota Act restricted the number of new immigrants to 3 percent of the number of residents from each country living in the United States as of the 1910 census. The rationale for the immigration policy was to protect jobs for Americans; however, it was actually a result of President Warren G. Harding's capitulation to the pressures mounted by the Immigration Restriction League, which his successor, President Calvin Coolidge, reinforced by supporting legislation—the Johnson-Reed Act—with even more severe controls. This was our country's policy of national origin discrimination.

As a child, I interacted with the children of these immigrants. Like other black children, however, I was subjected to instances of racial scapegoating that apparently stemmed from the tendency of ethnic whites, who had been once ghettoized and victimized, to look down on African Americans. Members of the black community saw that the families who came from English, Welsh, German, and Scandinavian areas understood themselves as occupying a preferred status, while those who hailed from Italy, Greece, Russia, and the Baltic and Slavic countries, and against whom quota restrictions were directed, were seen as "foreigners." Many came to adopt the racist attitudes of those who had biases toward them.

These white ethnic groups—themselves recent arrivals in the city—sought to align with others whose skin was white and refused to make common cause with the black migrants, the other target of discrimination. I often thought how stupid this was in light of what I had heard about the rise of the Ku Klux Klan in Youngstown at the very time my parents and thousands of other blacks arrived from the South.

The Klan made for common conversation among the people in my world. There was much talk of how major political figures of the day marched in hoods and robes in parades to protest the presence of the immigrants from southern and eastern Europe, Russia, Ireland, and those of the Catholic and Jewish faith. The Klan appeared to have been at its strongest in 1924 at about the time my parents arrived in Youngstown. The Grand Dragon of Ohio was Clyde W. Osborne, a lawyer I came to know later when he was retained to defend Jack DuRell, the operator of DuRell's Restaurant. While a college student in 1948, I sued DuRell for refusing me service. Osborne was a well-known lawyer. During his leadership as Grand Dragon of Ohio in the 1920s, the Klan bought a four-acre farm to use as a staging ground for parades, cross burnings, and other violent acts that ultimately required the governor to declare martial law and deploy the National Guard.

The Klan was so strong in the area that it succeeded in electing a mayor in Youngstown as well as in the surrounding towns of Niles, Warren, Girard, and Struthers. The Klan reinforced its campaign against hiring immigrants and blacks through its control of various public entities, including boards of education. There were notable moments of resistance, as was the case when protesters ripped Klansmen's hoods off as they marched along Youngstown's streets, exposing the Klansmen's faces and identities. By 1926, the Klan began to lose political clout. Catholics asserted political power and elected one of their own, Joseph Heffernan, as mayor. With an eye toward shaming the Klan, Heffernan in later years "outed" those among the city's power brokers who had once belonged to the organization. Still, it is a sad irony that many of the groups who were targeted by the Klan came to adopt its very ideas and views about the African Americans who settled in Youngstown. Their attitudes were often manifested in their resistance to blacks who sought to use public swimming pools and who made efforts to win access to decent housing and jobs.

Making Ends Meet During the Great Depression

At the time of my birth in 1926, my family lived in a tiny house at the rear of 129 Court Street, on Youngstown's east side, an area known as Smokey Hollow. We soon relocated to the lower south side on what was known as Garlick Street, named for the Garlick family that came to Youngstown from Vermont in the late 1800s. Once in Youngstown, Henry Manning Garlick founded banks, a brokerage house, and United Engineering and Foundry, which was one of the largest machine-making firms in Mahoning County. Prior to entering World War II, the United States began to provide weapons for the Allies, and United Engineering and Foundry converted its equipment to the manufacture of casting machines, sizing and embossing presses, foundry mold machines, foundry machines, and dies. It had operated for years in Youngstown and though its founder was from a group of New Englanders who were staunch abolitionists, the company never saw fit to hire black workers. Decades afterward and during my years as executive director of the Youngstown Fair Employment Practice Committee in the late 1950s, I was unsuccessful in breaking the color line at that company.

Garlick Street, a steep hill, was unpaved. Our house sat in the middle of the block, and we experienced gravel and mud slides during heavy rainstorms. President Franklin D. Roosevelt's New Deal solved this problem. In the late 1930s the Works Progress Administration (WPA) provided jobs that benefited our neighborhood, and luckily for us WPA workers laid cobblestones on our street. Coinciding with that improvement, our street name changed to Rockview Avenue. Many of the WPA workers who transformed the street were neighbors and members of our church.

The WPA went a long way toward relieving the pain caused by the Depression, which left one-third of the population of Youngstown without jobs. Among the ranks of the jobless were recent immigrants and first-generation neighbors who found themselves in the same boat as the jobless blacks. My father lost his job when the steel mills shut down in 1932. Six years of age at the time, I still remember my parents' struggle to make ends meet and their reliance on odd jobs and welfare assistance. The city government issued what was known as "scrip"—a voucher that allowed my parents to make limited purchases in the neighborhood grocery store located on Marshall Street. The store was operated by Al Richards, a jolly, rotund man, who from time to time extended credit to us and our neighbors. The Allied Council operated a distribution center for staples like cornmeal, oatmeal, sugar, and dried milk, and for clothes like knickers and shirts for boys, and skirts and blouses for girls. The clothes clearly identified all who wore them as welfare recipients. But since so many people were in need, there was no stigma or sense of shame.

I remember going with my brother to the relief office to pick up our food orders and lugging the goods back home. My father, laid off from his steel-mill laboring job after already having had his hourly pay cut from 50 cents to 45 cents an hour, pounded the pavement in search of a day's work for whatever it would pay. My mother took in and laundered shirts for a neighbor, Earl Woolridge, who lived down the street and operated a tap-dancing studio in the Central Auditorium in the heart of downtown. In 1936 and 1937, one of my jobs was to walk to the dance studio on Tuesday with a basket to collect Woolridge's white shirts for my mother to launder, and return them on Thursday.

On one occasion, as she was sorting our family clothes for washing, she asked me to take my blue knickers to the basement with instructions to place them in the "soaking" tub. I mistakenly placed them in the washing machine with Woolridge's white shirts. Shortly thereafter, I heard my mother scream, asking, "What did you do?" At that moment I developed a severe stomachache. She ultimately went to see Woolridge to explain what happened, and offered to do several weeks of laundry without charge. He was very understanding and did not impose any sort of a penalty. My brother caused my mother no similar pain. He reliably hustled through the neighborhood collecting ashes from homes of people who had coal-burning furnaces, as well as tin cans and taking them to a dump. There were also happy occasions, such as when my mother would send us to the Ward Bakery to buy "day-old" bread. This respite from the coarse cornbread made from the yellow cornmeal we received from the relief center was a real treat.

As the Depression deepened, my mother found other ways to supplement the meager family income. The McCrackin family owned a number of houses around the city. Our Rockview Avenue house was one of them. To assist with the rent, my mother would put in a few days of housecleaning every few weeks at the home of one of the McCrackin brothers, who lived in a suburb of Youngstown known as Austintown. She took a streetcar to the end of the line and then walked nearly a mile to the family's stately brick house. At the end of the day, she returned to us, her day's labor discounted from the rent. Sometimes, Ruth McCrackin drove her to the bus stop or even all the way home. We welcomed our mother back with hugs, not only because we were delighted to have her back home but because she carried a bag full of food sent from the McCrackins' pantry.

My mother also supplemented the family income by working a few evenings a week as a matron in a downtown theater, attending to the ladies' restroom for several hours, usually from six to nine p.m. My father landed a job at the same theater as a janitor, cleaning up after the last showing at about eleven p.m. Early the next morning, he was up and out again seeking a day's work wherever he could find it, most of the time sandwiched in between washing windows at downtown businesses. Today, we would describe my parents as "multitasking," especially my mother. My father worked hard, but my mother's activities were more creative. In the dead of winter when the WPA workers were paving our street, she invited them to deposit their lunch pails inside our house and to enjoy their lunches in the warmth of our kitchen. We had a coal-burning stove because the gas company had disconnected service when we could not pay the bill. She would warm the coffee from their thermos bottles on that stove to help them through those cold days.

My mother's outgoing and friendly personality enabled her to earn extra income by distributing J.R. Watkins products (various ointments, salves, condiments, and extracts useful for cooking) to neighbors and to people she had met through church membership and service at the West Federal Street YMCA. I well remember her use of the phrase "canvass the neighborhood," which meant that she was seeking new customers. As I got a bit older, she sent me by streetcar and bus to the office of the company to place and pick up her orders. This had to be done on the spot because we did not have a telephone. Back at home, I helped her organize orders, which she then, using the streetcars and on foot, delivered to her customers.

As I waited at the J.R. Watkins Company office for the orders to be prepared, I often overheard the conversations of the white men who worked there and those who hung around the building. They delighted in disparaging black people. Their favorite target was the renowned prizefighter Jack Johnson, who once had no peer in the boxing ring. The men denounced Johnson, who was often in the company of white women and even married to one. This was the heyday of the incomparable heavyweight champion Joe Louis, however, so the white men asserted that Louis had better "stay in his race" when it came to his choice of women. Even though I was in my pre- and early teens, I was well aware of the racist mind-set of those white adults who considered themselves superior to African Americans.

My mother's people skills also secured her a job at the recently founded black weekly newspaper, the *Buckeye Review*, published by the black lawyer and civil rights activist J. Maynard Dickerson. She became the subscription manager for the paper. This connection, and her involvement with the Ladies' Auxiliary of the West Federal Street YMCA, forged the relationship that eventually led Dickerson to take note of me as a ten-year-old and to become my mentor.

My parents, both in their early twenties, confronted a difficult challenge in transitioning from their rural life in Virginia to the harsh urban realities of Youngstown during the Depression years. My father was a strong-willed individual, determined to be the decision maker with respect to family matters. This extended to raising four young children and handling the finances—including money generated by the multiple jobs my mother held. This worked until my mother gained a greater degree of independence and when her contribution to the family income equaled or exceeded my father's. I was in junior high school when my family came apart. They told us about their impending divorce the night before they were to appear in court. I was not capable then of understanding the strain that the efforts to provide economic support and an improved quality of life had placed on their relationship. If there were serious disputes or disagreements between them, my parents kept this from us. We knew that they differed on occasion, but no more than what we witnessed of parents in the households of our playmates. Considering the way in which the Depression forced my father to work multiple jobs and my mother to do the variety of tasks she undertook in order to make ends meet, it was almost inevitable that strains would develop.

My siblings and I, on occasion, played the "card" that children sometimes do of pitting one parent against the other. I thought my father lacked understanding and was too demanding. So I would go to my more empathetic mother in the hope of gaining solace. My mother often related stories her grandmother told her of her childhood—of fleeing to the "big house" on the farm of the slave owner, her biological father, for protection from discipline. It often worked for my great-grandmother, I was told. Seldom did it work for me, though my mother had a way of dismissing me, after hearing my complaints, with hugs and words of encouragement. Since I took every opportunity of escaping to the park in order to play baseball and engage in other summer pastimes, thereby avoiding my chores, my parents considered me to be a bit lazy. My brother, on the other hand, was much more diligent, and he was constantly praised for being "smart."

For a period after my parents divorced, my mother and sister roomed with Mrs. Willa Jenkins, who was known to us as "Aunt Jenks." She was a kind person with a physical ailment that required the use of a crutch. She spent much of her day in her living room on a chaise longue and passed the time playing solitaire. My brother and I lived with my father in an apartment on Plum Street, a few blocks away. My older sister had already dropped out of high school and was married. My father, being the rugged individualist he was, placed great store in owning property just as his family did in Virginia. He struggled to build a house in an area of the city known as the Sharon Line, which later became McGuffey Heights. Once the structure of his self-built house had a roof, we moved in, even though the basement was only gravel and without windows. The Sharon Line area of the city was remote from the core of the city and sorely neglected by officials, particularly with respect to enforcement of housing and health codes. There were many reasons, including my desire to continue attending my neighborhood school, James Hillman, that I balked at remaining with my father in the unfinished house.

There were considerable differences in the school I had been attending and that which served the neighborhood in which my father's new house was located. For one thing the all-black Sharon Line School suffered from a lack of resources, while my regular school was integrated and academically strong. No less important to me was the matter of my wanting to be with my friends. In order to attend Hillman, I used my mother's address at the home of Aunt Jenks—1039 High Street. Each evening, after she completed her job at the theater, I waited there for her and used her bus pass to go to my father's house for the night. Early the next morning, I went to the neighbor's well, drew two pails of water, tried to heat it on a coal stove, and took a modified bath before walking to the bus stop to board a bus into town to my mother's house, where I left the bus pass for her. From there I joined my friends for our mile-long walk to Hillman Junior High. The inconvenience of sharing the bus pass with my mother was well worth it, given the difference between the schools. Hillman's gym classes were welcome because they afforded an opportunity to take a warm shower.

Hillman was racially integrated although with a mere sprinkling of black students. All the authority figures were white. I nonetheless felt a special "ownership" in Hillman Junior High because I was selected to sing with the student choir at the groundbreaking ceremony several years before. I will never forget the dean of boys, Walter Oswald, who was regarded by many of us as being particularly hard on black students. During one summer, his son was the victim of a fatal attack by several black teenagers. We speculated, with much fear, on our fate when school opened that fall. To our surprise, we had misread Mr. Oswald, for he proved to be extraordinarily kind to all of us.

The bus routine pained my mother so much that she asked my brother and me whether we would help with expenses if she were able to convince Robert McCrackin, the owner of our old house on Rockview Avenue, to rent to us again. We assured her that we would. She was able to obtain secondhand furniture for the house, and my brother and I moved back in with my mother. Having our own bedrooms, hot running water, and a coal-burning furnace was a true luxury. Moving back to the house at 113 Rockview Avenue with my mother restored a degree of order to our lives that we had not felt since my parents divorced. My brother and I kept our promise: we got after-school and weekend jobs, although my brother was much better at keeping the promise than I was. I settled for a job at a neighborhood gas station washing cars on weekends while my brother hustled to do a number of jobs after school and on weekends. In the summer months, at about age sixteen or seventeen, I worked at the Youngstown Sheet and Tube Company as a bricklayer's helper. It was the "helper" part of the job that appealed to me, though I soon learned that being a "helper" meant a bit more lifting than I had imagined. I also witnessed racial distinctions in yet another form.

Fellow employees included the adult men we looked up to, fathers and other relatives of our friends. They performed the same dirty, hot, laboring tasks that we did. The white "straw bosses" and "pushers" called them by their first names and often made them the butt of pranks and the targets of racially tinged jokes. The disrespect shown to these men disturbed me. These men were the fathers of my friends, officers in our church, and in other respects pillars of our community. Even though that is the way things were, I did not feel that I had to like it, and I did not. The next summer I fared much better with a cleaner job as a pipe fitter's helper with another company.

My Neighborhood in Black and White

Because my neighborhood was racially mixed, I regularly saw a form of societal schizophrenia in which the two races engaged and disengaged. A block from our house was an eating and drinking establishment called the Balboa Grill. The proprietors were friendly, but only to a point. I got to know them from hanging out at a gas station where they had their cars serviced. A few white neighbors patronized Balboa, but none of the blacks ever crossed its threshold, except to occasionally perform janitorial functions. Most of the patrons came from across the city and were obviously not members of the white working class. My black neighbors had no choice in the matter: they were excluded because of color. There was no doubt in anyone's mind who was and who was not welcome in that establishment.

Our next-door neighbor, Marie Myers, a widow of Irish extraction, worked at Balboa as a cook. She provided us with gossip about the goings-on in the grill. Occasionally, she shared some of the steaks and pastas she brought home. While she had three sons and two daughters, only one of the daughters lived with her, and only one of her sons was our age. Her other sons lived independently and worked at jobs in the steel mills and later joined the navy. Our black neighbors took note of the jobs they were able to land that were not available to people of color. Though we were friendly with the Myers family as we grew up—black and white children played together, and adults were civil—there was not a great deal of socializing beyond some porch conversations. Seldom did adults cross the threshold of a house occupied by another race.

Other white neighbors—two unmarried women we then called spinsters—the Armstrongs, lived on the other side of us. Seldom did more than friendly greetings pass between them and my parents, though my brother and I frequently ran errands for them. Other white families on our side of the street were the Hallewells and the Browns, both quite friendly. There were three black families across from us who had little or no contact with the white neighbors on our side of the street. Of course, our black neighbors, including those who lived around the corner, were all in frequent communication with one another. Membership in the nearby churches and common social interests drew many of our black neighbors together.

My black friends and I enjoyed playing with the white children in the neighborhood. We played ball in the street and in yards, climbed trees, picked fruit from the apple and peach trees, ran through nearby woods, and did all of the things that boys and girls of our pre–high school ages enjoyed doing. Black parents never questioned our choice of white playmates, nor did the white parents seem to limit the freedom of their children. There was, however, one notable exception. The grandmother of Bobby Apple, one of our white playmates, constantly resisted his determination to play with us. On one occasion, when she glanced out of the kitchen window and noticed him playing with black boys, she came to the back porch and bellowed, "Bobby, get in here!" Embarrassed, he then told us, "I have to go." We all felt sorry for him but nevertheless continued what we were doing, but I came to realize how people I knew to be decent, such as my white playmate Bobby Apple, who wanted so badly to play with us, had their wishes overridden by bigoted adults. On the other hand, the Gibbs family, immigrants from Scotland, permitted their son to play freely with us. I realized in this case that some white families had the strength to resist the societal pressures of racial discrimination and to treat people as people.

When we got older and engaged in organized sports with children from other neighborhoods, we congregated at a nearby playground, Volney Rogers Field in Mill Creek Park—a beautiful natural park, with lakes, walking trails, handicraft programs, softball fields, and tennis courts. Here everyone seemed to accept "the rule" that certain places and activities were okay and others were off limits to us. The playground represented an approved place for all kids. However, this was not true of the city's pools and its amusement park, known as Idora Park. I knew this exclusion was not right. My lifetime refusal to be defined as inferior traces back to those early experiences in my neighborhood.

The summers of my preteen and teen years were for the most part exciting. The activities kept the neighborhood youngsters very engaged. While the activities on the playground were open with regard to race, on Tuesday mornings something else occurred. The playground supervisors took the white kids for swimming lessons at Borts Pool, one of the seven city-owned pools. We black kids went on nature hikes through the park, or remained behind to work on handicraft projects, since we were not allowed at Borts Pool, which was located on the west side of town in an area largely inhabited by whites. I was offended by the practice and talked about it to the officials and to my black friends. Most of the black and white kids accepted the arrangement as the way things were supposed to be. Few thought to protest. The all-white playground staff was kind and thoughtful. The playground supervisors were usually college students, or public school teachers. The deputized park policemen who oversaw the playground established an easy relationship with all of us, black and white. Most of them were college football players home for summer vacation. Being college football players naturally gave these white athletes a preference when it came to summer employment.

Reflecting on the school system in my hometown, which was theoretically nonsegregated, as were most of the school districts in Ohio, I became conscious at a young age of the limits of permissible interaction between the races. The fact that black children were in the same school buildings and in the same classrooms as white children did not alter the racial reality we faced on a daily basis. From grade one through law school I never at any time had a black teacher or professor. I well remember the various superintendents who presided over the Youngstown schools during the time I was a student. They made annual visits to the various school buildings and classrooms. On those special days, everything had to be clean and polished. The first superintendent I recall was George Roudebush. He was followed by George Bowman, who went on to become president of Kent State University. The succeeding superintendents continued to make annual classroom visits. They never appeared to question the problematic image of the total absence of black teachers, black principals, black secretaries, or even black custodians.

In "mixed" schools and neighborhoods, I could see that black children were much more sophisticated when it came to matters of race. We learned early on the rules of racial etiquette and, with rare exceptions, complied with them, sometimes even with a good deal of humor. I do not recall a time when I was not aware of the fact that people who looked like me were treated differently—sometimes with condescension and at other times with the intent to demean and exclude. My parents and other adults provided us with coping skills to soften the impact, thus helping us to preserve our self-esteem. Yet the unrelenting assault on my dignity and that of my black friends was both direct and subtle. That realization sparked within me a sense of resolve to use the law to attack the system for what it was doing to people, rather than lash out in rage or wallow in despair. I inwardly and occasionally outwardly rejected the stereotypes that reinforced and gave legitimacy to presumptions of white superiority and black inferiority.

My youthful efforts at societal reform did not focus solely on racial discrimination. Indeed, the first effort concerned my own life and character. When I was around ten years old, I was taught a lasting lesson about the sacredness of trust and the value of respecting it. I violated the trust of a coffee-shop owner by attempting to steal a cupcake when I thought he was not looking. The lesson resulting from the humiliation has never left me. A group of my friends hung out in a coffee shop a block from my home, operated by Ted Metzger, a young white man in his twenties. He was a warm, affable person who aspired to become an Ohio state patrolman. He liked me and my buddies, and he permitted us to idle away our time in his small restaurant. His living quarters were located in the rear of the building separated by a curtain. On one occasion, egged on by friends, I reached behind the counter and helped myself to a cupcake. At that very moment, Metzger appeared at the curtain. He looked at me and said, "Put it back and get out." I cannot describe my embarrassment and pain as I slowly walked out onto the street with my friends trailing behind.

After a day or two, I mustered up enough nerve to return to the coffee shop and asked Metzger if I could speak to him. He invited me to take a seat in a booth with him. I said I wanted to apologize, that I was deeply sorry and would never do that again. In those days many of my friends called me by my middle name, Raphael. He said, "Raphael, I thought I could trust you. You let me down. If you have learned a lesson, you are welcome to come back." With that, he reached for my hand, and as we stood, he gave me a pat on the shoulder. That was a moment I have never forgotten. To this day, the notion of receiving something of value without permission or without paying for it is unthinkable. Yet, I also learned more than this. Metzger had taught me something about human character and the power of truth, forgiveness, and reconciliation.

My second effort at reform concerned my own community. I was sensitive to the existence of vice in Youngstown's black community, particularly the gambling enterprise known as "the numbers" or "the bug." The subject of much conversation among Youngstown elders, this form of organized gambling was also known in such larger cities as Cleveland and Chicago as the "policy racket." Racial ghettoization in large cities made blacks sitting ducks for the numbers because participation was available to those with very little money. Men and women with hardly more than pennies, nickels, and dimes played the numbers, while persons of greater means could and did play for larger stakes. The enterprise flourished through the cooperation of the gambling operators, politicians, and police. In

Youngstown, the numbers was operated by gambling syndicates or "bankers" who "licensed" several politically connected blacks to operate as their agents in their own neighborhoods. This led the *Vindicator*, my hometown's daily newspaper, to editorialize periodically against such gambling. The articles usually triggered a police crackdown on the "pickup" men. Little did I realize then that such crackdowns were a ruse that the gambling operators and the police played to mask corruption.

The "numbers racket" was a big and lucrative business. Betting revolved around the final stock-market prices reported each weekday on the financial page of the daily newspaper. A combination of three numbers on a line contained in a certain bracket of the stock report would form the payoff numbers. Winning amounts were based on the size of the wager made. Those who had the right combination of numbers "hit," and pickup agents arrived at their homes with the cash winnings—usually five times the amount of the initial bet. By bracketing with a box one's chosen numbers, the bettor had the chance, if lucky, of doubling the winnings if any combination of those numbers turned up. When a person "hit" the numbers, the good news spread throughout the neighborhood and a celebration often followed. Written aids with hints as to likely winning combinations were made available to assist players. The most common came in the form of dream interpretations, usually found in Dream Books. Tip books could be purchased in barbershops, beauty parlors, and other vendors that served the black community. Also, combinations of numbers, it was said, could be found in subliminal, hidden messages in the comics of weekly black papers like the *Pittsburgh Courier* and the *Chicago Defender*. Though ministers sometimes preached on Sunday mornings against playing the numbers, their message usually drew snickers from congregants and much humorous commentary, particularly in regard to the readiness of the clergy to accept people's winnings in their collection plates. Operators of the numbers banks became wealthy, with some of them spreading their profits inside the community. Most important, however, a condition of their remaining in business was to share the "wealth" with corrupt public officials.

After the Youngstown *Vindicator* carried a story blasting the city administration and the police for looking the other way with regard to the numbers, I decided to respond. Though I was not more than ten or twelve years of age, I organized nine of my friends to go to the office of Mayor Lionel Evans in city hall to report what we knew of the schedule and routes followed by the pickup men. As the ten of us (nine boys and one girl) entered the waiting room, the mayor's secretary, Jack Blystone, asked why we wanted to talk to him. I explained that we could not discuss our concerns with anyone but the mayor. We were thereupon seated in the conference room around the largest glass-topped table I had ever seen. Shortly thereafter, the mayor appeared, accompanied by Blystone. I told him that we had been reading the newspaper accounts of the numbers operations in the city and that pickup men came through our neighborhood at a certain time every day. He expressed absolute amazement and asked his secretary to send for Chief of Police Carl Olsen and the head of the Juvenile Bureau, Paul Kidder. Upon their arrival, the mayor asked me to repeat what I had previously reported to him. I did. They too expressed absolute shock, promising to look into the matter right away. At that point, Mayor Evans, who was a huge man of Welsh descent with a ruddy complexion topped by a head of thick, snow-white hair, asked if we would like to tour the police station. We eagerly agreed. Mayor Evans thanked us for the information and declared that he would "stand behind" us all the way. We were then escorted next door to the police station, where we first saw the paddy wagon before going upstairs to the cells that held prisoners. This was a rather scary sight. Our final stop was in the police identification bureau, where we were allowed to play with the fingerprinting equipment and handcuffs. Before dispatching us to the street to return home, the chief of the juvenile bureau issued this word of caution: "Be careful, boys; and I do mean, be careful."

We went first to the home of Marcellus Bowman, one of our group, to report, quite proudly, what we had done. His mother listened but soon became agitated. I assured her that the mayor made an explicit promise to "stand behind" us. She retorted: "That's the problem. When you need him, he'll be so far behind that he won't be any good to you." The following day, the Youngstown *Vindicator* carried a front-page story about "The Secret Ten" and our visit to city hall and the police station to report on gambling activity in the neighborhood. When my mother, and the other parents, saw the story we were severely chastised and told that we were not engaging in child's play. That ended the sleuthing of "The Secret Ten."

I had yet another direct experience with the numbers operation a few years later. Matthew Blakely operated a barbershop in our neighborhood. As soon as I was able to free myself from the ordeal of having my father inflict pain on me with his clippers, I began going to Blakely's shop. On one occasion, as I sat in the barber's chair halfway through the haircut, two plainclothes Vice Squad detectives entered and began to open cabinet drawers in search of numbers slips. Blakely, a constant pipe smoker, had trouble controlling his pipe, which rattled between his teeth from fear. His hands shook uncontrollably as he continued to cut my hair. The detectives, after finding what they wanted, told Blakely to "go ahead and finish." He tried as best he could, but my head paid the price. After removing the cloth from around my neck, Blakely declined to accept payment from me, put on his jacket, and off to jail he went. What this police charade did to that elderly and physically handicapped man was shameful. I say this because I learned many lessons by observing the pretense of controlling local gambling. Later as a lawyer, I got to know the operators of the numbers racket, and learned of the collusion that existed between them and the police. My respect for law enforcement took a severe hit. The blacks who were running these activities had tie-ins with the white "bankers" who had the real political clout. It was to the politicians that these minor "businessmen" paid tribute. Some of them tried to use their assets to enter legitimate businesses and become regarded as upstanding citizens. Yet what they were doing, which made criminals of them, has since been legitimized. On countless streets all over the country people line up to play the lottery in hopes of striking it rich. Some consider it hypocritical that local and state governments now do the very same thing for revenue that those numbers runners did when they came through our neighborhoods collecting nickels and dimes from poor people hoping to make a "hit."

Given that most of the public authority figures in my life were white, it was important for me to be exposed to strong men and women of color—people of integrity and character. In the latter regard, the West Federal Street YMCA and the Third Baptist Church represented the two pillars of my neighborhood and the larger Youngstown community, for it was in those institutions that I saw people who looked like me doing significant things. The segregated branch of the YMCA was dedicated to serving the needs of the city's black citizens. It was built in 1926 from the beneficence of the Julius Rosenwald Foundation. A Jewish philanthropist and founder of Sears Roebuck & Company, Rosenwald provided funding for the construction of black YMCA branches across the nation. Simeon S. Booker of Baltimore, the secretary of the West Federal Street Y, had moved to Youngstown to head up the conversion from the old Booker T. Washington Settlement to the new YMCA. Booker and his wife, Reberta, became its heart and soul. In addition to the programs normally associated with a YMCA— swimming, boxing, and basketball—the Bookers brought the black community's leadership into the institution through its Committee of Management. Invariably, a leader of the white establishment from the Central YMCA occupied a seat on the committee with these black leaders and served as a conduit to the Central YMCA leadership.

Reberta Booker's leadership skills aided her husband and were particularly apparent through her work organizing the Ladies' Auxiliary. This women's group was effective in supporting the programs of the Y by organizing and conducting a weekly Well Baby Clinic in cooperation with the health agencies of the city and hosting social events in connection with public activities spearheaded by the Committee of Management. My mother was a friend of the

Bookers and an ardent supporter of the activities of the Ladies' Auxiliary. Each Wednesday morning, she rode the streetcar and bus to the YMCA to assist Dr. W.P. Young and the other physicians who donated their services to examine babies. Another of my mother's activities at the Y was the social hour that followed its Sunday afternoon forums. The weekly forum was the brainchild of Secretary Booker. Through it, members of the Committee of Management introduced to the Youngstown community the outstanding leaders of black America. My mother took me with her to these meetings. I do not recall why I was the only one of her four children to attend, but I never missed a forum.

Many of the early black families who reached Youngstown via Maryland and Washington, D.C., were Virginians who became members of Third Baptist Church, founded in 1872. My parents did the same when they arrived in 1923. The church served as the center of my family's life. Regular attendance at Sunday school and morning worship services each week was a must for me and my siblings. What was known as Junior Church and musical events offered us opportunities to develop self-confidence by demonstrating leadership roles with peers under the watchful eyes of our elders. The church's programs and activities were fashioned to help in the adjustment to the challenges confronting family members, most of them newly arrived from the South. The Sunday morning worship service drew the attendance and participation of my parents, as well as the parents of most of my playmates.

A cluster of black churches in close proximity served the community. From a ritualistic standpoint, the Sunday services varied only modestly. Most important to my friends and me was the opportunity to socialize, broaden friendships, and absorb the teaching that adults at the respective churches offered. We visited back and forth on Sundays. The churches supplemented one another's youth programs. Oak Hill Avenue AME Church sponsored Boy Scout and Girl Scout troops. Sully Johnson was a dedicated Scout leader who did wonders with the boys in the Cub and Boy Scout programs. Gertrude Guilford, the mother of my close playmates, worked tirelessly leading the Girl Scouts, a program that drew participation from girls regardless of whether they were members of the church. Dedicated women led the various youth programs at Third Baptist Church. The head usher, Maude Frye, was looked upon as the church "policeman." She rode herd on those of us who chose to sit in the balcony following Junior Church. Whispering and gum chewing were absolutely forbidden. As we moved into our early teen phase, the attractiveness of persons of the opposite sex at the other churches accelerated the pace of interchurch visits and increased Mrs. Frye's scrutiny at Third Baptist.

Simeon Booker, head of the West Federal Street YMCA, and his family, were members of our church. This was largely due, I think, to the Virginia-Baltimore roots that he and many of the founders of the church had. "Mr. Booker," as we first called him, had come to the city from a Baltimore community center, following his graduation from Virginia Union College in Richmond. By then our minister, Dr. Harper, had returned to Third Baptist Church from a Philadelphia pastorate. Later, after Booker became ordained as a Baptist minister, he was chosen as an assistant to Dr. Harper. I was a great admirer of Reverend Booker because of his YMCA and civic work. Much later, during my college years when I was employed at the *Buckeye Review* I would see Reverend Booker each Monday after he became pastor, when he personally delivered his church notices for inclusion in the next issue of the paper. One of his great strengths was that of a communicator. His namesake, Simeon Booker Jr., made a name for himself as a journalist. Chief of the Washington bureau of *JET* and *Ebony*, Booker Jr. was a Neiman Fellow at Harvard before becoming a "regular" at the White House briefings. Soft spoken, Reverend Booker was a constant source of encouragement to me and numerous other young people. On one occasion he accompanied me to a Baptist state convention in Cleveland, where I appeared in an oratorical contest at historic Sardis Baptist Church.

His dual roles in the community as secretary of the West Federal Street YMCA and as assistant pastor and later senior pastor of the church benefited both organizations. Often, when notables came to the city to speak at the Sunday afternoon forum meetings, they attended Sunday morning worship service. Reverend Adam Clayton Powell Jr.'s appearance at a Sunday morning service caused a considerable buzz. Celebrity appearances were not limited to forum speakers. I recall one occasion when Duke Ellington's presence in a balcony seat was acknowledged by Reverend Booker and the excited reaction of the congregation. He was performing at the downtown Palace Theater.

As I grew older, I struggled to understand the role of religion in society. In particular, after returning from the service in World War II, I was disappointed by what I sensed to be reluctance in my church to aggressively take on the glaring evil of racism and social injustice. There was a much greater emphasis on the afterlife than on contemporary problems. I had made it my priority to seek out and follow a social gospel that respected the dignity of all human beings—God's children—and to strive to relieve their suffering while in their earthly setting. In searching for ways to vindicate a belief in a social gospel that addressed problems of segregation and inequality, I visited a variety of other denominations, which offered a different religious emphasis. My search led me to explore Catholicism and Unitarianism, but ultimately led me back to the church of our family, where, in the words of an old hymn, "I first saw the light." I continue to regard Third Baptist as my church home. I concluded that I could best attack the social problems by remaining there. The Reverend Dr. Morris W. Lee, whose pastorate exceeds fifty years, hails from Virginia, as did his predecessors. His pastorate, to me, came to represent the commitment to a social gospel I longed for.

I often recall my early years at Third Baptist Church and now have a profound appreciation for the role it played in shaping my life, honing my coping skills in ways that prepared me for my future endeavors. The hymns and spirituals seem to have had a more lasting influence on me than did many of the sermons. The messages I take from such songs as "This Little Light of Mine" and "Brighten the Corner Where You Are" have become watchwords. In terms of the opportunities church afforded me—thinking on my feet and the art of oral advocacy—had their roots in the speaking programs I was encouraged to participate in at a very early age. As I moved to leadership roles in youth organizations that included presiding at meetings, a foundation was laid that enabled me to perform similar functions as a high school and college student.

3

Becoming a Civil Rights Activist

I had heard and read about lawyers, but I had never met a black one until I went to my first YMCA forum. I well recall the sight of a number of impressive-looking black men in vested suits—guest speakers from Youngstown, Cleveland, Washington, New York, Chicago, Pittsburgh, Atlanta, and many other places. They brought inspiring messages of hope to our local leaders and community members. We were, after all, still living in the period of *Plessy v. Ferguson*'s separate-but-equal doctrine. That doctrine permeated and enveloped our lives, even though we were in the North. Though young, I could relate to the speakers' discussions on discrimination nationally and in my own hometown.

I questioned why none of the parents of my schoolmates, or even my own father, who was a custodian at two downtown movie houses, could get a job at my school. My father left home at eleven o'clock each night and worked until daybreak, sweeping up empty popcorn boxes and candy wrappers from messy theater floors. At other times he worked outdoors in the cold. At my church, black women taught us in Sunday school but could not teach in the public school system. Through the Sunday forums, I learned why and how race prejudice becomes institutionalized. I became acquainted with a long list of nationally and internationally renowned leaders engaged in the fight for racial justice in America. After hearing each speaker, I eagerly reported to my neighborhood friends what I had heard and experienced. Seeing and listening to distinguished men and women of color made me wish that some of the whites I saw from time to time in the neighborhood could meet these figures too.

The formal part of the forum program was followed by a reception in the first-floor lounge of the Y, where beautifully gowned members of the Ladies' Auxiliary served tea and crumpets, mints and nuts. My mother stood at one end of the table and poured tea. At the other end, I snuck handfuls of nuts and mints, much to my mother's embarrassment. During the reception, program participants often engaged me in conversation, asking my name, age, school, grade, and aspirations. Such an incident occurred when the Youngstown lawyer J. Maynard Dickerson introduced himself to me. I remembered his name from my mother's signing on as subscription manager for his newspaper business. At the forum I could not help but notice this impressive-looking man who sat sideways in his chair on the stage. I later learned that he had a hip impairment, the result of a failed surgery. He positioned his body in order to lean on his cane. When he rose to speak at the podium, his English was so precise that I was transfixed. His usual role was to preside over the meeting or at times introduce the main speaker.

That this lawyer paid attention to me as a youngster made me feel special. He always saw to it that I met and shook the hand of the principal speaker. I shall never forget when Dickerson introduced me to Walter White, the executive secretary of the NAACP. Walter White confused me when I first laid eyes on him. I thought, based on his ruddy skin, straight white hair, and blue eyes that he was white, yet as he spoke his racial identity slowly became clear, for he made frequent references to "We Negroes." He fought for anti-lynching legislation and led efforts to outlaw the poll tax in the South that had disfranchised millions of African Americans. As head of the NAACP, White was arguably the most powerful black leader on the national scene. Through Maynard Dickerson, I met many black leaders at the forum.

In addition to being a lawyer, Maynard Dickerson was an entre-
preneur who had established a commercial printing company and
founded a weekly newspaper in 1937, the *Buckeye Review*, to serve
the black community of Youngstown. The city's main daily newspaper, the Youngstown *Vindicator*, showed little interest in the
black citizens of Youngstown, limiting its coverage to the racially
defined column "Interesting News Notes for Local Colored Folks."
Written by the popular local black personality R. Burns Harvey,
the column contained an eclectic mix of announcements on black
events. Bundled together were civic events and weddings, chitter-
ling and chicken dinners, as well as an event called "Blessed Cab-
bage Night." The *Vindicator*'s confining of black news to a separate
column came increasingly to be perceived in the black community
as an indignity arising from a fundamental disrespect for people of
color. It served to emblazon the badge of racial inferiority upon
black readers first placed by Supreme Court Justice Roger Taney in
the infamous *Dred Scott* case.

In 1937, when Dickerson expanded his commercial printing business to include a weekly paper, he did so in addition to his law practice and as the city's first black assistant prosecutor, a position to
which he was appointed in 1928. A trailblazer, Dickerson became
the first black person to serve as a chief city prosecutor in 1943. In
1948, the governor of Ohio appointed him to serve as vice chairman of the powerful Industrial Commission of Ohio. In that position Dickerson opened doors for countless young black attorneys
and civil servants to enter state government at levels previously
unattainable.

As I look back on the late 1930s through the 1940s, I realize
that I witnessed the unfolding struggle of whites in power being
forced to come to grips involuntarily with social and political change.
Through his weekly editorials in the *Buckeye Review* and his activism in the NAACP, Dickerson forcefully set forth objections to
the *Vindicator*'s segregated column, as well as its editorial position
on the city's policy of excluding blacks from taxpayer-supported
swimming pools. This led to meetings with William F. Maag Jr.,
editor and publisher of the *Vindicator*, and Francis Wise, city editor,

in the latter half of the 1940s. I was permitted to attend some of the meetings. Those of us who joined Dickerson also had to contend with backfires ignited by black apologists who felt that a segregated column and one night of roller skating at Rayenwood Skating Rink on a segregated basis was better than none at all and also that a Jim Crow swimming pool was preferable to none.

When R. Burns Harvey's health failed, the *Vindicator* quietly dropped his column and began to distribute news about black people throughout the newspaper, with a notable exception, the "Society" section. It remained lily white for a considerable time thereafter. Even so, the pages of the *Buckeye Review* and local NAACP activists continued to attack the practices of the *Vindicator*. On July 7, 1948, the *Vindicator* riled the black leadership enough to demand a meeting with Maag, after an editorial asserted:

Old Youngstown residents foresaw what would happen when a few Negro leaders, backed by some well-meaning white friends and others not so well-meaning, planned a campaign to force acceptance of Negroes in all of the city's swimming pools.

The result was bound to be, first, a series of local disturbances, and then the exploitation of Youngstown Negroes by groups seeking to capitalize upon such a rich opportunity. . . . Their economic and social status has been steadily rising; it must continue to do so in order that they may have the kind of life which, as Americans, they have the right to expect . . .

Better relations, however, do not come by violence. They are not promoted by strong arm methods. They are not helped by reformers who urge young Negroes to go in masses to the swimming pools nearest their homes and insist upon swimming there, regardless of neighborhood sentiment. Granted that they have the legal right; everyone has rights which he does not find it wise to exercise.

The tenor of black protest heightened considerably after the *Vindicator* endorsed segregated swimming pools. However, an increasing number of whites began to express their discomfort over segregationist policies. Groups such as the Interracial Committee and the Intergroup Goodwill Council allied themselves with the NAACP branch. A newly arrived Episcopal clergyman, John Burt, began to speak out in sermons about the moral and constitutional monstrosity that the *Vindicator* editorials embodied. Reverend Burt was the rector of the prestigious St. John's Episcopal Church, located on the edge of downtown Youngstown, across the street from Youngstown College. Burt's critique carried influence. The publisher of the *Vindicator*, William F. Maag Jr., was a vestryman at St. John's, as were many of the establishment figures of the city, including Judge John W. Ford, a member of a leading family. Those sermons drew me, a Baptist, as well as a number of my friends to services at St. John's to hear and to meet Reverend Burt. Several other prominent ministers, newly arrived in the community, began to give sermons with the same call for change. These powerful voices began to attract more and more attention. I was encouraged by Dickerson to report on these developments in the pages of the *Buckeye Review*.

Supportive white clergymen faced opposition from members of their congregations. Neither the Catholic Diocese of Youngstown nor the various parish priests who served the neighborhoods where the various swimming pools were located at the time joined in the call for change. However, it did not take long for Father James Malone, superintendent of the Diocesan Schools, to speak out on a broad range of social issues. He later became Bishop of Youngstown Diocese and in that capacity placed the Catholic leadership squarely on the side of racial and social justice.

It was not long after those resounding voices of protest that *Vindicator* editorials sent forth a different message. When our delegation met with Maag, the only concession he made was to say that the July 1948 editorial could have been better written. The very thought that a newspaper, whose existence is protected by the First Amendment, would argue for withholding from African Americans the exercise of their constitutional rights conveyed so reprehensible a message that the paper's honor was called into question. And I am sure that it became clear to Maag and his chief editorial writer Francis Wise that the *Vindicator* had to reclaim its honor. Reverend

Burt and the other clergymen, with their moral pleas, provided a way.

Another conflict I observed involved the superintendent of schools versus leaders of the civil rights community, including my mentor, Maynard Dickerson. I was there as president of the NAACP Youth Council. The meeting took place in the office of Superintendent Paul C. Bunn, a distinguished-looking white-haired educator. He was very much on the defensive as the case for hiring black teachers was laid out. Superintendent Bunn gave the timeworn excuse that no qualified persons were available. This excuse was rejected. The case for hiring black teachers continued to be pressed beyond that meeting until Mary Ella Lovett was selected as an elementary teacher, followed by Elizabeth Lynch Caldwell. Miraculously, other "qualified" persons were found to teach in the Youngstown schools, first in the elementary grades, and later, with the hiring of James Ervin, a graduate of Kent State University, at Hayes Junior High School. Ervin eventually became a principal. Witnessing those confrontations provided lessons that proved useful throughout my life. For this, I shall forever be grateful to J. Maynard Dickerson. He stood out as the most powerful African American in the entire valley and one of the most significant in the state. He did not shirk from using the *Buckeye Review* to challenge the racial status quo.

Of the many contestations, one that drew national attention involved the National Amateur Baseball Federation (NABF). Youngstown had always been a favorite of the NABF because of the quality and the number of its ball fields. The Youngstown Parks and Recreation Commission was noted for its available ball diamonds, and thus the commission looked forward to hosting the national baseball tournament. However, for African Americans the problem with the NABF was its racial ban that kept teams with black players from participating. Plus, the fields on which the games were played were public facilities, supported by the taxpayers of Youngstown. Black leaders took the initiative and were joined by liberal white religious and labor leaders in the demand that either the racial ban be lifted or the tournament be taken to another city. Thomas Pemberton, the superintendent of the Parks and Recreation Commission, was a personal friend of the head of the NABF, a man named Doik Novaro. Pemberton also had a strong relationship with Esther Hamilton, an influential columnist for the Youngstown *Vindicator*. Hamilton strongly defended Pemberton, as did the editorial writers. Through the pages of the *Vindicator*, they also attacked those who criticized the NABF's discriminatory practices.

In the face of the formidable defense that surrounded the NABF, as well as Pemberton and the city's Parks and Recreation Commission, Maynard Dickerson through the *Buckeye Review* continued to keep the public abreast of the controversy. However, some members of the black community appeared disinterested, even as it became a subject of considerable national debate. As was often the case, a form of resignation continued to hang heavy over those who felt that racial discrimination was impervious to change. It was this mind-set that permitted the city's exclusionary polices to persist for as long as they did.

My role as a reporter for the *Buckeye Review* and my activities in the NAACP's Youth Council drew me into the campaign to snatch the welcome mat from under the NABF. At this same time I was involved in an effort to end the Parks and Recreation Commission's segregation policies in regard to swimming pools. Dickerson, a strong supporter of the new mayor, Ralph W. O'Neill, successfully lobbied him to press the commission. The mayor made clear to the commission that unless the NABF opened up the tournament, it must stay away. The baseball ban was lifted at the first game of the tournament on a Saturday afternoon at Bailey Park. I accompanied Dickerson and Mayor O'Neill to witness the game, which featured the Sheriff Smith team of Akron with its black pitcher. A tiny but significant step for the 1940s.

I spent years observing Dickerson in his law practice, his printing and publishing business, and civil rights activities because he and his wife, Virginia, a childless couple, took me under their wing. He was always open with me and encouraging, but even as a

teen I was not immune to his frank criticism or his sometimes painful commitment to the truth. He demanded change everywhere he
thought it was needed. I was in junior high school when I made the
request to write a column for the *Buckeye Review*. He agreed. I then
sat at a typewriter to peck out my first column, "Sports Shorts." My
desire to play football when I reached South High School had
piqued my interest in sports.

After typing my first column, I presented it to Dickerson for
edits. His confrontation was now with me, as he took out his tri-
color ballpoint pen—the first time I had ever seen one—and proceeded to use the red ink. When he finished, the pages looked like
a bloody mess. He paused, looked at me, and then asked, "What
grade are you in, son?" I said, "The eighth." He then asked, in rapid-
fire, cross-examination style: "What have you been doing in school
with your time? What courses have you taken? What grades do
you get? How did you make it to the eighth grade?" I was stunned
into silence, and stuttered something about my courses and grades.
He cut me off with this sharp observation: "Son, you don't know
how to write. You *can't* spell." He added, "These mistakes deal with
things you should have already learned. It's not too late to catch
up—if you work hard. If you are willing to be serious and buckle
down, I will help you." I assured him that I wanted to learn and welcomed his help. He let me know that I could not be thin-skinned,
because he would not be concerned with sparing my feelings. Upon
my assurance, we, in effect, entered into what now would be characterized as a mentor/mentee pact. That pact lasted until the day of
his death in August 1976.

We began with a reading program of magazines and newspaper
articles. Several days a week he brought home copies of the *New
York Times* and the newspaper *PM* that carried columns by the nation's leading political writers, such as Arthur Krock and Max
Lerner. He also gave me a pocket dictionary. The purpose of reading the columns, he pointed out, was not for me to absorb the in-
tricacies of the policy arguments they contained, but to broaden
my vocabulary and comprehension, and understand word deriva-

tion. "When you see a word you don't understand, look it up, damn it," he said.

Dickerson's demanding style was challenging, to say the least, but I was eager to learn. One incentive was the opportunity to do a sports column and later to inch my way into writing news stories for the *Buckeye Review*, all carefully edited by Dickerson, of course. The lessons learned began to carry over to my classroom writing assignments. The improvement and confidence I gradually acquired helped me to achieve something else—maintaining my grades at a sufficient level so as to enter high school eligible for participation in football.

In the process I learned a crucial lesson. My teachers in elementary and junior high school had been only minimally concerned about my learning. Their primary concern—and what seemed to determine my ability to advance to the next grade—was the fact that I was not disruptive. I had been taught by my elders to be pleasant and polite. This seemed to go a long way with my teachers. I also revealed an intellectual curiosity. As far as Dickerson was concerned, politeness, while important, was no substitute for correct use of the English language, both spoken and written. The independent research that I began to engage in put me in good stead with my teachers, and served me well in undergraduate and law school.

In the Military

During World War II, all males were required to register with local draft boards upon reaching their eighteenth birthday. Those classified 1A were deemed qualified for service. I was classified 1A and upon graduation from high school in January 1945 was ordered to report for service in March. On the day I was to report for induction, I went to Dickerson's office in city hall. My mother could not bring herself to accompany me to the Erie Railroad train station for a farewell; that task fell to my mentor. We walked the two

blocks from his office, engaging in small talk. We arrived at the
station, which was swirling with other draftees, black and white,
headed for induction in Cleveland, Ohio. At eighteen years of age,
and never having been away from home for an extended period of
time, I was filled with anxiety. Yet, standing on the platform waiting to board the train, Dickerson passed along his parting words
to me: "Good luck, Sonny. Don't do anything that will make us
ashamed of you." His words were both reassuring and challenging.
They said many things to me about being responsible and exercising good judgment. I was about to enter the U.S. Army when a
war was raging on two fronts, uncertain of what I would eventually face.

In advance of reporting for induction I had written to the army
seeking to be enrolled in the Army Air Corps flight-training program at Kessler Field, Mississippi. The response was not encouraging, since the army had capped the number of black cadets to be
accepted. This was a white-imposed quota system that did not
seem to give offense to those in power. Tokenism was the order of
the day. The Army Air Corps held a special appeal for me because
of the heroic feats of the Tuskegee Army Airfield's 99th Pursuit
Squadron, and the 322nd Fighter Group under the command of
General Benjamin O. Davis Jr., which had been regularly chroni-
cled in black newspapers. As I read of the heroism of black airmen,
I learned about the pressure being applied by black leaders on
the government to open more doors of opportunity for service in
the military free of segregation and discrimination. William H.
Hastie, an NAACP stalwart and legal strategist, accepted the position of civilian aide to President Roosevelt's secretary of war,
Henry L. Stimson. Colonel Campbell C. Johnson was appointed
as special aide to the director of Selective Service, Lieutenant
General Lewis B. Hershey, an appointment that did not alter the
segregated nature of the military. Hastie, frustrated over the
failure of Secretary of War Stimson to move more rapidly to end
discrimination against black soldiers, resigned in protest. Such was
the climate within the military when I left Youngstown for the
Cleveland induction center.

Upon arrival in Cleveland, I was processed with several hundred other draftees, and from there we boarded a train for Camp Atterbury, Indiana. After a few weeks I was sent to basic training at Sheppard Field, in Wichita Falls, Texas. Camp Atterbury was the threshold through which I passed into a totally segregated living environment. I was stunned to see the freedom that Italian prisoners of war enjoyed at the base. The PX and base theater were open to them, while the service clubs and theater were not available to those of us who were black, except on a segregated basis. These were among but a few of the conditions that the military maintained and refused to change.

Finding myself in the totally segregated barracks, dining halls, and service clubs, and viewing whites across a color barrier, was traumatic after having lived in an integrated neighborhood, playing with and going to school with white kids. Just as I had experienced in civilian life where authority figures were usually all white, the military officers—noncommissioned and commissioned—were white. Despite protest by our national leaders, the segregated conditions remained deeply entrenched and pervasive.

We went by bus from Camp Atterbury to Indianapolis, where a troop train awaited us. After departing, the train made a stop at Union Terminal in Cincinnati. Since the inductees were segregated, and the train reflected that fact, it was not necessary for us to do what civilians did when they traveled southward through Cincinnati—that is, change to Jim Crow coaches. We were already in compliance with that requirement, thanks to the army. In basic training, the drill sergeants did not address us in normal tones—they barked commands. Nearly all of our white commissioned officers were Southerners. This was a subject of much comment among those of us who came from the North. The sole black officer in our unit was Alfred Cain, a sergeant major who also served as an assistant in the chapel. A number of us turned to him for emotional support.

While we were on the drill field in Texas on the morning of April 12, 1945, an announcement came over the public address system that brought all activities to a halt. President Franklin D.

Roosevelt had died at his summer home in Warm Springs, Georgia. We were stunned. After returning to the barracks, we listened intently to our radios as more details were reported, including the fact that the new president was a Missourian, the former vice president, Harry S. Truman. President Roosevelt was a "god" to all of us. The new president, our commander in chief, was an unknown. To say we were wary would be an understatement. The fact that he was from Missouri—a former slave state and site of the Dred Scott trial—concerned us.

It was also while still training at Sheppard Field in Texas that news reached us of the deaths of Hitler and Mussolini, which coincided with the end of the war in Europe. Our excitement upon hearing this mixed with a high degree of anxiety over whether we would now be shipped to the Pacific Theater. All of this occurred within the context of our second-class treatment as black servicemen. The NAACP, under the leadership of Walter White and Roy Wilkins and lawyers William Hastie and Thurgood Marshall, continually protested such unfair treatment, but morale was poor, and many black servicemen remained cynical. They looked to the NAACP to press the case for fairer treatment, even to the extent of seeking to be placed in combat rather than being limited to labor battalions and other support roles. Some, however, questioned the strategy of our leaders pressing for the right to fight. I remained in the camp of those arguing for full integration and equal treatment in *all* phases of American life. That included the military.

By August 1945, things changed significantly. I had been transferred to Wright Field in Dayton, and I was there when the United States dropped the atomic bomb on Hiroshima, followed by one on Nagasaki. We knew that the end was in sight and began speculating on when we would be discharged. Initially, my duties at Dayton's Wright Field entailed the humbling job of collecting garbage from the various mess halls on the base. Even so, I regarded it as good duty because I began early in the morning and was finished early in the afternoon. That left the rest of the day to play softball and engage in other recreational activities. I later was assigned to the PX, where I stocked shelves with canned goods. In addition to these duties, I tried out for and was chosen to play on the base football team. We traveled on military planes to other bases for games. An army captain from Green Mountain, Vermont, who was serving as head coach made full use of my experience as a South High School varsity team member. His attitude was a welcome contrast to a number of the Southern white officers.

Weekend leaves permitted me to go home to Youngstown, which I did by hitchhiking. Because I had a deadline for reporting back to the base, my return trip was always on a Greyhound bus. On one occasion I visited the base travel office at Wright Field to obtain a ticket for a trip to Youngstown. The representative, to my surprise, was a young woman of color. When we finished our transaction she told me that she was Elizabeth Casey, formerly of Gallipolis, Ohio, and that her fiancé, Theodore Bost, was from Youngstown. I knew Bost. Our families were close friends, members of the same church, and his cousin Joyce Bost and I had attended high school together. Elizabeth went on to tell me that he had been court-martialed for mutiny, while stationed in Guam, along with another Youngstowner, 1st Sgt. Blair Harvey, whom I also knew. After that, whenever we saw each other she and I talked about their plight. I passed along information about the soldiers to the NAACP through Maynard Dickerson, who was president of the Ohio State Conference of Branches at that time. As it turned out, Thurgood Marshall and the national officials already had information on the Guam situation. The black troops were given the most dangerous assignments connected with handling ammunition. When their protests went unheeded, they decided to withhold their labor by remaining in their barracks rather than reporting for duty. This led to the charges of mutiny. Bost and Harvey drew long terms at hard labor and dishonorable discharges. Through pressure from Stateside, the sentences were modified and they returned home.

While serving at Wright Field, I also accepted an invitation from an NAACP official, Miley Williamson, who was then secretary of the Ohio Conference of NAACP Branches. With the state organization planning to hold its annual meeting in Dayton and my mentor, Maynard Dickerson, as the president, I knew his fine hand was at work though he never admitted it. Since the war had ended, and attention was being given to postwar activities, Williamson asked me to address the conference on the subject "What the Returning Negro Soldier Expects." By this time it was clear that duty abroad was foreclosed and I, among others, were just "marking time." Though I had just passed my twentieth birthday, the delegates listened most respectfully as I laid out my thoughts on the subject.

It was not long after that my unit was reassigned to the Newark (New Jersey) Air Force Base. We were quartered in Quonset huts in Weequahic Park in the heart of the city. I performed various duties on the base and on some evenings a number of fellow soldiers and I would take a train over to New York City, where we frequented the nightclubs. On Easter weekend, a few of us took the subway to 125th Street in Harlem, where we found free lodging in the YMCA gym. The next morning I worked my way up Eighth Avenue to 137th Street in order to attend worship services at the famous Abyssinian Baptist Church, with membership over ten thousand, pastored by Reverend Adam Clayton Powell Jr. It was the largest church sanctuary I had ever seen.

I found a seat in the balcony, where I was entranced by the size and the quality of the choir and its musical renditions. A number of ministers were seated on the pulpit, which was bedecked with Easter lilies and other flowers. After announcements, music, and a period of meditation, Reverend Powell, in a dramatic moment, strode to his place on the pulpit, raised his arms toward the congregation, and took charge. I was awed by his charismatic, magnetic presence and the history and majesty of this great church. Little did I know at the time that I would one day find myself connected to this history in a very personal way when I married the granddaughter of the renowned Reverend Charles Satchell Morris, who in 1908 had recruited Reverend Powell's father, Adam Clayton Powell Sr., to succeed him as pastor of Abyssinian Baptist Church.

Realizing that we were young, inexperienced, and away from home for the first time, concern about sex and venereal disease was a constant refrain voiced by military authorities. Movies were shown and printed materials were distributed, especially when we were leaving the base for town. Whenever we went to New York, the MPs kept a watchful eye on us, knowing that we were prey for the flocks of "ladies of the evening" waiting for our arrival. Located strategically throughout the city were "Pro-Stations," where servicemen were urged to go to obtain condoms as a precaution, and treatment after the fact. Ringing in my ears were the parting words of advice from Maynard Dickerson as I was about to board the train at the Erie Railroad Station in Youngstown for induction into the army. Undoubtedly, this was part of the reason for the warning that he so diplomatically offered to me, his eighteen-year-old charge.

It was during this period that soldiers were able to travel to Pompton Lakes, New Jersey, to the training camp of boxing champ Joe Louis. At one point Louis sauntered over to the section in which we were seated near ringside and said in a joking manner, "It's 'bout time you put those uniforms down." That was also the summer when Branch Rickey broke the color barrier in major league baseball by signing Jackie Robinson to play for the Montreal Royals, the Triple A minor league team of the Brooklyn Dodgers. When Montreal came to play the Jersey City Giants, we were in the stands. After the game, some of us GIs gathered at the dressing-room door, along with Jackie's bride, Rachel Robinson, to await his exit. After showering and changing into street clothes, Robinson stepped out, with perspiration on his brow, and politely autographed our printed programs. The historic nature of the event we were witnessing was yet to dawn upon us.

As the summer of 1946 waned, we GIs kept watch for our discharge orders. Finally, the orders were cut and we were directed to prepare to leave Newark and report to Fort Mead, Maryland, to be mustered out of the Army Air Corps on October 7, 1946. I was transported to Washington, D.C., to board a Greyhound bus bound for Youngstown.

Nearly a decade after leaving the service I was involved in Adlai Stevenson's 1956 campaign for the presidency. One of the rallies I chaired featured the then-retired Joe Louis. After I introduced him he spoke to the crowd about the reasons he was supporting Governor Stevenson. I later had the pleasure of driving him to the Youngstown Airport.

My College Years in Postwar Youngstown

Obtaining a job was foremost on the minds of most returning soldiers. Others were eager to take advantage of the GI Bill and go to college. Benefits included payment for tuition, textbooks, and fees, and a monthly stipend of $75. I lived at home with my mother and stepfather and performed household chores in lieu of rent. My duties in the print shop and for the *Buckeye Review* brought me $25 per week—sometimes. There was no car in the picture, so I walked everywhere or used public transportation. Maynard Dickerson's disability did not permit him to drive, so I assisted his wife, Virginia, with a variety of duties that included driving. The Dickersons also occasionally allowed use of their car for my own purposes.

I never doubted that I would go to college. With the aid of the GI Bill, the only question was where. Because of my ties with the Dickerson Printing Company and the *Buckeye Review*, I decided to remain in Ohio and attend what was then Youngstown College. It later became a state university. I reengaged with the NAACP Youth Council, wrote sports stories for the *Buckeye Review*, and began to learn the ins and outs of the newspaper business—selling advertisements, sending out vouchers, keeping track of the income on daily sheets, making bank deposits and paying bills, taking in printing orders, assisting in the shop, and delivering orders. When classes began, I had to organize my week so as to perform these duties around my class schedule.

At Youngstown College, I took what was called a pre-law course that included the basic subjects required of freshmen. I commuted to the campus by public transportation three days a week. My classes were spread over the course of the day, often into the evening, which allowed me to use the library for study periods. I operated on several time tracks in order to meet all my obligations. Social activities, including those associated with Scroller Club (the organization one joins before becoming a Kappa) and later Kappa Alpha Psi fraternity, were very limited. Saturdays and Sundays were devoted to study. After my freshman year, I was better able to adjust my time to allow for participation in community and civil rights activities.

Many of the civil rights activities centered on issues that arose on campus. These led to the formation of a college chapter of the NAACP. Forming such a group was a natural response for those of us returning from World War II. The returning veterans' resolve was strengthened by their war experiences; we were less tolerant of discriminatory practices. For example, some returning vets, including those who had been students prior to World War II, felt direct action was required in response to school policies that excluded black students from the cafeteria and from dances, parties, and other social events. In fact, shortly before my enrollment at Youngstown College, black vets challenged cafeteria exclusion practices with direct-action tactics. The college administrators hastened to institute the required reform. Racist practices appeared in a more subtle form when I arrived at the college. For example, the "Student Activity Book," which held tickets to extracurricular activities, reflected the effort to preserve the social structure that had existed prior to World War II, before the arrival of relatively large numbers of black students. The college was struggling financially and welcomed the money pouring in from the Veterans Administration under the GI Bill. In their stupidity, however, they thought they could have it both ways—hold on to the past, and take advantage of the government subsidy.

When I received my Student Activity Book, I compared it with that of a white friend, John Muntean. We noted that several tickets had been removed from mine while his was intact, with tickets for various social events. After checking with other students— white and black—and noticing the pattern, we went to the Business Office for an explanation. We were passed from assistant to assistant until we finally met with the business manager. No one would admit knowledge of the problem. We decided to take the matter up with the school president, Howard W. Jones. President Jones was very approachable. He listened to our expression of outrage, and our intention to file a complaint with the Veterans Administration. We were prepared to let the chips fall where they might, pointing out that there was likely criminal conduct involved. We contended that the college was possibly committing a fraud on the federal government by receiving payment for activities denied to students. President Jones begged us to forgo taking any such action and said, in pleading tones, "Oh, don't do that. That's going to get me in trouble with my board." Relying on President Jones's promise to correct the situation, we withheld filing a complaint with the VA. When the Student Activity Books were next issued, they were fully intact for black students. (The main library on campus is named for its then board chair William F. Maag Jr., publisher of the Youngstown *Vindicator*. Today, overlooking the library lobby are two portraits—one of Maag and the other of an alumnus, Nathaniel R. Jones.)

In between classes and on the days I had no classes, I continued to work with the *Buckeye Review*. I monitored issues that affected the black community, gathered news, and wrote stories. Later I began writing weekly editorials. I "doubled in brass," so to speak, because in addition to my reporting and educational duties, I became involved in the production phase by working in the shop, where I learned to operate the Linotype machine. I also proofread the stories and assisted in laying out the pages to be printed on the huge Miehle flatbed press. Publishing a paper on a weekly basis was grueling work and my work as a reporter required me to make rounds of the police department, city hall, and the courthouse.

Along with publishing the newspaper, the Dickersons' printing company printed commercial tickets, invitations, handbills, placards, business cards, and letterhead. In the evening, while Charles Satterwhite, Lillian Singleton, and other production workers worked on the paper, I helped Dickerson manually set type for the commercial orders. Burnice Hall and Dickerson operated the printing presses while I often organized, stacked, and wrapped the orders for pickup or delivery. My responsibilities soon expanded to include ordering and purchasing newsprint, ticket stock, and related materials needed for filling the orders. The Dickersons taught me all aspects of the printing business as well as the newspaper business. Everything from preparing the receipts for delivery to making bank deposits became a part of my job. Handling the checkbook, paying bills, and writing salary checks each week were also my responsibility.

Those duties were sandwiched between my class schedule and day work. My new responsibilities with the printing company opened an entirely new vista for me and afforded an insight into the management side of life. Even in this regard, the issue of race discrimination became apparent to me. The ability to compete for printing business on a large scale was inhibited because of the refusal of the printers' unions to admit blacks. Most companies refused to do business with us because they placed orders with only union shops. Thus, we could not compete. Fortunately, within the black community, where the union's discriminating policies were understood, the union requirement was ignored.

As far back as I can recall I was an avid reader of magazines and newspapers. In particular, the black newspapers supplemented my reading of the Youngstown *Vindicator*, which had taken over another daily newspaper called the *Youngstown Telegram* in the 1930s. Black newspapers were published on a weekly basis and made their way through the homes in my neighborhood. The popularity of such papers as the *Pittsburgh Courier*, Cleveland's *Call and Post*, and the *Chicago Defender* stemmed as much from the comic strips they carried as the news they reported. I appreciated the availability of the black newspapers, comics and all, because of the serious and in-depth news stories they carried about the subjects I heard discussed at the West Federal Street YMCA forums. I learned much and gained inspiration from the various columnists, some of whom I had met when they spoke at the forums. My exposure to racial issues through the black press sharpened my ability to recognize discrimination in my own community.

One of the matters that riled me was the discrimination practiced by the Youngstown Hospital Association and the two facilities it operated, known as the North Side Unit and the South Side
Unit, both of which had nurse training schools. The laboratory of
the hospitals, under the direction of Dr. Arthur Rappaport, also
had training programs for medical technologists. I was troubled
over the absence of young black women in these programs. Women of
color who wished to become nurses had to go to other cities to
obtain that training. I began to write stories about the shameful
policy of exclusion. Those articles resulted in a call from Murial
Dunlap, the newly appointed director of the School of Nursing of
the Youngstown Hospital Association. She read some of my *Buckeye Review* stories condemning the exclusion of black women from
the School of Nursing.

An interview with Ms. Dunlap was arranged. She stated that she
intended to change that policy. She had come from New York, where
she had directed a nurse training program that recruited and trained
African American women with great success, and had every intention of doing the same in Youngstown. True to her word, in 1951 she
recruited Carol Sue Bacon and Willa Conoly to the nurse training
class. On the occasion of the "capping" ceremony, I photographed
and reported on the history-making ceremony. A year later I became
ill and was hospitalized with miliary tuberculosis in the sanatorium
for a year and was cared for by these nursing pioneers as they went
through their three-year training cycle in the hospital system.

After regaining my health, a call from Isy Young, a youth adviser
at my church, alerted me to the selection of the first black medical
technician trainee to be accepted at the Youngstown Hospital Association. Her name was Eloise Carter. She had come from St. Louis
and was living at the Central YWCA. Young asked if I would call
on her and introduce her to people in the community. Being that
we were both single, I was only too happy to oblige, and was even
more interested in spending time with her myself.

One Sunday I borrowed the Dickersons' car to take Eloise out to
dinner. We drove through a rainstorm toward Lake Milton, some

twenty miles west of Youngstown. Just as the rainstorm subsided, we stopped at DuRell's Restaurant in the suburb of Austintown. With the sun setting, a rainbow appeared and the evening turned beautiful. As we entered the restaurant, no one offered to seat us. After an awkward few minutes we saw an unoccupied booth and took it. We sat, and sat, and sat—unapproached by any of the waitresses. I finally got the attention of a waitress serving a table next to our booth as she attempted to slide past us. I, tapping her on the elbow, asked "May we have a menu?" She replied, "Well, wait just a minute," and kept moving. Moments later a woman came and asked, in a harsh tone, "What is it you want?" I said, "We want a menu." She said, "Well, you can't have one." Somewhat incredulously, I asked, "I can't have a menu? Are you in charge here?" And she replied, "No." At that point I demanded to speak to whoever was in charge. Pretty soon a man with a swagger approached, wearing white pants and a T-shirt. He asked, "What's the problem?" I said, "There's no problem. I just want to know why we can't have a menu." He said, "I think you know the reason." I said, "No I don't, tell me." He replied, "Well, it's pretty obvious. We're not going to serve you." By this time I was determined to draw him out further. I said, "Oh, really? Are you aware of the Ohio civil rights law?" After he replied, "Yeah," I said, "You still say you're not going to serve us?" When I next asked, "What's your name?" He replied, "I don't have to tell you that." As we stood to leave, I remarked, "We'll find out."

By that time the restaurant customers had noticed the scene. Some appeared to be in shock and even embarrassed. I'm sure that for many of them it was the first time they had seen this type of encounter. But no one said anything. We started toward the door, with the manager following. Upon reaching the door he spoke again: "What's that you said about that law?" I replied, in a tone loud enough for all to hear, "It's a law that could put you in jail for what you just did." He said, "Well, you understand. You know why we have to do this." I said, "No, I don't. Do you know there are people who look like us fighting in Korea so that you can keep this place open?" He said, "Yeah, but it's really not my fault." I said,

"Well, we'll see." We left. I was well aware of the Ohio laws against discrimination in places of public accommodations. It is one thing to know about the laws, but quite another to act on them.

As an officer of the NAACP Youth Council I had tried to motivate our members to challenge segregation in all forms. Suddenly I was confronted with my own personal decision as to whether to seek a legal remedy for an obvious act of racial discrimination. Eloise and I could have let this incident slide. No one would have known about the insult unless we chose to reveal it. But there was the matter of pride and self-respect. A couple of days later I went to see a lawyer, William Howard, who had been a partner of Maynard Dickerson. I told him that Eloise and I wanted to file a suit. He sent a letter to the restaurant owner, Jack DuRell. When he did not respond, we signed an affidavit that set the stage for a civil suit. Howard prepared the papers, which we signed, and they were served on DuRell. The suit was based on a statute that provided for damages of $500. I hadn't told Dickerson about the episode, and when he learned about it he was annoyed with me for filing the suit. I knew he would have discouraged me out of a sense of protectiveness. At that stage of my college work he did not want to see me entangled in litigation, although he was a staunch civil rights person. He felt I was being unduly influenced by Eloise. He asserted, "You know, she's here now, but she's going to be gone tomorrow. You have to think about your future." The case languished. It did not come up for trial until after Eloise had gone back to St. Louis. Attorney Howard contacted me with news that the lawyer for DuRell wanted to know if we were willing to settle the case. "The statute calls for judgment up to $500," DuRell's lawyer wrote, "If you make a demand for $300 or $350 we could probably avoid a trial." We settled the case for $300. After the attorney fees, only a little money was left, but I had made my point.

Our NAACP Youth Council had begun to engage in sit-ins at the downtown restaurants. Our sit-ins had the advantage of being supported by law, as contrasted with the Southern sit-ins that challenged segregation laws in the 1960s. On some levels, appeals to the law gave us greater self-confidence, although the breadth of racist practices demanded no less a frontal attack on the public sector—taxpayer-supported swimming pools, movie houses, and other places of public accommodation such as restaurants, hotels, amusement parks, and skating rinks. The NAACP Youth Council focused on the Brass Rail restaurant on East Federal Street in Youngstown, since it refused to serve African Americans. We kept going there, sitting at the counter, and getting turned away. We later filed a complaint with the city prosecutor and had the owner summoned with a warning that if it happened again a warrant would be issued under the criminal provision of the Ohio Civil Rights statute. We continued to protest. A group went to that restaurant one day and ordered soup, which, when served, was too salty to be edible. I phoned our family physician, Dr. William Young, who advised us to "just stay there." He left his office and went to the medical supply store, where he purchased several test tubes. Upon joining us at the restaurant we poured the soup into the test tubes, which he then took to the chemist at city hall, two blocks away, to have it analyzed for salt content. The report led us to conclude that the proprietors were playing dirty tricks. We promptly reported this to the city prosecutor, who invited us to file a criminal complaint. When the proprietor later appeared in the prosecutor's office and realized that he was on the verge of being arrested, he broke into tears and pleaded with us to forgo pressing charges. He promised to change and that everyone would be welcomed in his restaurant. We withdrew our complaint but continued to monitor the restaurant.

A few weeks later I received a complaint at the *Buckeye Review* about Idora Park discriminating against blacks in a variety of ways. They felt welcome at the amusement park only on days set aside by corporate underwriters like Ward Baking Company and Isaly Dairy Company. On those special days, blacks could enjoy the rides and other amenities without discrimination—except for the swimming pool. The dance hall was also open in the afternoon for dancing. However, a rope was strung across the middle of the hall to demarcate the area for black people on one side and white people on the other. Uniformed officers stood nearby to enforce the separation.

We had argued in the columns of the *Buckeye Review* that blacks should not participate in such racially restricting events. But, kids being kids couldn't resist the lure and wanted to enjoy the park, even if on a limited basis.

One evening John Carney, the young white man who headed up the newly formed civil rights group, and I decided to test the complaint that black patrons of Idora Park were being served beverages out of paper cups whereas white patrons were being served out of ceramic or glass. While this practice may have seemed minor to some, it represented to me an instance of the badge of slavery being applied to people of color. This was intolerable. Carney and I went to the park and approached a concession stand from different directions. Carney placed his order and was served his beverage in a ceramic cup, as were other whites. When I ordered my drink from the other side of the stand, the kid proceeded to fill my order in a paper cup. I said, "No, no, no. I want the same kind of cup he has," and pointed to John. A summer worker, he was just a kid; he replied, "I can't." When I asked the reason, he said, "I'm not allowed," adding he was so instructed by "the boss." I pressed him further: "You mean you can't serve me in that kind of cup because I'm colored? Because of my color?" He said, "Yeah." I then asked to see his boss. By that time, Carney had come around to my side and joined me in the questioning, noting, "You served me in this cup." He was told, "I know, but I'm not allowed to . . ."

John and I walked over to the park office seeking the manager, Max Rindin. We asked the secretary to see Mr. Rindin. When he appeared, we identified ourselves: John from the newly formed Intergroup Goodwill Council and me from the *Buckeye Review*. We related our experience. Quite flustered, Rindin said, "Well, I don't have anything to do with those vendors. We just rent them the space." We let him know that in our view he was responsible. We told him that I was doing a story for the *Buckeye Review* and that he wouldn't be too happy with it. He said, "Well, it's really not our fault because I don't have any control over it. I'll get in touch with them and tell them what they have to do in the future." I wrote the story, leading with a blazing headline. From time to time Carney and I would check, as would other people after reading the story. We became satisfied that the discriminatory practice, indeed, had come to an end there.

While I was a college student, my fraternity, Kappa Alpha Psi, confronted the racist policies of the Hotel Pick-Ohio, a very popular site for social and civic events, located in downtown Youngstown. The manager, Del Courtney, was an extremely popular figure in town, always the subject of glowing stories in the daily newspaper. The powers that be catered to him. The hotel's Crystal Ballroom was often rented out for dances and banquets. As did other fraternal organizations, Youngstown College's Kappa chapter chose it for its Sweetheart Ball. As the head of the chapter, I called the manager's office and reserved a date for the event, providing the essential information to the manager's assistant: Kappa Alpha Psi Fraternity Sweetheart Ball, the date, et cetera. Advising me that the date was available, the assistant invited me to come in and work out details. When I went to finalize the details and leave the deposit, the manager's assistant balked, stating, "Oh, there must be some mistake because the ballroom has been rented to another group for that time." I said, "How can that be? I called, reserved the date, and was told that all we had to do was come down and leave a deposit." "Well," she said, "I'm sorry." I responded that we would not let the matter end there. I then wrote a story and threatened to contact the home office of Pick Hotel chain in Chicago. After the story ran, Del Courtney placed an urgent call to me and asked for a meeting, which I agreed to. Shortly afterward, the matter was resolved, the dance was held, and the policy underwent a change. Another small step.

There was reason to be hopeful about change, even though some of our victories came more easily than others. Rayenwood Skating Rink in Youngstown presented a relatively easy hurdle to overcome. Operators were determined to limit black use to Monday night. I wrote stories about this pattern of "Black Night" that urged young people not to patronize it. The inclination for some was to ignore our suggestions and override our objections. Uniformed, off-duty, white police officers worked at the rink to enforce the Jim

Crow policy. The skating rink, however, soon succumbed to our continued pressure and brought "Black Night" to an end.

Not all victories came quite so peacefully. When I joined a group that sought to test the racial policy at the North Side Swimming Pool one hot Sunday afternoon, we were unable to gain admission. As we stood at the ticket window demanding to be sold tickets, a dozen or so white thugs descended upon us swinging fists and clubs. We fought back. I demanded that a park policeman get the names of the assailants. He feebly requested one or two to identify themselves. All they did was give false names, laugh, and flee. Later in the afternoon I went to the home of a friend who attended the high school that served the area. We looked through his yearbook in the hope of recognizing some of the attackers. Sure enough, I did recognize one of the leaders of the group. Arrests followed. Although their sentences were suspended, they had to pay a fine. This was another instance in which we used the law to make our point. There appeared to be one racial incident after the next, forcing us to seemingly claw our way, step-by-step, in the years before 1954—before *Brown v. Board of Education*. And yet despite what seemed at times to be battles at every turn, we were conscious of a new day dawning in postwar Youngstown. We emboldened ourselves with the knowledge of Ohio's civil rights laws and with a determination never to return to past racial practices.

Pathway to a Career in Law

I enrolled in Youngstown College's night law school in 1951. However, my "legal training" had begun much earlier in the front row of the forums of the West Federal Street YMCA. It was there that I was introduced to the issues and challenges of America's racial realities. It was there that I became conscious of the fundamental ways that the law was being distorted to tightly screw racist principles into the hardware of American institutions that affect voting, housing, public accommodations, health benefits, jobs, education, and recreation. This convinced me, in turn, that law was essential to uncouple those institutions from the attitudes and societal practices that denied African Americans their basic constitutional rights. Indeed a moral sense about this has guided my thinking and hardened my resolve through each phase of my life, from the earliest time up to and including my period of civil rights advocacy, to the years of my federal judgeship, and in the responsibilities I performed as chief diversity and inclusion officer for Blank Rome LLP, the law firm I affiliated with upon retiring from the bench.

As I've said, it was through the YMCA forum program that I came within the orbit of national figures. My mentor, J. Maynard Dickerson, saw to it that I had personal contact with the featured speakers. While not all of them were lawyers, all addressed racial injustice and issues that were connected to the law and the courts. They included NAACP giants like Walter White, Thurgood Marshall, and Roy Wilkins; educators Benjamin Mays, Mordecai Johnson, and Charles H. Wesley; psychologists Kenneth Clark and Mamie Clark; and the leading advocate for fair housing, Robert C. Weaver. Conversation with many of the speakers continued at Dickerson's home in the form of post-lecture social festivities. I recall at such an occasion Walter White's discussion of his meetings with President Franklin Roosevelt, Eleanor Roosevelt, and Supreme Court Justice Felix Frankfurter. It was fascinating to hear about the behind-the-scenes efforts to overcome the refusal of the Daughters of the American Revolution to permit Marian Anderson to sing in Constitution Hall. This led to Anderson's dramatic Easter Sunday morning performance on the steps of the Lincoln Memorial. Having arisen early with my family to hear Anderson's concert on the radio, as did a record-breaking number of Americans, it was nothing short of a rendezvous with history to listen to White's description of what it took to make this appearance possible.

The shelves in the Dickersons' home were lined with books dealing with the history of race and what the Swedish social scientist Gunnar Myrdal's study called "An American Dilemma."[1] Several of the researchers and scholars who took part in the Myrdal study were Dickerson's friends and lecturers at the YMCA forum.

Foremost among them were Dr. Kenneth C. Clark and Dr. Robert C. Weaver. Kenneth Clark and his wife, Mamie, founded a research center in New York City that, among other things, studied the effect of segregation on black children. A key instrument of their study involved the use of black and white dolls and black children's reactions to them. It showed the damage done to black children's self-esteem by racial segregation. So compelling were the results of that study that the Supreme Court footnoted it in *Brown v. Board of Education*. I was able to hear Kenneth Clark discuss his study in an intimate and informal setting at a reception in his honor in the Dickerson home. Years later, in the 1970s, when I was in charge of the NAACP's legal program directed at ending Northern school segregation, I called upon Clark's expertise in the Coney Island School desegregation case that I was litigating in federal court in Brooklyn. Clark's commitment to school desegregation in the face of powerful attacks by black separatists, on the one hand, and anti-busing groups on the other, never wavered.

Robert Weaver earned his PhD from Harvard and formed part of Thurgood Marshall's "dream team" of desegregation strategists. I heard him speak in Youngstown on housing discrimination in the 1950s shortly after the Supreme Court struck down restrictive covenants in the case of *Shelley v. Kramer*. I had the honor of escorting him to meetings and a television interview. His directness in telling local real estate and banking officials that they had been "bad boys" by maintaining restrictive practices drew red faces. After all, Weaver, who had held high-level positions in the Roosevelt and Truman administrations, was no one to tangle with. In the 1960s, President Kennedy would appoint him to be administrator of the Federal Housing Administration (FHA). Under President Lyndon B. Johnson, Weaver became the first black to serve in the cabinet, holding the position of secretary of Housing and Urban Development (HUD).

My focus on a law career sharpened further after meeting Thurgood Marshall, who came to Ohio when the city council of Warren, Ohio, located fourteen miles from Youngstown, attempted a legislative sleight of hand to prevent blacks from using its city-owned swimming pool. The officials attempted a different strategy than the one that was used in my hometown. The city's mayor and city council proposed to the Warren NAACP branch, headed by its fearless and spunky president James Culver, Ada Berryman, and other black leaders, that they accept a one-day-a-week use of the city's only swimming pool. The branch rejected the proposal. After this, the city entered into a lease with a hastily formed group of whites who established a nonprofit organization called the Warren Veterans Swim Club. The lease arrangement required that the swim club, in addition to segregating blacks, share a portion of its proceeds with the city. The "private" club would establish criteria for membership, which, of course, meant whites only. Culver and his associates sought the counsel of Dickerson, who by then had become president of the Ohio State Conference of NAACP Branches. Dickerson mobilized the legal redress team of the Ohio State NAACP to lead a legal challenge to the lease arrangement. In addition to Dickerson, the team included his law partner, William M. Howard, a distinguished graduate of the University of Michigan Law School; William Brooks, an outstanding lawyer of the Columbus, Ohio, bar; and J. Franklin Spruill and W. Howard Forte of Akron, Ohio.

This case offered me the opportunity to observe strategy sessions on various desegregation issues with the NAACP. Some of the sessions included Thurgood Marshall. His arrival always stirred enormous excitement. The phone calls from lawyer to lawyer, city to city across Ohio, beamed the message: "Thurgood's coming, Thurgood's coming." An aura of excitement always surrounded Marshall. He was a walking bank of legal knowledge. His impact on the lawyers drafting the papers for filing in the Warren swimming-pool case was powerful because of his vast experience. Their briefs were tightened through multiple revisions. What to me seemed repetitious was a reflection of the experience of a civil rights litigator who had prepared and overseen legal drafting in cases all over the South. The lawyers soaked up references in legal briefs and court opinions that Marshall brought in his briefcase, and in some instances, combined them with drafts of documents the local lawyers had previously prepared. I well remember William Howard, one of the

Youngstown lawyers, sparking a spirited discussion over the term "invidious," which was totally new to me. The discussion of that term and how to make it apply to the conduct of the Warren, Ohio, city officials in leasing the swimming pool to the Veterans Swim Club was key to the case the NAACP felt it needed to prevail under their Fourteenth Amendment claim. As these lawyers discussed and debated language and phraseology and legal points, I watched and listened. The finished products were readied for final typing and filing. Though the city's one-day-a-week proposal for blacks to use public facilities was nothing less than a discriminatory screen, it began to be pushed by other Northern cities. And it had the effect of often splitting a black community between those willing to accept crumbs and those who felt they were entitled to a full slice, which became the fate of the "Black Night" roller-skating option in Youngstown.

The Warren case was tried before a Trumbull County Common Pleas judge who rejected the arguments of the NAACP. While the decision was a setback, the lawyers lost no time in preparing an immediate appeal to the Seventh District Court of Appeals. For some reason, which I do not recall, the judges of that court recused themselves, making it necessary for the Ohio chief justice to designate judges from another appellate district. A hearing was shortly scheduled for the appellate judges to entertain the argument. All this occurred prior to the Supreme Court handing down its historic 1954 *Brown v. Board of Education* decision that outlawed public school segregation. To be able to sit at the feet of these skilled and resourceful lawyers and witness their meticulous preparation inspired me with a determination to walk in their shoes. Their respect for the law and the courts, even when the cards had been stacked against the interests of black people, stood as a testimony to their faith in the belief that, if they persisted, the law could be an instrument of positive societal change.

What was even more compelling for me was the startling outcome of their brilliant appellate advocacy. It was on July 8, 1948, that the Eleventh District Court of Appeals rendered its powerful opinion. The opinion minced no words; it was a ringing pre-*Brown* reaffirmation of the meaning of the Fourteenth Amendment's equal-protection clause. The Ohio appellate court said to the city of Warren, "The power to lease does not include the power to discriminate against members of a minority race in the exercise of a constitutional right." It added: "It is our conclusion, therefore, that the Veterans Swim Club, a corporation not-for-profit, was a mere agent or instrumentality through which the City of Warren operates the swimming pool ostensibly for the veterans of all wars of the United States but actually only for war veterans of the Caucasian race."

I called that decision to the attention of my political science class at Youngstown College for the simple reason that as a black World War II veteran, I believed that the powerful judicial conclusion struck home. The audacity of the city fathers of Warren sprung from the fact that in earlier times their gambit would have worked. Believing that they could get away with such a maneuver reflected the mind-set of pre–World War II white public officials and white citizens. Unbeknownst to them, however, much was going on in the country on a number of fronts to challenge the way law was being used to circumscribe the rights of black Americans. As I have mentioned, most notable in the same year of 1948 was *Shelley v. Kramer*, in which the U.S. Supreme Court struck down the enforceability of racial restrictive covenants. Having fought for democracy abroad, African Americans now demanded it for themselves. I became ever more determined to join the ranks of lawyers.

These experiences enriched my early understanding of the law, but I also had a personal reason for wanting to become a lawyer. At the age of thirteen, I saw my father in a jail cell for being in arrears in his child-support payments. He had pleaded with the lawyer for the Humane Society to release him so he could resume his job and make up the support payments. Needless to say he had difficulty obtaining a new job. Years later, after my parents' divorce, my mother's remarriage, and while a college student, there was another encounter with the criminal justice system. Tom Fasula, the sheriff of Ashtabula County, fifty miles from Youngstown, held my stepfather in jail on a very limp petty larceny charge involving a wheel of cheese found on his produce delivery truck. The justice of the peace (JP) in Ashtabula County summarily sentenced him to ninety days and levied a $500 fine, with no trial and no access to legal counsel. The JP lacked the guts to exercise his independent judicial authority and reconsider the abuse of my stepfather's constitutional rights because he was afraid of antagonizing the county sheriff, who wielded tremendous political power. After a weekend of wrangling, the sheriff relented, picked up the phone, and called the JP to say, "I'm letting him go." I was perplexed. That is not the way I had been led to believe the justice system was supposed to operate—a judge bowing to a sheriff—but it was the reality in Ashtabula County and many other counties in America. These examples demonstrated to me how the criminal justice system insulates itself from the Constitution's guarantees of due process and equal protection when dealing with the powerless.

Once in law school, I combined my studies with experiences quite unusual for most students. The day after the director of the Fair Employment Practice Committee (FEPC) resigned and took a job in Pennsylvania, Maynard Dickerson alerted me that the mayor was going to call me. Sure enough, Mayor Frank Kryzan phoned and asked if I would consider being appointed director of the FEPC. I accepted and served in that position throughout my law-school days. This was a tremendous opportunity. I did a number of things with the FEPC, including broadening its mandate. I created a human rights subcommittee to initiate investigations into employment discrimination. We conducted educational programs in the schools and for employers. Although the enforcement mechanism was nonexistent, some headway against discrimination was made.

While I was serving in that position I was appointed to the Mahoning County Welfare Advisory Board by the county commissioner to succeed Episcopal priest Father Walter Payne Stanley, who had recently died. All of this meant my days were very busy. I attended classes three nights a week. Friday nights, Saturdays, and Sundays were mostly devoted to studying. My social life was quite limited. Work on the *Buckeye Review* took on a very secondary role. I wrote a few editorials but did none of the reporting I had done earlier.

The advisory board proved to be a very interesting and stressful experience. I saw things that were just plain disheartening. Programs during the pre-Medicare era depended on the state to provide a certain amount of the welfare budget, and the county an additional amount. These funds had to be stretched. The needs were great and the funding didn't stretch to the point where it could adequately meet the needs. The board conducted a number of studies, one of which was of the County Home, which was being managed by a political appointee and his wife. The health conditions were less than optimal. On Thanksgiving and Christmas, ministers, rabbis, and civic leaders served meals to the patients and residents. This gave all the participants a "feel good" sense of contributing to those who were sorely in need. But that was only for the moment.

It was during my second year of law school when my numerous activities took their physical toll. After I attended a Cleveland Browns football game under frigid conditions on December 28, 1952, doctors diagnosed my extraordinarily high fever as resulting from a rare and usually fatal form of tuberculosis known as "miliary." They ultimately admitted me into the Mahoning County Tuberculosis Sanatorium in a semiconscious state. Fortunate for me, a series of "wonder drugs" had come onto the market. I was treated with various combinations of them with results that were deemed to be a miracle. In fact, so dramatic were the results that medical authorities refused to release me for several months. After a stay of nearly a year, I was discharged. I returned to my law studies. This was a turning point in my life—the timeliness of the new wonder drugs and the disease that brought me to the point of death and placed my law school career at risk. I believed that I must have been spared for a purpose.

During my rehabilitation at the sanatorium I took note of conditions and practices that stirred my ire. For instance, I was offended by and made no bones about expressing my disapproval of the racial segregation of patients. I also found offensive a degree of occupational segregation among the staff. Rotating through the sanatorium were student nurses from the city's hospitals whose schools of nursing had just recently accepted the two black women trainees

I mentioned earlier. Two male student nurses worked there as well. The nursing supervisor on my floor, Hannah Haberly, was a devout member of the Seventh-day Adventist faith. She claimed that her religion did not permit her to allow the male student nurses to administer shots to female patients. When I learned of this I protested to Sally Bray, the director of nursing, who took no action.

Accordingly, the male student nurses passed up treating the female patients on my ward. When my protest fell on deaf ears, I refused to comply with Haberly's order to "turn your sunny side up," when she entered my room with needle in hand to give me a shot in my posterior. When I persisted in defying her, she summoned her superiors, Sally Bray and Dr. Sartarelli, my treating physician, who implored me to end my resistance. Only upon being assured that the male student nurses would no longer be discriminated against did I relent. My complaints about patient segregation, however, went without redress until after I was discharged.

4

Family, Marriages, and Faith

During the early phase of my law school days I burned the candle at both ends. With classes in the evening, I carried on, though at a reduced pace, the numerous activities of a professional, political, and community nature in addition to meeting my law school responsibilities. I also wove into my schedule an ad hoc social life that included activities of the Kappa Alpha Psi fraternity, and a number of Saturday lunches with a close female friend, Ann Marie D'Agostino. Ann Marie had tutored me in foreign languages, which helped me gain admission into law school. However, when it became clear that her parents frowned on the friendship, we limited our public socializing. She was from an Italian American family that lived in Campbell, Ohio, a community east of Youngstown. She ultimately married a young banker, and parented two sons. We remain friends.

Being a single young man I was often the subject of matchmaking. In addition, I found myself serving as best man or usher at the weddings of countless friends. My mother humorously remarked that I would never find a wife because I was too busy getting others to the altar. In reality, bachelorhood served my purposes because I was able to avoid serious romantic entanglements. I was already overextended with many duties. Clearly burning the candle at both ends had contributed to the rundown physical condition that precipitated my serious illness. As law school drew to an end, I attempted to ease up on some of my outside activities. My failing the bar exam forced me to come to grips with the limits of my ability to multitask successfully. In preparing to retake the bar exam, I cleared the deck and buckled down. My social life became nonexistent. I accepted the Dickersons' invitation to move into their Columbus, Ohio, home in order to be free from all distractions.

After repeating the bar exam in 1957, I nervously awaited the results and busied myself by returning to my FEPC job and community and civic activities. A college classmate, fraternity brother, and close friend Jim Cox urged me to come to Los Angeles and to join him at our fraternity's national convention. Having moved there the previous year, he assured me that I would enjoy the fantastic social scene of which he was a part. The bar exam grades were to be released during the period I was to be in Los Angeles. I had asked my mother not to call me unless the news from the Ohio Supreme Court was good. Jim's girlfriend, a popular Los Angeles educator-musician named Bette Alston, provided entrée to many cultural and social groups in the city. Bette introduced me to the friends whom she thought would catch my eye. At one point, she said, "I have just the person for you—Jean Graham. She is Shirley Graham's niece. Do you know Shirley Graham? She's married to Dr. W.E.B. Du Bois." I had long known of the writer Shirley Graham and her iconic husband. Knowing that I was going to meet the niece of Shirley Graham and W.E.B. Du Bois stirred more than ordinary curiosity.

I met Jean at the home of her sister and brother-in-law, Ruth and Herbert May. Also present were Jean's parents, Ruth and Lorenz Graham. We sat together in the living room, talking and waiting for Jean to enter. And then, Jean appeared—petite, gorgeous, and smiling. She and I went to dinner and afterward enjoyed the music of the great Earl Grant. Before the evening ended, I asked if she would be my date for the remainder of my fraternity's social events. To my delight, she agreed. Early one morning after one of the parties, a phone call came from my mother who asked to speak to "Attorney" Jones. This is how I learned that I had passed the bar examination. The rest of the day was one of celebration, which lasted for the rest of my stay in Los Angeles.

Jeanie and I began a steady stream of correspondence after I returned to Youngstown. She was in the process of completing her Bachelor of Arts degree in social work at the University of Southern California. Several years before, she had received a nursing degree while living in New York. After her graduation from USC, she visited Youngstown. My mother and other members of my family were eager to meet the one person who seemed to have captured my eye. It was not long after her visit that I proposed marriage. She accepted. Plans proceeded for a wedding on November 8, 1958, in the beautiful rose garden of her parents' home in Los Angeles. It was an impressive affair, attended by her aged maternal grandmother, Mrs. Sadie Eugenia Morris, widow of Dr. Charles Satchell Morris, who pastored Harlem's historic Abyssinian Baptist Church prior to Dr. Adam Clayton Powell Sr. A number of former Youngstowners then residing in Los Angeles joined my mother at the wedding.

Following the reception, Jeanie and I left for a brief honeymoon in Encinada, Mexico. After a week, we returned briefly to Los Angeles to bid farewell to family before flying off to Youngstown. We took up housekeeping in the Dickerson home, made available to us by their move to Columbus, Ohio. Parties and receptions kept us busy. I was also active in the drive for a statewide FEPC, especially since Ohio had recently elected Michael V. DiSalle as governor. I had worked as a campaign volunteer before heading to California for the wedding. During his campaign DiSalle promised to push hard for the enactment of a state FEPC. Early in December 1958, now Governor-Elect DiSalle invited Jeanie and me to join other supporters for a reception in his hometown of Toledo, Ohio. I knew that if Governor DiSalle were successful in pushing the state law through the Democratic-controlled Ohio legislature, I would be most likely asked to join his staff. That made the Toledo reception particularly important.

Jeanie and I had taken a trip to Columbus to celebrate Christmas with the Dickersons in 1958, but she felt faint on our return. This prompted us to make a visit to Dr. Henry Ellison, a new friend. His diagnosis: she was pregnant. We were as shocked as we were thrilled. Of course, we prepared to be teased by our friends, who were inclined to engage in the game of "gestation arithmetic." However, given that I'd arrived in Los Angeles just two days before our November 8 wedding, and the fact that we had not seen each other since July, we jokingly suggested to our teasing friends that if they proceeded to "do the gestation math," their assumption would not hold up.

The pregnancy was not an easy one, and Ellison surmised that there might have to be a premature birth, perhaps at the end of the seventh or during the eighth month. As it turned out, the doctor's call was correct because just past midnight on August 1, 1959, Jeanie went into labor and after a tough twenty-four hours, just past the next midnight, a four-pound, eleven-ounce baby girl was delivered, whom we named Stephanie Joyce. Because of her small size, she had to remain in the hospital for several days. Jeanie's mother was visiting with us from California, and she was a big help as we tried to get ourselves organized. Other relatives pitched in. Friends poured in the first few evenings.

But there was a problem. I had noticed, from the time of delivery, a change in Jeanie. Normally very sweet and outgoing, she became uncharacteristically agitated, anxious, and indecisive. I took leave from my job in order to help with the chores. Even so, things deteriorated to the point that we had to reach out for professional help. At that time I had not heard of postpartum depression. The decision was made that Jeanie would make a two-week trip to Los Angeles to spend time in her family home. During that time, we were in daily contact. Sometimes she seemed like her old self; other times she was distressed and wanted to be reassured that she would be returning to Youngstown. My unease was deepening. I made plans to fly out to visit and return both Jean and baby Stephanie to Youngstown. Two days before my departure, a telephone call came from one of my brothers-in-law, Campbell Johnson, Jr. He said, "You had better come out right away. Jeanie is in the hospital." His tone suggested the gravity of the situation.

I made plans to take the next flight, which did not depart until that evening. Upon arrival in Los Angeles early the next morning, Campbell and another brother-in-law, Herbert May, met me. I asked about her condition, "Is she still okay?" We raced to the hospital, where my father-in-law was standing outside her hospital room. She was in a coma, kept alive with the assistance of a breathing machine. The doctors and nurses talked with me, explaining that she had overdosed on pills. Persistent questioning of the doctors about her chances finally drew an answer: "If I were a betting man, I'd say fifty-fifty." As the day went on, they became more optimistic and predicted better odds. Our spirits were lifted. The reports we were getting were increasingly optimistic, to the point of telling me that Jeanie was breathing without assistance. But then, just as I was prepared to return to the hospital at midnight, an urgent call came from my father-in-law, who shouted, "Nate, come quick!" I knew what that meant. On my arrival on her floor, several nurses hustled me into the room, where I saw two doctors. One of them brushed past me as he headed for the door. I confronted the other one with the question, "Is this it?" He snatched off his mask and said, "We tried everything." I stood, frozen, at the side of Jeanie's bed. It seemed like an eternity before members of our family entered to escort me from the room. My father-in-law went immediately to the phone to call the family. An almost fairy-tale chapter of my life came to an end with Jeanie's death, and another was beginning with me assuming the responsibility for the care of our two-and-a-half-month-old baby girl.

My wife's twin sister, Joyce, and my mother-in-law pleaded with me to entrust Stephanie to their care in California. They assured me that they would take good care of her, and that I could have her at any time I wished. I felt she was my responsibility, and I intended to take her home with me. My mother and my younger sister, Jean Wooten, who had two young daughters, prepared a beautiful nursery in my mother's home. My stepfather, James Rafe, could not have been more excited about having a baby in the house.

I resumed my duties as executive director of the FEPC, became involved in the 1960 presidential campaign of John F. Kennedy, and worked part-time as a reporter and editor on the *Buckeye Review*. This was all made possible because of the wonderful care my mother, sister, and friends provided to my daughter. Most evenings I picked her up, kept her until bedtime, and then returned her to my mother's home. Often on weekends, she stayed with me at my home. I was still in the Dickerson home on Oak Hill Avenue. It was also the location of the printing company and the *Buckeye Review* newspaper.

Lorenz B. Graham, the father of my late wife, Jeanie, was a distinguished author of children's books, as was his wife, Ruth. They had met in Liberia when he was a secretary to his grandfather, the president of Monrovia College, and she was there as a missionary. They were doting grandparents who adored their new granddaughter Stephanie, and at every opportunity after Jeanie's death, during their trips east, they stopped in Youngstown to visit her. On one occasion, after several years had passed, Graham took me aside for a chat. He praised my parenting of Stephanie and could not say enough good things about the love and attention my mother provided. At that time, my mother had moved into her sixties. He said, "Son, I think there is a time when a child could benefit from a young mother. You should not hesitate to begin thinking about remarriage."

Bearing in mind this "release" I received from my late wife's family, I began seeing Evelyn Jane Velez—whom everyone called "Jean"—a wonderful young woman, a single mother of a daughter, Pamela, three years older than Stephanie. I had known her from afar. An honor society student at South High School in Youngstown, she worked as a registered nurse at Woodside Hospital in Youngstown. Our time together with our girls increased, and by then I had been appointed an assistant U.S. attorney. We decided to marry. The ceremony took place in St. Patrick's Catholic Church.

Weeks before the ceremony I learned of a house that was being foreclosed on and would be sold at a sheriff's sale. The house was located on the north side of the city in one of the upscale neighborhoods. I knew the neighborhood because when I was executive director of the city's FEPC and Human Relations Committee, I had investigated the case of white neighbors who sought to block efforts of the first black family to move into a newly purchased house three doors from it.

On the date of the sheriff's sale I was scheduled to be in trial in federal court in Cleveland. I asked my fiancée if she would attend the sale and make a bid. She did, and our bid was accepted. Soon we became owners of a beautiful house into which we moved the day of the wedding. That we had a relatively new six-room house in a wonderful neighborhood served by an excellent school launched our marriage in great style. There was much joy as we continued to focus on our young daughters. My service as an assistant U.S. attorney had me commuting between Youngstown and my office in Cleveland. However, as years passed, stresses and strains became a part of the relationship. When faced with the move to New York after I'd become NAACP general counsel, Jean was strongly disinclined to join me. After commuting from New York to Youngstown for a year, I felt the need to relocate east. While Jean was on a trip to the Caribbean, I signed a contract to purchase a house in Ridgewood, New Jersey. When I picked Jean up at Kennedy Airport we drove to Ridgewood to see the house. She liked it and the community, located twenty miles from New York. However, as the time to move approached, her reservations deepened. My duties required extensive travel, which caused trouble for the relationship. Things got no better, and during the tenth year of our marriage I was served with divorce papers. Needless to say, it was a painful end to our marriage for both of us and for our two girls. A sense of failure encased me. Yet a blessing I enjoy is the continuing love of my stepdaughter, Pamela Velez. To her, I am still "Daddy," which brings me great joy and gratitude.

Life after the divorce was not easy. The large number of cases for which I had responsibility sat pending in courts throughout the country. In addition, there were wide-ranging administrative duties connected with being the chief legal officer of the NAACP. I had to address the needs and requests of national board and staff, along with the organization's 1,700 branches. As a consequence, I pressed

on with all of this while at the same time coping with the responsibility of being a dad to a daughter who was about to enter her
teens. Again, I don't know how I would have managed without the
support of my mother and sister, who alternated traveling from
Youngstown, Ohio, to Ridgewood, New Jersey, when I had to travel,
and my devoted administrative assistant, Mabel Smith.

In March 1975, I married Lillian Hawthorne at a ceremony in
Rockville, Maryland, at the home of mutual friends. I had met her
many years earlier when she was a teenager (then Lillian Graham—
no relation to my first wife) in Youngstown, and I had returned
from serving in the Army Air Corps. In the intervening years, she
had married and divorced. Lillian and her three sons, Bill, Rick,
and Marc, relocated to Rockville, where she took a teaching position with the Montgomery County school system. On some of
my trips to Washington, D.C., Lillian and I would have dinner.
My NAACP duties often took me to Washington, where I worked
closely with Clarence M. Mitchell, director of the NAACP
Washington Bureau, and his legal counsel, J. Francis Pohlous, on
legislation and issues involving various agencies of the federal
government.

From her days in Youngstown, Lillian had developed a deep interest in the NAACP, serving for a while as senior adviser to the
youth council. I found it refreshing to spend time with a person
with an involvement in the NAACP, and who understood the importance of my civil rights work. During this time I was coping as
a single parent, complicated by my travel in connection with numerous cases in various cities. My ability to make such trips was
severely cramped by my desire to avoid imposing unduly on my
aging mother and sister, who took time away from their homes in
Youngstown in order to assist me with Stephanie. Later, in recognizing the circumstances under which both Lillian and I were
coping with our respective child-care needs and mindful that our
acquaintanceship extended back over the years, I felt comfortable
asking her to marry me. I was not at all certain what her answer
would be when I asked because, if she accepted, it would mean a
move for her and her sons to the New York area to join my daughter

and me as a family. I nevertheless proposed. She accepted. I had sensed from her sons that they had a good feeling about me, as did her parents. After completing her teaching contract with the Montgomery County schools, she moved to New Jersey with her two younger sons (the eldest was in Youngstown with his father) to join my daughter and me. Our families, after the expected number of adjustments, became a close unit. My life with Lillian covered the exciting years of my general counselship with the NAACP, and all of the twenty-three years as a judge in the U.S. Court of Appeals for the Sixth Circuit. The latter period involved a move from the East Coast to Cincinnati, the seat of the court. Cancer claimed her life in November 2011 after thirty-six years of marriage.

Lil and I were gratified by the successful professional and personal achievements of our blended family. Bill and Marc are successful lawyers in Atlanta, and Rick is an IT expert in Cincinnati. Our six grandchildren, Lauren, Tayler, Christopher, Brooke, Cory, and Sydney, have grown into outstanding young adults.

My daughter, Stephanie, has built a successful career and an interesting, rich life. After high school, she enrolled at Smith College in Northampton, Massachusetts, and she took a year off to study at Tuskegee University in a different educational environment. She explained that every year of her educational life she had been either the only student, or one of a handful of students, of color. Her choice of Tuskegee proved to have been an excellent one. She was accepted in the Tuskegee community—town and gown—in a way that enhanced her personality and sense of self-esteem. In her spare time, Stephanie obtained a job as assistant to the Commodores, the Tuskegee-based singing group whose performances and recordings were the national rage. Commodores lead singer Lionel Richie and his family embraced her as one of their own and they continue to enjoy a warm and cherished friendship. Over time, Richie has also included me in his family circle—in fact, he thanked me in the acknowledgments on one of his albums, a special treat for me.

Following her graduation from Smith, Stephanie worked as a reporter at the *Cincinnati Post* before enrolling at the University of Cincinnati College of Law. After earning her law degree and passing the bar, she joined a white-shoe Cincinnati firm as the first black associate—where she faced the "trip wires" that minority lawyers often confront when they break the ice in majority white firms and that, fortunately, I was able to help her navigate. After four years, she became a law professor at the Northern Kentucky University's Chase College of Law.

It was as a law professor that she met Arkansas governor Bill Clinton and began a friendship that continues to this day. She played a major role in the 1992 primaries and the general election campaign. After Clinton's election as president, she joined his administration, serving as education secretary Richard Reilly's regional representative. She also performed special assignments for the White House, traveling around the world with President and Mrs. Clinton.

Having that kind of access to the president, Stephanie was able to arrange for members of our family to become close to him and to the First Lady. On one occasion during a campaign stop in Youngstown, my wheelchair-bound, ninety-one-year-old mother had a conversation with President Clinton as he knelt beside her. From that time on she would brook no criticism of him by anyone, and was known to talk back to the television set when she did not like what was being said about him.

Stephanie later became chief of staff to Representative Stephanie Tubbs Jones, served as chief judiciary counsel to Senator John Edwards, was appointed executive director of the National Urban League Policy Institute, and started a successful consulting business. As I write, she is now senior counselor to the secretary and chief opportunities officer at the U.S. Department of Transportation, serving under Secretary Anthony Foxx, who was one of my law clerks early in his career. And, very important to me, she has maintained a strong, loving relationship with her late mother's family, who have always kept Stephanie, me, and our extended family in their warm and nurturing embrace.

5

Political Solutions to Racial Tensions

After passing the bar, I kept my $6,000-per-year position as executive director of Youngstown's FEPC. The position had expanded to embrace responsibilities beyond employment. The city faced a variety of racial and intergroup tensions that I encouraged the mayor and our committee to resolve. Mayor Frank X. Kryzan, whom I constantly sought to sensitize to these issues, recruited me to assist him by writing drafts of speeches on employment's connection to housing, law enforcement, and educational problems because such a connection had become clear to the members of the FEPC. Complicating the effort was the fact that the ordinance establishing the FEPC did not include enforcement powers. As we developed strategies for obtaining voluntary compliance with the objectives of fair employment, the interconnection of the city's history of racial discrimination in education and housing became apparent. Particularly vexing were various white ethnic groups, many of which were first-generation American and had also been "ghettoized." They engaged in scapegoating when it came to their black fellow citizens. This was reflected in the politics of the city, which was rapidly becoming dominated by white ethnics. For example, the public school system readily hired members of once-disparaged white ethnic groups as teachers, but steadfastly refused to hire black teachers.

The limited effectiveness of the city's FEPC fed my frustration and fueled the desire by Youngstown's black leaders to join in the effort to enact a statewide FEPC. My mentor, J. Maynard Dickerson, who was serving as president of the Ohio State Conference of NAACP Branches, was at the forefront of this effort. He collaborated with a number of black and white leaders, including Cincinnati lawyer Theodore M. Berry and our state senator from Cleveland, Howard Metzenbaum. However, by the time the state law was passed in 1959, with a major push from Ohio's new governor Michael V. DiSalle, I had abandoned the idea of joining the state agency and opted instead to enter the practice of law and open my own law office.

This decision was most upsetting to my mother. Her unease stemmed from her life in the South, the Depression, and from migrating to a city that was not hospitable to black professionals. She asserted, "Colored lawyers starve to death. You have a baby to support." I tried to assure her that I would earn as much in the practice of law as my FEPC salary. Combining the fees from my practice with the income from the *Buckeye Review*, I was confident that I could match, and perhaps exceed, that salary. In order to allay my mother's concern, a suggestion was offered by my stepfather. He said, "Son, is it possible that you could get a night job at the post office?" I knew that many black professionals often had to take post office and other government jobs to survive, but I felt confident that I would be able to be successful in the practice of law. My confidence stemmed in part from my familiarity with the courts after having "shadowed" my mentor when he was the city prosecutor and a practicing lawyer, and from covering the courts as a reporter. The profile I had built by virtue of civil rights work, especially serving as executive director of the city's FEPC, emboldened me to launch my law practice with the assurance that I would be able to meet my parental responsibility.

The Rising Tide of Politics

I was energized by the nation's exciting political climate. As a college student, I was involved in the presidential campaign of 1948 in which President Harry Truman, who had succeeded the fallen Franklin D. Roosevelt, was opposed by New York governor Thomas Dewey. I organized house rallies and meetings in various venues around the city, seeking out young people as well as some of my college classmates. I was able to connect, through J. Maynard Dickerson, with Congressman William L. Dawson, the powerful black political leader from Chicago who had been tapped as vice chairman of the Democratic National Committee. One of his top lieutenants was a black journalist named Louis T. Martin. Maintaining a line of communication to Dawson and Martin allowed for the networking of blacks at the level of national politics.

Years and many administrations later, in 1979, Martin played a key role in my being appointed by President Jimmy Carter to a seat on the U.S. Court of Appeals for the Sixth Circuit.

My transition from being an avid Adlai Stevenson supporter to a John F. Kennedy supporter began while attending the Democratic National Convention in Los Angeles in August 1960. Stevenson had lost to President Dwight D. Eisenhower in 1952 and 1956, and the chance of his becoming the Democratic standard-bearer once again appeared bleak. On the eve of the convention, the various civil-rights groups held a huge rally in Los Angeles' mammoth Masonic Auditorium. From high in the balcony I scanned the cavernous auditorium looking for a vantage point. I chose the stage entrance. Before I knew it, I was in the wings, near the holding rooms. I could see some of the dignitaries onstage already lined up in their seats. Senator Hubert Humphrey was at the podium. He had been preceded by Mrs. Eleanor Roosevelt and an array of notables. Presiding at the event was Clarence Mitchell, director of the Washington bureau of the NAACP. While I stood there, the Kennedy entourage arrived in the holding room. It included Sargent Shriver, who introduced himself to me as "Sarge Shriver, Jack's brother-in-law." That prompted me to conclude that Kennedy's brother-in-law was a police officer working as part of his security detail. Later I heard him arguing with Harris Wofford and other members of the Kennedy team about Kennedy's just-concluded speech, a speech that did not match the earlier rip-roaring, barn-burning speech by

Humphrey. Shriver said to Wofford: "Dammit, this crowd wanted a Hubert-type speech. Jack can't give a Hubert-type speech." It was then that it dawned on me that Shriver was a major player and not a part of the security team.

Another recollection about that occasion was what happened as Kennedy waited to be escorted to his seat on the stage—exactly nothing. Kennedy, while in the holding room stood with his elbow resting on a high window ledge, peering outside. Surrounding him, quiet as church mice, stood a number of his black supporters— Frank Reeves, a Washington, D.C., lawyer; Marjorie McKenzie, wife of prominent Washington, D.C., lawyer Belford Lawson, who was national president of the Alpha Phi Alpha fraternity; and several others. As Kennedy looked out the window, he tapped his teeth with his finger. The others said nothing. How strange the silence, I thought.

The presidential campaign of 1960 between Senator John F. Kennedy and Richard M. Nixon opened the eyes of at least some of the local white political leaders. Even after Kennedy garnered the Democratic nomination, the Kennedy campaign began to take note of the reality that the only way that Nixon could be beaten was with the overwhelming support of black voters. Some of the traditional black supporters had gone over to Eisenhower in the '50s. So concerned were William Dawson and Louis Martin that they warned the Kennedy campaign of the lukewarm support of many blacks. Sargent Shriver, lawyer Harris Wofford, and Louis Martin, were the civil rights "point people" charged with "selling" Kennedy to black voters. They convened a meeting in New York City in late summer of 1960 for the purpose of bolstering Kennedy's appeal. J. Maynard Dickerson's link to Dawson and Martin gave me special access to this conference, which included a "who's who" of black political leaders, including: Congressman Adam Clayton Powell; the influential Harlem political leader Raymond Jones; Congressman Charles Diggs of Detroit; Cecil Poole, who was serving California governor Pat Brown as his pardon attorney; and Jean Murrell Capers, a powerful member of Cleveland's city council. This was a heady moment for me, a young small-town lawyer, to be rubbing shoulders with these black political titans, as well as white ones like James Roosevelt, Hubert Humphrey, Governor G. Mennen Williams of Michigan, and many other leaders who did not compromise the commitment to civil rights.

I guess it was my nose for news, plus a natural curiosity to know what was going on, that led me to hang around the fringes of huddles and discussions and to observe at the New York conference the heated exchange in the hotel lobby between Congressman Powell and Sargent Shriver. As the two stood face-to-face, Powell suddenly turned on his heel and stormed away, with Shriver in pursuit. Upon Shriver overtaking him, the two spoke in hushed tones and shook hands before parting. The dispute had something to do with the rally for Senator Kennedy that Powell organized for the next afternoon in front of Harlem's famous Theresa Hotel. The event did come off with Kennedy and his wife, Jacqueline, sharing the stage with Powell and other national political leaders. It was a typical Powell show. For me, the gathering was historic because of a pledge that Senator Kennedy made. He promised to transform the Justice Department so that it would in fact be a citadel of justice. Existing civil rights laws would be vigorously enforced, he said, and new ones proposed. Blacks would be appointed as federal judges and to positions in the Justice Department.

The advice of the black and white leaders who gathered at the New York conference provided Kennedy with information and effective strategies for responding to the cascading civil rights developments in the South. The jailing of Dr. Martin Luther King shortly before the 1960 election created an opportunity for the Kennedys—John F. and his brother Robert—to put to good use the information they received. Pictures of a handcuffed King being led from a courtroom by Southern deputy sheriffs to prison to serve a six-month term at the notorious Reidsville Penitentiary in Georgia stirred blacks all across the nation. Evidence that the conditioning process at the New York civil rights conference had taken hold was displayed by the prompt and unprecedented actions of candidate Kennedy and his brother, Robert. Senator Kennedy placed a dramatic telephone call to King's wife, Coretta, that turned Kennedy's fortunes with black voters. News of the call shot across the country like a rocket. In the call Senator Kennedy is reported to have said, "I know this must be very hard for you. I understand you are expecting a baby, and I just wanted you to know that I was thinking about you and Dr. King. If there is anything I can do to help, please feel free to call me." Mrs. King replied, "I certainly appreciate your concern. I would appreciate anything you could do to help." Robert Kennedy reportedly called the judge, who agreed to immediately release King on bail. I closely followed these developments. King's father's reaction foretold the impact the telephone call would have on the election. The elder King, a lifelong Republican, was quoted in the press as saying, "I've got all my votes and I've got a suitcase, and I'm going to take them up there and dump them in his lap."[1]

In 1961, shortly after the John F. Kennedy administration took office, my mentor Dickerson phoned me from the state capital to report on his lunch with his political "regulars," who included John Fontana, one of Senator Stephen Young's "men on the ground." Fontana had mentioned to him that the senator wanted to recommend an African American to serve as an assistant U.S. attorney in Northern Ohio. This led to my meeting with Howard Metzenbaum, then a powerful state senator. I had previously met Metzenbaum through Dickerson, who had a long relationship with him. In fact, Metzenbaum, who went on to become a progressive, long-serving U.S. senator, had early on played a major role in Dickerson's appointment to the Industrial Commission of Ohio. The Dickerson-Metzenbaum relationship provided the crucial launching pad for my career, and on a trajectory that would lead ultimately to my appointment as a federal appellate judge.

When I went to Cleveland to meet with Metzenbaum, he promptly placed a phone call to Senator Young and, in my presence, urged that I be recommended to Attorney General Robert Kennedy for the position of assistant U.S. attorney. What I did not know at the time is that Ohio's governor Michael V. DiSalle had put a different plan in motion. Few had closer ties to the Kennedys than DiSalle, whose political base rested inside the Cleveland political machine, as well as in other Democratic strongholds in

Ohio, including his hometown of Toledo. He was formidable in my home county of Mahoning, which had a heavy turnout for Kennedy. DiSalle sought the president's appointment of an African American to a higher position, namely that of "the" U.S. attorney for the Northern District of Ohio. His candidate was the African American lawyer Merle M. McCurdy of Cleveland, who rose to prominence on the local, then national, level until his sudden death at age fifty-six in 1968. McCurdy served as assistant prosecuting attorney of Cuyahoga County in the 1950s and in 1960 became that county's first public defender. Impressed with McCurdy, Governor DiSalle decided to go to bat on his behalf, and in 1961 Kennedy named McCurdy U.S. Attorney. Kennedy's appointment of Cecil Poole in 1961 to U.S. attorney for the Northern District of California had marked the first time that a black person held the position of U.S. attorney in the continental United States. McCurdy was next. This, however, put my appointment to be an assistant U.S. attorney on hold.

While the position of U.S. attorney had been considered a political perk for white lawyers in Ohio, a messenger's job in that office was the best that a black person was previously able to get. When past U.S. attorneys in Ohio were questioned as to why they were not appointing blacks, even as assistants, the answer invariably was, "We cannot find a qualified Negro lawyer." Sumner Canary, a former U.S. attorney, affronted black lawyers when he continued to insist that they couldn't measure up. McCurdy's appointment and his superb performance refuted that excuse.

After McCurdy was confirmed and sworn in, I awaited developments on my pending appointment to his staff. The next two appointments were both well-connected white lawyers. These appointments raised questions among my friends and supporters. Among those with questions were Congressman Michael J. Kirwan; newly appointed federal Judge Frank Battisti; and a prominent Youngstown businessman, William J. Cafaro. Judge Battisti offered to inquire of McCurdy about the status of my appointment. Kirwan also went to Robert Kennedy, who had previously cleared me. Battisti was told by McCurdy that he was going forward with white lawyers for the first vacancies to avoid the appearance of black favoritism. That explanation brought a spirited response from Judge Battisti, who told McCurdy that he should feel a special obligation, if not to advance the fortune of Negro lawyers, to at least not penalize them. Battisti then invoked the names of Congressman Kirwan, Senator Young, and Ohio's second senator, Frank J. Lausche, who were on record with the Justice Department as supporting me. McCurdy promised to promptly attend to the matter. Shortly thereafter, he received additional clearance from the Attorney General's Office. He then called me, and things began to move on a fast track. Having been in attendance at the New York rally when John Kennedy promised a black audience that he was going to diversify the Justice Department, I felt as though I was part of a historic moment. My position called for a starting salary of $7,500. However, McCurdy said, "I think I can start you at $9,600." And he did. For 1961, that was a highly respectable level of compensation. McCurdy had spent his professional time honing his courtroom skills. He aided me in improving mine. One couldn't have had a better teacher. He came to look to me for assistance in meeting the demands being made upon him by community organizations because the significance of his appointment made him a role model. That relationship is what led him to urge me to go with him to Washington, D.C., to serve with the Kerner Commission.

The Kerner Commission

A wave of civil disturbances in a number of the nation's cities was precipitated by violent encounters between members of the black community and the police. As these disturbances raged, the loss of lives and property damage shocked the nation, prompting President Lyndon Johnson and governors to deploy military forces in an effort to restore order. To get at the causes of these disruptions, which came at a time that many civil rights initiatives were being enacted, on July 29, 1967, President Johnson issued Executive

Order 11365 in order to create the National Advisory Commission on Civil Disorders, which came to be known as the Kerner Commission. A few weeks afterward, McCurdy informed me that he had been in Washington, D.C., in response to an urgent call from Attorney General Ramsey Clark. He continued, "Ramsey and the president want me to be the general counsel of the 'Riot Commission.' There is a meeting of the commission tomorrow morning, which I cannot make because of an important matter pending here. I want you to cover the meeting for me." Not seeing my role as anything more than filling in for my boss, I agreed to do it. I left for Washington that very night in order to be on time for the early morning meeting. Being the first person to arrive at the commission meeting room on 16th Street gave me an opportunity to study the nameplates at the seat of each commission member—Governor Otto Kerner of Illinois (after whom the commission was informally named), New York mayor John V. Lindsay, NAACP executive director Roy Wilkins, Senator Edward W. Brooke of Massachusetts, Senator Fred R. Harris of Oklahoma, Congressman William M. McCulloch of Ohio, Congressman James C. Corman of California, Atlanta police chief Herbert Jenkins, United Steelworkers of America president I.W. Abel, Kentucky commerce commissioner Katherine Graham Peden, and Litton Industries CEO Charles B. Thornton. As I read the names, the senior staff began to drift into the room. I was surprised that they all seemed to know who I was. They welcomed me, stating, "We're glad to have you on board." The influential Washington lawyer David Ginsburg was the staff director. Other members of the senior staff included David Chambers; Henry B. Taliaferro; John Koskinen; and Ginsburg's deputy, Victor Palmieri. It began to dawn on me that my friend and boss Merle McCurdy had *assigned* me to the general counsel's staff of this important group. In a telephone report to him, I prefaced my comments with the observation: "They think I have signed on already." He merely chuckled and added, "May I add my welcome?" The decision as to whether I was going to join the commission had already been made for me. I was to serve as deputy general counsel.

I could not help but feel a sense of urgency connected with the work of the Kerner Commission. President Johnson's charge to the commission team was unequivocal in its demand for answers to three questions: What happened during the disturbances that rocked the nation's major cities? Why had the rioting occurred? And what must the nation do to keep it from happening again? Many in law enforcement and the media blamed the urban disruptions on "outside agitators," "Communists," and "radicals" of one form or another. It became clear from our fieldwork, however, that the "activists" were of the homegrown variety—in other words, not outsiders but the residents of the riot-torn cities.

Commission members Mayor Lindsay and Senator Harris embarked on "walking tours" in several of the cities. Based on their limited exploration and with the support of senior staffers, Lindsay and Harris urged the commission to organize and dispatch fact-finding teams to the various cities affected by the disturbances in order to do in-depth studies. The teams went into Atlanta, Cincinnati, Newark, Plainfield, Detroit, and Los Angeles. They initially encountered great difficulty in getting the residents in these areas to talk to them. Community members refused, for a period of time, to communicate with our field investigators because of their distrust of the police and any federal investigators. To meet this problem, the commission had to reconstitute the teams to ensure that they included persons skilled in communicating with residents who had lost faith in their leaders.

At times McCurdy and I headed field teams, as was the case in Atlanta, Cincinnati, Los Angeles, and in Plainfield, New Jersey. All the teams urged the commission members to use care in labeling persons as "rioters" and "agitators." Such mislabeling fueled the feelings of distrust that we encountered in the field and impeded our efforts to get at the basic causes of the eruptions. I was among those who argued within the staff and to the media that ghetto residents were too often mislabeled and castigated as "rioters" rather than understood as "victims." I found myself seeing variations on the same patterns of racial discrimination that I had experienced in Youngstown and Cleveland in regard to swimming pools, bowling alleys, restaurants, the amusement park, and the denial of summer jobs to black teens while their white schoolmates found employment. Moreover, lax housing-code enforcement and strained police/community relations contributed to explosive conditions. I drew upon my work as a reporter for *The Buckeye Review* and FEPC director, investigating the dismissive way complaints of discrimination and injustice against those who were poor and black, and even some who were not so poor but still black, were handled by those in authority with the ability but not the willingness to make changes. My past experiences prepared me to help the teams dispatched to the ghettos to understand the anger they would encounter. It was important for team members to see and comprehend the poverty and despair in those communities. Every urban community—those that experienced disorder and violence and those that escaped it—harbored deeply held racial grievances, irrespective of their economic status.

While in the field, the inquiry into events brought McCurdy and me into contact with fascinating people. For example, in Watts we spoke to the black-nationalist leader known at the time as Maulana Ron Karenga, the founder of Kwanzaa, a celebration observed by many African Americans after the Christmas holiday. McCurdy and I met with him in late 1967, when the Kwanzaa observance was in its infancy. Karenga was not at all eager to talk to us. Although we had made an appointment to meet him at his headquarters in Watts, he kept us waiting for a considerable period of time before coming out to greet us. We had the feeling that he was suspicious of us and hoped that we would tire of waiting and leave. Karenga finally appeared in the rather dimly lit, spacious room where he obviously held group meetings. His head was shaved and his high-top shoes unlaced. In our meeting with Karenga, he slowly became more comfortable and began to discuss the frustration over lack of jobs for Watts's young people, issues with the schools, and problems the community had with the police. Karenga spoke on behalf of those described as militants. Once we began to engage him in conversation about his concerns, he opened up and provided valuable insights and perspectives.

The job of the field teams was to write a report documenting the grievances and other ideas expressed by those we encountered. This report was sent to the commission offices for analysis and evaluation by consultants, staff, and commission members. McCurdy and his general counsel's staff identified particular issues from those reports that could be expanded upon in hearings before the commission. Our job was to then schedule hearings in order that testimony could be presented to the commission. We believed the president's charge to the commission could not be met unless the members had the opportunity to directly hear from and question individuals who could provide expertise and also real-life perspectives on the triggering events that so rocked the urban areas of the nation. However, it was not always easy to persuade individuals to testify. Dr. Kenneth Clark, the eminent psychologist, agreed, though reluctantly. His testimony was very illuminating and provided a backdrop for most of the commission's final recommendations. In a soft voice dripping with frustration and anguish, Dr. Clark stated:

> I read that report . . . of the 1919 riot in Chicago, and it is as if I were reading the report of the investigating committee on the Harlem riot of 1935, the report of the investigating committee on the Harlem riot of 1943, the report of the McCone Commission on the Watts riot.
>
> I must again in candor say to you members of this Commission—it is a kind of Alice in Wonderland with the same moving picture reshown over and over again, the same analysis, the same recommendations, and the same inaction.[2]

It took effort to persuade Dr. Martin Luther King, who was one of our final witnesses, to testify at the commission hearing. Focusing less on the violence, King addressed what he deemed to be the overriding issues of poverty, hunger, and the Vietnam War. Roy Wilkins pressed him on the Vietnam issue and specifically on King's contention that the country could not meet the needs of urban poverty while still conducting the war. Senator Edward Brooke sought King's views on a range of domestic problems we had investigated.

Other members appeared to be simply delighted to have his views on the record as a means of adding credibility to our recommendations. McCurdy and I faced other challenges in regard to witnesses whose testimony we believed would be helpful. In order for the commission's report to have credibility, it was our opinion that Stokely Carmichael's views had to be considered. Because he was a founder of the Student Nonviolent Coordinating Committee (SNCC) who constantly challenged the system, we felt it important to meet with him. The only way we were able to elicit his views—since he viewed anyone connected with the federal government as being tied to the CIA—was to meet at a private home of one of our staff members he knew and trusted. That person was Lawrence A. Still, the deputy director of information of the Kerner Commission, who once worked for *Ebony* and *Jet* magazines. Our staff was not pleased with Carmichael's demeanor. He ignored the fact that he was in a private home with young children upstairs within earshot of his words, which were often foul and profane. He sat on the floor with his boots unlaced and as he spoke, he would roll from side to side. But our need to get his perspective made it necessary to overlook his behavior and dwell only on his views.

Another challenge we faced came with calling as a witness Judge William Matthews, of the Hamilton County (Ohio) Municipal Court. Our field reports relating to events in Cincinnati and complaints of the arbitrariness of his sentencing prompted the commission to authorize McCurdy and me to issue a subpoena for him to appear to explain his policy of automatic jail terms for persons arrested for what he described as "riot-connected" offenses. We noted that African Americans were taken from their front porches and homes by police and National Guardsmen and jailed. Judge Matthews declared to the media that all such arrestees would receive ninety-day sentences. During Judge Matthews's testimony, McCurdy displayed his cross-examination skills in questioning the justification for jailing people without regard to mitigating factors associated with their arrests. He and members of the commission pressed Judge Matthews about his lack of concern for several mothers who were arrested with no arrangements made for their young children left at home and unattended. We concluded that this type of judicial abuse exacerbated the distrust of citizens rather than built respect for the law.

The recalcitrance of witness George Meany, president of the AFL-CIO, educated commission members about the discriminatory practices of labor unions. In the hearing Meany was questioned about construction jobs in black neighborhoods that were held by white workmen while blacks remained unemployed. Meany minced no words in letting Roy Wilkins know his displeasure at this line of questioning. Wilkins merely smiled.

Perhaps the most unlikely witness, the famous entertainer Eartha Kitt, sought to make her views available to the commission just as the hearings were concluding. She persuaded Chicago congressman Roman Pucinski to ask commission chair Governor Otto Kerner on her behalf. Kerner agreed to the request, and not desiring to extend the hearings any longer, accommodated the congressman by inviting Ms. Kitt to present her views to the legal staff in a private session on January 18, 1968. She was already scheduled to come to Washington at the invitation of the First Lady, Lady Bird Johnson, who had organized an event on the same day—the Women Doers' Luncheon—to discuss ways to make the nation's cities safer. McCurdy and I arranged a morning session at the commission offices in order to facilitate Kitt's event at the White House that afternoon.

The head of our congressional relations unit, Henry "Boots" Tolliver, in addition to McCurdy and those of us on the legal staff wondered what Eartha Kitt would say to assist the commission. I was the only member of our staff who had ever met Ms. Kitt, but that had been twenty-three years earlier in 1945. That meeting took place when I was stationed at Sheppard Field in Texas during World War II. She was a member of the famous Katherine Dunham Dancers, who were touring military installations entertaining the troops. At that time, she was seventeen years old. Following their performance, she and her troupe visited with the GIs. She and I later began corresponding, and in one of her letters she invited me to come to a pre-Broadway opening of a show in New Haven, Connecticut. My income as a private did not provide the

means of traveling to Connecticut. My recollection of our correspondence is clear. Her letters were written in broad strokes with
green ink, in a style most unique, and signed "Kitty." At the time
we met, her professional name was Kitty Charles, though the
return address on the envelopes bore the name Eartha Kitt. With
the passing of time, our correspondence ceased. As I helped my
colleagues at the commission to better understand who this person was on whose behalf Congressman Pucinski was lobbying,
there was, quite understandably, a swelling of the ranks of the
staff willing to "adjust" their busy schedules to take part in the
interview.

Upon her arrival at the Shoreham Hotel late the night before our
meeting, I met Ms. Kitt in the hotel lobby to give her a briefing in
advance of her meeting with the staff. The manager and I escorted
her to her suite. McCurdy arrived a short time later.

The staff interview the next morning was rather unremarkable,
given the intensity of Congressman Pucinski's persistence that she be
heard. The gist of her case was an argument for more job creation
for inner-city youths as an antidote to gang violence. We concluded
the interview before she appeared ready to leave out of concern that
she be on time for the White House luncheon.

Later that evening, as I attended a meeting in Warrenton, Virginia,
of high-ranking military officers involved in quelling a number of
the disturbances, I overheard a general mention the name of Eartha
Kitt. When I inquired as to what prompted the mention, he gave
me a wry smile and mentioned an earlier incident at the White
House. Anxious to know more about it, when I was delivered back
to Washington at midnight, I immediately went in search of an
early edition of the *Washington Post*.

On the front page of the *Post*, I saw a large, three-column-wide
picture of Eartha Kitt and Lady Bird Johnson spread across the
top and above the fold. The cutline read: "Mrs. Johnson talks with
Eartha Kitt before a confrontation at a White House luncheon
over the Vietnam War."

What baffled me as I read the first lines of the story was that in
urging the commission to take her statement Eartha Kitt had told

me—and Congressman Pucinski had told David Ginsburg, the staff director—that she was going to the White House to discuss ways to beautify the cities. Nothing was said to us about the Vietnam War. Yet, we should have known from our work in the cities that the Vietnam War controversy hovered over all of the commission's efforts and was of passionate concern to Ms. Kitt. The story's actual headline was "Eartha Kitt Confronts the Johnsons." A subhead added: "Startled First Lady Responds to Singer's Attacks on War."[3]

The *Washington Post* story and pictures were similar to the Associated Press accounts that ran in virtually every newspaper in the country. They described Eartha Kitt as seemingly being in a nonconfrontational mood as she arrived at the luncheon in the private dining room on the second floor of the White House. Some fifty guests were in attendance, and Ms. Kitt was seated near the podium. The topic for discussion was to be "What Citizens Can Do to Ensure Safe Streets." Three women spoke, including Katherine Graham Peden of Kentucky, a member of the Kerner Commission. They each addressed the issue from different perspectives, which displeased Ms. Kitt as being irrelevant. When the floor was opened for discussion, Mrs. Johnson noticed her hand was raised and nodded in her direction. Her first words were, "As the program got under way, I think we have missed the main point of this luncheon. We have forgotten the main reason we have juvenile delinquency."

At that moment, which was after dessert, President Johnson made a surprise appearance. In his comments, the president spoke in defense of police and declared that "there's a great deal we can do to see that our youth are not seduced and the place to start is in the home." The fireworks started as the president prepared to leave the room; Ms. Kitt arose and blocked his path as she asked: "What do you do about delinquent parents? Those who go to work and are too busy to look after their children?" His response was that Congress had "just passed a Social Security bill that gives millions of dollars for day-care centers." That apparently did not satisfy Ms. Kitt, for reports are that she interrupted him with this question:

"But what are we going to do?" The *Washington Post* story stated that he responded with some impatience as he walked out, "That's something for you women to discuss here."

During Ms. Kitt's deposition, one of her principal complaints was the amount of taxes that people had to pay, which she argued was an impediment to job creation for youths in urban areas. That type of thinking, however, ran counter to the conclusion of the commission.

In discussing her views with us prior to going to the luncheon, Kitt had been calm, good-natured, and appreciative of the opportunity to be heard. Reading the stories in the *Washington Post* and in other newspapers prompted me to wonder what could have set her off. That was the state of play the following morning when I was told by our public relations director that Liz Carpenter, Mrs. Johnson's top assistant, had been on the phone all morning seeking answers for Eartha Kitt's reactions. I was alerted to expect a call momentarily from the White House. When Miss Carpenter reached me she got right to the point: "What did y'all talk about to Eartha Kitt over there," she asked in her deep Texas drawl. She cross-examined me about Ms. Kitt's mood, what we discussed, and, in particular, whether the issue of the Vietnam War had been raised. As of that time, the full impact of events at the luncheon had not become clear to me. I responded by assuring her that our discussion was positive, that we had a transcript if she wanted to review it. I stated that when McCurdy and I escorted her to the waiting White House limousine, she was in good spirits. In fact, I volunteered details concerning my meeting with her at the Shoreham Hotel upon her midnight arrival. As it turned out, the media had already identified me as having had the midnight meeting and that Ms. Kitt was later visited by Stokely Carmichael.

At the time the commission began its work, there was a desire to publish an interim report by December 1967, to be followed by the final report in June 1968. However, the public appetite for answers was so strong that the commission decided to accelerate the schedule by issuing a single report by March 1, 1968. Emerging from the process of analysis and drafting was attention to the ways, as the

commission stated, "the structure of discrimination has persistently narrowed his [the Negro's] opportunities and restricted his
prospects." Also, the report confirmed that recent European immigrants or their recent descendants "gained an economic foothold
and thereby enabled their children and grandchildren to move up
to skilled, white-collar and professional employment" while the
black migrants from the South, such as my father, "found little opportunity in the city." Descendants of European immigrants, who
arrived in urban communities at about the same time as African
Americans, "tend to exaggerate how well and quickly they escaped
from poverty." Their move into the middle class was facilitated by
the whiteness of their skin, while blacks—adults and youths—were
denied opportunities, remaining mired in ghettos. The report recognized as well that "America's urban-industrial society has matured;
unskilled labor is far less essential than before."[4]

Nor did the trade and craft unions guarantee fairness to blacks, who
had to fight within the unions, and sometimes against the entire
white leadership, which reflected the racism of the general society.
These and many other frank statements in the Kerner report, of-
ficially titled *Report of the National Advisory Commission on Civil
Disorders* (1968), stirred much reaction across the nation.

The record made by the commission's investigation in order to
answer the second charge received from President Johnson with
respect to the disorder, "Why did it happen," led the commission
to the inescapable, yet to many people shocking, conclusion found
on page five of the report:

> White racism is essentially responsible for the explosive mixture which
> has been accumulating in our cities since the end of World War II.
> Among the ingredients of this mixture are:
> - Pervasive discrimination and segregation in employment, edu-
>   cation and housing . . .
> - Black in-migration and white exodus, which have produced the
>   massive and growing concentrations of impoverished Negroes
>   in our major cities . . .

- The Black ghettos where segregation and poverty converge on the young . . . [5]

It was painfully clear that the dry rot resulting from decades of disparities, neglect, and educational deficits would require drastic intervention, as the report declared: "Only a commitment to national action on an unprecedented scale can shape a future compatible with the historic ideals of American society. . . . The major need is to generate new will—the will to tax ourselves to the extent necessary to meet the vital needs of the Nation."[6]

Doubtless, the heated debate between members of the commission over the cost of new social programs being advocated, in light of the costs of the Vietnam War, helped to drive that conclusion of the report. During the considerable debate, the comments of David Ginsburg, the staff director, gave the commission members pause. He argued, "This is the wealthiest nation on Earth. We can afford both guns and butter." Everyone at the table knew that though the words came from Ginsburg, they were, in reality, the words of Lyndon B. Johnson. Ginsburg was unmistakably the White House's presence on the commission, and he kept the White House apprised of our efforts. It was the field investigations and hearings that opened commission members to accept the Ginsburg argument about the federal government's duty to step forward. The field studies and investigations that informed the commission's views took into account the anatomy of the disorders, including the precipitating events. Of the disorders, it was a wonder that there were so few—twenty-four disorders in 1967. Given the social dynamite that was spread so broadly across the nation, our probe sought to find what triggered the disorders in some cities and not in others.

The riots and subsequent Kerner Commission thrust both McCurdy and me onto the national stage to a degree neither of us anticipated. As we talked about the rising racial tensions after decades of neglect, we shared with each other our awareness of being involved in a profoundly significant undertaking that had serious national and historical implications. Tragically, Merle McCurdy died suddenly in May 1968, shortly after the release of our report. The mission proved sobering and urgent, but it afforded the opportunity to participate in a significant historical drama—to drill down deeply into the piles of "social dynamite" stored up in American cities, and to do so at the command of the president of the United States. This obligated me to share some of what became apparent when we pulled back the curtains in the various cities that we visited and also to share insights that did not make their way into the pages of the official report. I am still queried about my work with the commission because the answers the Kerner Report offered remain relevant today. I strongly feel that its insights remain relevant nearly fifty years later.

6

Cutting My Teeth as NAACP General Counsel

After leaving my position as an assistant U.S. attorney and deputy general counsel of the Kerner Commission in 1968, I returned to the practice of law in my hometown. Soon after arriving in Youngstown, I plunged once again into civil rights efforts, launching a membership drive for the NAACP local branch. In many respects, the NAACP is a bottom-up organization; its policies are formulated in consultation with local and state units based on the problems members confront in their own communities. Members' dues and the work of the branches are central to the organization's survival. Thus in 1969, I agreed to organize the opening of the membership rally and invited Gloster B. Current, the NAACP's director of branches and field administration, to be the principal speaker. I first met Current when he led the extremely active Detroit branch in the early 1940s, before Walter White recruited him to head the national membership department. I knew Current to be an inspirational speaker, and more recently I had turned to him for assistance in lining up witnesses to testify before the Kerner Commission. The far-flung network of the NAACP had proved to be of great value to the commission.

Current had obviously spoken to the NAACP's executive director, Roy Wilkins, about my work in Youngstown, since not long after his departure Wilkins invited me to meet with him in the national office in New York. During the course of our meeting, he offered me the position of NAACP general counsel. He noted that the position was currently vacant and that he had held off filling it until satisfied that he had the right person. Wilkins then expressed his belief that I was that person, based on having worked with me on the Kerner Commission and having known me, as he put it, to be a "child of the NAACP." I am certain that Wilkins's confidence in me was also based on Gloster Current's report on his visit to Youngstown. Current was a member of the team charged with finding a replacement for Robert L. Carter, and while he would never confirm my suspicion, the broad grin that came over his face when I put the question to him was confirmation enough for me. Wilkins's request that I carry on the responsibilities once held by Thurgood Marshall, Robert Carter, and other legal giants came as both an honor and an absolute surprise.

The decision to accept the position was not an easy one. I was offered a salary of $25,000 a year to be general counsel. This was considerably less than I was making in attorney's fees from my practice in Youngstown. In addition, I faced the difficult reality of having to relocate my family to New York, with its higher cost of living. I sought the advice of several people, including Frank J. Battisti, a federal judge appointed by John F. Kennedy. Battisti was a close friend, and he had previously taught me in law school. "What's your problem?" Battisti asked when I presented him with my dilemma. I replied that the problem was whether I should take the job. He put the question to me again, "Yes, but what is the problem?" I answered that I was, for the first time in my life, making a respectable amount of money and did not want to forsake what seemed like a promising law practice. I will never forget his response: "Listen to me, an offer such as that is a Call. One doesn't reject a Call. You have a duty to accept it. If you don't like it after working at it for a while, you can always walk away. If you don't accept it, you will forever wonder about your decision." I appreciated his candid advice and within hours telephoned Roy Wilkins to accept the offer.

However, I was unprepared for the response by my mentor J. Maynard Dickerson. He had assumed that I would *not* take the position. After telling him what I had done, he voiced his concern that I would find myself in the meat grinder of the organization's office politics. His reaction, given his long involvement with the NAACP, surprised me. One of the many gifts I received from my mentor during my youth was my introduction to the NAACP, so I was shocked to see a look of absolute disappointment on his face. At that moment I realized I would have to perform superbly in order to prove the correctness of my decision. I know now that Dickerson sought to shield me from the internal squabbles he had observed within the NAACP hierarchy. He feared that I was not ready for the rough-and-tumble maneuverings he had seen take place. That concern was not totally without basis, as I soon came to learn.

An example: unlike me, Dickerson was keenly aware of the confusion and factionalism surrounding the separation of the NAACP Legal Defense and Education Fund (LDF) from the NAACP proper. Because "NAACP" appears in the title of both organizations, most people continue to be confused, not realizing that the two became legally distinct in the late 1950s when the NAACP's legal department under Thurgood Marshall moved into a separate space and took on a separate tax-exempt status. The break was murky but not particularly problematic because Marshall operated within the organizations with ease, wearing two hats—one as general counsel of the NAACP and the other as director counsel of the NAACP Legal Defense and Education Fund. The responsibilities at the time were interchangeable and there was no real division in the performance of the responsibilities of the two entities, since the same person performed both jobs. The contention arose in 1961, after Marshall resigned to become a judge on the U.S. Court of Appeals for the Second Circuit. The NAACP board sought to appoint his replacement as the LDF director counsel, but was advised by tax lawyers that it lacked authority in regard to the separate tax-exempt entity. The question of who would be Marshall's successor rested solely in the hands of the newly constituted LDF board, which appointed Jack Greenberg as director counsel.

The news of Greenberg's appointment came as a jolt to Robert Carter, who had been second in command to Marshall. Carter had successfully argued *Brown v. Board of Topeka, Kansas*, at the trial level and in the U.S. Supreme Court. Unknown to most people, because of the towering image of Thurgood Marshall, it was actually Carter who was the principal strategist in the *Brown* case. Tempers flared when the press began to erroneously describe the *Brown v. Board of Education* case as having been won not by the NAACP but by the different LDF entity, even though it had long been understood that those lawyers litigating the case were NAACP lawyers. The NAACP, as a membership organization, never yielded on the issue that it was the organization that brought to the courts and won *Brown v. Board of Education*.

Dickerson had followed this controversy, but his alarm in regard to my becoming NAACP general counsel stemmed from far more than this. The very event that created the opportunity for me to be appointed general counsel began amid tremendous dissension associated with the firing of legal staffer Lewis Steel by the NAACP's national board of directors. Steel's article "Nine Men in Black Who Think White," which appeared in the *New York Times Magazine* in October 1968, openly criticized the remedial timing of the Supreme Court's decision in *Brown v. Board of Education*.[1] The negative depiction of the Supreme Court was more than the NAACP's national board could take. Winning the *Brown* case was the most significant Supreme Court victory ever achieved by the organization. The *Brown* decision reversed the pernicious separate-but-equal doctrine pronounced in *Plessy v. Ferguson* in 1896, the case that nullified the guarantees set forth with the ratification of the Fourteenth Amendment's equal protection clause. The *Brown* decision was precedent over and beyond education. The sit-ins and boycotts of the 1950s and 1960s were accompanied by decisive court cases that rested on *Brown*. For example, the legal battle against segregated public transportation led by black Tuskegee, Alabama, lawyer Fred Gray and NAACP lawyer Robert Carter during the Montgomery Bus Boycott was affirmed by the Supreme Court, thus bringing the boycott to its victorious end. The court cited *Brown* as precedent. The wide-ranging ramifications of *Brown* were huge. Furor arose within the NAACP family because of perceptions of Steel's having belittled the courageous justices who gave us *Brown v. Board of Education*. Worse yet, they were made to appear racist, as the title of the article suggests. The article so infuriated the NAACP board that it demanded answers and explanations from Dr. John Morsell, Wilkins's chief deputy, and it ordered General Counsel Robert Carter to fire Steel. In the face of Carter's refusal, the board took actions to dismiss Steel. This led to the resignation of Carter and the entire legal staff. It took a year for Roy Wilkins to fill the vacancy. Fortunately, two legal staff lawyers, Barbara Morris and June Franklin, returned to their posts and continued to work on several important cases in progress. It is only fair to say that Lewis Steel did *not* write the article's headline. However, many in the legal community, and certainly NAACP board members, disdained the characterization of the Supreme Court as consisting of "men in black who think white." At the very least, those words were deemed "ungracious."

By the time I joined the NAACP, Carter had become a practicing attorney and law professor. The fierce circumstances of his departure along with his legal staff complicated my arrival. Anger over what had been perceived as unfair treatment of Carter and his staff led to a boycott of the organization by a number of civil rights lawyers. Supporters of Carter spoke harshly of the NAACP and of me for taking the job. Only a few of the critics actually knew me, but nevertheless felt that I was a traitor to the cause of civil rights lawyers, for coming to the aid of the organization under those circumstances. Such anger partially explains the chilly reception directed at me by the New York press corps during my initial press conference. The director of public relations, Henry Lee Moon, and his deputy, Warren Marr, had scheduled the press conference to present me to the New York and national media. They hoped this publicity event would satisfy some of the curiosity surrounding the new lawyer from Ohio who had been chosen to occupy the hot seat.

Although the press conference proved to be a real test for me, I was told by my NAACP colleagues and by members of the press, with whom I later became friendly, it was a test that I passed. I was pressed hard by some reporters to explain why I would leave a promising law practice in Ohio and put my reputation at risk. I argued that I grew up in the NAACP and as a youngster was privileged to sit at the feet of civil rights giants who firmly believed in making the country respond to the promise of the Thirteenth, Fourteenth, and Fifteenth Amendments and to the historic "Call" of 1909, which led to the founding of the NAACP. In response to their insistence that the NAACP legalistic approach was much too slow and had lost favor with the angry masses, I replied that while direct action had its place, it could only succeed if accompanied by systemic and institutional changes that incorporate the values and commands set forth in the Constitution and the civil rights laws. As general counsel I intended, much as Thurgood Marshall did, to make the nation confront the reality of those constitutional commands. But I was not unaware of the challenges ahead. After all, lawyers like Carter, Steel, and the others who had left the NAACP had achieved respected reputations on the national civil rights stage. While I had a long NAACP track record in Ohio, at the time I stepped into the job of general counsel my slate as a civil rights lawyer was clean and whatever was to be written on it would be pretty much up to me.

Roy Wilkins assigned Mabel Jackson Smith to be my secretary shortly after I arrived at the NAACP. She had served him for a decade, was secretary to former executive director Walter White for ten years, and was secretary to the national board of directors. More than anyone, she made it possible for me to succeed in the initial years and to avoid the problems that formed the basis of Dickerson's concern about my taking the position. After becoming my administrative assistant, Mabel Smith was an excellent resource because of her knowledge of the organization and of those who occupied positions of power within it. She knew all of the personalities and traps, and she continually guided me away from the latter.

I early on came to understand the various power centers in the organization. One of the most influential and dedicated leaders of the branch structure was Mrs. Hazel Dukes, president of the New York State Conference of Branches.

The voluminous mail presented to me on my arrival included legal papers that dealt with pending litigation. Crucial to me in meeting this challenge was Matthew Perry Jr., an experienced and courageous civil rights litigator from South Carolina who helped the NAACP out of trouble with the courts during the period when the organization was without a legal staff. In terms of NAACP internal politics, Matt Perry bridged the gap between the so-called Young Turks—the group determined to dethrone Roy Wilkins because of his commitment to the traditional NAACP methods—and the loyalists who defended Wilkins and his approach. A most effective broker, Perry communicated skillfully with both militant and traditional factions in the NAACP, with those who sought direct-action tactics and nonviolent confrontation as well as with those who advocated litigation and legislation. He was highly respected in South Carolina—even by the segregationist lawyers and judges he challenged. In 1975, Perry, with the support of Senator Strom Thurmond, was appointed to a seat on the U.S. Court of Military Appeals. Later, when President Carter picked him to be a U.S. district judge in Columbia, South Carolina, both senators of that state, Thurmond and Fritz Hollings, supported his nomination. The respect the South Carolina senators, particularly Thurmond, held for Perry helped smooth the way to my own confirmation as a federal appellate judge in 1979. All of this flowed from a momentous change in the political landscape. African Americans had at last been brought into the Southern electorate by the passage of the Voting Rights Act of 1965. One thing was sure: Thurmond, and other white candidates, could count votes.

Defending Black Militants

The late 1960s ushered in a black militancy impatient with the litigation tactics of the NAACP. Yet I remained convinced of the correctness of Roy Wilkins's leadership style, which was sufficiently nuanced and strategic to withhold punches at times and offer olive branches when warranted. There was never any doubt in my mind as to where my loyalty rested. Wilkins vested complete trust and authority in me. In this I had the support of the national board, including many of the Young Turks. Some may not have viewed me warmly early on, but they came to know that I brought a lifetime of dedication to the organization's mission—one that combined both the legal approach to full equality and the advocacy of the indispensable, active role that members of the organization had to play in order to effect change. I never lost sight of the fact that the membership base fortified the leadership as it pressed for changes in laws and policies nationally, in various states, and local communities. I grew from the wisdom of Roy Wilkins. Wilkins refrained from doing what often occurred when black power was on the ascent, which was to define who was and was not a "legitimate" leader. As he stated in a speech to the National Negro Publishers Association in 1969, "No one man can speak for all Americans" and "no so-called race leader in the traditional sense can be expected to possess the wisdom and the skill to speak and act for all segments of Negro life." Such a perspective enabled me to serve effectively as counsel for people who espoused a variety of causes in the freedom struggle.

Before I moved to New York, a phone call from Roy Wilkins to ask if I could fly to Los Angeles immediately caught up with me in Cleveland, even though I had not as yet begun my duties. This became my first assignment as general counsel, and it involved the defense of black students who advocated black power and Black Studies courses on college campuses. On some levels this seems ironic. Although Wilkins had empathy for black youth, he was unsympathetic toward those who exploited their impatience by calling for separate campus facilities. He denounced ideologies of black separatism and insisted that blacks needed to learn "what the white boys learn" in order to compete. Contrary to what many may believe, however, the legal arm of the NAACP served those who utilized peaceful civil rights strategies as well as those who utilized the disruptive tactics of black militancy in the late 1960s. This was the case in August 1969, when twenty-four students of color had been indicted in connection with a "takeover" of the fifth floor of the Administration Building at San Fernando Valley State College the prior year. They were desperately in need of legal counsel. After gathering some additional information I rushed to Los Angeles to assess the situation.

In the late 1960s, students' tactics for winning concessions on campuses included the dramatic act of seizing buildings. This was often done with little thought of the legal consequences. Criminal laws were beginning to be enforced by some law enforcement and political officials, over the occasional objections of educators. Tensions certainly ran high on the campus of San Fernando Valley State College, where African American and Latino students protested their treatment on campus. Students had employed the tactic used in other such confrontations, seizing control of the Administration Building and holding hostage a number of key administrators. When the takeover was quelled, twenty-four students were arrested and later indicted on more than one thousand felony counts, including multiple counts of kidnapping. The chief prosecutor was assistant Los Angeles district attorney Vincent Bugliosi, who would soon gain worldwide fame for his prosecutorial zeal in the Charles Manson case for the murders of actress Sharon Tate and six others in Benedict Canyon, a part of the San Fernando Valley. Assigning Bugliosi to the San Fernando case meant that the State of California intended to make examples of those students.

Because the San Fernando students had no financial means to retain counsel they appealed to the NAACP for help. Virna Canson, California's state NAACP director, joined with officers of the Los Angeles branch in an urgent request to Wilkins—thus his call to me. Branch officers had heard that I had just agreed to become general counsel and assumed, mistakenly, that a fully functioning legal staff was in place. On arrival in Los Angeles, I met with an impressive group of lawyers whom Virna Canson had assembled. Halvor Thomas Miller Jr., Morgan Moten, Loren Miller Jr., Benjamin James of San Francisco, and Nathaniel Colley Sr. of Sacramento were among the lawyers who volunteered their services. They briefed me on the facts of the case and the resources that would be needed to provide an effective defense for the students. This was a first-class team of lawyers. Loren Miller Jr.'s father was a nationally known NAACP lawyer, having won a significant restrictive covenant case in the U.S. Supreme Court.

We shaped the defense strategy for the students, fully cognizant of the tough legal and political battle ahead. I drew upon insights gleaned from my work with the Kerner Commission. For example, one of the most difficult lessons for the power structure of a community or an institution to learn is that when reasonable leaders of the aggrieved are ignored or discredited, they will be pushed aside by constituents and replaced by more radical and extreme voices. The Kerner Report made this point, and I came to recognize it many times during my litigation experience with the NAACP. The San Fernando Valley State College situation revealed that the drama and tension associated with the takeover could have been avoided had the officials heeded the demands for change made by student representatives early on. The black and Latino students, without question, had legitimate grievances for which they found no redress from school officials. In pressing their defense our legal team drew attention to these and other grievances. Fortunately, the involvement of the NAACP helped to defuse the situation and salvage the lives and careers of many of the students who faced felony indictments. Almost a year after the student takeover, college officials were prepared to pay heed and, as a result, significant changes took place, including establishing a Pan African department and implementing ethnic studies programs. The school administration learned an important lesson, even if embarrassingly tardy, and the college is a much better institution because of it.

Defending Black Servicemen

My early years as general counsel also focused on the important problem of racism in the U.S. military. My preparation for stepping into this arena traces back to the lectures at the West Federal Street Y forums when I was a teenager. In the 1930s and early

1940s, the topic of blacks in the military became a popular subject of discussion during the month of February, when we celebrated Negro History Week (today Black History Month) and when we observed Race Relations Sunday. A by-product of that experience was my becoming an avid reader of black newspapers and their coverage of the campaign to win entry of African Americans into the various branches of the armed forces during World War II. Blacks pressed for the right to fight in the hope that white America would reward their loyalty with first-class citizenship. Once in the service, however, black troops faced barriers of discrimination that kept them in segregated units, denied them opportunities to advance, and made them targets of an unfair military justice system. Especially after the draft, the dramatic increase in the military's practice of discrimination against black troops during World War II led to numerous calls to the NAACP for legal assistance. As I knew firsthand, knowledge of the wrongs done to African Americans in the armed forces echoed from black social organizations, churches, and the columns of the black press.

Thus I felt part of a longer tradition of offering legal defense for black servicemen, when in 1971 Roy Wilkins dispatched me and a legal team (consisting of Temple University law professor Robert Reinstein and Howard University law professor Charles Fishman) to an air force base at Goose Bay in Labrador. Our job was to defend five black airmen who were being "railroaded" by their base commander. Our investigation uncovered "nitpicking" reflective of both overt and subtle racism. We were able to get the charges dismissed with the airmen being permitted to transfer, and the base commander being reassigned.

My next assignment that year took me, along with Julius Williams, the director of the NAACP Veterans Affairs, and NAACP lawyer Melvin Bolden to West Germany in order to study problems connected with the large number of black soldiers receiving less-than-honorable discharges. The study led to the significant NAACP report *The Search for Military Justice*.[2] We toured bases in and around Berlin, Frankfurt, Stuttgart, Mannheim, Munich, Mainz, Wiesbaden, Karlsruhe, and Heidelberg and interviewed more than five hundred black enlisted men, in addition to several hundred white officers and civilians. The Pentagon facilitated this assignment by providing us with access to key personnel. We were met by army colonel Andrew Chambers and his aide, an army major. Colonel Chambers appeared to be the embodiment of military efficiency as he briefed our team at the airport upon our arrival. His staff handled our luggage and transported us to an off-base hotel. We had declined the army's offer to house us at a military installation, since we felt that our independence and objectivity might have been questioned, if we were "guests" of the army. The eagerness with which the military was prepared to cooperate took us off guard, however we later cautiously accepted offers upon our arrival in Berlin.

As we rode to town, Colonel Chambers appeared to be a mix of military formality and cordiality. His light skin color and hair texture, which was noticeable from under his military cap, along with his slight Southern accent, led me to wonder whether he was black or white. Curious as to his racial identity, I decided to pose a "test" question: "Are you a frat man?" I asked. He replied, "Yes sir, I belong to the Kappa Alpha Psi fraternity." Coincidentally, this was also my fraternity, and with that, we shook hands again, and in doing so, exchanged the "grip" accompanied by wide grins. From that point on, my paranoia evaporated and the remainder of our trip took on a level of trust that led to a productive inquiry. Colonel Chambers would later retire with the three-star rank of Lieutenant General. He and the now-retired four-star general and former secretary of state Colin Powell ascended the ranks of the military together.

Our most crucial informant as to conditions in West Germany was the black army captain Curtis Smothers, a member of the Judge Advocate's General (JAG) staff and an outspoken opponent of many of the practices that the black troops complained about. In addition to his judicial duties with the JAG Corps, Captain Smothers taught a weekly class in government at Heidelberg University. A graduate of Morgan State College in Baltimore, the young officer held a law degree from American University in Washington, D.C. Smothers put his military career at considerable risk when he persuaded several other black commissioned and noncommissioned officers to join him in signing a petition to the Pentagon calling for a court of inquiry to look into conditions affecting black servicemen. The petition was dated Christmas Day, 1970. It rattled the Pentagon, causing a number of people to fear for Smothers's future. Fortunately for him, Roger Kelly, the deputy secretary of defense, arranged for his transfer from West Germany to the Pentagon, where he joined the office of Secretary of Defense Melvin Laird. Upon completing his tour of duty, Smothers entered the private practice of law in Oakland, California.

In addition to the twenty-eight-year-old Captain Smothers there was another unsung black hero in this saga—the *New York Times* reporter Thomas Johnson. Through a series of articles, Johnson featured the plight of black servicemen in West Germany, calling explicit attention to the positive role of Smothers. The first black reporter to be hired by the *New York Times* in 1966, Johnson later wrote about racial disparities throughout all branches of the armed forces. His strong writing was based upon personal interviews in West Germany. Reading his stories, I was reminded of the role played by black journalists in World War II. For example, Walter White, P.L. Prattis of the Pittsburgh *Courier*, and other African Americans traveled to war zones in search of eyewitness accounts. Simeon Booker Jr. of *Ebony* and *JET* magazines did much the same during the Vietnam War. In the case of Thomas Johnson and the *New York Times*, the NAACP benefited from the role of this top journalist from the world's most powerful newspaper.

Wilkins and I presented the NAACP report on West Germany at a press conference at the New York Sheraton Hotel, and I later completed the written report with the assistance of Williams and Bolden. Wilkins transmitted our report to Defense Secretary Laird on April 22, 1971. Once the NAACP became involved in getting to the bottom of the problems, Johnson and the *New York Times* continued to feature stories on the plight of black soldiers in even greater depth. There were two principal reasons why it was important to get maximum news coverage. For one, it said to the black servicemen that they were not alone; second, it sent a signal to officials in Washington that their policies were being carefully watched. Excerpts that bore Johnson's byline on February 15, 1971, reported on a New York press conference that resulted in our investigative trip:

> Nathaniel R. Jones, the general counsel for the National Association for the Advancement of Colored People, called yesterday for black civilian lawyers to be sent to West Germany to defend Negro soldiers facing military trials there. At a news conference at the Park Sheraton Hotel, Mr. Jones said that he had found that black soldiers often had little faith in white military defense lawyers. He added: "I have talked to more than 100 white lawyers in the Judge Advocate General's office in Germany and they all shared a feeling of utter frustration in getting black clients to confide in them."[3]

Johnson died in June 2008 at the age of seventy-nine, but not before seeing, during his lifetime, many changes that his reporting helped to bring about.

My focus on black servicemen did not cease when the West German investigation ended. The NAACP faced an onslaught of black veterans seeking to get their less-than-honorable discharges upgraded to honorable. The effect of a less-than-honorable discharge was so disqualifying with regards to future rights and opportunities that it was equivalent to receiving a lifetime sentence.

Our report, which focused only on the army in West Germany, sparked Secretary Laird's desire to appoint a Department of Defense task force in order to investigate military justice in all the branches of service. I co-chaired the eleven-member Department of Defense task force with Lieutenant General Clair E. Hutchins Jr. Hutchins was at the time commanding general of the 1st Army. A battle-tested leader, his experiences included service under General Douglas MacArthur. The DOD team comprised top legal thinkers in the different branches of the armed forces and the federal judiciary, leaders of government offices, representatives from civil rights organizations, and experts in the field of human relations. We endeavored to document the extent to which racial and cultural bias occurred in the military. We also sought to identify clearly the causative factors. The task force conducted investigations at military installations in the United States, Europe, and in the Pacific, and developed a methodology for best capturing the conditions of the black servicemen.

Of the thousands of African American youths who served in the Vietnam War as a result of the draft, a disproportionate number received a less-than-honorable discharge, known as Article 15. They were based on the accumulation of minor infractions. Such an accumulation in one's file could lead to the far more punitive "dishonorable discharge," if convicted at a court-martial. Unaware that a court-martial was a trial proceeding, not a conviction, many black servicemen presumed the court-martial itself to be a foregone conclusion of guilt and conviction. Thus many chose a nonjudicial option. Little did they realize how crippling the effect of the less-than-honorable discharge would be on their lives as civilians. They found themselves ineligible for post-service GI benefits and disqualified from the educational benefits and employment opportunities available to others under the GI Bill.

The willingness of those we interviewed, whether enlisted personnel or base commanders, to be forthcoming and candid brought energy to our efforts. I had learned from difficulties with the Kerner Commission interviews that it was important to win the confidence of the "victims" of the system under scrutiny. That we accomplished this to a considerable degree gave important credibility to the findings and recommendations of the task force. On returning to the mainland, our staff began the arduous task of preparing a report. I took heart from the resolve of Secretary Laird to get a firm grip on race-relations issues. After long hours and many days, we completed the draft of the report. While we did not reach unanimity on each point, we were able to blunt sharp differences. Lieutenant General Hutchins proved masterful in prevailing upon the military members to rethink many of the traditional views they harbored. Major General George S. Prugh Jr., judge advocate general of the army, wielded much influence. Rear Admiral Merlin H.

Staring, judge advocate general of the navy, wrestled with a number of the recommendations. The navy was the last of the armed services to "see the light" on the issue of race. However, Admiral Staring was an enlightened lawyer who recognized and accepted facts when they became clear. General Clyde R. Mann, director of the judge advocate division of the Marine Corps, proved the most resistant. He chose to write separately on some of the issues with which he was in disagreement. The most receptive and progressive of the judge advocates general was Major General James S. Cheney Jr. of the air force.

I played the combined roles of advocate and mediator as I moved between the military officers and the civilians. Each side had strong views about what the military should and should not do to correct conditions. Given my civil rights background, I had to keep the confidence of civilian members while not alienating the military members. At times I found myself sorely tested. But in the end, the entire group took pride in our finished product. We presented the four-volume *Report of the Task Force on Administration of Military Justice in the Armed Forces* to Secretary Laird and the public on November 30, 1972, some eighteen months after our NAACP report.

The following excerpt from the report illustrates the depth and scope of our efforts:

> The point which the Task Force wishes to make here is that the overall problem of racial discrimination in the military and the effect of that problem on military justice is not a Negro problem, a Mexican-American or a Puerto Rican or a white problem. It is the problem of a racist society.
>
> It is clear to us that many white individuals entering the military service come with severe disabilities resulting from being raised in a racist society. What those disabilities are, exactly, is not as well documented in their case as it is in the case of the young black citizen. Perhaps this fact reflects the fascination of even well-intentioned American scholars for the victim, rather than the perpetrator of racial discrimination.[4]

I felt it imperative that we also address the way in which the Armed Forces Qualification Test (AFQT) determined the likely success or failure of a serviceman. African Americans scored markedly lower on this test, and so their fate was sealed from the very beginning of their service. A disproportionate number wound up in "soft core" career fields and infantry units. Whites, on the other hand, were assigned to the occupations that offered technical training with promotional opportunities. This occupational segregation produced much frustration, leading to disciplinary problems. The army's way of handling those caught up in the disciplinary system was to ease them out with less-than-honorable discharges. Much the same occurred in the air force.

The report quoted the words of a black serviceman:

When you come in, you take the AFQT. If you haven't had a good background and a good high school or college education or experience in electronics, into supply and transportation and other "soft core" areas you go. I graduated from high school in 1955. I got a substandard education, compared to the white NCOs my age. They can progress because their better education put them into another career field, where the progression rate is faster. No matter how hard I study, I can't advance now. On a promotional exam for the few slots that do open up in my field—which is top heavy with black and white NCOs—I have to score damn near perfect. In the administration field, which I am in, my score has got to be phenomenal, or I am out of it, in terms of promotion. That is what is killing us.[5]

The skepticism about me and the anger over Robert Carter's departure, when I first took the position of NAACP general counsel, vanished as I established my reputation on the steady wave of issues that emerged involving student protests, military justice, school desegregation, employment and housing discrimination, and police excesses. I gradually persuaded new and former lawyers to reengage in the struggle on behalf of the NAACP and its members. Robert Carter, whom I had met during the 1940s when he came to Ohio, was cool toward me only for a brief period. We forged a good relationship over time, and after I joined him as a federal judge, he said to me, and to others, that he was glad that I took the NAACP job. Likewise, my mentor, J. Maynard Dickerson, came increasingly to accept my decision as favorable reports of my work reached him. I felt a deep sense of satisfaction when, as general counsel, I was able to utilize Mr. Dickerson's experience at a time when he had been eased out of his powerful position in state government at an advanced age. His long experience as a civil rights lawyer and counselor proved invaluable to our litigation team.

Two Unique Cases Beyond Litigation

I recognized early during my career as NAACP general counsel that my duties would entail more than litigating civil rights. As the chief legal officer for the organization, I found myself frequently called upon for legal advice and counsel on policy issues that affected the corporate welfare of the NAACP. This was the case when one day a call was routed to me from Oscar Bernstein, a New York lawyer who wanted to talk about the estate of the famous author Dorothy Parker, who died on June 7, 1967.

I had heard and read about Dorothy Parker in connection with New York's Algonquin Hotel and its celebrated Round Table of writers. The group included such noted American authors as Heywood Broun, Dashiell Hammett, Franklin Pierce Adams, Robert Benchley, Marc Connelly, George S. Kaufman, Harold Ross, Robert E. Sherwood, and John Peter Toohey. Their liberalism and, for some, leftist ideas had subjected them to attacks from conservatives and even "witch hunts" by congressional investigations launched by the House Un-American Activities Committee during and after World War II.

In her last will and testament, Dorothy Parker named Dr. Martin Luther King to be the original beneficiary of her estate, with the NAACP a successor beneficiary in the event of the death of Dr. King. I have often wondered why she named the NAACP and have concluded that it was most likely her respect for the organization's former longtime executive secretary, the legendary Walter White. In addition to being one of the most prominent champions of racial equality from the 1920s through the 1940s, White had begun to move in New York's literary circles during the Harlem Renaissance years of the 1920s. Parker was certainly familiar with him and the work of the NAACP. More than this, however, Parker was known for civil rights advocacy. She gave a vivid indication of her racial views in her short story "Arrangement in Black and White," which appeared in the *New Yorker* in 1927. With biting satire, the story criticizes the condescension and prejudice of whites who think of themselves as liberal in regard to race relations.[6]

At my meeting with lawyer Oscar Bernstein, it soon became clear that he represented not the wishes of Dorothy Parker but rather those of her friend, the noted playwright and political leftist Lillian Hellman, who considered Parker's bequest to be a terrible mistake. Hellman believed that she should have been the object of Parker's generosity and remembrance, stating that she could not envision the Dorothy Parker whom she knew and for whom she had done so much to have named the NAACP as beneficiary. Considerably to the left of the NAACP, Hellman regarded the organization as having a relatively weak record on behalf of liberal causes. Bernstein was thus acting on Hellman's behalf, when he tendered a proposal to the financially strapped NAACP for the sale of the holdings of her estate, specifically her papers and royalties. I promised to consider the request and get back to him. Being so new on the job, I did what I was to find myself doing with considerable frequency: consulting with more seasoned colleagues. I had a concern because of the financial plight of the organization. The sum of $25,000 sounded like a lot of money at that time. In fact, it equaled my annual salary.

I first spoke with Roy Wilkins, who knew of Dorothy Parker and Lillian Hellman. His reply was, "You're our lawyer." I next sought the advice of his chief deputy, Dr. John Morsell. He too knew Parker and Hellman and commented, "You don't want to make Lillian angry. She is very influential; we have to be careful about this." I then sought the counsel of Max Delson, a highly re-garded New York lawyer and a member of the NAACP's national board of directors. As I explained the situation to him, he suggested immediately that we consult Andrew Weinberger, one of the part-ners in his law firm of Delson and Gordon and an expert on literary property matters for writers, composers, and artists. As it turned out, Andy Weinberger was just what the NAACP needed. Delson and Weinberger were quick to suggest an inventory and later pointed out that the real value of Dorothy Parker's bequest far exceeded the $25,000 offered by Hellman.

Hellman's lawyer had led me to believe that the estate consisted of writings primarily of a sentimental value to a dear friend such as her. However, Weinberger's search and review of the inventory of Dorothy Parker's literary properties revealed a virtual treasure trove. The experience taught me a lesson on the importance of being careful and solicitous of others' expertise before making a de-cision. From that time until I left the NAACP, I read with consid-erable interest the section of the organization's financial statement that referred to receipts from the Dorothy Parker estate. Over the years the bequest had helped brighten the fiscal picture of the NAACP.

There is one final page to the Dorothy Parker story. Although her body was cremated by the Ferncliffe Crematory in Hartsdale, New York, two days after her death in 1967 and well before the NAACP's knowledge of her bequest, her ashes remained unburied for more than twenty years. Since Lillian Hellman made Parker's funeral arrangements, it was assumed by most people that she also took care of the burial of the ashes. However, Hellman simply left Parker's ashes at the crematory, ignoring the bills for their storage. In 1973 Hellman instructed the crematory to package the remains and to send them off to her lawyers at the O'Dwyer and Bernstein firm, where they were placed in a file cabinet and remained for fifteen years.

It was not until 1988 that this matter became public. I was on the federal bench and thus no longer involved with the NAACP.

The NAACP had moved its headquarters from New York to Baltimore. Benjamin Hooks, then the NAACP president and CEO, exercised the organization's rights of ownership to the Parker estate and claimed Parker's ashes. Hooks, in collaboration with the mayor of Baltimore, Kurt Schmoke, agreed to dedicate a location on the grounds of the national headquarters of the NAACP as her final resting place. Representatives from Howard University's School of Architecture created a garden of white pines on the premises, and on October 20, 1988, following tributes to Dorothy Parker, a forty-pound urn was lowered into a circle of brick. The circle was meant to evoke the Round Table at the Algonquin Hotel. On a wall on the grounds appears a plaque with the words:

> Here lie the ashes of Dorothy Parker (1893–1967) humorist, writer, critic, defender of human and civil rights. For her epitaph she suggested "Excuse My Dust." This memorial garden is dedicated to her noble spirit which celebrated the oneness of humankind, and to the bonds of everlasting friendship between black and Jewish people.

Another intriguing case during my early years at the NAACP involved Clarence Norris, the last "Scottsboro Boy." The Scottsboro story has found a special place in the history of American jurisprudence and for those who pursue racial justice in our legal system. The case originated on March 25, 1931, when nine black youths, ages twelve to nineteen, who had hopped a freight train in Alabama, were arrested in Scottsboro, Alabama, and charged with the rape of two white women on the train. The criminal justice system whipsawed the boys through Southern state courts and federal courts. Initially, all but the youngest boy, who was twelve years old at the time of the arrest, were sentenced to death. With respect to Norris, he had three trials, receiving the death sentence each time. The case drew national and international attention throughout the 1930s.

Legal defense fund-raising rallies by groups sympathetic to the black youths were held all across the nation in the 1930s. During those years of the Great Depression, the American Communist

Party and its International Labor Defense (ILD) stood at the forefront of the case. With the injustices that arose in the Scottsboro case the Communists seized opportunities to bring blacks into their ranks by putting a spotlight on American racism and condemning our entire system of justice. Lawyers from the various Communist-front organizations tangled with NAACP lawyers over who should represent the defendants, and the Scottsboro Boys became pawns in an ideological struggle. Most black Americans followed the boys' fate in the courts as well as the political tug-of-war between the Communist Party and the NAACP.

The case's notoriety coincided with the offer of Walter White to Roy Wilkins in early 1931 to leave his position as editor of the *Kansas City Call* to become assistant secretary of the NAACP. From the time of the arrests Wilkins maintained an interest in aspects of the Scottsboro case. Seldom was there a discussion of racial justice among African Americans that neglected to acknowledge their story. The Scottsboro case put the entire criminal justice system on trial, and the various federal court rulings it produced during appeals resulted in a refinement of American constitutional jurisprudence relating to fair trials by state courts. I had heard about the Scottsboro Boys my entire life, but to come face-to-face with a principal actor in that great drama exceeded my wildest imagination.

After I became general counsel in 1969, from time to time I noticed a man being escorted into Wilkins's office for brief periods. Staffers seemed to recognize and acknowledge him, although he was never introduced to me. This changed on January 26, 1971, when the man decided to tell the two top NAACP leaders, Roy Wilkins and Dr. John Morsell that he was tired of being a fugitive and wanted to go back to Alabama to turn himself in. Wilkins beckoned me to his office for a talk with his visitor—a man called "Willie" Norris, but actually he was Clarence Norris, the last survivor of the Scottsboro Boys. After fifteen years in prison, during which time his death sentence had been overturned, Norris was placed on parole with the requirement to remain in Alabama. Norris fled the state, however, and ultimately made a home in New York. During our meeting Wilkins explained that Norris was wanted by Alabama officials. This fugitive from the law had found his way to the NAACP's headquarters years earlier, and the organization had for some time been a source of help to him, financially and otherwise. Initially the officers of the association were not fully aware of his illegal status. The NAACP never made an inquiry as to how he got to New York. Whatever brushes he had with the law in New York over the years—and there were several—none ever resulted in his identity being uncovered.

When Norris made his decision to return to Alabama, he was residing in Brooklyn, with his wife and children. During our meeting, Norris stated to me that he was tired of living as a fugitive and wanted to surrender to Alabama officials. A conversation with his daughter had prompted this decision. Ironically, his daughter had learned about the Scottsboro Boys in school one day and returned home with the question as to whether their family was related to the Scottsboro Boy with the last name of Norris. Norris and his wife decided at that time to reveal his real identity to their daughter. Her question had sufficiently unnerved him to the point of seeking advice and assistance from the NAACP. It was then when Norris went to see Wilkins and Morsell to inform them of his desire to surrender to Alabama authorities that I was asked to offer advice and develop a strategy that would assist him. I immediately brought into the conversation a highly capable and committed young lawyer on my staff, James I. Meyerson, who assumed primary responsibility for the case. Along with Wilkins and Gloster Current, we urged Norris to go slow and promised to assist him in every lawful way we could. One strategy we hit upon, mindful that the governor of Alabama was the arch segregationist George C. Wallace, was to contact New York's governor Nelson Rockefeller. We hoped that Rockefeller would persuade Governor Wallace and Alabama officials to allow Norris to remain in New York under the supervision of its parole officials. But because of an interstate pact, states are required to turn over fugitives to the states from which they fled, so Governor Rockefeller was powerless to assist us.

The very thought of having to deal with George Wallace, particularly on a matter as racially sensitive as the Scottsboro case, became a source of great concern. As governor in the early '60s, he defied the orders of the federal courts and stood in the schoolhouse door to block black students from enrolling at the University of Alabama. In the presidential primary campaigns of 1968 and 1972 he spread his racist venom in the Northern states. In some states Wallace's message served to ignite the racism waiting to be aroused in the North. The decision as to Norris's freedom rested in Governor Wallace's hands, so we really had no choice but to place our trust in this segregationist governor. Meyerson and I prepared letters of appeal for Wilkins to send to a number of prominent New York officials, including the first black New York appellate justice, Harold Stevens, and black lawyer Percy Sutton. I gave Meyerson the responsibility of connecting with our Alabama branch. He worked prodigiously and creatively. The branch leaders directed him to Assistant Attorney General Milton Davis, Donald Watkins, Judge Alvin Holmes, and other influential officials. They also connected him with the Alabama attorney general, William J. Baxley, who agreed to work with the NAACP and the Governor's Office. Other persons instrumental to our efforts were two veteran Alabama lawyers—Morris Dees, a formidable champion of civil rights, and Fred Gray, who represented Rosa Parks, Martin Luther King Jr., and Aurelia Browder in their landmark cases.

In the effort to spare Clarence Norris a return trip to an Alabama prison, I found myself in periodic conversation with him. He spoke about his life of anguish for a crime that neither he nor the other eight defendants committed. He told a chilling story of multiple trials and appeals and the long years on death row. There were times, I am certain, that he became impatient at the pace at which we were moving. I had insisted that we proceed with great deliberateness so as not to politicize the situation and create a backlash.

In an October 25, 1976, letter to the Board of Pardons and Parole, Alabama's attorney general William J. Baxley recounted the zigzag route that Clarence Norris took through Alabama's criminal justice system. The Scottsboro Boys had been tried on three separate occasions on the charges of rape. At each trial the evidence and testimony of the witnesses were substantially the same, with the significant exception that one of the alleged rape victims, Ruby Bates, retracted her testimony after the first trial, admitting that she had perjured herself and that there was no rape. Victoria Price, the other so-called victim, testified at the last Norris trial that she was raped by him and his co-defendants. When Attorney General Baxley set forth the highlights of her testimony, he argued and the judge agreed, that the two-hour time slot between the alleged brutal rape and the doctor's testimony as to his physical examination of Price showed no scientific evidence to corroborate her accusation. Attorney General Baxley concluded his impassioned argument by asking for a "full and complete pardon" for Clarence Norris.

On October 25, 1976, the Alabama Board of Paroles and Pardons declared Norris a free man and Governor Wallace signed the official pardon. Norris received the news by telephone. A month later, Roy Wilkins, who had lived with the case since it first hit the press in 1931, accompanied the Norris family and the NAACP legal team to Montgomery. We gathered at LaGuardia Airport early on the morning of November 29, 1976, for our flight to Montgomery. I continued to feel slightly uneasy out of fear that our plans might somehow go awry at the very last moment, especially since we were returning Norris to the jurisdiction of Alabama. After all, we were dealing with a governor whose administration was famous for its hostility to African Americans.

As we took each additional step in the process, my unease lessened. Upon arrival in Montgomery, we were met by state NAACP officials and representatives of the Attorney General's Office. It was on that day that Norris received the official document declaring his full pardon. At the historic Dexter Avenue Baptist Church, where Martin Luther King Jr. served as pastor during the Montgomery Bus Boycott twenty years earlier, we were joined in celebration by a delegation of members of the state legislature and civil rights leadership. Wilkins was among those who spoke to the church's packed audience. Norris had returned to Alabama a hero, and his emotion was palpable. In addition to Norris, another person to show great emotion in our party was Roy Wilkins. No living person, except Norris and his family, had so long an affiliation with the celebrated case. Wilkins, as I earlier noted, first read of the arrest of the nine black youths as he and his wife were deciding whether to leave Kansas City for the opportunity to join the NAACP leadership in New York. Once at the NAACP, Wilkins immediately began to push Walter White to get involved in the Scottsboro defense and not leave this legal battle to the Communist Party and its International Labor Defense lawyers. With pressure from Wilkins and with some exasperation, White said to him, "Roy, the Scottsboro case is your baby." And so it continued to be until 1976, when Norris was awarded a full pardon.

After the church rally, Attorney General Bill Baxley and lawyer Morris Dees took several of us to lunch at a nearby restaurant, where we ran into Governor Wallace. The governor briefly joined us at our table for what turned out to be a pleasant conversation. As he prepared to leave, he shook my hand, gave me a friendly nudge, and thanked me for coming to Alabama, adding, "I'm not such a bad fella." Under the circumstances, I had to agree. I thanked him and asserted, "We appreciate everything that you have done." Roy and Aminda Wilkins and I left for the airport and returned to New York.

Later, when the others returned, Meyerson and I joined Norris at the ABC studios of *Good Morning America*. The host, David Hartman, proved to be a most sensitive interviewer of Norris. He guided Norris through the telling of his experience of being arrested, wrongfully charged, convicted, and as a Scottsboro defendant who faced the electric chair three times. Norris told of being on death row, at times coming within hours of being executed. He startled Hartman and even those of us who had been involved in obtaining his pardon, when he answered Hartman's question as to whether he was opposed to the death penalty. Norris said, "I favor it." When asked why, he responded, "Sometimes it is necessary." That answer set our heads spinning.

In his classic autobiography *A Man Called White*, the NAACP leader Walter White, who had gone to Scottsboro, Alabama, to test the climate, gave this account:

Seldom have I seen an atmosphere so charged with racial hatred and the lynching spirit. We knew that the conviction in the lower court of the nine Negro boys was inevitable in such an atmosphere. The most we could hope to accomplish would be inclusion in the record of as much evidence of the innocence of the defendants as was possible, and the notation of violations by the Court of the constitutional rights of the defendants' due process protection as the basis of appeal from the inevitable guilty verdict.[7]

Walter White's vivid description captured the raw racism that infected and dominated the American justice system. On October 25, 1976, however, the record of evidence held sway in the pardon board's pronouncement of Norris's innocence. Clarence Norris died on January 13, 1989. In November 2013 the state of Alabama granted a blanket pardon posthumously to all of the Scottsboro defendants. This chapter in one of America's most shameful abuses of justice had finally come to a close.

Black-Jewish Relations

The YMCA forums I attended in my youth had the intended effect of charging and recharging my batteries to believe in the dignity of the human being, collaboration, and the possibility of social and political change. In retrospect, that was the first layer on my foundation of being able to think beyond my own neighborhood and immediate circle of friends.

It was that experience that sharpened my sensitivities about the willingness of others to join in the struggle for change. I came to realize, even then, that in a society such as ours, some basic truths had to be recognized: Blacks had to be reinforced in their belief of their innate worth as human beings and citizens of the United States, which I later learned was under challenge in the infamous *Dred Scott* case; and that our status as "persons" in a pluralistic society required blacks to reach out and enlist white allies of differing religious and ethnic groups in the cause.

Among the white faces I would see at the forums and whose voices I would hear consistently in the various other meetings I attended when the issues of social justice were being addressed, were those of the Jewish faith. There were others, of course, but Jews participated not only as individuals but they often also brought strong organizational support to those of us seeking social change. In 1909, Jews were instrumental in the founding of the NAACP, and their names were signatories to *The Call*.

My responsibilities as general counsel carried me over a large section of the nation as I visited local NAACP branches. When it came to efforts to effect change, there was constant political, financial, and legal support in varying degrees from significant elements of the Jewish community. In noting their role, I do not intend to overlook others who were essential members of the coalition of the concerned.

Nationally, there did come a time in the early 1970s, when strains appeared between blacks and their Jewish allies. There was disappointment with the objections that some national Jewish organizations and individuals leveled against aspects of affirmative action as it related to admission policies of colleges and universities, though a few organizations remained staunch supporters. What was troublesome for blacks was the refusal of objecting Jewish groups to draw a distinction between fixed traditional quotas and remedies that used numbers as a part of goals and timetables. Jewish resistance caused blacks to lump their position with whites who had historically blocked black advance. It drew a bitter backlash from within the black community by those who preached "black power" and cited that as justification for "black separatism." Try as many of us did to bridge the gap, the groundswell of bitterness was horrendous.

As an official of the NAACP, I cast my lot with those who attempted to bridge the rift between Jews and elements of the black community. The task was formidable and was often met with a response that cited the "unreliability" of Jews as allies when it came to sensitive issues. They would note that as long as blacks were targeting corporations and labor unions, the two groups were as one. That was also true when it came to sit-ins, efforts to end seg-regated bus and train travel, and attempts to obtain voting rights and jobs in plants or factories, and efforts to gain access to places of public accommodation. However, when the campaign for access to colleges, medical schools, and law schools began to use goals and timetables, the unity ended. Jewish abhorrence of quotas formed the basis of their withdrawal and, indeed, resistance. Black efforts to explain that the numerical goals were not quotas hit a stone wall of Jewish opposition. Voices in the black community resented the implication that Jews seemingly regarded the professional schools that produced doctors, lawyers, and engineers as their special prov-ince. I was among those who tried to argue against that notion, and at the same time tried to convince our erstwhile Jewish allies that their adamant opposition to the affirmative methods to diversify professional schools was not only ill founded but was seriously damaging the historical bond that existed between the two groups. Staunch Jewish allies such as the civil rights labor lawyer Joseph Rauh, who served on the national board of the NAACP, and who teamed up with the head of the NAACP Washington bureau, Clarence Mitchell Jr., to lead the lobbying efforts that brought about the enactment of the 1964 Civil Rights Act and the 1965 Voting Rights Act, strove to keep many of the national Jewish or-ganizations neutral on some aspects of the legislation. In this they were joined by longtime NAACP president Kivie Kaplan and Ar-nold Aaronson of the Leadership Conference on Civil Rights. I particularly appreciated the role they played when we were litigat-ing the *Bakke v. Board of Regents* and the *Bradley v. Milliken* cases when they were before the Supreme Court.

Another instance of my sensitivity to preserving and strength-ening relations between the black and Jewish communities oc-curred in a speech I gave while general counsel of the NAACP at a Fisk University conference on Black/Jewish relations. Substitut-ing for my colleague Dr. John Morsell, who was terminally ill, I concluded with his observation:

Fortunately, there is a positive factor at work in Negro-Jewish relations—above and beyond the close and analytical scrutiny which both are accustomed to render to the issue of their relationship. This is the working partnership which has developed among professionals in the respective organizations and among officials and academicians, whose daily pursuits bring them into close and continual contact.

The antennae of representatives in those categories are highly sensitive: they respond to warning signals with consultations; efforts to mediate tension spots; and attempts to achieve formulations which will accommodate both sets of interests, without requiring excessive compromise at either end.

I remain convinced that if the words of Dr. Morsell are heeded, the future of Black-Jewish relations will be enhanced and restored to where they once were.

7

Desegregation and the Road to the North

Shifting Legal Strategies—from Plessy *to* Sweatt *to* Brown

W.E.B. Du Bois's prescient assertion that the twentieth century would be defined by the problem of the color line was never more evident than in the NAACP's fight to eliminate segregation in public education. The legal strategy for school desegregation had never been static. It evolved over the decades of the 1930s and 1940s through a series of meaningful court decisions culminating in *Brown v. Board of Education* in 1954 and 1955, which mandated the elimination of racial segregation "with all deliberate speed." I first watched from the sidelines as this endeavor unfolded and then joined the fight, helping to guide the strategy as the NAACP's general counsel decades later. Involved with Northern urban cases in the 1970s, I sought to prove that discriminatory public policy in many sectors of society led to school segregation and to protect transportation—for example, busing as a legitimate means for converting from segregation to desegregation to achieve equality of education.

As early as the 1930s, NAACP lawyer Charles Hamilton Houston maintained that "equality of education is not enough," because "there can be no true equality under a segregated system." While this fundamental goal of true equality has never changed, the NAACP's legal strategy to attain it did indeed change. Houston began to combat de jure segregation not at the level of primary and secondary public schools but at the level of state-supported schools of higher education, and specifically their post-baccalaureate degree programs in law, education, and graduate studies. In 1935, his initial strategy attacked not the constitutionality of separate but equal but the failure to make "separate" truly "equal." Houston and his protégé Thurgood Marshall knew the depth to which racism had penetrated and infected colleges, universities, and other American institutions. They also knew that appeals to fairness and equity would do little to influence segregation's defenders. It was Houston who urged the NAACP to take a realistic perspective in regard to the limits of what could be expected from the legal system, given the Supreme Court's sanction of segregation in its 1896 decision of *Plessy v. Ferguson* and the continued lack of sympathy on the part of state and federal judges to arguments against the constitutionality of racially separate schools. Historian Genna Rae McNeil notes that Houston's strategy of protracted litigation through a series of "positionary tactics" cumulatively set legal precedents and thereby established the "groundwork" for the outcome in *Brown*. This was a brilliant, if counterintuitive, plan of insisting on strict adherence to the "separate but equal" doctrine of *Plessy*. In requiring that "separate" must be truly "equal," Houston and Marshall demanded something they knew to be virtually impossible. There could be no cheap way to equalize the separateness, and the courts seemed to agree that ordering the creation of a separate school for blacks was not a legitimate alternative. The NAACP lawyers began to win significant cases—Donald Murray's admission to the University of Maryland Law School in 1935; Lloyd Gaines's admission to the University of Missouri Law School in 1938; Ada Lois Sipuel's and George W. McLaurin's admission to the University of Oklahoma in 1948 and 1950 respectively, and Lyman Johnson's admission to the University of Kentucky's Graduate School in 1949.

However, this strategy shifted course in 1950, when the state of Texas sought to convince the Supreme Court that its establishment of a separate law school for black applicant Heman Sweatt complied with the "separate but equal" requirement. The case *Sweatt v. Painter* revealed the lengths that the state was prepared to go to keep its law school "lily white." The state of Texas had sought to circumvent the U.S. Supreme Court's ruling in the Oklahoma cases of *Sipuel v. Board of Regents of University of Oklahoma*, and *McLaurin v. Oklahoma State Regents*, by establishing a "separate law school" for Heman Sweatt to attend. Sweatt brought suit against the University of Texas when it denied him admission to its law school. In conversations I had with Roy Wilkins, he told the story of the *Sweatt* case, which he related in his book, *Standing Fast*.

He wrote that the year in which the NAACP brought the *McLaurin* and *Sipuel* cases they were also helping "an intense, balding student named Heman Marion Sweatt sue the Board of Regents of the University of Texas for admission." Sweatt was a graduate of Wiley College in Marshall, Texas. He also studied at the University of Michigan. He was encouraged by Walter White and Thurgood Marshall to apply to the University of Texas Law School. He did, but was turned down. In noting how long it took to litigate the *Sweatt* case, Wilkins described the attempt of Texas officials to "fix Sweatt up with some teachers in a basement in Houston" as though that would provide him an equal legal education. However, "the pitch was so ridiculous that a group of indignant white students got together and organized an N.A.A.C.P. chapter. It was the first chapter at a lily-white college in the South."[1]

Thus when Marshall argued *Sweatt v. Painter* in the Supreme Court, he declared with confidence that segregation itself was unconstitutional. Moreover, by this time, the separate-but-equal doctrine in higher education cases was under such serious question that it aroused a considerable degree of judicial discomfort. The Supreme Court articulated what an acceptable constitutional standard required—spelling out a standard of equality that Texas had not met and could never meet. Chief Justice Fred Vinson dropped a bombshell by tiptoeing even closer to overruling *Plessy v. Ferguson* with these words: "What is more important, the University of Texas Law School possesses to a far greater degree those qualities which are incapable of objective measurement but which make for

greatness in a law school. Such qualities, to name but a few, include the reputation of the faculty, experience of the administration, position and influence of the alumni, position and standing of
the alumni, standing in the community, tradition and prestige."
This opinion dealt directly with the definition of "equality." It also
said, "We cannot find substantial equality in the educational opportunities offered white and Negro law students by the state. . . .
A law school, the proving ground for legal learning and practice,
cannot be effective in isolation."[2]

The *Sweatt* case also benefited from Houston's persuasiveness
with the Justice Department. He prevailed upon the federal government to file a powerful brief that called the case one that would
test "the vitality and strength of the democratic ideals to which the
United States is dedicated." In 1950, Marshall declared that every
education case should directly challenge the segregation laws involved. All branches and units of the NAACP were so instructed.
Further clarification came from the NAACP board in 1950, when
it resolved that "pleadings in all educational cases . . . should be
aimed at obtaining education on a non-segregated basis . . . no other
relief will be acceptable." The new theory was first tested in the
South Carolina case of *Briggs v. Elliot*. The shift was seismic. All
school desegregation litigation by the NAACP thereafter proceeded
on a new theory: segregation is, per se, a violation of the Fourteenth
Amendment. The overturning of *Plessy v. Ferguson* came to fruition
four years later with *Brown v. Board of Education*—the result of
Houston's and Marshall's careful blend of idealism and realism.

When one considers all of the social, political, and legal challenges facing black parents, community leaders, and attorneys in
the 1940s and 1950s, one cannot help but develop a deep and enduring respect for their courage. It was Judge J. Waties Waring and
those remarkable lawyers who wrestled the state of South Carolina
over school segregation—and won. Most important historically,
though, is that it was in *Briggs* that the black community took the
mammoth step of shifting their collective goal from merely seeking
"equal" bus transportation, school facilities, pay for teachers, and so
on, to an all-out frontal assault on the institution of segregation.

Houstonian jurisprudence lay at the core of the historic *Brown* opinion authored by Chief Justice Earl Warren. Houston maintained, "Since education is a preparation for the competition of life, poor education handicaps black youth who, with all elements of American people are in economic competition."[3] Houston was convinced that failure to eradicate inequality in the education of black youth would condemn the entire race to an inferior position within American society. Chief Justice Warren in *Brown* conceded the truth of Houston's point by holding that "we conclude that, in the field of public education, the doctrine of 'separate-but-equal' has no place. Separate educational facilities are inherently unequal. Therefore, we hold that the plaintiffs and others similarly situated . . . are . . . by reason of the segregation complained of, deprived of the equal protection of the laws guaranteed by the Fourteenth Amendment."[4]

I remember well that day in May 1954 when the Supreme Court announced its opinion in *Brown*. I was attending night law school at Youngstown University and first learned of the decision from Dickerson, who was notified by the NAACP national office. Elated, I went to class and informed my law school classmates of what a momentous decision this was. My enthusiasm did not arouse a similar reaction in them, perhaps because it was not an issue that they had been following to the same extent that I had been. I looked forward to further developments from national civil rights leaders. It didn't take long.

The Atlanta Declaration

Following the monumental victory in *Brown v. Board of Education* on May 17, 1954, the first official NAACP response to the historic decision came from the NAACP leadership gathered in Atlanta just days later. In the Atlanta Declaration, the leadership pledged all of its resources toward the full implementation of the decision that overturned *Plessy v. Ferguson*'s separate-but-equal doctrine issued fifty-eight years earlier.

The NAACP leadership at that time declared:

We, as representatives of the National Association for the Advancement of Colored People, from seventeen Southern and Border States and the District of Columbia, have assembled here in Atlanta, Georgia, May 22–23 (1954), for the purpose of collectively developing a program to meet the vital and urgent issues arising out of the historic United States Supreme Court decision of May 17, banning segregation in public schools. . . . All Americans are now relieved to have the law declared in the clearest language . . . segregation in public education is not now only unlawful; it is un-American.[5]

On the heels of the Atlanta Declaration, the NAACP called for all of its units, North and South, to engage in the struggle to implement the decision. The victory was hailed in a resolution adopted by delegates at the Forty-Fifth Annual Convention in Dallas, Texas, on July 3, 1954. It said:

Whereas, the school segregation cases decided by the Supreme Court on May 17, 1954 . . . although directed specifically against State imposed segregated public education, have wider implications. Racially restrictive practices where they exist in the North, although rarely dependent upon law, do the same harm as the Southern segregation which the Supreme Court outlawed. . . .

That, in order to implement this resolution, we recommend that all Northern NAACP branches immediately examine their school systems for the following: (1) the existence of predominately or exclusively all-Negro schools resulting from deliberate segregation either reflecting residential segregation or gerrymandering of school districts; (2) discriminatory general educational standards, all educational services and those special classes available to children in predominantly all-Negro schools as compared with those available in other schools in the system; (3) school expansion programs locating new schools which, because of segregated residential patterns, would result in predominantly or exclusively all-Negro schools; and

(4) any non-discriminatory policy in the employment and assignment of Negro teachers and administrators.[6]

Each succeeding year, delegates to the National Convention of the NAACP reaffirmed their support of the principles of the Atlanta Declaration and the resolutions adopted in 1954. It was this series of resolutions that prompted Northern NAACP branches to press me to act against school segregation in the North.

My predecessor, Robert Carter, had instituted a number of suits in the early '60s in Northern cities such as Gary, Indiana; Cleveland, Ohio; and Cincinnati, Ohio. The success was spotty. Judges were loath to regard the *Brown* decision as a command to desegregate on the grounds that the racial imbalance in those districts was caused by acts unrelated to state action. *Brown*, these cases held, required proof of "state action," such as statutes or constitutions mandating racial segregation. The causation was said to have created de facto, not de jure, segregation. Courts held that de facto segregation did not meet the Fourteenth Amendment's "state action" requirement to permit federal courts to exercise jurisdiction.

However, by the time I became general counsel, pressures were building within the organization to address segregation in Northern schools. (Contrary to the shocking misreading of those Northern cases by Reagan-appointed judges and Justice Clarence Thomas, racial imbalance can be segregation if proof shows it was caused by intentional racial policies.)

Before any court-imposed remedy could be obtained, plaintiffs had to prove intentional acts of segregation in these Northern school systems. This was true even with the *Keyes v. School District No. 1* (Denver) presumption, which arises when segregation is shown to exist in a significant portion of a school district, allowing a court to presume that the entire system became segregated by virtue of those policies. This proved to be more of a task than individual, often impecunious, plaintiffs could show. Help was needed. Requests for financial assistance were made to the NAACP.

Complicating the problem for black plaintiffs was the range of tools with which school officials could arm themselves. School boards had, for example, the financial resources provided by tax-payers to employ top legal talent, ready access to the media, and the ability to exert considerable political leverage. They could engage in forceful legal resistance in the courts, and ignite backlash, even within the minority community, through the use of such buzzwords as "forced busing" and "white flight." They were experts on convincing some blacks that desegregation was bad for them. Nevertheless, the desire of black plaintiffs to challenge segregation in the public schools moved forward.

In several of the school desegregation cases, parties discussed the possibilities of settlement in order to avoid a costly trial. We were always open to settlement. The basic condition that school boards had to agree to before there could be a settlement was to admit that the current condition of the school system did not comply with the requirements of the Fourteenth Amendment, or in other words, were segregated. If they would make that admission, the court could make a finding of unconstitutionality. Such a finding would then be the basis for orders of remediation that could include pupil reassignment and educational components to correct the educational harm that segregation created.

Absent an agreement, it was necessary to go to trial to prove the causes of the segregation. The resulting orders were aimed at remedying constitutional violations. This was not voluntary affirmative action. Yet in the public mind, due largely to the resistance campaigns mounted by school districts and opponents of desegregation, there was often a belief that court-ordered desegregation was the same as affirmative action. The latter occurs when there has been no proof of unconstitutional conduct. Affirmative action is a voluntary change in policies and practices as distinguished from changes compelled by judicial fiat.

For example, the plans involved in the famous *Bakke* case did not arise from a court finding against the California Board of Regents. Had there been a finding by the court, or an admission by the regents, the plan put in place could have withstood a court challenge.

Alan Bakke sued the Medical School at the University of California at Davis for adopting a special admissions program with a specific number of seats designated for minority students. There was no judicial finding of discrimination. That controversy exposed the racism that lurked in the midst of the affirmative action plans and the nation's unreadiness to accept this historical fact. Lines were tightly drawn. The Supreme Court, in a 1978 ruling, reversed the case by holding that explicit use of quotas with no predicate finding of discrimination did violate Alan Bakke's rights. His admission was ordered. However, the court went on to hold that race could be used as one of the factors in the admissions program as long as it was only one of several factors considered. We all breathed a sigh of relief and felt that use of race in affirmative action plans would survive.

On the day of the decision I went up and down the West Coast holding press conferences assuring our clients that affirmative action was still alive. It was not until the *Bakke* affirmative action controversy that many blacks and others who had been "taken in" on the "forced busing" issue began to understand that as a remedial tool, busing was a red herring and that as a desegregation tool, it was indivisible from remedial techniques needed to correct other forms of discrimination. They came to understand that to compromise on the busing issue in school desegregation cases was to create a vulnerability for the remedies needed in the related areas of employment, housing, voting rights, and the entire array of affirmative action programs. They came to realize that the problem was really race—not a bus—since white pupils by the millions had been and were still being transported to school by bus all over the country. The *Bakke* case and other affirmative action cases demonstrated that where the remedy was racial, resistance was certain to follow. The real heroes of the 1970s were those litigants, students, parents, and judges who did not and still do not compromise on the issue of race-based remedy. A contention of mine is the simple fact that a right without a remedy is no right at all. To pretend otherwise is to engage in wheel spinning.

As we explore the actions of the 1970s aimed at overcoming racial segregation in urban schools, particularly in the North, it is
helpful to understand the strategies that evolved. First, it must
be noted that in taking on urban or metropolitan school systems,
where plaintiffs were required to prove intentional racial discrimination by public officials, an enormous allocation of resources was
necessary for research that often required specialized skills beyond
that usually relied upon in an ordinary civil rights case. The metropolitan or interdistrict approach to school desegregation therefore
posed an even more complex set of problems for litigators in the
1970s. The Detroit experience (*Bradley v. Milliken*, discussed in
detail later) best demonstrates those complexities.

Contemporaneous with the Northern litigation was the case in
Atlanta. The events looming in Atlanta in connection with the desegregation litigation there nearly caused the unraveling of the
strategy and the successes that our Northern litigation was experiencing. The widespread press coverage it received—including
headlines in the *New York Times* and the *Washington Post*—ensured
it would have nationwide repercussions. In addition, years later, it
came close to blocking my pathway to the bench.

The Atlanta School Case

The Atlanta school case, *Calhoun v. Cook*, was being litigated at
the time the NAACP launched the major cases in the North. When
some of the theories that our lawyers were developing in the
Northern cases led to court findings of de jure or official causation,
elements of resistance in the South and North banded together to
stage their most spirited fights at the gates of remedy. The policies
and practices that created liability for segregation were no longer
a subject of serious debate. We had the proof. One of the tools of
remedy that married the South and the North—the reassignment
of black and white pupils through the use of transportation, which
came to be known as "busing"—was seized upon as an effective
weapon with which to counterattack. Northern congressmen and

senators introduced anti-busing amendments. I engaged in a major television debate with a then-youthful Senator Joseph Biden of Maryland, who had coauthored the 1978 Eagleton-Biden anti-busing amendment.

There were groups in Atlanta trying to get some black leaders to accept a compromise offered by friends of the school board that would undercut our basic theory in the Detroit case *Bradley v. Milliken*. Doing some behind-the-scenes prodding was a powerful judge who was sitting on the U.S. Court of Appeals for the Fifth Circuit, Griffin Bell, whose record had not shown him to be a friend of school desegregation. It was only weeks after I'd made an argument in the Detroit school case before the en banc Sixth Circuit Court of Appeals in February 1973 that the deal was struck that came to be known as the Atlanta Compromise. It traded the goal of pupil desegregation for an increase in black administrators in the school system. What I was faced with, from an organizational standpoint, was a war between the principles undergirding the 1954 Atlanta Declaration and the new Atlanta Compromise, the latter of which embraced separate-but-equal, the very segregated conditions that *Brown* had declared to be unconstitutional. My argument before the Sixth Circuit had urged that the same remedial principles being enforced in the South should be applied in school districts in the North.

Countering the earlier shift in the Nixon Justice Department position was *Swann v. Charlotte-Mecklenburg Board of Education*, an important pronouncement from the Supreme Court on the issue of neighborhood schools, on quotas, and the use of transportation or busing. The litigation efforts challenging dual systems for white and black students had, by the 1970s, reached urban or metropolitan school systems of significant size. Those in charge of the systems were slow to act and in most cases did not act without private plaintiffs initiating litigation. In *Swann*, the court considered and approved the use of race-sensitive remedies, questioned the sanctity of neighborhood schools, and called transportation for busing an integral tool of public education. This highly significant opinion, authored by Chief Justice Warren Burger, declared:

Absent a constitutional violation, there would be no basis for judicially ordering assignments of students on a racial basis. All things being equal, with no history of discrimination, it might well be desirable to assign pupils to schools nearest their homes. But all things are not equal in a system that has been deliberately constructed and maintained to enforce racial segregation. The remedy for such segregation may be administratively awkward, inconvenient and even bizarre in some situations; and may impose burdens on some; but all awkwardness and inconvenience cannot be avoided in the interim period when remedial adjustments are being made to eliminate the dual school systems.[7]

It is clear that the Supreme Court had matured immeasurably since *Brown II*, when it decreed, some think naively, that desegregation should proceed with "all deliberate speed." *Brown II*, in 1955, was a decision that resulted from the Supreme Court's consideration of a timetable for implementing its 1954 decision that declared school segregation was a violation of the Fourteenth Amendment. Significantly, in the face of continuous, serious and, in some cases, simpleminded challenges, the Supreme Court refused to retreat from its basic holding in *Brown I*, that "in the field of public education the doctrine of separate-but-equal has no place." Thus, the Houston-Marshall strategy remained on track into the 1970s in spite of the stubbornness of its foes.

Repercussions

When the media learned of the Atlanta Compromise, they recognized the contradiction and sought out Roy Wilkins to confirm that the NAACP had, indeed, renounced the position it had been embracing since the time of the 1954 Atlanta Declaration. Jon Nordheimer, a reporter for the *New York Times*, reached Wilkins by telephone and engaged him in a general philosophical discussion about black pride. The reporter, without any reference to any particular case, drew from Wilkins this observation:

Our general position has been there is no sacrifice of racial pride or loss of education if blacks go to school with blacks. If the school board agrees to the improvement in education and a program that leads to meaningful equalization of the educational process, black children will not suffer by attending an all-black school. However, an integrated education where whites and black children can learn about each other in the classroom setting remains a desirable goal, if not an exclusive one.[8]

Even the NAACP regional director for Region V that included Atlanta, Mrs. Ruby Hurley, a non-lawyer, took the bait and stated that the NAACP Legal Defense Fund (LDF) lawyers handling the case, by pushing for a desegregation plan that included pupil reassignment, were acting contrary to the wishes of the Atlanta branch. She saw merit in trading off desegregation of schoolchildren in exchange for a superintendent's position and other administrative and teaching jobs. A hard-fought series of cases in the South had won from the Supreme Court approval of the remedial principles we were building on in the North. These remedial principles shifted the burden of compliance, once a constitutional violation was proven, to school officials to remove vestiges of segregation, root and branch. For a unit of the NAACP to agree to a deal whereby the children would remain locked into segregated schools in exchange for granting jobs to school administrators was intolerable.

This whole matter fell solidly into my lap. Mindful of the holding of the Supreme Court in *Brown* about the unconstitutionality of state-imposed segregation of children, our own Atlanta Declaration, and the consistent resolutions of the convention delegates over the years, it was clear to me that the Compromise could not stand. An immediate clarification from Wilkins was necessary to put to rest any notion that the NAACP was backing off from its historic belief that segregated education, when induced by official action, was inherently unequal and, therefore, unconstitutional.

My legal team was bewildered at this turn of events. Branch officials in a number of Northern cases, particularly Detroit, were virtually pounding on my door demanding explanations as to what the Wilkins statement meant for their own cases. Other newspapers took their lead from the *New York Times* headline "NAACP Shifts in School Fight." The *Washington Post*'s Susanna McBee did a major story that tracked the *Times*, three days later with, "NAACP Accepts Atlanta Proposal with Less Busing." Her piece repeated the *Times* quote attributed to Wilkins even as it carried a subsequent clarification, released by Wilkins and Bishop Stephen Gill Spottswood, chairman of the national board of directors. In NAACP-ese, a telegram message was sent to the branch that demanded immediate action: "We call upon the Atlanta Branch Officers and Executive Committee Members to reverse its approval of the Plan submitted to the Court."[9]

Of course, in the midst of this maelstrom, columnists rushed into print with variations of the *New York Times* and *Washington Post* stories. One of the most vigorous and unrelenting challengers was a black *Washington Post* columnist named William Raspberry. His column of Wednesday, February 29, 1973, was headed, "The NAACP: Moving to Defuse the Busing Issue." In his piece he stated that by agreeing to the Compromise, the NAACP was "now saying that integration and quality education, while both desirable, are separable items, and that the latter is the overriding priority. I am trying to resist premature handsprings. After all, a later 'clarification' may reduce the Atlanta business to a one-time aberration. But, if the NAACP really has made the turn, it is a major victory for racial sanity and yes, for integration as well."[10]

This was a major crisis that I did not feel I could allow to relegitimize what the Supreme Court had, after fifty-eight years of litigation, declared to be unconstitutional. If that happened, what we thought had been a historic victory would have been nothing more than a fantasy. It was not enough for people to be singing hosannas over the striking down of segregation only to fold at the barriers of remedies.

I had no alternative but to press my concerns with Wilkins and to seek a way to limit the harm. In a February 26, 1973, memo to him, I stated:

There have been repercussions to the Sunday *New York Times* story on the Atlanta school case from our lawyers handling the Detroit and Indianapolis litigation. When I return to the office, I would like to have a chance to discuss it with you and to see in what way a clarification can be issued that will limit the chance of that settlement being misconstrued by the Supreme Court and Judges currently considering our other cases in which the position we have argued is in contrast to that asserted by the Atlanta Branch.[11]

We did meet, and I outlined in considerable detail the proof we had developed to convince the courts of the ways in which Northern districts had brought about massive racial imbalance. So powerful was this proof of segregation that these districts mounted only a token defense. They saved their serious firepower for the remedial phase, knowing full well that they would pick up many allies with their emotional George Wallace–type harangues against busing and appeals to the understandable racial pride of blacks by contending that black children do not have to sit next to white children in order to receive a quality education. For the NAACP to validate those arguments, as the Atlanta Compromise would do, would pose a risk that could not be allowed to go unchallenged. Wilkins understood, as few did, what was being sought and he immediately swung into action with his repudiation of the Atlanta Compromise. That was not the end, however. It later became necessary to remove the branch president, Lonnie King, when he refused to abide by the National Office directive.

Request to Recant

Before that drastic action was taken, I wrote King a long letter on February 28, 1973, explaining why it was necessary for him and the branch to disavow the deed. One problem for King was that he was the branch official with whom Fifth Circuit Court judge Griffin Bell had spoken in an attempt to broker the deal. That a federal judge would inject himself into pending litigation, particularly one who during the period of "massive resistance" went across the

South advising states on ways to delay complying with the *Brown* mandate, stirred the ire of desegregation lawyers, to say the least.

In my letter to Lonnie King, I laid out the case against the compromise:

> Outlines of the plan . . . raise serious questions as to whether it conforms to the declared policy of the NAACP . . . is binding upon all branches and units of the Association. . . .
>
> I am suggesting that the Atlanta Branch consider anew its action on the school desegregation plan. . . . Mr. Wilkins has had no communication from the Atlanta Branch in this final development. I am certain that our office would be interested in a detailed explanation of the factors that caused the Atlanta Branch to act as it did, in view of our policy and requirements of the law.
>
> For myself, I am handling the Detroit case. I am in touch with the lawyers in the Richmond, Virginia, case which will be heard by the U.S. Supreme Court. Each one of these attorneys is apprehensive that judges will be influenced by the Atlanta agreement. The reply of the Atlanta Branch, giving the reasons for its actions, will be invaluable in assessing the situation. Please advise me of the action of reconsideration by Monday, March 5.[12]

Not surprisingly, many white Atlantans and a disappointing number of the black middle class saw no harm in using poor black children as pawns for getting better administrative jobs. King cited the popularity of the compromise as justification for it without realizing what would happen to the children who would be locked into segregated schools in violation of *Brown* or the generations that would follow. The support King claimed that there was for the deal did not deter us from demanding its rejection as we were required to do if we were going to be true to *Brown* and the resolutions adopted annually by NAACP delegates. That is why Wilkins followed up with a mandate to King and the executive committee of the branch to repudiate the deal. Their failure to do so, following demands and a hearing, led to the removal of King and members of the executive committee. In this the national board was in full support, and replacements were selected to fill the various posts.

Bridging a Gap with the Enigmatic Derrick Bell

In addition to marshaling legal and financial resources to keep up the litigation campaign against Northern school districts, it was a struggle to keep our ranks strong. A number of strategically placed blacks, including Ron Edmonds and Derrick Bell Jr., joined the anti-busing efforts and published widely read articles and books that were critical of our desegregation efforts.

A few words about Professor Derrick Bell. I was a longtime admirer of his. We graduated from college the same year, both served in the Army Air Corps, worked for our hometown NAACP branches, and later moved to the national NAACP staff. As an NAACP-LDF lawyer, he handled major cases throughout the South before becoming an anti-poverty lawyer under the Office of Economic Opportunity. He then went into academia, becoming a member of the Harvard Law School faculty. He clearly was a star.

Professor Bell was particularly critical of the strategy that my colleagues and I put into place in Northern school cases. How someone with the impressive civil rights and academic credentials of Derrick Bell could miss the logic, rationale, and reason we were following baffled me.

In order to prove that the racial imbalances in the Northern school districts were not the result of happenstance but derived from policies and practices of an official nature, our research teams and lawyers thoroughly examined the history of the school district. The evidence we developed persuaded the various judges to agree we were dealing with de jure rather than de facto segregation. In the process of developing our proof we offered the testimony of educational experts, who described the degree of harm suffered by black children. After establishing the constitutional violations, the courts then invited proof as to the type of remedies that would be required to correct the harm. The Supreme Court had held in the *Swann* case that remedies had to be narrowly tailored, and that the nature of the violations would determine the scope of the remedy. In other words, before the remedial powers of the court could be exercised, a violation must be shown. It was at that point that the remedial powers of the court could, in addition to reassignment of pupils and teachers, compel the expenditure of funds that they had heretofore refused to expend on the education of black and poor children.

I never doubted that Professor Bell shared the NAACP's interest in the education of black children. However, the step he appeared willing to waive was a most important one, from a constitutional point of view—that is, to push for desegregation of the pupils to the greatest extent feasible. Atlanta NAACP officials were willing to forgo that most important step, a step that ignored the essence of the Houston thesis, "Failure to eradicate inequality in the education of black youth would condemn the entire race to an inferior position within America's society in perpetuity" and the basic holding of *Brown* that segregated education was inherently unequal.[13]

To keep faith with what was required by *The Call* and the Constitution, I, as the general counsel to whom the litigation program was entrusted, could not, any more than Houston or Marshall or Carter, allow the NAACP to break with its obligation.

My rebuttal was that the remedies Professor Bell wrote about—in the movement away from desegregation—are not available except when purposeful racial discrimination has been proven. When segregation is proven, the educational deficiencies are traceable to that unlawful policy. Therefore, the remedy can go further than pupil reassignment and include educational components.

We used the *Brown*-driven fact-finding against school systems as a basis to obtain a variety of improvements beyond pupil reassignments. A couple of excerpts from my *Yale Law School Journal* essay in response to Professor Bell follow:

> The courts up until now have evidently understood, as Professor
> Bell apparently has not, that segregation is itself the deepest educa-

tional harm because it is the result of institutional racism and a condition of state-imposed racial caste.

Desegregation would in fact go a long way toward eliminating the educational damages with which Professor Bell is concerned. . . .

Professor Bell's argument, moreover, curiously seems to blame civil rights lawyers for a "decline" in the "great crusade to desegregate the public schools." It is true that in academic circles, to say nothing of the political realm, the merits of busing have been much questioned of late, but in those cities and towns where integration has occurred with the support of local public officials or school board members, the transitions have been successful. . . .

If on the other hand, Professor Bell means to claim that black support for desegregation has declined, this is a more serious charge. Professor Bell correctly points to cases in Atlanta, Boston and Detroit. However, Professor Bell fails to specify any factual evidence of the extent of those "increasing number of defections within the black community." What is even more disappointing is that Professor Bell has apparently closed his eyes (and his ears) to the ranting and raving of mobs agitated by anti-busing statements and code words from no less an officer of government than the President of the United States. The overwhelming number of blacks favor desegregation and oppose segregation as an affront to their humanity. That some blacks question the desegregation process must be attributed to this shameful demagoguery.[14]

My debate with Professor Bell occurred during the heat of the litigation war in which the NAACP was engaging. At the heart of each of our positions was a profound concern for the welfare of black children who were being cheated. For an academic of the stature of Professor Bell to validate the Compromise—a compromise so harmful to the black children of Atlanta, and one that would have an effect far beyond the city—made it necessary that there be a sharp response from the NAACP.

What I feared would happen to remedies for constitutional shortcomings and even voluntary efforts at correcting wrongdoing has come true. We are at a point now where Professor Bell and I would be of one mind reacting against Chief Justice Roberts's comment in a recent Texas redistricting case involving the Voting Rights Act, that "it is a sordid business, this divvying us up by race."

Following our written debate published in the *Yale Law Journal*, Professor Bell offered this conclusion: "Mr. Jones need not accept my assessment of black parental priorities, and his letter makes clear his belief that my criticism is unwarranted. But to the extent that his statement reflects a new recognition of the importance of educationally oriented remedies, the interests of those he represents will be better served, and the conflict between integration ideals and client interests will be headed toward resolution."[15] In fact, the twin objectives of combining pupil desegregation with educational components were always at the heart of the strategy the NAACP pursued.

The Fight Moves North: The Hillsboro School Case

Many Northerners assumed that the *Brown* ruling applied only to the South, and that whatever racial "isolation" existed in their Northern schools did not arise from law. But black parents and anyone else aware of the realities of education in the North knew better. In 1956, litigation in the federal courts involved the schools in my home state of Ohio. The case *Clemons v. Board of Education of Hillsboro, Ohio*, which relied on the *Brown* precedent, not only helped to shape the legal strategy I later employed as general counsel of the NAACP but also reflected my boyhood experiences attending schools that were tainted by the stain of segregation, even though they were not segregated as a matter of statutory or legal declaration. Like most school systems across the Northern states, my hometown schools were theoretically nonsegregated. However, clear rules and proscriptions limited the interactions between blacks and whites. Even when black and white children took classes in the same school buildings, racial discrimination could be seen on a daily basis, although it appeared to go unquestioned by white students, their parents, and the teachers. I have pointed out earlier that I never had or saw a black teacher at any of the schools I attended— a condition predicated on black inferiority and white superiority. People who perpetuated these precepts clung to them even when civil rights lawyers cited evidence that the various laws that legislatures in Ohio and elsewhere had at one time, intentionally and purposely, mandated a denial of education to black children and that the current condition was a vestige of that period. This blind, dogged resistance was shared by judges who, with the exception of the heroic few noted in this memoir, stubbornly refused to take proper note of the lingering effect of those early discrimination laws. They, as well as the larger white society, too often ignored the historical effects of racism on other contemporary thought and actions. For some judges, this kind of behavior served as what I came to regard as judicial "sleight of hand"; I first saw this gambit in action when it was employed by the trial judge in the Hillsboro school case.

My firsthand view of the *Hillsboro* case began long before it reached the courts. Years earlier, in 1945, Dickerson, who as president of the Ohio State Conference of NAACP branches, wrote to Thurgood Marshall, chief counsel for the NAACP, requesting assistance from the national office to fight school segregation in Ohio. On December 5, 1945, at the urging of his boss, Executive Secretary Walter White, Marshall responded to Dickerson, writing, "Mr. White spoke to me about the program of the NAACP to fight the tendency toward segregated schools in Ohio. We are more than interested in cooperating in such an effort." This was prior to *Brown*.

Marshall followed up his letter to Dickerson with a personal visit in 1946 to the meeting of the Ohio State Conference of NAACP Branches. During that meeting with representatives from thirty-one branches, and after conferring at length with a team of lawyers from across the state assembled by Dickerson, Marshall assured those present that their efforts would have the full support of the national legal staff. That commitment reflected an understanding of the historical fact that pupil segregation in the Hillsboro, Ohio, school district was an outgrowth of laws enacted by the Ohio legislature in the 1800s. Indeed, Hillsboro demonstrated the seamless connection between racial motives that stitched together Southern and Northern school segregation.

At the time Congress granted Ohio the right to hold a Constitutional Convention in 1802, as a prerequisite to being granted statehood, the 1787 Northwest Ordinance required that "schools and the means of education shall forever be encouraged." The State Constitution of 1802, in response to the Act of Congress that authorized the Convention, commanded that "schools and the means of education shall forever be encouraged by legislative provision." In 1817 the legislature passed an act, amended in 1818, regulating the investment and use of the lands reserved for the benefit of education. Later, on January 22, 1821, the legislature enacted another law "to provide for the regulation and support of common schools," which laid the foundation for a state system of common schools. It did not take long for racial discrimination to rear its ugly head. In 1829, a mere eight years later, and sixty-seven years before *Plessy v. Ferguson*, the Ohio legislature passed a law specifically barring black and mulatto children from the public schools. In 1838, the legislature passed another exclusionary common-school act that limited school funds to the education of white children only. Although the state legislature outlawed public segregation in Ohio in 1887, in Hillsboro the vestiges of this long history of racial discrimination continued after the laws were no longer on the books.

Hillsboro is located in the southwestern part of Ohio in Highland County. Census figures put the county's population in 1950 at 28,188, and of Hillsboro itself, at 5,126. Primarily a rural community, only 2.6 percent of the county population was black. Majority racial attitudes had a distinct Southern cast, based on historic local struggles over the abolition of slavery and collisions with abolitionists who hid fugitive slaves. The Fugitive Slave Act was vigorously enforced in Ohio. In fact, bounty hunters roamed the streets of Cincinnati in search of escaping slaves. The Ohio laws and the Southern Ohio court system worked together in the effort to capture and return escaping slaves to their "owners." The federal court undergirded the entire process of returning fugitives to slavery. It is little wonder, then, that a legal system that did not hesitate to reinforce slavery would have no problem lending support to policies that denied education to free citizens of color. Racial prejudice ran rampant in the communities in that region. Hillsboro was one such community.

According to historian Susan Banyas, the Hillsboro schools in 1950 consisted of one integrated high school, two all-white elementary schools, and one all-black elementary school that was established before segregation became outlawed in the 1880s. In 1951, the Hillsboro Board of Education desegregated the seventh and eighth grades by moving them out of the elementary schools and into the high schools. But the lower grades remained segregated. Black parents then sought the NAACP's help in their efforts to end segregation in their elementary schools. They seemed to make some progress for a short time, but then the board reversed its position and rezoned the city, making Lincoln School 90 percent black, thereby ensuring that segregation would continue. As I was to see in all of the later Northern school cases, officials argued that the black students would fare better in a racially isolated educational environment. This was not news to me; during my time in elementary and high school I encountered white school officials who claimed that blacks preferred segregation.

Despite this setback, black parents continued to push for integration while white parents resisted, including resorting to vandalism and destruction of property. Indeed, when one considers all the social, political, and legal challenges facing black parents and children, and community leaders and attorneys, in the 1940s and 1950s, one cannot help but develop a deep and enduring respect for their courage and persistence. For example, after Philip Partridge, a former county engineer, burned the Lincoln School, the school board insisted that the black children continue to report to the fire-damaged building. In response, black residents organized a boycott and devised a strategy to integrate the other two elementary schools by attacking the board's zoning scheme. On September 22, 1954, three months after the *Brown* ruling, the NAACP filed a lawsuit in U.S. district court in Cincinnati asking the court to prohibit the school board from compelling the black children to withdraw from the white schools they had "integrated" and return to the segregated Lincoln School. Marshall and Dickerson put together a stellar legal team led by Constance Baker Motley of New York. Later in the 1960s, Motley represented Charlayne Hunter and Hamilton Holmes in integrating the University of Georgia, and James Meredith in integrating the University of Mississippi. She would go on to become America's first black female federal judge after serving as president of the Borough of Manhattan. Joining her on the Hillsboro case were Ohio lawyers James McGhee of Dayton and Harvard-trained Russell Carter, also of Dayton.

Federal District Judge John H. Druffel denied the relief sought, on grounds of its being premature. This was but the first of countless rebuffs encountered by those who sought to apply *Brown* to the North. The NAACP appealed to the U.S. Court of Appeals, asking it to direct Judge Druffel to issue a ruling. After the appellate court directed the trial judge to show cause for not ruling, a visibly irritated Judge Druffel held a hearing and then denied relief to the black plaintiffs in a decision that was totally devoid of legal analysis. He wrote, "The good faith and sincerity of the Board of Education and its Superintendent of Schools, Paul Upp, in their endeavor to overcome what they concede is temporary segregation, is amply supported by the record." His order on "good faith" and "sincerity" is illustrative of the judicial sleight of hand associated with a lack of respect for the black children, their situation, and their cause.

These skirmishes took place before the Supreme Court came down with its *Brown II* ruling in 1955, which required desegregation "with all deliberate speed." School districts, including the Hillsboro School Board, put their own interpretation on that phrase. History and experience now show "with all deliberate speed" to have been a license for obstruction and delay. Only when the Southern states' disguise of delay was exposed did the Supreme Court years later, in the case of *Alexander v. Holmes County Board of Education*, abandon the "all deliberate speed" mandate for immediate implementation. And only then did desegregation begin to move forward with alacrity. That phrase not only had significant ramifications for school desegregation, it also came to affect me deeply on a personal and professional level because of a controversy that eventually led to the firing of an NAACP lawyer and my hiring as general counsel, at which point I took the litigation baton from my NAACP predecessors—Charles Hamilton Houston, Thurgood Marshall, and Robert Carter.

8

Beyond De Facto/De Jure

The Northern School Desegregation Cases

When Roy Wilkins offered me the position of NAACP general counsel in 1969, he invoked the names of former colleagues and my heroes Marshall and Houston. Wilkins obviously knew what he was doing in reminding me that I would be following in their footsteps. I had long been impressed by Houston's philosophy on education and his resolve to remove barriers that blocked blacks' access to it. His credo became my watchword: "Equality of education is not enough. There can be no true equality under a segregated system."[1]

Long before that time, I had committed myself to use the powers of the law and the courts to do what the Constitution required. This commitment was quickly called to active duty when I found a number of Northern school desegregation cases virtually on life support at the time I assumed the position. The legal strategy under which those cases were proceeding gave me considerable pause as a result of what I had seen happen in the 1964 *Craggett v. School Board* case in Cleveland and the 1965 *Deal v. Cincinnati School Board* case. Those two cases demonstrated the difficulty of convincing Northern federal judges that *Brown* applied to school districts beyond Ole Dixie and the Border States. Judges had readily accepted the fiction of a de facto/de jure distinction, which had the effect of perpetuating the expansion of school segregation. De jure segregation is segregation that is set forth in law, while de facto segregation arises from the effects of customs and practices, even though not mandated by law. My predecessor, Robert Carter, who had successfully argued *Brown* in the U.S. Supreme Court and was the principal author of the brief, brought the *Craggett* and *Deal* suits on behalf of the respective Cleveland and Cincinnati NAACP branches. In the Cleveland case, Carter was joined by a first-rate team of lawyers (now all deceased): Louis Stokes, who later became a U.S. congressman and one of the most dedicated public officials I ever knew; his brother Carl B. Stokes, who went on to make history as the first black mayor of Cleveland; Jack Day, a leading litigator; and Russell Adrine, a longtime NAACP lawyer.

At the time of the *Craggett* case I was serving as assistant U.S. attorney in Cleveland and sat in on much of that trial. I also saw firsthand how Judge Kalbfleisch's lack of sympathy for the desegregation position of the NAACP manifested itself in many of the courtroom rulings and in his treatment of Carter. Carter, who later became a federal judge, once told me that he had never been treated so rudely by a judge in any of his appearances in Southern courtrooms.

With this contemptuous judicial demeanor fresh in my mind, I felt that repeating the approach used in *Deal* and *Craggett* would be unsuccessful. I had no doubt that the earlier strategy would have yielded more defeats under the legal doctrine of res judicata, which bars a re-litigation of the same issue once a decision has been rendered. Thus, I decided, much to the consternation of the previous lawyers, to recast our approach in the pending cases. I also realized that the financial resources required to accomplish this shift of strategy were going to be hefty. Nevertheless, even though the NAACP was seriously strapped for funds, I felt we had no choice. Special appeals were made by the NAACP Special Contribution Fund to foundations and organizations for tax-exempt grants to underwrite the costs of the legal research on which we were embarking.

The introduction of various legal precedents set in the Southern cases, when combined with the evidence of Northern racial policies, stirred up a political firestorm. So inflamed did the atmosphere become that Northern politicians and the Supreme Court majority itself finally withdrew from the clearly established precedents. Thus, the scenes shifted on the education litigation front and my own role transformed from that of a sideline observer to that of a participant.

When I took over as general counsel in 1969, there was mounting pressure on the NAACP legal department to provide advice and counsel on school desegregation to an increasing number of branches located in large and middle-size Northern cities. A series of Northern school cases that I embarked upon at the insistence of residents of various communities across the North forced us to confront the legal barriers erected by judicial precedents in the *Deal* and *Craggett* cases that racial isolation was the result of happenstance and not the acts of public officials and institutions. Therefore, the courts were held to lack jurisdiction to remedy segregation.

Communities presented most compelling issues. Those that drew our attention appeared to be in a position to advance most effectively the NAACP's strategy to slow down the galloping segregation in the North. They included Detroit and the Ohio cities of Dayton, Columbus, Youngstown, Cincinnati, and Cleveland. The Boston branch of the NAACP had been struggling with the segregation issue for some time and also wanted us to weigh in. Members in Los Angeles, Pasadena, and San Francisco were also pressing their branches to take action. This was also true in Grand Rapids and Kalamazoo, Michigan. New York City schools were also operating in violation of *Brown v. Board of Education.*

Since we were already engaged in the Midwest cities of Benton Harbor, Michigan, and Milwaukee, Wisconsin, and were developing research techniques in the Detroit case, as discussed below, the decision was made to give immediate priority to the Michigan and Ohio cases. At the same time, the Lawyers' Committee for Civil Rights Under Law had agreed to partner with the Boston NAACP branch and our national office in a suit against the Boston School Committee. This partnership was a tremendous lift because of the powerful legal talent provided by the Lawyers' Committee.

The ability to attract top-flight legal talent was a godsend. It made our team very competitive, given the barren state of the staff when I commenced my duties. Those who were initially critical of the NAACP over the firing of Lewis Steel were no longer harboring criticisms of the organization or of me, and had blessed our litigation efforts that restored the NAACP to a position of preeminence. The lesson I learned from Thurgood Marshall was to pick the brains of the top lawyers and put them to our use. This process went forward even as I tended to the political and public relations aspects of other cases, including Detroit and Cleveland.

In each case, we encountered a wide range of problems in proving the claims of wrongdoing being made against school districts, and the resistance those school districts raised to avoid making the required changes. The financial and emotional strains were staggering.

Each of the individual cases had unique aspects to them but they also had several common threads. Most notably, the school segregation we sought to eliminate was caused and/or perpetuated by a history of housing discrimination that was allowed to weave itself into the very fabric of the community. And the school officials consistently sought to absolve themselves of any culpability for the segregation by falling back on the "neighborhood school" defense, arguing that the children were assigned to schools based not upon their race but upon where they lived. In each case, we strove and usually succeeded in proving that the neighborhood patterns were the result of governmental action. A third common factor was the manner in which some courts and opponents of our desegregation efforts submerged the constitutional issues under the misleading blanket of "busing cases."

School desegregation litigation activities required probing deeply into the interplay of politics, race, and law in the North. After our team was able to prove that the de facto shield protected school systems in the North from judicial accountability, a new wall of defense was erected. Attention shifted from the constitutional wrongs that occurred to black children to the very remedy the Supreme Court had approved of in the Southern cases—namely the transportation of pupils (or "busing"). The cure was now called an evil. Few bothered to explain that the requirement to provide transportation was actually mandated by state laws because of the distances from homes in segregated neighborhoods to integrated schools. Moreover, there was also a lack of understanding that the "root and branch" duty to eliminate the pervasiveness of school segregation required pupil reassignments that extended over considerable distances.

As is evident in the opinions in cases in Detroit, Cleveland, and Boston and other communities, the court-ordered remedies included more than pupil reassignment and transportation. A major component of remedy consisted of what we called "soft core" or educational elements designed to eliminate the effects of inferior education inflicted by segregation.

A description of these cases that spanned my ten years at the NAACP and beyond would require a separate book. They also interlock and connect in ways that make it difficult to discuss them in isolation. However, I will here discuss a few of the key cases to provide insights into the overall problem of Northern school segregation and the strategies we employed to combat it.

Detroit: *Milliken v. Bradley*

On the eve of the National NAACP convention in Cincinnati in 1970, I received an urgent telephone request from William Penn, executive director of the Detroit NAACP branch. The emergency stemmed from the fact that Governor William Milliken had signed legislation designed to block the implementation of a voluntary desegregation plan that was put together by Detroit's new superintendent, Dr. Norman Drackler, who had an informed view of the needs of urban education. His plan was approved by a majority of the Detroit School Board. It would have resulted, for the first time, in a relatively small number of white students (1,800 out of 290,000 students), being assigned to black-majority schools. A fierce political backlash from white parents was seized upon by political opportunists, which resulted in the state legislature enacting Act 48, which became law upon receiving the governor's signature. It blocked the desegregation plan from taking effect.

I convened a meeting of Detroit NAACP branch officials and representatives of the Detroit School Board in my hotel suite to discuss the options available to them. I deferred a final decision on Governor Milliken's actions pending a second meeting to be held in my New York office. In the meantime, I assembled a legal team to join me in evaluating the situation.

At that follow-up meeting, on the advice of a group of school desegregation litigators, I committed the NAACP to initiate legal action to enjoin the enforcement of Act 48 on grounds that it was unconstitutional and to urge the federal court in Detroit to order the school board's plan implemented. It was in my office in New York that George Bushnell Jr., counsel for the Detroit School Board, exploded in anger when I informed the group that it would be necessary for us to name the Detroit School Board as a nominal defendant. The very thought that his client, the entity that sought to carry out a desegregation goal and inspire better education for children, would be named a defendant led to his tirade that included a threat to "whip [our] asses" in court.

Bushnell's outrage did not alter the decision to bring suit, which was assigned to Judge Stephen Roth of the U.S. District Court for the Eastern District of Michigan. We presented our applications for a temporary restraining order (TRO) and preliminary injunction. The judge reacted with considerable irritation. Upon denying the request for a TRO, he scheduled a hearing on the preliminary injunction request. However, this would not happen until after the semester began. We needed emergency relief. We filed an immediate appeal with the U.S. Court of Appeals for the Sixth Circuit and telephoned the chief judge, Harry Phillips, at his Nashville, Tennessee, chambers. Judge Phillips directed the court clerk to schedule an emergency hearing for Cincinnati before a three-judge panel. Days later, after an oral argument, the majority of the panel agreed with us that Act 48 was unconstitutional because it interfered with local attempts to comply with the Constitution's Fourteenth

Amendment's equal protection clause as determined in *Brown*, in the same manner as had been done in the South. It was a form of interposition and nullification. The case was thereafter remanded for a full trial on the segregation claims we had set out in our complaint.

During the forty-one-day trial, Judge Roth's hostility melted and on September 27, 1971, he decided in our favor. The record in that case created a formula for breaking down Northern urban segregation by linking the evidence of state and local school board policies and practices and residential segregation. Opponents to desegregation continually sought to blur the evidence. The evidence we presented to Judge Roth exposed the anatomy of Northern urban segregation and proved the de facto/de jure distinction to be nothing more than a myth.

On appeal, a three-judge panel of the Sixth Circuit, and later the court sitting en banc, upheld Judge Roth's findings. The court concluded, "This record contains a substantial volume of testimony concerning local and State action and policies which helped produce residential segregation in Detroit and in the metropolitan areas of Detroit. In affirming the District Judge's findings of constitutional violations by the Detroit Board of Education and by the State defendants resulting in segregated schools in Detroit, we have not relied at all upon testimony pertaining to segregated housing except as school construction programs helped cause or maintain such segregation."[2]

Although we were at first a bit puzzled by the Sixth Circuit's treatment of the findings of housing segregation, we understood that the court was avoiding the appearance of revising the precedents of the *Deal* and *Craggett* cases, barred by res judicata. Thus the finding of wrongdoing in this case by the state was enough to distinguish it from those cases and permit the court to approve Judge Roth's order that the state participate in the interdistrict remedy. The court of appeals agreed and held that the only feasible desegregation plan would require pupil assignments that crossed the boundaries between the city and suburban school districts. The court concluded that an effective desegregation plan should not be hemmed in by artificial barriers, especially where, as here, the state government had helped create and maintain racial segregation through the reliance on artificial boundaries. All-out relief required an interdistrict approach since, consistent with precedents in Southern cases, liability was found against the State and local district. Chief Judge George Edwards framed the judicial challenge in this way: "The instant case calls up haunting memories of the now long overruled and discredited 'separate-but-equal' doctrine of *Plessy v. Ferguson*. If we hold that school district boundaries are absolute barriers to a Detroit school desegregation plan, we would be opening a way to nullify *Brown v. Board of Education* which overruled *Plessy*."[3]

The defendants and some suburban school districts joined in appealing to the U.S. Supreme Court. This case was achieving a high level of legal, educational, and political significance across the country.

The circumstance that led to me becoming NAACP general counsel—the resignation of Carter and the legal staff—had forced me to quickly reach out to other lawyers for help. A bonding took place over time, and when the Detroit case reached the Supreme Court, I felt that a highly formidable appellate team had been forged. Even so, the passion stoked by the challenge that awaited me upon assuming my position created an urgency I'd never anticipated.

The legal and research teams that came together to assist in litigating the Detroit and other cases were of a quality and degree of competence that far exceeded the meager compensation I was able to offer.

Once the case reached the Supreme Court, and after a number of strategy meetings with the trial team officials of the Detroit branch, and my consulting members of the NAACP National Legal Committee, it was agreed that J. Harold (Nick) Flannery and I would make the argument. Flannery, who had been a star of the Justice Department's civil rights division, was also representing the NAACP in the Boston school case. We spent months preparing in New York and Washington, reviewing the trial and appellate record, drafting briefs, mapping out our arguments and performing dry runs before mock panels.

In February 1974, we arrived in Washington for the Supreme Court appearance. Although I had been in the Supreme Court a number of times, this was to be my first argument, and my adrenaline was high but I was confident in the strength of our case and my ability to present it. NAACP leadership, including Board Chairman Bishop Stephen Gill Spottswood, were in the chamber to offer their support. Flannery and I divided the argument. He graphically demonstrated the multiple evidentiary grounds and precedents for upholding Judge Roth and the Sixth Circuit. My portion of the argument was aimed at demonstrating the necessity and feasibility of the interdistrict remedy.

> The nature of the violation . . . led to the containment of 133,000 black children in 133 core [black] schools surrounded by a ring of white schools . . . [In considering remedy], the [district] court concluded that the ratification or acceptance of any of the [Detroit-only plans] would have led [to] perpetuation of a black school district [still] surrounded by a ring of white schools.[4]

At the conclusion of the arguments, our team felt that we had presented a strong case and were optimistic about our chances of prevailing. Our spirits were bolstered even further when, upon our exit from the Supreme Court chamber, we were met with loud and lusty cheers from a group of Nick Flannery's law students, to the obvious displeasure of Supreme Court security, who did not appreciate this breach of decorum in the halls of the Supreme Court.

But our optimism was short-lived. Six months after the argument, I returned to the chamber and sat in shock as I listened to Chief Justice Burger and Justice Potter Stewart read their majority and concurring opinions—opinions that bore little relation to the arguments that Nick Flannery and I made or to the evidence produced in the case we had tried. The decisions by the trial court and the appellate court met a fate in the Supreme Court that proved to be a turning point in the judicial implementation of school desegregation.

While its 5–4 decision affirmed the Supreme Court findings outlawing intradistrict or single district segregation, the Supreme Court reversed the portion of the lower court's holding that dealt with the interdistrict metropolitan remedy that would have involved suburban schools. Writing for the majority, Chief Justice Warren Burger declared, "We conclude that the relief . . . was based upon an erroneous standard and was unsupported by record evidence that acts of the outlying districts affected the discrimination found to exist in the schools of Detroit."[5] In fact, we never alleged that the suburban districts engaged in segregative acts that affected Detroit. Instead, we alleged—and proved in trial and on appeal—that the State of Michigan did so act, and as such, could be ordered to use its powers to correct the resultant harm.

For the Supreme Court majority to ignore the record and the law that gave the state control over local education in Michigan, including the suburbs, was flat-out wrong.

Research of the papers of Supreme Court justices revealed the role of Justice Lewis Powell in virtually taking over the drafting of the majority opinion from Chief Justice Warren Burger, following a memorandum-driven tug-of-war. The majority opinion wound up attributing to suburban educational districts—created by the state itself—a degree of independence heretofore unrecognized. Districts were accorded by the justices a sovereign status that therefore led them, as Justice Brandeis once said, to deny as judges what they knew to be true as men. That is illustrative of the extent the Supreme Court majority deviated from precedents. It was a profound and stunning limitation on the reach of the *Green* and *Swann* cases. It was as though the opinion were based on a different trial. I was simply astounded at what was clearly a result-driven opinion, probably the most abominably dishonest opinion on race since *Plessy* in 1896.

Justice Potter Stewart, an Ohioan, provided the critical fifth vote, describing the "containment" of black children within Detroit as caused by "unknown and perhaps unknowable factors."[6]

He was unable to discover, he wrote, any evidence in the record that would lead to a conclusion that "the State or its political subdivisions have contributed to cause the situation to exist," or that the situation was caused by "governmental activity." As noted in the book *The Brethren*, "the majority was no longer concerned about the education of black children in a segregated urban school system. Its concern now was the convenience of white suburban children."[7] By so obviously ignoring the specific findings of fact made by Judge Roth as to the causes of the segregated conditions in the Detroit metropolitan schools, Justice Stewart yielded to a sense of white entitlement and, in so doing, severely damaged the courageous judicial record on civil rights he had developed over the years. Moreover, the Supreme Court majority itself showed its intellectual dishonesty when it refused to follow the suggestion of Solicitor General Robert Bork to take the legally appropriate step of remanding the case to the district court for additional evidence to clarify any confusion over how a plan including the suburban schools would work. The court's majority, by refusing a remand, revealed an intellectual and racial cowardice, intermingled with a tinge of Dred Scottism—in this case, an assumption that black schoolchildren were not entitled to an education of equal quality to that afforded to suburban white children. Given that the decision in the *Milliken* case was 5 to 4, had Justice Stewart, consistent with his previous school desegregation opinions, urged his Supreme Court colleagues to remand, it is possible that we would have broken the back of urban school segregation. However, that majority decision compelled us to limit the scope of the remedy we sought in other pending cases. For most urban areas, that meant preserving or expanding public school segregation and with it, inferior education.

The four dissenting justices in *Milliken*, fortunately, did not allow the majority's opinion to stand unchallenged. Justice Douglas, for one, declared: "When we rule against the metropolitan area remedy we take a step that will likely put the problems of blacks and our society back to the period that antedated the separate-but-equal regime of *Plessy v. Ferguson*."[8] Yet that is exactly what the Supreme Court majority did.

No one was more prophetic than another of the dissenters, Justice Thurgood Marshall, whose words continue to resonate to this day. He wrote:

> Today's holding, I fear, is more a reflection of a perceived public mood that we have gone far enough in enforcing the Constitution's guarantee of equal justice than it is a product of neutral principles of law. In the short run, it may seem to be the easier course to allow our great metropolitan areas to be divided up each into two cities, one white, the other black—but it is a course, I predict, our people will ultimately regret.[9]

The shameful fact is that the highest court in the land had denied to public education and its patrons—black and white—a channel through which they could receive the healing air of the guarantees of the Constitution's Fourteenth Amendment. The consternation over the state of public education was born of the Southern Strategy, which was determined to return the nation to the period when the rights of blacks could be nullified by political interposition and judicial fiat.

Milliken II

While this interdistrict decision was a serious setback, we were relieved that the Supreme Court did not do more to impede our efforts against segregation within single districts. We proceeded with cases elsewhere with generally favorable but limited results.[10]

The remnant left in the Detroit case for remand was to fashion a single-district remedy. After the trial court ruled on the single-district remedy, the case, in 1977, found its way back to the Supreme Court in *Milliken II*. The issue on the second appeal was whether the state, having explicitly been found culpable (along with the local board) of maintaining segregation within Detroit, could be required to share in the cost of the remedy. Specifically, the Supreme Court addressed the issue of the Eleventh Amendment and the state's contention that it was shielded by that amendment from having to pay the funds ordered by the district court and affirmed by the Sixth Circuit. Having been found liable by the Supreme Court, the state could be required to help pay the cost of remedying the effects of the dual system, which extended to underwriting the cost of ancillary educational relief. The contradiction between the two Supreme Court opinions was apparent. In *Milliken I* the court ignored the complicity of the state in maintaining segregation in Detroit. Yet, in *Milliken II*, the justices had no trouble in fixing the state's obligation in helping to pay for correcting the harm done to the children of Detroit. Therefore, Michigan was ordered to pay half of the $56 million for vocational programs and to make annual payments of $5.8 million for such educational relief as in-service training, reading programs, guidance and counseling, and community relations.[11]

Milliken II provided needed benefits to all children in the urban district, which was heavily composed of minority students. The court did what the political branches in Michigan had refused to do—support the rights of minority children to receive quality education.

However, despite the benefits that flowed to the Detroit children from the litigation, it was clear that the Supreme Court's first *Milliken* decision had severely impaired our efforts at obtaining interdistrict relief in other cases.

Judge Skelly Wright of the U.S. Court of Appeals for the District of Columbia sounded an early warning of the dire consequences if the Supreme Court reversed metropolitan-wide relief in *Milliken*. Speaking at the Harvard Law School on the twentieth anniversary of *Brown* in 1974, an event which I attended, Judge Wright predicted that if the Supreme Court were to hold that interdistrict relief was impermissible, "the national trend toward residential, political and economic apartheid" would not only be "greatly accelerated," it would be "rendered legitimate and irreversible by force of law."[12] How true.

Milliken jarred my faith in the ability of the legal system to correct racial injustices. It was the most stinging setback on the school desegregation road since the *Brown* victory. It is difficult to avoid the conclusion that the racist virus from the absolutely profane rationale of Justice Roger B. Taney in the *Dred Scott* case had infected and influenced the rationale used by Chief Justice Burger and some of his majority colleagues.

As I compare the bogus rationale employed by Chief Justice Burger in *Milliken*, I realize how fortunate the nation is that he was not chief justice at the time of *Brown*. The result, I fear, may have been for the Supreme Court to affirm rather than overturn *Plessy*. My reason is simple: in *Milliken*, though Burger prefaced his opinion with praise of *Brown v. Board of Education*, he struck down the remedy needed to give it meaning. That approach rendered *Brown*'s constitutional holding a virtual nullity, because the rights declared in *Brown* are meaningless without a remedy to enforce them. The primary goal of the Burger majority was to preserve the status quo—that is, segregation. It was, therefore, meaningless for Chief Justice Burger to preface his noble-sounding opinions with a reaffirmation of *Brown* and then proceed to erect a barrier to a remedy. The current Supreme Court majority, at the urging of Chief Justice Roberts—a majority that includes, ironically, the successor to Justice Thurgood Marshall, who argued successfully to overturn *Plessy*, Justice Clarence Thomas—is turning back the clock to *Plessy*'s separate-but-equal jurisprudence.

While faking a reaffirmation of *Brown*, the Supreme Court, in reality, gutted the means of enforcing it, thus demonstrating how a right without a remedy was reduced to being no right at all.

Dayton: *Brinkman v. Board of Education*

The long, dramatic, and at times tragic saga of the Dayton school system reminded us all of the high stakes and enormous sacrifices involved in the fight for equality.

Even at the time of the trial in 1972, eighteen years after *Brown I*, forty-nine of Dayton's sixty-nine public schools were nearly all segregated—black or white. Seventy-five percent of its black pupils attended black schools that had less than 1 percent of Dayton's white students in a system that was 42 percent black. Eighty percent of Dayton's classrooms were virtually one race.

Those statistics described the segregated state of the Dayton school system that prompted Superintendent Wayne Carle and his board majority to draft a voluntary desegregation plan, working with a group calling themselves the Committee of 75. And it was that plan that drew opposition from a group that called itself Save Our Schools (SOS). Their opposition led to the ouster of the majority favoring desegregation. The new successor majority promptly rescinded the desegregation plan. It was that action that caused the Dayton branch to urge the national office of the NAACP to join in a suit.

Mrs. Miley Williamson, local branch president, urged us to file suit in an effort to defend the city's voluntary desegregation efforts. She was a close friend of Walter White who had worked closely with Roy Wilkins and Thurgood Marshall and had other powerful local allies, including lawyers James McGee and Russell Carter; Leo Lucas, a force in Dayton political circles; and C.J. McLin, a prominent Dayton funeral director. Together, they constituted a formidable force. We filed suit in 1972.

After opening statements at trial were concluded, we called our first witness to offer testimony about housing segregation in Dayton. The trial judge, Carl B. Rubin, declared in a scolding tone that no such evidence would be admitted. Paul Dimond, our counsel, persisted and was again reprimanded by the judge. By that time the court was about to recess for the day. The next morning at the opening of the session, I addressed the judge, stating that housing evidence was a crucial element of our case and therefore we asked that he certify the disputed issue of housing evidence for an immediate appeal to the Sixth Circuit Court of Appeals.

Faced with that motion, the surprised judge cleared his throat and declared that we had misunderstood his rulings and that Dimond could proceed.

The segregative acts we went on to prove were committed by the Dayton Board of Education over many years and led to findings of constitutional violations. Once that record was established, the

judge was then required to consider means of remedying the violations. He on several occasions refused to fashion a constitutionally
adequate plan to deal with the extent of segregation that existed in
the system.

In no other case did our lawyers encounter the type of obstinacy
and intimidation by a judge that we did from Judge Rubin in the
Dayton case. Given the irrefutable segregation history of the Dayton schools, it was perplexing to my legal team why a Northern-
based federal judge went to such lengths to derail the introduction
of evidence that would put such an indefensible history on the record. Yet it took the Sixth Circuit Court of Appeals and ultimately
the U.S. Supreme Court to constantly correct Judge Rubin's erroneous knowledge of the jurisprudence of *Brown v. Board of Education*
and its progeny.

His negative attitude was consistent with that displayed in 1965
when, prior to becoming a judge, he, as chairman of Cincinnati's
Civil Service Commission, opposed changing the mayor's Friendly
Relations Committee to a Human Relations Commission with
investigatory powers.

Our lead counsel, Louis Lucas of Memphis, whose bona fides as
a school-desegregation litigator for the Justice Department placed
him at the head of the class, continually drew the wrath of the recently appointed, inexperienced Judge Rubin. The way the judge
responded to Lucas on numerous occasions with threats of sanctions reflected his unfamiliarity with civil procedure rules and civil
rights law. Fortunately, there was always the Sixth Circuit Court
of Appeals to which we could repair. And each time we did, we
prevailed. The Dayton case was proceeding along with the litigation in Detroit, Cleveland, and Boston, among others, which made
me rely heavily, and with confidence, on the superb talents of our
legal team.

Interestingly enough, one of the Sixth Circuit panel members,
Judge John W. Peck, had been the trial judge in the earlier *Deal*
case. To his credit, he joined with Chief Judge Harry Phillips and
Judge William E. Miller, both Tennesseans, in recognizing the myth
of Northern de facto segregation and in reversing Judge Rubin.

The record findings of Judge Rubin themselves made the point. Yet in a strange turn of logic, he sought to apply the doctrine of attenuation—that the current conditions were so remote in time from prior actions as to have no present effect. This was a similar analysis of the constitutional misdeeds of the school boards that occurred in the Grand Rapids case in 1973 and the Youngstown case in 1978 by Judges Engel and Contie, which are discussed below.

An example of Rubin's contorted logic was cited in the Supreme Court's 1979 opinion in the Dayton case:

> Prior to *Brown*, physical isolation of Black students ended, swimming pools were no longer restricted, and Black athletic teams competed on an equal basis with all other Dayton High Schools. . . . Both by reason of the substantial time that has elapsed and because these practices have ceased, the pre-*Brown* discriminations will not necessarily be deemed to be evidence of a continuing segregative policy.
>
> Dunbar High School was intended to be and did in fact become a Black high school until it closed in 1962.[13]

And there were other factual findings made by the trial court that were beyond dispute. Again, Judge Rubin had trouble coming up with a remedial plan that would comport with *Brown* and the Constitution. The Sixth Circuit Court of Appeals had to continue nudging the trial court to revisit his approach. This led Judge Rubin to appoint Dr. Charles Glatt, a desegregation expert, to provide guidance in drafting a plan. Dr. Glatt was a person of great experience, having assisted the court in the North Carolina case of *Swann v. Charlotte-Mecklenburg*. He had the confidence of the Ohio State Board of Education in analyzing the situation as it existed in Dayton in 1970–71.

Tragically, Dr. Glatt was murdered by a racial terrorist as he worked on a new plan in the office assigned to him in the federal courthouse. Afterward the judge ordered armored doors to be installed in his own chambers and directed that other security measures be implemented in the courthouse by the General Services Administration. Attending Dr. Glatt's funeral with other members of our team gave us a renewed awareness of the perilousness of the desegregation effort, even in the North. Nevertheless, we resolved to press on. Some of us pondered the question: did the stubbornness of the trial judge in failing to fashion a constitutionally adequate remedy encourage the assassination of Dr. Glatt?

We ultimately prevailed in the U.S. Supreme Court in the Dayton case.

Cleveland: *Reed v. Rhodes*

Unlike other school cases across the country, the Cleveland school case arose in a territory with which I was already very familiar. The proximity of my hometown of Youngstown to Cleveland often found me and my fellow townsmen trekking to the "big city" for a variety of political, social, athletic, and entertainment events, and I was a frequent visitor to Cleveland Stadium, where I covered the Indians and Browns games as a reporter for the *Buckeye Review*. My professional entry onto the Cleveland scene had occurred when I took up my duties as the first black assistant U.S. attorney in 1962 in the federal courthouse in Cleveland. That afforded me an opportunity to learn much more about that city than I had from my previous trips.

My position as an assistant U.S. attorney gave me much access to several of the federal judges on the court, including U.S. District Court Judge Gerald Kalbfleisch, a conservative Eisenhower appointee from Mansfield, Ohio. We often engaged in informal conversations on various topics; during these conversations, Judge Kalbfleisch made clear to me his aversion to court-ordered desegregation. My perspectives of the historical basis for desegregation—a discussion that he encouraged—fell on deaf ears.

As I noted earlier, my position also allowed me to observe one of Kalbfleisch's trials, *Craggett v. Cleveland Board of Education*, the city's first school desegregation case, which was tried by my predecessor, Robert L. Carter, general counsel for the NAACP from New York. Watching the evidence unfold in the *Craggett* case not only provided me valuable insights into the operations of a large Northern school district, it allowed me to see how Kalbfleisch's stubborn refusal to admit crucial evidence on behalf of the plaintiffs made the result a foregone conclusion. The judge threw out the case on grounds that Northern school officials had no affirmative duty to eliminate "de facto" segregation, which is how he characterized Cleveland's segregation. This case would later help to inform our strategy when the NAACP once again stepped into the Cleveland school desegregation fight.

Almost immediately after I accepted the NAACP general counsel position in 1969, I began receiving requests from the Cleveland branch for legal assistance in their school desegregation efforts. I deflected those requests for years for several reasons. I decided to concentrate on the Detroit case and other litigation that was taxing our limited resources. I also had reason to believe that the Cleveland case would be so clear-cut that a settlement was likely without a trial.

However, after constant urging by James Stallings, the executive secretary of the Cleveland branch, and members of the education committee, I agreed to join in settlement negotiations with school officials. I first consulted Maynard Dickerson with a request that he ask his friend William Hartman of Squire Sanders and Dempsey, the law firm that represented the school district, to set up a private meeting.

James Hardiman, our chief local counsel, and I met with lawyers for the Cleveland Board of Education and Superintendent Paul Briggs to discuss resolving the case through a consent decree. (Consent decrees result from an agreement by adverse parties to a set of facts and a remedial plan without the need to offer proof or requiring a ruling by a fact finder, namely a judge.) I had several reasons to be optimistic about a swift and favorable outcome: the Cleveland School Board president, Arnold Pinkney, was a friend; a majority of the board of education was black; and the newly hired Superintendent Briggs had a reputation for being a staunch champion of quality education. All of this suggested that the problems could be resolved by a consent decree. I was wrong. Except for the Boston case, the Cleveland school case was the most consistently contentious and bitterly fought school desegregation case I confronted during my years at the NAACP.

During this initial meeting, to my surprise, Superintendent Briggs was outraged and flatly refused to entertain any notion of settlement, considering it a personal affront. The talks quickly broke down and on December 12, 1973, we filed a lawsuit in the U.S. District Court in Cleveland. Under the rule of the court on "relatedness," it was assigned to Judge Frank J. Battisti, who had already heard two major Cleveland-area housing discrimination cases. Judge Battisti and I hailed from the same city, Youngstown, Ohio, and he had been one of my law school instructors. What made the school case qualify as "related" was that discriminatory housing practices and policies constitute a major part of the proof of segregation in Northern cases, especially when the defense to be asserted was that school districting should be tied to neighborhood housing patterns. That was a standard defense theory when school boards sought to justify school segregation.

Cleveland officials, led by Briggs, had been watching the developments in the other Northern cases and the success we were having in the courts. At the time we filed the Cleveland suit, *Bradley v. Milliken* had been tried and was pending in the Supreme Court. Briggs and his team surely knew that the *Milliken* trial judge had concluded that the pervasive racial isolation in Detroit resulted from the same policies and practices that had contorted the Cleveland schools and formed the basis of the conclusion that nothing less than an interdistrict or metropolitan-wide remedy would provide an adequate solution. But instead of working with us to fashion a remedy, they dug in their heels and fought.

Despite our best efforts to work out an agreement prior to trial, Briggs rejected any notion of settlement and, along with some members of the board of education, launched an all-out attack upon the suit and on those of us involved in preparing the suit on behalf of the Cleveland NAACP branch. Since several of the legal team were non-Clevelanders, Briggs and some board members played the "outside agitator" card.

Forced to concede in our face-to-face meetings that the statistics on racial isolation and their "causation" were irrefutable, Briggs resorted to another line of defense: an abhorrence of "massive cross-town busing," which he claimed would be educationally disruptive. In this approach, he portrayed himself as having a special concern for the well-being of black children. He consistently refused to confront the evidence that showed the actions, policies, and practices of predecessor boards and superintendents, along with policies of the State Board of Education, had cheated black children for decades and had deepened racial isolation in the schools. He also ignored the legal precedents recently laid down by the Supreme Court in the 1970 case of *Swann v. Charlotte-Mecklenburg Board of Education* and 1968 *Green v. New Kent County*, which held that the neighborhood school was not sacrosanct and that the school boards were under an affirmative duty to eliminate segregation "root and branch." According to the *Swann* court, when school segregation results from violations of the constitutional rights of children, remedies may be "administratively awkward, inconvenient and even bizarre . . . and may impose burdens on some" if necessary to meet the obligation to desegregate, which remains the paramount consideration.[14]

Of course, Briggs's continual push against comprehensive remedies both exploited and was reinforced by the wave of anti-busing fever sweeping the country at the time. The intent was to delegitimize the force of the *Swann* and *Green* decisions.

Briggs used his friends in the media such as William O. Walker, publisher of the black weekly newspaper the *Call and Post*, and Thomas Vail, publisher of the *Cleveland Plain Dealer*—the largest and most powerful newspaper in Ohio—and various allies in the black and business community for whom he had done a number of favors, to warn that the suit would defeat the board's ability to provide "quality" education. He also reached out to his friends in the national arena.

Most notably there was a schedule of interviews he suggested to the respected *New York Times* columnist James "Scotty" Reston, who wrote a column that reflected the Briggs line. Interestingly, Reston did not see fit to reach out to the NAACP or our lawyers, who knew what the case was all about, to get another perspective. Though Reston was regarded as one of the nation's preeminent columnists, he fell into the same trap as local neophyte scribes often did: hopscotching over the constitutional violations to decry the remedial medicine that the law requires. I fired off a response to Reston in an attempt to set the record straight. He never responded, and he never visited the subject again in his column.

One other dramatic encounter is worthy of note. A few days before the trial, William O. Walker told me that the black leadership of Cleveland would be meeting in his conference room that evening, as they did periodically, to discuss issues of concern to the Cleveland black community. He invited me and our legal team to attend. I knew of this group from my earlier days in Cleveland. I had also known of Walker from his leadership in black Republican circles. And I knew that to be included in the Walker inner circle was something many people coveted, so I agreed.

Shortly after our arrival, we sensed a tone of unease in the group. There were "huddles" among some of those assembled, after which Walker disinvited our white team members and directed them to leave. When I protested, he responded, "This is a black meeting." I declared that if they left, we would all leave. At that point, a powerful Democratic political figure, George Forbes, who was president of the Cleveland City Council, emphatically reinforced Walker's directive. So we all left.

We regrouped in the parking lot and debated whether we had done the right thing. I said that the most powerful members of the black community were in that room and questioned whether we should forgo an opportunity to educate them about the case. We decided that Father Austin Cooper, James Hardiman, Tom Atkins, and I should return. And we did. This meant submitting ourselves to a period of profane and vicious verbal onslaughts. A couple of the attendees volunteered to run the non-Clevelanders out of town. But then tempers cooled and they agreed to hear us.

Atkins and I began to carefully describe the nature of the research we had gathered with regard to the policies and practices of the current and former school boards and former school superintendents. We previewed the evidence we would present at trial, and outlined the governing legal authorities. As we continued, the mood in the room underwent a change. The city council president, George Forbes, began to ask questions of the school board president, Arnold Pinkney, probing the extent of his knowledge of these facts. So moved was Forbes by our presentation that he reminded his hushed colleagues that he was from Memphis and had attended segregated schools. As to "busing," he said the black students in Memphis were denied transportation while white students rode modern buses to their schools. He went on to declare that he was not impressed by the picture the school board was painting about the threat of "massive cross-town busing" that was likely to take place in Cleveland. He then said to me that he would support the suit in any way we thought would be helpful. "I can sit on the members of council and keep them quiet, or I can become a vocal advocate." My response at that time, and during a later telephone conversation, was that it would be helpful if members of the city council simply stayed on the sidelines and not join in the anti-busing tirades. Council President Forbes was true to his word and played a most constructive role during and after the trial.

The trial was split into two phases—liability and remedies. In the liability phase, we presented incontrovertible evidence showing that the segregative actions were caused by policies and practices of the school board and the state educational officials, in combination with private acts of discrimination by banks and realtors. This evidence came from the school board's own files, documented housing evidence, and from records produced by the state. In addition, we introduced witnesses who gave shocking anecdotal testimony that described their experiences with the segregated system.

Students who were in the "intact busing" program (see below) provided riveting accounts of the humiliation they experienced.

As a result of our evidence, carefully presented at trial, the judge identified more than two hundred instances of intentional discriminatory actions in violation of the Fourteenth Amendment of the Constitution. Included among them were:

1. The practice, from 1969 to 1973, of assigning most black teachers to predominantly black schools.
2. Temporarily expanding, through use of portable classrooms, the overcrowded black schools when the overcrowding could have been alleviated by simply revising attendance zones to permit attendance of black students at nearby underutilized white schools within feasible transportation distance.
3. Intact busing of black students to white schools where they were contained in a segregated arrangement within those schools. When some of the black and white students struck up friendships in violation of instructions, they were disciplined by teachers.
4. School capacity figures being manipulated to present misleading descriptions of the situation to the public.
5. Administratively permitting special transfers as a convenience to white parents.
6. Creation of "Optional Attendance Zones" to facilitate white students opting out of schools when racial percentages began to shift.
7. Racial assignments of faculty and staff to match the racial composition of the student body.
8. Incorporating into attendance policies of the system the segregated housing patterns of the neighborhoods in the face of evidence that such segregation resulted from governmental action.
9. Adopting the practice of holding half-day classes for black children as a means of dealing with overcrowding in violation of state law rather than reassigning students to underutilized adjacent white schools.

We also proved that, during the initial phase of the intact busing, the black children were segregated from the white children. Later, responding to vigorous opposition of the black parents, the students were sprinkled throughout the classrooms in the building, while at the same time, the black and white students were not permitted to interact with one another as individuals. The black students first reported to their neighborhood schools, where they would board buses that would transport them to be "integrated." At the end of the day they re-boarded the buses to be returned to their "home" school. Each Friday was awards day, when teachers would present to students an appropriately colored star for them to place next to their names on a chart. These stars were awarded on the basis of a child's performance during the week. One of the students testified that, since the names of black students were not on the chart because they were not considered regular students, the teachers placed the stars on their foreheads.

Much of this testimony came as a distinct shock to many in the Cleveland community who had been on the fence about the wisdom of the lawsuit. As the testimony unfolded during the trial, support began to grow for the plaintiffs and for Judge Battisti, who was so much under siege by anti-busing forces that he required twenty-four-hour security from the U.S. Marshals.

The school board's defense was more political than legal. Rather than eliminate segregation, they attacked the remedy, the plaintiffs, and the judge and sought to pit elements of the black community against one another. This they did with unrelenting fervor.

An example of the ferocity of their attack on the desegregation remedy—even before the court's judicial findings—can be found in a number of behind-the-scenes shenanigans the superintendent orchestrated. In one instance several black parents, aided by a popular black legal figure in the Cleveland community, Jay B. White, filed a motion to intervene in order to challenge our representation of the plaintiffs and the NAACP. They sought to prove that we were not acting in the best interests of the members of the plaintiff class. At a hearing called by the judge to receive evidence from the lawyer for the proposed intervenors, it became embarrassingly apparent that he and they were actually pawns of Superintendent Briggs. Needless to say, the motion was denied.

The scope of the constitutional wrongs visited upon black children was so broad that the remedy would have to be equally broad and encompass the entire district. Unable to refute the findings themselves, in an effort to forestall remedies and to whip up popular opposition, the school board and the superintendent converted the case from one dealing with the Constitution into a "busing" case. Justice Marshall later described this trick when played by his Supreme Court colleagues in the Detroit case, as "conjuring up a largely fictional account of what the District Court was attempting to accomplish."[15]

The bitter resistance Briggs and his minions mounted against the desegregation remedies that the judge ordered told the story. Judge Battisti directed that there be a system-wide plan of actual pupil desegregation to eliminate the pattern of identifiably black and white schools. The pattern of one-race schools would have to be substantially eliminated to the maximum extent feasible for the system to be constitutionally correct. This part of the judge's order was consistent with the requirements laid down by the Supreme Court in the Southern *Swann* and *Green* cases.

The evidence of harm to the black children under the segregated system administered by the school board required a second remedial step to be taken, because pupil reassignments would not be enough. The remedial order formulated by Judge Battisti also called for the desegregation of administrative and certified supervisors, teachers, and noncertified personnel, and development of creative educational curricula, including innovative reading and other programs designed to correct the effects of prior segregated schooling. Other forms of ancillary relief were calculated to remedy the academic deficits of prior segregation and to ensure that existing and future programs would be administered in a nondiscriminatory fashion. Given the resistance of the school officials, the judge felt that to maintain a secure integrated school environment in which the rights of all students would be protected and guaranteed under the power of the court order, a strong order was necessary.

Judge Battisti directed that specific educational components had to be a part of the desegregation plan. The plan would have to provide for such things as testing and tracking, counseling and career guidance, magnet and vocational school programs, school-community relations, transportation, and staff desegregation.

One would have thought that the Briggs administration would have eagerly embraced these innovations, particularly in light of the fact that the state of Ohio was ordered to underwrite a substantial part of the costs. These were programs that the state had heretofore refused to fund. Without question, every student in the school system would have benefited from these court-decreed educational offerings. After all, Superintendent Briggs and his supporters on the board had talked constantly about "quality education" being their goal. Yet they continually defied the court's order. So intractable was their resistance that the judge found it necessary to appoint a Special Master to implement and oversee the implementation of the order. The person designated, Daniel McCarthy, was not an educator but a tax lawyer. At first, we thought that McCarthy was a curious choice. Yet we soon came to realize that what was needed in that position was someone with the ability to dig into the financial records of the school district and untangle the financial mess that the Briggs administration had created through questionable practices, including, of course, the contracts related to the program of building schools on top of the segregated neighborhood housing patterns. It was this tangled financial mess that led the school board to dodge its responsibilities by arguing that it lacked funds to underwrite any of the desegregation expenses.

The struggle between the court and the school board went on for years, even after the departure of Briggs. Seeking to untangle the mess was Edward "Ted" Mearns, a professor at Cleveland's Western Reserve School of Law. In 1980 Judge Battisti named Donald Waldrip, a Cincinnati school superintendent, to implement the desegregation plan. His success was limited. He was followed by a desegregation expert who had worked on the Boston school desegregation plan, Dr. Alfred Tutela, who nevertheless struggled with the Cleveland system. The turmoil fostered by the Briggs reign carried over to successive administrations. The development that stunned the city was the suicide of a fifty-eight-year-old successor superintendent, Frederick D. Holliday, who had come from Plainfield, New Jersey. On a Saturday he went to the tower of Aviation High School, located on Cleveland's lakeside, and shot himself. His suicide note was a plea for a new direction. He wrote: "The purpose seems to be lost. Use this event to rid yourselves of petty politics, racial politics, greed, hate and corruption. This city deserves better."[16] I am convinced that the misdeeds of the city's school administrators and their resistance to change drove Holliday to his death.

The original decision in *Reed v. Rhodes* was handed down in August 1976. In May 1978, I withdrew from further participation, following President Carter's announcement of my nomination to be a judge on the U.S. Court of Appeals for the Sixth Circuit.

The Youngstown and Grand Rapids Cases

A common thread for most of the Northern school cases we tried during this period was the marked similarity of the proof we offered; in each of the cases, we detailed the segregative policies and practices that had been pursued over time by the local boards of education and the state departments of education, most of whom operated in lockstep.

But the Grand Rapids and Youngstown cases differed from the others in one important way. In most of the other cases, federal trial judges found that state-directed segregative policies and practices resulted in the creation and maintenance of racially identifiable schools on a district-wide basis in violation of *Brown v. Board of Education*. These findings triggered the same desegregative remedies that the Supreme Court had ordered in the Southern cases. But not so in Grand Rapids and Youngstown.

Although presiding over different trials in different states, Judge Albert Engle in Grand Rapids and Judge Leroy Contie Jr. in

Youngstown, by rejecting our argument on attenuation, employed almost identical methods of flawed legal analysis, which led them both to reach the same conclusion: that the policies and practices pursued by those school districts in the past were too "attenuated" or disconnected to be a cause of current segregative acts and, therefore, the *Brown* precedent did not apply.

Each of those federal district court judges was appointed to the bench by President Richard Nixon, whose aversion to school desegregation was well known. Both judges were later elevated to the Sixth Circuit Court of Appeals—Engle by President Nixon and Contie by President Reagan, who also shared Nixon's anti-desegregation bent—after earning their political spurs by adhering to a judicial philosophy that squared with that of the two presidents who held sway over their professional futures. In fact, Contie's appointment to the circuit court was a partial fulfillment of Reagan's campaign promise to bring about "sea change" to the federal bench. Although we took very different roads, they converged and eventually put the three of us—Engle, Contie, and me—together on the Sixth Circuit Court of Appeals.

Contie and Engle reached their erroneous conclusions despite the fact that, in each trial, we stripped away the mask that exposed the link between state powers and local districts' implementation of state requirements. This proof was the basis for our urging judges to apply the *Keyes v. Denver School District No. 1* presumption, blessed by the Supreme Court, to wit: that if state/local policies resulted in segregation in a significant portion of a school district, the court could presume that the entire district was similarly affected.

Some of the policies we proved to exist related to the location of schools and the fixing of attendance boundaries in ways that kept white and black students segregated. Some of those practices had existed for such an extended period of time that the courts seized upon them as not being a proximate cause of the current conditions. The judges analyzed each act of segregation in isolation, and concluded that the initial act was too remote in time to have contributed to the current condition of segregation.

Having gone to school in the Youngstown school district and experienced firsthand the facts our trial team documented, I was particularly confounded by Judge Contie's approach. We had painstakingly assembled the history, extending over a period of three decades, including documentation from school board minutes and other school board records. Yet Judge Contie refused to recognize the cumulative effect of segregative acts. Rather he treated historical incidents in isolation, and then concluded that these acts, in their isolated state, did not create segregation. Moreover, he excluded from consideration evidence of policies and practices that occurred before May 17, 1954, when *Brown* was decided. Thus, the district was exonerated. He did at least consider the failure to hire black teachers to be state action, violative of the Fourteenth Amendment, and ordered a remedy.

The same type of proof that was offered in Youngstown had earlier been presented in the Grand Rapids case, presided over by Judge Engle, with the same result—school board exoneration. It was clear to me that Judge Engel and Judge Contie were unsympathetic to school desegregation cases and had hit upon a formula for preserving the status quo. Their mind-set was adopted by Justice Potter Stewart in the *Bradley v. Milliken* case in 1974.

While I was stunned by the results in the Grand Rapids and Youngstown cases, there was always the Sixth Circuit Court of Appeals.

Bearing in mind that the Sixth Circuit, geographically, extended from the Canadian border on the north, to the Alabama and Georgia borders at the southern end, and spread from the Allegheny Mountains on the East to the border of Indiana on the west, I had been impressed by the positive racial impact of the many court decisions that came from that circuit. One of the judges, Judge Pierce Lively—from Danville, Kentucky, the home of Centre College, the alma mater of the late John Marshall Harlan, who wrote a stinging dissent against separate but equal in *Plessy v. Ferguson*—carried on the Harlan tradition in his many opinions on civil rights. From Nashville, Tennessee, came Judge Harry Phillips, who approached civil rights cases with the courage and independence demonstrated by

Justice Harlan and Judge Waties Waring, the South Carolina federal judge who had angered Southerners with his insistence that racial segregation was unconstitutional. Waring's reasoning encouraged the NAACP legal team to shift its strategy from pushing for equalization of separate facilities to a total elimination of segregation, root and branch. It was Judge Phillips who wrote the opinion that struck down Michigan's Act 48 on grounds that it was aimed at nullifying the efforts of the Detroit Board of Education to deal with segregation in that system.

For these and other reasons I had hopes that the Sixth Circuit Court of Appeals would reverse Judge Contie's decision in the Youngstown case, since it ran contrary to Southern precedents and other holdings in Northern cases. The appeal occurred when I was on the bench, and I had recused myself from all such cases at the time of my appointment.

The appellate panel for the Youngstown case consisted of three judges who, along with me, had been appointed by President Carter in 1979. They were Judges Cornelia Kennedy of Michigan, Bailey Brown of Memphis, and Boyce F. Martin Jr. of Kentucky. I assumed that Judge Kennedy, based upon her record as a district judge, would find a way to uphold her fellow University of Michigan Law School colleague. Judge Brown's record was not as clear-cut, but I thought, in light of the precedents in the other Ohio and Michigan cases, that he would find error in the analytical process used by Judge Contie in his refusal to apply the *Keyes* presumption. Most certainly, it seemed to me, that Judge Martin, whom at that time I did not know very well but who was deemed to be fairly liberal, would vote to reverse. As it turned out, he and the rest of the panel accepted Judge Contie's flawed analytical process.

Their opinion exonerated the district court's reasoning on the grounds that "the District Court was sufficiently cognizant of the controlling cases and legal principles." This was a virtual replication of the "back of the hand" that Judge Druffel had given to black plaintiffs in the Hillsboro case in 1954 when he credited the school superintendent with acting in good faith.

I have since gotten to know Judge Martin better and observed him mature into a strong, liberal federal appellate colleague. I am certain that he would like, if he could, to withdraw the reasoning and result reached in the Youngstown case. Though I was a Sixth Circuit Court of Appeals colleague at that time, I never discussed the opinion with him or with any member of the panel. To me, the issue was not that Judge Contie did not know the precedents but that he failed to follow them. The reasoning by the panel, had it been adopted by the Supreme Court in the 1954 *Brown* case, would have left us with *Plessy v. Ferguson*'s separate-but-equal doctrine.

Cincinnati: *Bronson*

The evidence being developed in the Detroit and Boston cases encouraged our researchers to begin looking more favorably on the persistent requests that came from Cincinnati to the NAACP National Office. The nature of the evidence varied only slightly from that considered by the court in the 1965 case brought on behalf of Tina Deal by my predecessor, Robert L. Carter. The difference was in its packaging. In the 1960s, there had been a reliance on a presumption that racial isolation resulted from actual governmental action. In *Bronson*, the cause of the racial isolation was actually based on governmental policies and practices. There appeared therefore, to be good and sufficient reasons to proceed on the new theory we had relied on in the other Northern cases.

As I noted earlier, Ohio presented a number of the most challenging cases in which we demonstrated how discriminatory housing policies were incorporated into school attendance policies. This linking of the public aspect of housing segregation as a form of state action came as a surprise to many who had no sense of the city and state's racially discriminatory history and its connection to private housing discrimination. It was that interrelationship that persuaded me to yield to the insistence of members of the Cincinnati, Ohio, community to "bring *Brown* to Cincinnati." The only problem with that request was the barrier erected by the legal precedent created by the decision in the case of *Tina Deal v. Cincinnati Board of Education* and the financial costs associated with organizing the research required to prove causation.

In the *Deal* case, Judge John W. Peck had ruled that whatever segregation there was in Cincinnati was "de facto"—that is, not the result of law. In order to go forward, we had to distinguish *Bronson* from *Deal*. Judge Peck had ruled in the *Deal* case that segregated housing, not school policies, was the cause of Cincinnati's segregated schools, and without proof of school involvement the federal court lacked jurisdiction over the school board. That decision was upheld by the Sixth Circuit Court of Appeals in 1966. The only way my legal team and I saw to get around that decision was to dig deep into the school and housing records and show a linkage to schools to develop a "de jure" record on a metropolitan basis to broaden the scope of relief we would seek. We concluded that a metropolitan-type suit, in which suburbs, districts, and the state would be parties, could be shown that would confer jurisdiction on the federal court. Through the efforts of the Cincinnati NAACP branch, a number of potential plaintiffs were identified, led by Charles and Jeanette Bronson, the parents of eleven-year-old Mona Bronson.

Our legal and research teams were quite formidable. Leonard Slutz, Elizabeth McKenna, Solvita McMillan, William Caldwell, Teresa Demchak, William Lamson, Robert Brown, Tom Atkins, Louis Lucas, Theodore M. Berry, and William Taylor were the core of the team. Funds were raised locally, and nationally, through the NAACP Special Contribution Fund. Local volunteers such as Regine Ransohoff, a member of one of Cincinnati's oldest and most respected families, pitched in, along with civil rights leader Marian Spencer and her businessman husband, Donald Spencer.

They unearthed the racial history of Ohio and Cincinnati, and the role of state agencies, including the legislature, in first excluding black children from the schools, and then segregating them. Cincinnati's was a shocking case study of how school segregation was developed and sustained in the North.

Unfortunately, because *Milliken* dealt a severe blow to our metropolitan theory, the future of the Cincinnati case seemed doomed. In an effort to salvage as much desegregation as we could, we intensified our review and discovery in the hope we could convince school officials to enter into serious settlement negotiations. The story of the Cincinnati case from that point on is a remarkable saga. Although I had the responsibility for policy decisions at the time we filed the suit, my judicial nomination caused me to recuse myself from this and all cases. The litigation responsibilities were then turned over to Tom Atkins and the other top-flight desegregation lawyers.

Through all this time, even after I withdrew from the case, I remained convinced that the history of Ohio's treatment of its black children was a story that must be told. To properly understand *Bronson*, its context had to be understood.

The case was finally reassigned to Judge Walter Herbert Rice in Dayton, who explored the possibilities of a settlement. I followed with deep interest the press reports of the steps being taken by my former NAACP colleagues and officials of the Cincinnati Board of Education to settle the case without a trial. Having been deeply involved at the early stages of the case, and given my familiarity with the racial history in Ohio generally, and in particular, Cincinnati, I hoped fervently for a resolution of the case without a trial. A trial would have resulted in the airing of decades of dirty linen, much of which was unknown to people currently working to improve conditions in the community. It would have been unsettling to the community. Contrary to rantings of desegregation's foes, a federal court is without power to act against school boards in these instances without first making findings of facts and conclusions of law about unconstitutional policies and practices. An exception is thus made when the parties themselves agree to skip that step of offering proof. In that event, the court is empowered, on the basis of the agreed facts, to act. The judicial power of the court is then invoked to correct the wrongs.

Press reports in the *Cincinnati Enquirer* and the *Cincinnati Post* kept score on the starts and stops of settlement negotiations. To

facilitate the settlement efforts, Judge Rice had requested the mediating services of Senior Judge David S. Porter. As the trial date
neared, Judge Porter, meeting with no success in bringing the parties to agreement, returned the matter to Judge Rice, who then set
a firm date to commence a trial. He urged the parties to continue
their talks in the interim.

It became a matter of public knowledge that the NAACP legal
team had reached out to the Ohio attorney general, Anthony Celebrezze Jr., and Governor Dick Celeste with a request for the state to
become more directly involved in the settlement attempts. Over the
final weekend that preceded the scheduled beginning of the trial,
reports leaked that Governor Celeste instructed appropriate state
officials to cooperate to settle the case. When word of that development reached Judge Rice on the morning of the trial, he agreed
to delay the beginning of the trial until the afternoon to allow the
parties additional time to negotiate. As the talks proceeded, Judge
Rice postponed the trial on a limited basis, a half day at a time. As
the talks continued, I noticed the lawyers and potential witnesses
as they moved about the federal courthouse.

NAACP lawyers had prepared a powerhouse case that cited misdeeds committed by state and local officials going back to the 1800s.
The defense of the board's conduct was being handled by veteran
school board lawyer John Lloyd. When the case took another turn,
and it appeared that negotiations would replace litigation, the
Cincinnati School Board brought in two prominent African
Americans—former common pleas judge William McClain, who
had been involved in the *Deal* case, and John Andrew West, now a
judge on the Hamilton County Common Pleas Court. Other
school-board counsel were John Concannon and his staff. In the
event that school officials would agree with plaintiff's counsel to
confer upon Judge Rice jurisdiction to handle the remedial part of
the case without first requiring a full-blown trial on liability, I felt
that the community could possibly be well served.

There was one serious last-minute problem that had to be averted
before the settlement discussions could go forward. During the
weekend before the trial was to begin, the NAACP's Tom Atkins

released a copy of his planned opening statement to a reporter for the *Cincinnati Post*, the city's afternoon newspaper. His thinking, as he later explained, was to ensure that the education reporter would have an opportunity to thoroughly grasp the scope of the NAACP's case and the proof that would be offered. He felt it important that the reporter be briefed in order to have a firm understanding of the theory and evidence. Northern cases produced the type of evidence that required reporters who could master its complexity and the relevant legal principles. When it became clear on the morning the trial was to begin that it would be postponed to allow settlement talks to continue, which would put the opening statement on hold, a state of panic overtook the legal team. They feared that the tone and substance of Atkins's opening statement was such that any chance for a successful negotiation would be blown sky-high if it reached print, and the school board would feel compelled to dig in to defend itself.

I well remember the moment because Atkins appealed to his cocounsel, the veteran Cincinnati legal icon Theodore Berry, for advice as to how to avert what seemed to be an impending catastrophe if the *Cincinnati Post* carried Atkins's opening statement. It was an occasion when only someone with Berry's stature could gain an urgent audience with a powerful newspaper publisher with a request to virtually "stop the presses." In this instance, the publisher, William Burleigh, took a phone call from Berry, who explained that it was in the interest of the community that settlement talks proceed, that if Atkins's strong historical narrative were published, the settlement talks would be destroyed. Through the timely action of Burleigh, the story, including Atkins's opening statement, was pulled, the settlement talks proceeded, and ultimately the 1984 Bronson Settlement was a result.

Distilled to its essence, the Bronson Settlement provided for the following: the ending of racial isolation in the low-achieving schools and the reduction of racial isolation district-wide. In this regard, the parties agreed upon a student measurement formula called the Taeuber Index, named for its creator, Dr. Karl Taeuber, for determining the degree of racial assignments in the schools.

Dr. Taeuber had been used as an expert in a number of school desegregation cases for which I had responsibility. Additional settlement provisions included: expansion of existing alternative programs and the creation of new ones, with the state committed to pay $35 million over a seven-year period; maintenance of open enrollment policies under which students could transfer to any school in the district except schools whose racial isolation would be worsened by such transfers; development of tests and policies free of cultural bias, and development of fair disciplinary practices; targeting seven chronically low-achieving schools for improvement, and developing plans for spending a minimum of $5 million to improve the basic skills of students; improving access to after-school extracurricular activities, including bus transportation to and from students' neighborhoods when necessary; and establishing and maintaining district-wide racially balanced staff in each school.

The settlement provided for a court facilitator or monitor, and a community-wide task force. An outstanding educator, Dr. Robert Evans, was chosen as monitor. The task force consisted of prominent citizens with deep educational concerns. They included Louise Spiegel, Marian Spencer, my late wife Lillian Jones, Nelson Schwab Jr., Reverend Duane Holme, Louise Bowen, Robert Brown, Carol Burrus, Hendrick Gideonse, Cheryl Grant, Karla Irvine, Patricia Johnson-Baker, Zakia McKinney, Patricia Timm, and Mark Vander-Laan. The task force performed for more than seven years, with periodic reports being made, through Dr. Evans, to Judge Rice. After a period of time, considerable discomfort was registered by some members of the Cincinnati Board of Education, who became increasingly agitated and insisted that Judge Rice terminate his oversight of their efforts. They particularly resented the scrutiny by the community-wide task force and Dr. Evans, who had grown increasingly critical of the slow pace of change. It apparently did not occur to those agitating for less oversight that to have the court terminate jurisdiction would mean that millions in state funds coming into the system would also be halted. Oversight was ultimately withdrawn, to the considerable distress of teachers and parents.

Judge Rice was determined to hold the school officials' feet to the fire. Even as the political heat was turned up by the elected school board members to discontinue his oversight, the judge stood firm. Finally, in 1991, in response to another request to release the board from oversight, he issued a final report card that took members of the school board to task for their "benign neglect."

In commenting on the board's final report card, Judge Rice made searing observations, which he combined with his decision to continue to maintain some degree of supervision. To the credit of the education reporters of the city's newspapers, the words of Judge Rice were brought to the attention of the public, which did not always happen in some of the other desegregation cases in which I had been involved.

The jurisdictional barriers that were overcome to enable Judge Rice to exercise constitutional powers of a federal judge proved to be of benefit to the entire system, and in particular, to minority children in the various underperforming schools.

The ultimate takeaway from the Cincinnati case is the highlighting of the impediments that black children face when trying to reap the benefits of *Brown* in the North. Atkins's planned opening statement put the spotlight on state complicity in creating and perpetuating segregated education in Ohio.

New York: The Weinstein Decision

Contrary to the reputation of New York City as the bastion of liberality, events in the *Lee v. Nyquist* case exposed some of the ugly racism on which the South was thought to hold a monopoly.

The 1972 case of *Jeffrey Hart et al. v. The Community School Board of Brooklyn, District #21*, which produced what has become known as the Weinstein Decision, was not, as some news reports stated, the first Northern, or even the first New York, desegregation case. There had been others, and this case built upon those precedents. The Brooklyn case was an attempt to desegregate a single school rather than an entire district.

The uniqueness of Judge Jack B. Weinstein's *Hart* decision involved the court's broad approach to a remedy that included re-shaping an area's surrounding housing patterns—in other words, integrating the actual neighborhoods as opposed to just the schools. Defenses often interposed in Northern cases pointed the finger at housing patterns. We faced that claim here too. Wein-stein presided over the proceedings not from the bench but from a seat in the well of the court. From there he could better scrutinize the enlarged maps of the areas surrounding the school that showed the deplorable streets over which students had to walk to reach their school. Judge Weinstein would note the signs of drug activity in abandoned buildings and, from his seat, would order that those buildings be demolished. Courts prior to this Northern case, while finding that housing and school segregation were interdependent, had limited their power of remedy to the schools alone. Weinstein's approach was an answer to school boards' interposing housing pat-terns as a defense, as was done in Cincinnati, Cleveland, and other Northern cases.

The NAACP filed suit in August 1972 on behalf of Jeffrey Hart, a black child who attended the school, and the Parent Associa-tion of Mark Twain School in Brooklyn, New York. I assigned a remarkably talented young lawyer on my staff, James I. Meyerson, to handle the litigation. Subsequently, Louis Valez, a Puerto Rican child, and Judith Glantzman, who was white, joined Hart as plaintiffs.

We alleged that the school was racially segregated and underuti-lized (in that there was excess capacity to accommodate students from overcrowded, nearby schools). Space limitation in schools often served as a racially neutral justification for excluding diverse students from a school. We sought an order that would enjoin the school district from carrying out and pursuing practices that had the effect of violating Fourteenth Amendment constitutional rights. Further, we sought, by means of the lawsuit, to obtain affirmative equitable relief that would require the New York school system to shape a plan that would end the segregation and underutilization of the school. Our efforts met with limited success.

This case taught us that even with a liberal judge (Judge Weinstein had been a member of Thurgood Marshall's *Brown v. Board of Education* team) it can be difficult to obtain meaningful desegregation.

As our efforts at desegregation went forward, considerable time had to be spent in fighting rearguard attacks by some community political groups. The same political dynamics are described in my discussion of the Atlanta Compromise.

Boston

Community reaction to the Boston school case was the most contentious and troubling of all the Northern litigation I was involved in.

It was the most dramatic example of a city with liberal traditions masking its racism until a court sought to convert its illegal school system into a constitutional one. The ugliness of the resistance to efforts to end school segregation in the Boston schools hardly varied from that which occurred in areas of the South, particularly Little Rock. It took a while for the nation's attention to shift to a location so physically remote from the South.

The virulence of the Boston reaction, a city long associated with America's struggle for freedom, startled the nation. It was in the Boston case where the strategy of resistance to school desegregation by our opponents seemed to come full circle. It is where the likes of Alabama governor George Wallace linked up with the Northern political flank. In Boston the black community presented a near solid wall of support for our efforts. This was largely due to the leadership of Tom Atkins. The shrillness of the opposition attracted media of all sorts and compelled us to fight a battle not only in the courtroom but on the public relations front as well.

It became increasingly apparent that racism in the North was, as it was true of the South, an element of the opposition to integration of schools. It was clear to me that meeting the Boston challenge required a maximum commitment of resources.

As I have noted, I faced a struggle to raise sufficient funds to keep afloat the increasing numbers of these Northern school cases. Even though our legal teams worked for a very minimal stipend, generating funds to pay their expenses of travel, lodging, witness fees, transcripts of depositions and transcripts of trial records, was an ongoing process. As it turned out, we were particularly fortunate in the hard-fought Boston case of *Morgan v. Boston School Committee* to have an unusually high quality of lawyering. Being associated with the first-class legal talent required to litigate for the Boston branch of the NAACP in bringing a school desegregation suit against the Boston School Committee was a dream come true for me. The legal resources offered by the Boston Lawyers' Committee bolstered the desegregation team immeasurably.

In Boston, the team was led by Thomas I. Atkins, about whom I cannot say enough. A Harvard Law School graduate, Atkins performed incredible feats in his lifetime. He was the secretary of community affairs in Massachusetts governor Francis Sargent's cabinet, and later served as executive director and president of the Boston NAACP branch. A person with a global view, his major at Indiana University had been Middle Eastern studies with an emphasis on economics. A strong policy disagreement with the U.S. government over the Middle East caused him to abandon his PhD studies at Harvard and transfer to its law school, from which he graduated in 1969. While still a law student, Tom Atkins ran for and was elected to a seat on the Boston City Council, being the first black to be successful in that role. He later made an unsuccessful bid for mayor of Boston. The NAACP's litigation campaign would not have fared as well as it did without the brilliant generalship of my friend Tom Atkins. Moreover, Atkins was my principal strategist in a number of the other Northern cases. His political judgment was invaluable. He played a major role in the Cleveland case, ultimately taking lead counsel responsibilities. As mentioned, at the outset of that case, he was with me when we attended the Cleveland meeting with black leaders, when William O. Walker invited the white members of our team to leave. Atkins's advice that we return to the meeting and present our evidence proved to have been a masterstroke. When I resigned my position of general counsel, he was my enthusiastic choice as a successor.

The LCCR lawyers came from some of Boston's most prestigious law firms. Among them were Roger Abrams, John Leubsdorf, Thomas Simmons, Robert Pressman, and Eric Van Loon. They were joined by J. Harold Flannery, who had served with the Civil Rights Division of the Justice Department litigating major civil rights cases in Mississippi and argued the *Milliken* case with me. This was as formidable a legal team as ever entered a courtroom to litigate a Northern school desegregation case—or any other case, for that matter.

In the courtroom of U.S. District Judge W. Arthur Garrity, the evidence presented was overwhelming. Documented evidence demonstrated the ways in which the Boston schools became segregated in the same way we proved segregation in Cleveland, Detroit, and other Northern cities. But outside the courtroom, politicians kept the pot stirred in the various neighborhoods, in particular, South Boston, just as was done in other Northern communities.

While I was personally engaged in various aspects of the litigation in Boston and elsewhere, I also retained the responsibility of ensuring that the strategic decisions that were made each step of the way conformed to the policies of the NAACP and dedicated to the principles set out in *Brown v. Board of Education* and its progeny. Moreover, I often had to travel the country for the purpose of articulating the rationale for the strategy we were employing. Court appearances and organizational matters occupied my weekdays, while many weekends found me on the road, attending meetings aimed at educating and inspiring the rank and file of the NAACP.

I was in Boston for the first days of the implementation of the desegregation orders. On the evening after the first day, some white parents were threatening to harm the black children on their arrival at the "white" schools. Black parents gathered at a Roxbury community center to plan a strategy for protecting their children.

A number of adult black men announced their intent to arm themselves and ride the buses the next morning. Boston mayor Kevin White arrived at the packed meeting hall and urged calm. The police would be in full force, he promised, and would protect the children. There were even calls for Judge Garrity to suspend the desegregation order.

As I stood near the stage at the community center, Tom Atkins entered. He was by far the most prominent black leader in Boston. I asked him if he was fearful about things getting out of control the next morning when the buses took the black children into South Boston. In a firm tone, he said that he was going to the stage and demand that the mayor guarantee that the police protect their children. After calming the crowd, he asked that the angry audience accept the assurances of the mayor and leave their weapons at home. Had Tom Atkins not waded through that aroused crowd and convinced the mayor that he had to act on the spot to reassure the black parents, I am convinced that there would have been bloodshed on the streets of Boston.

Atkins was far and away one of the brightest and most courageous individuals I met during my years at the NAACP. His commitment was total. His central role in Boston during that turbulent period compelled him to fortify his home in the Roxbury section of Boston in order to protect his wife, Sharon, and their children. One of the means he used was to run chicken wire over the windows to block Molotov cocktails. He also installed spigots throughout his home in order that hoses could be connected in the event of fires that arsonists might set. The fact that the Boston children entered their new school buildings without bloodletting did not settle matters. Inside the schools there was considerable unrest. White adults were using their children to carry on their battle to block desegregation. Atkins labored on this and other cases until felled by ALS in 2008.

Judge Garrity's decision, which, unfortunately, was read by too few people, sounded the death knell to a segregated system of schools that had successfully resisted all prior efforts by the state and federal governments to make it constitutionally legitimate. The decision, later upheld by the U.S. Court of Appeals for the First Circuit, hit the "neighborhood school" defense of the school defendants head-on and emasculated it. Opinion makers deserve a failing grade for refusing to seize the occasion to correct the massive degree of public ignorance as to the cause of school segregation. The interlocking thrusts by forces of race and politics are not only causative factors, but also impediments to the public's acceptance of remedies. On that point, Judge Garrity wrote:

> There are various answers to the defendants' arguments: first, it is now generally recognized that school officials' practices may have a substantial impact upon housing patterns; second, when school officials have followed for at least a decade a persistent course of conduct which intentionally incorporated residential segregation into the system's schools, that conduct is unconstitutional; and, third, when school districting and a neighborhood school system are fraught with segregatory exceptions, neither defense need even be considered.
>
> It is now generally agreed that schools and neighborhoods have a reciprocal effect upon one another. There is a substantial interaction: a school will cause the racial composition of the neighborhood to shift and vice versa. Both plaintiffs' and defendants' expert witnesses testified as to this. These phenomena have been recognized and discussed in many cases.

He continued:

> The defendants have, with awareness of the racial segregation of Boston's neighborhoods, deliberately incorporated that segregation into the school system. This has been accomplished through construction practices and facilities utilization. With respect to school construction, the defendants have pursued a pattern of building relatively small schools to serve defined racial groups. These practices were not founded solely upon private discrimination, but also incorporated unconstitutional discrimination by other governmental officials.[17]

Due to the firm-handed Judge Garrity, backed by a resolute court of appeals, desegregation proceeded. A notable exception was the violent resistance of South Boston High School. Black students were harassed and attacked by white students. Teachers and state police on duty at the school provided little or no assistance to black students. In instances documented by the NAACP, it was apparent that instead they were aiders and abettors.

As the situation worsened in South Boston, our lawyers gathered evidence for submission to Judge Garrity, with a request that the school be closed. Earlier, on November 18, a memorandum was filed by our counsel urging that the school system be placed in federal receivership. Among the allegations Judge Garrity found to be proven by us was segregated seating in classroom, in the cafeteria, and in detention rooms.

Racial incidents, reported by black students, went without official response. The school had the highest suspension rate and lowest pupil attendance. School officials failed to develop extracurricular activities for positive effect on student attitudes.

At the remedial stage, the judge stood his ground in insisting that Boston public schools conform to his orders, which were based on the requirements of the Fourteenth Amendment. A desegregation plan was adopted by Judge Garrity and ordered into effect in September 1974. The plan included an "educational" component to overcome the effects of segregation. With one exception, the plan promised to effectively desegregate schools in all sections of Boston. Known as Phase II, it also called for the creation of bi-racial parent councils.

The significance of Judge Garrity's action was to remind the public of the court's power to enforce its orders. It showed that in whatever guise resistance appears, courts are not without power to act.

We reached a crisis in that case once the litigation path became obstructed by the political opposition. Community resistance was present in many of the other Northern cases for which I was responsible, but never to the extent seen in Boston. We were always able to cope with developments that were based on local opposition.

When the powerful former congresswoman Louise Day Hicks, as well as the Justice Department, began to lend a sympathetic ear to the mobs and to incite other violators of court orders, the issue took on a seriousness not seen since Little Rock.

It cannot be repeated too many times that these cases afforded the various states opportunities to correct the harm that had been done to black children in segregated schools.

The Boston Intervention Controversy

A national furor was created when Attorney General Edward H. Levi confirmed on May 13, 1975, that the Department of Justice was considering filing a friend-of-the-court brief (aka an amicus brief) in the Supreme Court in support of a request for a cutback in the use of busing for school desegregation. Roy Wilkins and Clarence Mitchell, director of the Washington bureau of the NAACP, took the lead in seeking a meeting with Levi.

Because the executive branch—the White House and the attorney general—was seeking to place a chokehold around the neck of Judge Garrity to trim his exercise of judicial powers that judges were often required to use in Southern cases, a major crisis loomed. It was imperative that the issue be squarely met. Wilkins's directive to me was to prepare for him a comprehensive background status memorandum on school desegregation. The meeting was to include Attorney General Levi; Clarence Mitchell; and Joseph Rauh, counsel to the Leadership Conference on Civil Rights; and several others. It was to be followed with a meeting with President Ford at the White House. The delegation, though small in number, was powerful. Since I had been handling the laboring oar on school desegregation in most of these cases, Wilkins asked me to take the lead in outlining our concerns. I summarized the state of desegregation throughout the nation, particularly in the North.

As I concluded my summary, President Ford began to respond by making a reference to "forced busing." At that point my colleague,

Clarence Mitchell, who was held in such high regard in Washington that he was referred to as the "101st Senator," politely interrupted the president. He noted the long and friendly relationship they enjoyed when Ford was the Republican minority leader. President Ford readily acknowledged their warm relationship. Mitchell then obtained agreement from the president that in working with Southern members of Congress on civil rights legislation they discovered the importance of language. He then referred to my explanation of how the Northern school cases had been mislabeled as "busing" cases, rather than efforts to enforce constitutional rights, and that such mischaracterization had added to public confusion. Mitchell urged him as president to refrain from giving legitimacy to that mislabeling. President Ford apologized and thanked Mitchell for the clarification.

Our delegation chalked up President Ford's acknowledgment as a successful teaching moment that only one with the stature of Clarence Mitchell could have won. Our joy was short-lived, however, because within seventy-two hours, in a speech in Michigan, the president again attacked "forced busing." For the president of the United States to be unable, for whatever reason, to resist the temptation to be factually incorrect, was an indication of just how tight a grip resistance to school desegregation had achieved.

With passing years, I have been struck by the way that actions long forgotten and words long ago spoken have affected the lives of other people. In looking back at the document I drafted and presented, it is apparent that its emphasis was strongly influenced by my early exposure to the thinking and strategies proposed by national civil rights leaders. President Ford and many whites were encased in walls of racial tradition. Those influences remain fresh and active at all levels. My early experiences attending the West Federal YMCA forums helped prepare me for the challenge of speaking truth to power. J. Maynard Dickerson, the lawyer who took me under his wing when I was thirteen, a central moment in my life, mentored me about the importance of the elements of study whether it was reading, using proper grammar, understanding history, or developing the art of listening.

Nevertheless, it is with a sense of disbelief and awe that I, a person who grew up in a small steel town and graduated from Youngstown State University's night law school, was called upon to perform this task of drafting the briefing memorandum, and as it turned out to also participate in the discussion of a major national issue with the president of the United States.

The memorandum I prepared continues to be instructive as we struggle to preserve what is now left of *Brown v. Board of Education*. For that reason, I've included it as an appendix to this book.

Two weeks after this meeting, I issued a statement attacking legislative proposals President Ford had advanced that undercut the success we had enjoyed in a number of Northern communities. Among other things, I warned that the NAACP was prepared to challenge the Ford legislative proposals because they were (1) unconstitutional; (2) unprecedented; and (3) inconsistent with the administration's previous policies and positions. "What has happened," I asked, "to cause a reversal of . . . position?"

There was no letup in efforts by the federal government to repeal the progress made once efforts to implement the *Brown* decision in the North began. The strategy was to block the remedy for the obvious segregation that crept across the North.

Complicating and fanning the political fires that were ignited, in addition to anti-busing amendments proposed in Congress, were the questions injected by several high-profile blacks with access to the media and, in some instances, the media themselves. We had to counter the reaction of the media, including that of some black journalists, in our Northern efforts in much the same way that the NAACP and its legal team had to do during various phases of the Southern cases.

In the multiple cities where the cases were being tried by my litigating staff, the officers of the local NAACP branches and I always tried to cultivate a relationship with education reporters and writers in order for them to gain an understanding of the evidence being offered. Unfortunately, we were not always successful.

Supporters of the status quo often used elements in the media, unfamiliar with the record evidence in cases, to torpedo our efforts. The *Boston Globe* was one of the exceptions. Muriel Cohen, its education reporter, wrote pieces that informed rather than inflamed readers about the issues in the case. Editorial writers were, for the most part, another matter. Their editorials generally condemned our efforts.

Diane Ravitch, a writer for the *New York Times* whose articles were influential in educational circles, frequently acted as an echo chamber for opponents of desegregation. Her articles prompted me to fire off a strong letter of protest to her, and I later scheduled a meeting with her in order for me to explain the theory under which we were proceeding in Boston and other Northern cases. The findings of segregative acts by school districts, I felt, once understood, would be persuasive to her. While she listened politely and occasionally fenced with me, neither her views nor her reporting changed.

Another attack that I felt compelled to confront came from a prominent black columnist for the *Washington Post*, William Raspberry. His words were aimed at fundamental propositions of constitutional law and basic equitable principles that undergirded the precedents that gave meaning to *Brown v. Board of Education*. Thus, I wrote an op-ed rebuttal for publication in the *Washington Post*:

> The central issue present in the Boston case is whether lawful orders of a federal court, now affirmed by a unanimous Court of Appeals, are going to be obeyed, or whether the integrity of those orders will be flouted by hostile mobs. To be decided by this nation is whether we are to be governed by a rule of law or rule by mob. . . . Rather than continuing fruitless journalistic probes for legal distinctions that don't exist, it is time for all people of decent instincts to come together to preserve the fragile but essential rule of law.[18]

I note with considerable dismay how little some things changed in reporting on matters associated with the struggle to overturn segregation in the North from how things had been in the South. Opposition to our efforts in Northern school desegregation cases continued to take a curious turn. Racial bias was a principal reason behind it, but it was also disguised in various garbs, the most prominent of which was the concern for "quality education," as though desegregation and quality education were incompatible.

The State of School Desegregation in the Roberts Court Era

The legal department of the NAACP now shows promise of returning to the stature it held during the Robert Carter years and during my tenure, when the general counsel had a great deal of autonomy regarding litigation. With the assumption of the reins of the organization by new leadership with a different focus, at a time when there is a deconstruction of race-based remedies and precedents, driven by the Supreme Court's anti-Houstonian jurisprudence, the time has come for the NAACP to restore to its legal arm the power it previously exercised. This is an imperative. Justice Marshall, in his last major dissenting opinion before retiring from the court, left us with this warning:

> Power, not reason, is the new currency of this court's decision-making. . . . Neither the law nor the facts supporting Booth and Gathers underwent any change in the last four years. Only the personnel of this court did.
>
> In dispatching Booth and Gathers to their graves, today's majority ominously suggests that an even more extensive upheaval of this court's precedents may be in store. . . . [This Opinion] sends a clear signal that scores of established constitutional liberties are now ripe for reconsideration.[19]

That Justice Marshall was correct in his prediction is borne out by opinions of Chief Justice John Roberts and Justice Clarence

Thomas in the fairly recent Louisville and Seattle school desegregation cases, in which they argued for a new standard for the use of
racial remedies—a standard that virtually nullifies the long years
of remedies developed for use in racial discrimination cases—and
the Fourteenth Amendment itself. I saw this coming when I
read the memos that John Roberts, then White House counsel
to Reagan, wrote. As Chief Justice of the United States, Roberts
has moved from an in-house advocate to the position of decider-
in-chief. Protecting the powerful from the petitions of the lowly
seems to have been his creed. This style of jurisprudence was
also reflected by Justice Thomas in a number of his earlier opinions, condemned by the late Judge A. Leon Higginbotham. In
later chapters of this book, I will deal at greater length with these
persistent efforts to restore states' rights and what Judge Higginbotham warned this will mean for the Houstonian devotees who
believe that the law can provide a remedy for racial wrongs.

The deconstruction of racial remedies by the current Supreme
Court majority, led by the chief justice, who has devoted a substantial part of his public career to reversing Houstonian jurisprudence, is in high gear. Based on the pull of my conscience, I
therefore agreed to testify at the confirmation hearing before the
Judiciary Committee of Judge Roberts and raise questions for
the Committee to consider in order to head off his confirmation.
I stated to the Senate Judiciary Committee on September 15,
2005:

> While I appear in my own right, more importantly, I am invoking
> the voices of distinguished legal giants on whose shoulders I stand
> and whose voices have been stilled by time: Dean Charles Hamilton
> Houston, Justice Thurgood Marshall, Judge William H. Hastie,
> Clarence Mitchell, James A. Nabrit, Judge Spottswood Robinson,
> Judge A. Leon Higginbotham Jr., and many others who have my
> deep and enduring respect. . . .
>
> Since he was nominated by the president, serious questions have
> been raised concerning Judge Roberts's views about the relevance

and legality of remedies aimed at ending racial discrimination. Unfortunately, very few Americans know the history of the myriad ways the positive law—legislatures and courts—reinforced and perpetuated racial discrimination in America. It is up to this committee, therefore, to assure that, at the very least, the next chief justice of the United States understands that history and most importantly, why remedial action was and continues to be necessary.

One's fitness to be the chief justice transcends what so many have thus far focused upon—stellar academic achievements and a degree of unquestioned professional competence. The nominee's views and his unquestionably activist attempts to thwart the federal courts' efforts to dismantle the segregation schemes it had erected and sustained bring into play something much more fundamental than technical competence, given that he is being considered for a lifetime seat on the nation's highest court. The critical question before you is one of values, not competence.[20]

The verdict is in on this matter. The U.S. Senate failed its constitutional obligation—and the nation is all the poorer for it. President Obama "gets it" and, it is to be hoped, replaces the values missing in this discredited constitutional jurisprudence through his appointments. Maybe his appointees will check the reckless careening of governmental policy which threatens a return to states' rights.

Early on I received a request at the national office from the Arkansas branch of the NAACP. It involved Carnell Russ, who was brutally slain on May 31, 1971, while inside the Star City, Arkansas, police station after a minor traffic charge—his wife and children waiting outside in their car. A damage suit filed by his wife in federal court alleging that police denied Russ his civil rights was dismissed.

In a companion matter, the NAACP sued the attorney general over the failure of the FBI to seriously investigate the Russ matter. Though the NAACP did not prevail in that case, it was useful to have pressed that and other similar claims, because such requests are now seriously entertained as grounds for pursuing by the Trayvon Martin case in Florida and other acts of violence against blacks.

Much of what I set forth in these pages deals with the continuation of the Houston-Marshall and Carter efforts to implement the mandate of *Brown v. Board of Education* in the North. But there were other and broader responsibilities to be met. As *The Call* outlined, the problems confronting black America extended beyond the education sphere. The abolitionist Frederick Douglass, Charles Hamilton Houston, Thurgood Marshall, and Robert Carter constructed and reinforced the foundation that black Americans continue to depend on in achieving their quest for equal justice. Members in the 1,700 NAACP branches stretching across the nation came to regard the organization as a shield against manifestations of racism that were directed against them from a variety of institutions that governed their lives.

I knew about this dependency and expectation of local communities as a branch member. From my association with Dickerson, as an NAACP officer, and later my work in ferreting out causes of the urban unrest as a member of the Kerner Commission, my antenna was keenly tuned to the requests that came from local branches around the country. That led me to respond, for instance, to pleas from San Francisco when the police department was randomly jailing black youths, without probable cause, in what they called Operation Zebra. A federal lawsuit that we brought led to the issuance of an injunction against the San Francisco Police Department. Another successful federal lawsuit was filed against practices by the Philadelphia Police Department headed by Frank Rizzo. Police brutality in various cities, as well as miscarriages of justice in court cases across the country, led to requests for assistance, which I felt compelled to respond to.

Not only were abuses in the criminal justice system widespread, but it was necessary to use the 1964 Civil Rights Act, the 1965 Voting Rights Act, and the 1968 Fair Housing Act in bringing court cases that involved employment, voting, and housing discrimination. I was convinced of the necessity of responding to these requests, to the extent our limited resources permitted, because I early learned, and the NAACP understood, that due to the systemic nature of discrimination, issues of police abuse; manipulation in the courts; denial of housing, voting, and public services; and the presence of poverty often presented a seamless web that had to be severed. It was difficult for that to be done by individuals. Only the combined resources and approach of organizations and the government could be effective.

In looking back over the period of civil rights struggle commencing with Houston and Marshall, advanced by Carter, the decade of my stewardship at the NAACP, and the effective lobbying of Clarence Mitchell and his colleagues, I am convinced that it was the unstinting insistence of the lawyers in pursuing legislation and litigation that established civil rights legal standards. For the nation to move forward, there could be no compromise on the basic question of remedy. It was after I saw the effects of the Reagan administration's juggernaut in reversing hard-won precedents that I felt compelled to leave the court and assume another role.

From the days the NAACP first established its legal thrust, it was known as a civil rights organization whose primary function was to maintain a hard-core defense of civil rights. Over time, as it was presented with a variety of issues, it was tempted to reach out and engage in broader pursuits of a social justice nature. I remained of the view, however, that the NAACP was most effective when it concentrated on its basic mission. Other organizations had the experience and skills to best develop strategies and cope with the broader social-action challenges.

Unfortunately, today, the organization's expertise and history are drowned out by the cacophony of voices that outrace the NAACP to the TV cameras. The wisdom and contributions of a Walter White, Roy Wilkins, Thurgood Marshall, Gloster Current; the courage of Medgar and Myrlie Evers; the brilliance of Clarence and Juanita Mitchell and of William H. Hastie and A. Leon Higginbotham; the genius of Bayard Rustin; the pioneering work of Milwaukee's Vel Phillips; and the political acumen of Arkansas' Wiley Branton or the NAACP's own Ruby Hurley, to mention just a handful, receive little or no historical mention.

With the turn of events that has now taken place, and civil rights remedies and the Fourteenth Amendment now being stood on their heads, it is high time that leadership reemerge that will take on the campaign of nullification that is presently seeking to return the nation to the states' rights era.

9

The Road to the Court

For years after joining the U.S. Sixth Circuit Court of Appeals, I was asked how I became a judge.

I explained, especially to law students and curious lawyers, that I did not ever seek or set my sights on being appointed as a federal appellate judge. When I commenced my legal studies and joined the bar, the legal profession was infected with the same racial virus that limited opportunities to blacks as was found in other areas of endeavor. Even after the experience I gained while serving as a practicing lawyer, an assistant U.S. attorney, and assistant general counsel to a presidential commission, a desire for appointment to the federal bench was never on my radar screen.

Anger at the systemic changes that were being ordered by courts to uproot segregation and discrimination had spread to the North. White political majorities began to resist the thrusts of progress initiated by the NAACP and other civil rights advocates. President Johnson's Kerner Commission identified causes for this anger and the civil rights pressure for change. Thus the challenge to the civil rights groups grew in intensity. Becoming general counsel for the NAACP, the largest and oldest civil rights organization in the nation, represented an achievement that surpassed my fondest expectations.

Shortly after President Carter's election in 1976 he announced his appointment for attorney general, Fifth Circuit Judge Griffin Bell of Georgia. That nomination set off a firestorm.

Judge Bell's record as a judge on the U.S. Court of Appeals for the Fifth Circuit, and prior to that as an adviser to Southern governors who sought to impede school desegregation in their states, unnerved the civil rights community. Clarence Mitchell, the NAACP's principal lobbyist, assumed a leadership role with an assortment of civil rights groups, including the Leadership Conference on Civil Rights, in mapping a strategy of opposition to Bell's confirmation. Mitchell asked my assistance in developing information on Bell's judicial record. Following spirited hearings, Judge Bell was confirmed by the Senate by a sliver of a margin. It seemed unlikely that there could be a bridge built between Bell and the civil rights community. Though my role was minor, it was not unknown.

Two subsequent developments after the disappointment over Bell's confirmation caused the civil rights community to soften their view of the incoming Carter administration. First, Carter made it clear that African Americans would be appointed to key positions. Second, he created bipartisan judicial selection commissions for each of the twelve circuits to recommend diverse candidates to fill the seats provided by the recently enacted legislation creating new positions in the courts of appeal. With regard to the first matter, William Robinson of the NAACP Legal Defense Fund correctly predicted that a Justice Department appointment would soon be announced that I would find very pleasing. Shortly thereafter, it was announced that our mutual friend, Drew Days III would be named Assistant Attorney General for Civil Rights. Placing oneself back in time to 1976, that was huge.

Considerable hope was stirred by the caliber of people being appointed to the judicial selection commissions in the various circuits. Those two developments caused much of the acrimony around the Bell appointment to be muted. Even so, I never gave any thought to the possibility that I would become a contender for a judicial seat. While the executive order signed by President Carter creating the selection commissions was limited to the courts of appeals, he also urged senators, who play a key role in making recommendations to the president for district court judgeships, to also use bipartisan screening committees. Many agreed to do so.

President Carter's goal was to bring more diversity to the federal courts, particularly the courts of appeals, which are one level below the Supreme Court, and which, for all practical purposes, represent the final stop along the road for those seeking justice.

I had made numerous appearances before federal courts across the country during my days in private practice and as an NAACP lawyer. I never felt strange in a courtroom, although there were noticeable differences in the way various judges conducted themselves. Jurisdictions with a history of diversity generally set a different tone from those whose racial makeup was homogeneous. There was an occasion in the mid-1970s, on the eve of an appearance before the Sixth Circuit that a member of my team, Paul Dimond, said to me, "Nate, why don't you try for the Sixth Circuit?" I think I replied with some type of a quip, because flattering though it was, I did not take his suggestion seriously. I do recall later thinking that for such a suggestion to come from a colleague who had clerked for a Sixth Circuit judge, and who was working closely with me, that he must have thought that I would be up to the task. But beyond that, I gave no thought to it until several years later when I received the call from John Bustamante on June 28, 1978, the day that the Supreme Court handed down the decision in the famous case of *Alan Bakke v. Board of Regents of the University of California at Davis*.

The *Bakke* Case

As I mentioned earlier, the California Supreme Court caused an eruption in 1976 when it ruled that the affirmative action plan at UC–Davis violated Alan Bakke's constitutional rights. Because I was general counsel of the NAACP, the organization looked to me for a recommendation on an appeal, thus I became a major player in the national constitutional controversy. After a vigorous debate within the NAACP's national board of directors, a decision was made to intervene in the U.S. Supreme Court appeal of the state court decision as a friend of the court. I argued, unsuccessfully, in opposition to seeking Supreme Court review. My aim was to limit the reach of *Bakke*; I worried that a heightened profile could increase the influence of the case, particularly if we lost. My view was that we should allow that opinion to rest in California as an aberration—rather than take it national. Nevertheless, the NAACP directed that an amicus brief be drafted, joining a number of other organizations.

I had been directed by the board in advance of the ruling to schedule a series of press conferences in Los Angeles and San Francisco on June 28, 1978—the day the Supreme Court was expected to release its opinion. That date coincided with my scheduled arrival in Portland, Oregon, to begin preparations for the NAACP national convention.

The decision was released by the Supreme Court at about the very hour I arrived in Los Angeles. After reading it, I stated that we did not win but neither did we lose. I told our branches and the press that the NAACP was relieved that the U.S. Supreme Court, by sparing the consideration of race, that affirmative action was not dead; and that schools like Davis could continue using race as a factor in admission policies.

We knew that we had our work cut out for us: that the NAACP needed to reassure our constituency that affirmative action was alive, provided that certain procedures were followed. We had an obligation to help universities and employers resist efforts to oppose affirmative action. This all took place against the backdrop of the Sixty-Ninth Annual Convention of the NAACP that was to begin that week in Portland.

When I checked into the hotel, two phone messages awaited me. One was from a federal judge in Cleveland, my longtime friend Thomas Lambros. The other was from a black lawyer and businessman from Cleveland who was an adversary in a major school desegregation case that I was litigating for the NAACP, John H. Bustamante. Both calls related to the vacancy that had earlier that day been created on the Sixth Circuit Court of Appeals, brought about by the decision of Judge John Weld Peck to assume senior status. Bustamante was serving as a member of the Judicial Selection Commission for the Sixth Circuit. His was the first call I returned. He said that all he wanted was my permission for him to advance my name. When I balked, saying, "I'm swamped. I just got the *Bakke* opinion; it is going to keep me busy," Bustamante emphasized, "It is quite important that we move on this right away." I finally promised him that I would complete the papers but could not do so for two weeks due to my duties at the NAACP convention, followed by a Hawaiian vacation I had promised my wife.

After concluding my conversation with Bustamante, I returned Judge Lambros's call. He said, "You know, there's a Sixth Circuit seat open. I'm going for it and I just want to know if I can have your support." A brief pause was in order, after which I replied, "Judge, ordinarily you would have it but just moments ago I learned that someone had put my hat in the ring." He expressed surprise, but recovered enough to say, "Oh well, we'll have a little friendly competition."

As the NAACP convention got under way, I immediately told my colleague Clarence Mitchell about the telephone calls. He encouraged me to act swiftly. Having helped Thurgood Marshall through the judiciary committee thicket when nominated for the Second Circuit Court of Appeals by President Kennedy, the U.S. solicitor generalship, and later to the U.S. Supreme Court, Clarence understood the ins and outs of winning confirmation battles. From that time through to my being sworn in, he was my closest adviser.

After completing and sending my papers to the commission through Bustamante, I was invited to Cleveland to meet with a subcommittee of the commission. Then in August 1978, I was contacted by James Higgins, Sixth Circuit executive, who was serving as the chief of staff to the commission, acting on behalf of its chairman, Wilson Wyatt, a Louisville lawyer. Higgins invited me for an interview by the full group in Cincinnati. Following interviews, five names were to be submitted to the president.

My interview lasted nearly an hour. In preparation for the session I carefully reviewed the materials I'd previously submitted. The members seemed more interested in me as a person—how I viewed the role of a judge. After the interview, I thanked them, shook their hands, and departed.

The White House released the names the following week, and I noted that three of the five were sitting judges and the fourth was a law school dean. I felt doubly certain that a civil rights lawyer was no more than a token.

Several weeks later, while attending a conference at the New York Sheraton Hotel, I received a phone call from a friend who said he had it on good authority that President Carter had signed off on me for the judgeship. He cautioned against my saying anything about it. The president, he added, would do nothing about it in a public way until after the November election. Upon reentering the room I confided to Clarence Mitchell. Being the pro that he was about such matters, he said, "I will look into it," which meant that he would check with Louie Martin, another pro, who was serving as President Carter's special adviser and was a wonderful friend of mine. I urged that he do so. It was nearly midnight when I received a call from Mitchell. He related his conversation with Louie, who had asked Hamilton Jordan, the president's chief of staff. He confirmed that President Carter had indeed signed off on my appointment but would not move on it until after the November election.

Shortly after word of the president's decision leaked out, problems began. The November election came and went with no word from the White House. Ohio's two senators, John Glenn and Howard Metzenbaum, signaled the White House and the Justice Department that any one of the five names recommended by the commission was satisfactory. However, in mid-December, Martin advised Mitchell that an effort was being launched by some Clevelanders to derail my appointment. Most of the opposition came from powers committed to Judge Lambros. Mitchell had seen similar maneuvers, particularly in the context of Thurgood Marshall's appointment to the Second Circuit, and strongly objected to the idea that I step aside in favor of Judge Lambros in exchange for Senator Metzenbaum's promise to recommend me to succeed Lambros as a district court judge. "That's what they tried to do to Thurgood when he was nominated for the Second Circuit seat," Clarence told the White House and me. "You have been recommended for the court of appeals, and that is where you belong," he told me. The ostensible reason for trying to block my appointment was that I was "too controversial" in that I was overseeing a number of school desegregation cases, or "busing" cases, as my detractors labeled them. The delegation of Cleveland politicians, led primarily by some blacks, told a White House liaison team that if they insisted on me that there would be a "bloodbath" that would hurt the president's chances for carrying Ohio in his reelection efforts.

At that point I felt that Mitchell should take over the efforts on my behalf. My early skepticism was transformed into a stiff resolve to fight for the seat. With Mitchell working on my behalf I was confident things would work out. He teamed up with Louie Martin and Margaret McKenna, assistant White House counsel.

Mitchell never missed an opportunity to advance the ball down the field and always kept his eye on the big picture. A Cleveland-area congressman, Ron Mottl, was constantly introducing anti-busing amendments. Moreover, the Department of Justice tangled with him over fair housing issues in his hometown of Parma. In fact, a major fair-housing lawsuit was filed in federal court accusing Parma of engaging in shenanigans to keep blacks out. There was an employment angle to this, because the Ford Motor Company had an assembly plant in Parma and was required by presidential executive order and Title VII to hire blacks. Parma's housing policies were exclusionary and were negatively affecting Ford's efforts. Thus Congressman Mottl was in a fierce tug-of-war with both civil rights groups and the federal courts. Drew Days III, the assistant attorney general for civil rights, had authorized a suit against the City of Parma. It was being handled by a veteran civil rights lawyer, Robert Reinstein, who became a special assistant to Days, and a new, young lawyer, Theodore Shaw. Each of these lawyers has gone on to achieve fame and success as civil rights lawyers and legal educators. Mitchell saw the big picture of the Parma situation—the courts, jobs, housing, and school desegregation—which made it all the more imperative to him that President Carter stand firm on his intention to appoint me and other blacks to the bench.

At about the time this effort was heating up, Martin arranged a private meeting between the president and Mitchell. It was on the eve of the president's departure for a conference with the Israeli prime minister, Menachem Begin, and the president of Egypt, Anwar Sadat. He called me later that evening after their conference to report on their meeting. In reporting the events on this occasion he was uncharacteristically upbeat. In an almost blow-by-blow manner, he filled me in.

At the beginning, Mitchell expressed his deep appreciation to the president for agreeing to meet with him at a time when he was about to embark on such a historic mission. "Mr. President, I know you, as a Baptist, are a man of faith. I am a Methodist and also a man of faith; we both are Sunday School teachers. Would you mind if we begin with a word of prayer?" The president readily agreed. The two men grasped hands and bowed their heads as Clarence Mitchell led a prayer for, among other things, a positive and safe mission. Clarence then proceeded to mention the matters on his agenda that he felt required presidential attention. First, he said, is the matter of Nate Jones's appointment to the Sixth Circuit. He stated that some of the same kind of resistance that Justice Marshall encountered when he was nominated was building up. He said that the president interrupted with the observation that he knew Justice Marshall and of his excellent reputation as a lawyer and performance as a Justice. Mitchell assured the president I would bring the same kind of independence to the bench that Marshall had done. The president replied, "Clarence, I hear you loud and clear." At that point Mitchell discussed certain members of Congress who were continuing to load up the fair-housing legislation with anti-busing amendments as a means of killing the legislation. The president promised to look into the matter and take appropriate steps to remove all doubt.

I did not know how actively Attorney General Bell was registering his opposition to my appointment, but the role he thought I had played in opposing his confirmation as attorney general clearly displeased him. He mentioned it in his book by condemning the active role the White House was playing in judicial appointments. He complained that the White House senior administration personnel were intruding on Justice Department turf by insisting on greater racial diversity. Margaret McKenna was periodically made aware of the opposition of Attorney General Bell; however, it was to Assistant Attorney General Days that he expressed his views about my activities during his own confirmation skirmishes. Both tried to convince him to withdraw his opposition. After the holiday season, when the real reason for the opposition became apparent, support for me solidified, except for the handful of Clevelanders who were still strongly in the Lambros camp. They continued to press their campaign through Senator Metzenbaum.

National civil rights leaders were in constant touch with officials in the White House. Dr. Robert Green of Michigan State and the University of the District of Columbia had served as an educational expert in a number of the school desegregation cases. He helped to keep Ambassador Andrew Young and Coretta Scott King apprised of developments, and I found their counsel to be extremely helpful. When Senator John Glenn learned that the White House had decided to sign off on me, he assigned a key assistant, Reginald Gilliam, to work with Mitchell and me. That cooperation included a letter from the senator stating that he was fully in my corner. When Senator Metzenbaum heard about the letter, he became upset and demanded a copy of it, which I declined to provide. I told him that it would be more appropriate that he request a copy from his senatorial colleague himself.

There were a number of dramatic moments leading up to my nomination—too numerous to detail. Several, however, are memorable. Mitchell advised that the opposition being generated by the small group of individuals in Cleveland could be best countered by demonstrating the strength of support I enjoyed in the black community throughout Ohio. It was evident that the overall positive national response had impressed the Judicial Selection Commission and the White House. Ordinarily, that would have been more than enough—and had been enough until the visit by the Cleveland delegation. But the Clevelanders were endeavoring to create a political undertow that would deter President Carter from his goal of depoliticizing the judicial selection process. Clarence Mitchell came up with a means of countering that kind of gamesmanship. It involved a demonstration of support from lawyers from across the country. My opponents were overwhelmed by the display of national support. Thus, the White House staff remained steadfast and urged the president to not be swayed from his original decision to nominate me. Such a strategy would not have been necessary had the Cleveland political opposition not intruded upon the process.

One friend, Dorothy Burch, president of the Ohio State Conference of Branches, was particularly effective, as was Doris Sells of Cincinnati, a close friend of Rosalynn Carter. Dorothy Burch, Doris Sells, and their associates activated a network of black women that extended into most Ohio cities. A group from this network attended a Jefferson-Jackson Day Dinner in Mansfield, Ohio, that was to be addressed by Senator Metzenbaum. I am told that before the dinner a delegation approached him and asked why he was opposed to the president appointing me. During the exchange, the senator made reference to "you people," a racially demeaning expression, and the women took offense. I knew nothing about the plans of this group to meet with the senator, but learned that he was furious. It led to a very heated conversation between the two of us the following Monday morning, with him accusing me of "setting him up." He challenged my denial of not knowing anything about the incident. He asked, "What do you want me to do, call Griff Bell? I'll call him and tell him to appoint you." I said that I would like the senator's support but that this appointment was being handled out of the White House, not the Justice Department. He, with exasperation, said that he would make clear to the attorney general that he had no objections to me. In one respect, the Mansfield incident was regrettable because the senator and I had a good relationship that extended back to the early 1960s, when he recommended to Attorney General Robert Kennedy my appointment as assistant U.S. attorney in Cleveland. Furthermore, he had been a close political ally of my mentor, J. Maynard Dickerson, which went back to the days when they collaborated on ways of enacting an FEPC in Ohio. What happened in my situation, I sense, is that he had made a commitment to support Judge Lambros before he knew I was going to be involved and would be favored by the president. His sense of loyalty to Judge Lambros wouldn't let him back away.

While all of this was going on, I received an invitation to attend a White House reception that President Carter was hosting on May 17, 1979, to commemorate the twenty-fifth anniversary of *Brown*.

While I was at first reluctant to attend, due to the NAACP national board holding its own *Brown* celebration in Columbia, South Carolina, to salute the families who brought the *Briggs v. Elliott* case, Clarence Mitchell urged me to accept the invitation. He noted that for the past decade I'd had the major responsibility for directing the NAACP's school desegregation litigation and that the president was being most sensitive in commemorating the *Brown* cases. Once I had agreed to attend the White House ceremony, my in-house supporters, McKenna and Martin, went to see the president to point out that the celebration of the twenty-fifth anniversary of the *Brown* decision would be the ideal setting to announce my nomination. Martin, always having an eye for the dramatic, was mindful that as general counsel, successor to Thurgood Marshall and Robert Carter, I would be filling the shoes of those who gave us the *Brown* victory.

On the morning of May 17, I flew to Washington from Columbia, South Carolina, and met with Clarence Mitchell at his office before walking over to the White House for the event. We first encountered Louis Martin, who, in greeting us, said to me, "Hi, fella, I'm glad to see you." Next, we saw Margaret McKenna, whose face was beet-red, as she explained, "We're still working on the attorney general. He doesn't want to budge." Unsure as to what the president would do at the reception, Martin and McKenna decided to say nothing to me about it when they greeted me. Shortly thereafter, Mitchell and I, along with hundreds of invited guests, found our way into the East Room.

The president began his remarks with a touch of humor before moving to a discussion of the purpose of the occasion. He was delighted to be able to convene the group of people committed to the principles that the *Brown* decision set forth as true national policy. He went on as follows:

> In one area significant legal action is still necessary. We have to realize that the promise of equal opportunity in housing, if we are to make the educational benefits of the *Brown* decision as available to the Northern poor as they are becoming in the South.
>
> We need to amend the Fair Housing Act, to remove the burden and the expense of enforcement of the law from the shoulders of the poor victims of housing discrimination. I've urged Congress to give HUD, Housing and Urban Development Department, the power to resolve complaints directly, and to provide Secretary Pat Harris with cease and desist authority.

President Carter went on to discuss the appointment process:

> If you look around this reception, you'll see many of the 166 black Presidential appointees—appointments that I've been privileged to make. And there are also about the same number of black secretarial appointees here today. This is an unprecedented achievement, but we still have a long way to go together.
>
> I'd like to announce today that we'll continue this process. I will nominate, for instance, Nat[e] Jones, general counsel—[applause]— who's general counsel of the NAACP, to serve as a federal judge in the Sixth Circuit of our judicial system.

And we are trying to continue the process of letting qualified and motivated black leaders serve in policymaking bodies, in addition to the judiciary and the executive branch of government, the independent regulatory agencies. Marcus Alexis will be appointed as a new member of the Interstate Commerce Commission.[1]

Among those to whom the president was referring who were present in the East Room that day were the U.S. solicitor general Wade H. McCree; HUD secretary Patricia Harris; Eleanor Holmes Norton, chair of the Equal Employment Opportunity Commission; and Mary Frances Berry, chair of the U.S. Commission on Civil Rights. Many other cabinet officers, sub-cabinet officers, other agency heads and federal judges were on hand to take bows. It was a tribute to the influence of Clarence Mitchell that the two matters raised with the president during their Oval Office meeting—the need for amendments to the Fair Housing Law and my appointment—both found their way into the president's remarks.

When President Carter made the announcement, it was followed by a burst of applause. I had a momentary feeling that it was all a dream. The experience was numbing. The crowd's reaction drew a huge smile to the president's face. After all, presidents do not ordinarily announce judicial appointments in that fashion. Just as I was turning to say something to Mitchell, a huge set of strong arms embraced me from behind. They belonged to Jesse Jackson.

A reception followed the formal program. I stood in line for a long period of time accepting congratulations. Propriety and truth had me reminding the well-wishers that the applause and congratulations should be directed to our host, President Carter.

There was another, less than enthusiastic, response to the president's announcement. It came from my dear friend and a true national hero, Dr. Kenneth Clark. I had this exchange with him during the reception as we shook hands. He said his feelings were tempered because "we keep losing our lawyers." He took note of two of my NAACP predecessors, Justice Marshall and Judge Robert Carter. He lamented, "First it was Thurgood, then Bob Carter, and now you." I tried to assure him that I would always be committed to improving the opportunities of and protecting the constitutional rights of all children.

As soon as I was able to break away, I sought the assistance of a Secret Service agent to locate a telephone to inform my wife, Lillian. An elementary school teacher in the Ho-Ho-Kus, New Jersey, school system, she was summoned from the playground, where she was tending to her class. Anxiety gripped her as she, out of breath, reached the phone. For one thing, she was unaware that I had left South Carolina to go to Washington, D.C. I blurted out, "He did it. He did it." Her response was, "Who did what?" I replied, excitedly, "The president. He appointed me." Her relieved, and slightly annoyed, reaction was, "Oh."

The excitement surrounding the announcement reached her after she arrived home that evening when she received a phone call from a *New York Times* reporter. The national press coverage was extensive, including human-interest profiles in the *Washington Post* and the *Times*.

For me to be invited to the White House and have the president of the United States, who hailed from Georgia, a Southern state made infamous by bigots such as Herman Talmadge and his ilk, announce my appointment to a seat on the second highest court in the land, humbled me as nothing else ever has. A sea of congratulations poured in from all across the country. A story appeared in the *Cincinnati Post*, written by the chief of its Washington bureau, Barry Horstman, on the following day that bore the headline "Jones' Appointment Symbolic Triumph." I include excerpts from that story only to serve as a reminder of how much has happened in my lifetime, capstoned by the historic election of a black man, Barack Obama, as president of the United States in 2008. I do this in the hope that persons who may become disillusioned by contemporary developments will be inspired to stay the course. The story stated:

It was the 25th anniversary yesterday of the U.S. Supreme Court's historic *Brown v. Board of Education* decision, which declared segregation in the nation's public schools to be unconstitutional.

President Jimmy Carter stood in the East Room of the White House addressing several hundred civil rights leaders to commemorate the occasion. . . .

And then, as if to give a clear signal that he meant it, the president announced that he was nominating Nathaniel Jones, general counsel of the NAACP, to a federal judgeship on the U.S. Sixth Circuit Court of Appeals in Cincinnati.

Jones, standing among the crowd in the East Room, was as shocked as anyone. Although it had been known for months that he was a leading contender for the judgeship, he had thought that he was invited to the White House Thursday merely because of the *Brown* anniversary celebration.

"Obviously, the timing of the appointment was not just a coincidence," a White House aide said. "We thought it was a fitting way to commemorate the occasion and to show the president's commitment to advancing the principles of the civil rights movement."

As the NAACP's legal counsel for the past decade—a position previously held by Supreme Court Justice Thurgood Marshall—the 53-year old Jones was the chief legal spokesman for the civil rights organization.[2]

On the flight back to Columbia, South Carolina, to attend a reception hosted by Governor Richard Riley, Judge Matthew Perry, a native South Carolinian, introduced me to South Carolina senator Strom Thurmond, a prime author of the infamous Southern Manifesto. The senator reminded me that he was the ranking member of the Senate Judiciary Committee. I let him know that I was aware of it and that I knew I would appear before him, with "a fear a'trembling." He shot back, "Don't be concerned. Anyone who is a friend of Matthew Perry is a friend of mine." The following Monday Thurmond's assistant, Duke Short, phoned me in my New York office to reaffirm the senator's support of my nomination. He remained true to his word.

The Dixiecrat Party, formed in 1948, once nominated Thurmond as its presidential candidate. He ran a segregationist campaign. But thirty-one years later, he was offering to assist me, a former general counsel of the NAACP, an organization that was a one-time archenemy, in becoming a judge at the second highest level of the federal judiciary.

Confirmation

The details awaiting my attention were countless and would have to be addressed in a relatively short period of time. Preparing for my FBI interview was at the top of the list. Simultaneously, I needed to wrap up my active litigation and supervisory responsibilities in the school desegregation cases, including Dayton and Columbus, still pending in the U.S. Supreme Court. Mabel Jackson Smith, my administrative assistant, oversaw these crucial wrap-up activities. Of course, there were a number of cases at various stages still in our pipeline, including those affected by the Supreme Court's recent affirmative action decision in the *Bakke* case. Preparing reports for the relatively new CEO, Dr. Benjamin Hooks, and the sixty-four-member national board of directors were all on the front burner. James Meyerson and William "Rusty" Wells, my able in-house counsel and litigators, pitched in as they had so many times over the years to keep the legal program moving. Thomas Atkins proved himself virtually indispensable and took over the direction of the major desegregation litigation.

During the run-up to the confirmation hearing I kept in regular touch with Reggie Gilliam in Senator Glenn's office. I was also anxious to mend fences with Senator Metzenbaum, who had been smarting over the skirmishing that took place before President Carter's May 17 announcement. Senator Metzenbaum fortunately did not carry a grudge toward me, and his spirit of cooperation was most reassuring. He agreed to join with Senator Glenn in presenting me to the Judiciary Committee. Mitchell and I had been careful to always include Metzenbaum's name when handing out the bouquets. When time came for my testimony, I took my seat, flanked by Senator Glenn and Senator Metzenbaum, whose estrangement prompted them to enter the room through separate doors. Each spoke favorably of me and then took their leave.

With the confirmation process complete, my contacts with the Sixth Circuit court officials increased. My principal contacts were with the circuit executive, James Higgins, and the clerk of court, John Hehman. Court schedules were discussed, as well as housekeeping matters relating to my judicial chambers and other needs. My "class" of new judges included District Judges Cornelia Kennedy of Detroit and Bailey Brown of Memphis, and Kentucky State Court of Appeals Judge Boyce Martin Jr. of Louisville. A regular three-week session of the court was scheduled to begin on the morning of October 15, 1979, with my investiture slated for that afternoon.

Shortly after my confirmation, Chief Judge George Edwards Jr., before whom I had appeared a number of times as a lawyer, phoned me at my New York office. I had previously asked that he swear me in during my afternoon investiture. During his call he inquired as to whether I would accept an assignment to sit on his panel the morning before the public swearing-in ceremony. I reminded him that my ceremony was not to occur until 2:30 p.m. In his homespun manner of speaking, Judge Edwards replied, "Well, if you drop in to see me about eight o'clock, I'll give you an oath that will get you through the morning." The following day I received an overnight shipment of briefs on the case I was to hear. Opening the package and reading the briefs gave me a strange feeling. Due to the fast pace of disengaging from the NAACP, selling our house, and preparing for the move to Cincinnati, I had not yet come to grips with the reality that I was about to become a federal judge. Thanks to Judge Frank J. Battisti of Cleveland, I was introduced to his departing law clerk, a brilliant young man, Charles Moellenberg. I immediately asked him to become my first judicial law clerk. Faced with the request of Chief Judge Edwards that I sit on a case the very first day I was invested as a judge, I pressed Moellenberg into service.

Lillian had left for Youngstown, Ohio, a few days before, while I remained behind in order to attend a farewell dinner in my honor by the Bergen County (New Jersey) NAACP and to wrap up a few last-minute details before driving overnight to Youngstown. Late Saturday, my mother and other relatives headed for Cincinnati, where we were joined by many friends who arrived on Sunday. Our children, who were away at college, arrived about the same time at the Netherland Hilton Hotel.

Judge Damon Keith was kind enough to escort me to Chief Judge Edwards's chambers for the October 15 early morning oath taking. Following that event, he and the court clerk, John Hehman, showed me to what was meant to have been my "temporary" chambers—but which housed me for four years—to await the call to the robing room later in the morning. When the case on which I was to sit was ready to be called, I went to join the two other judges who were to sit with me. Even then, the momentousness of being transformed into a judge had not quite sunk in.

When entering the courtroom, under the existing court proto-col, the most junior judge is the first judge to ascend the bench, followed by the most senior, and the next most senior. The center seat was occupied by the presiding judge. The moment arrived for the three of us to make our entrance out onto the bench when a knock came at the door. When it opened, I, garbed in my new robe, led the other two judges to our seats on the bench. Sitting on that bench seemed so unreal. When the case was called, a lawyer for the appealing parties was the first to approach the lectern. The argument proceeded. I was anxious for counsel to address a partic-ular constitutional issue I had researched during my preargument preparation. It suddenly occurred to me that in my new role as a judge, I no longer had to wait. I could simply interrupt and ask the question, which I did—startling the advocate. He quickly recovered. With a deference that was almost embarrassing, he acknowledged me by prefacing his recognition of me with, "Yes, Your Honor . . ." I realized then with dramatic suddenness, for the first time, that I was, indeed, a judge.

Lighting Lights

From my earliest observations of courtrooms in my hometown, I was struck by the racial divide—a phenomenon akin to what I observed years later in South Africa under apartheid: positions of power and the exercise of authority were in white hands, with blacks largely confined to the prisoner docks. When I entered upon my service as a federal judge, I saw much the same general situation, modified only by my presence and the fact that while blacks may not have always been in the dock, they, nevertheless, were without power. That remained in white hands—the judges, clerks, marshals, probation officers, and the like.

There was no justification, for instance, for judicial chambers being staffed exclusively by white law clerks. It was a problem that I would soon take steps to address. There was a paradox in federal judges and federal courts enforcing civil rights decrees against public and private litigants with orders drafted by lily-white judicial staffs. As general counsel of the NAACP I had litigated civil rights cases in courtrooms all across the country and noted the contrasts between what I saw emerging in the Sixth Circuit and elsewhere. I had visited law schools nationwide and saw law students of color who were fully capable of performing as judicial law clerks. This reality flew in the face of the explanation for the minuscule numbers of blacks chosen.

Among my initial challenges was the need to organize my chambers staff, learn the routine of the court with regard to hearing schedules, and establish working relationships with the other judges. It was akin to joining a family. At the time I first joined the court, the sessions were three weeks in length, every few months. That had all of the judges in Cincinnati at the same time and afforded an opportunity for blending in with the "court family," as Chief Judge Edwards liked to describe us. He and his wife, Peg, worked very hard at preserving this sense of family among the judges. That included the judges lunching together at the University Club and in the evening having spouses join us for dinner. During the daytime hours several spouses volunteered their services with community organizations and agencies. Often, the spouses lunched together. Given that we were in Cincinnati for three-week periods, Lillian and I stayed at the Netherland Hilton Hotel with other judges prior to purchasing our home in Cincinnati. That furthered the sense of family. We were promptly embraced by the members of the court and their spouses. The lack of partisanship was impressive. Solid friendships had formed between judges I knew to be political and ideological opposites. For example, conservative Paul Weick, appointed by President Eisenhower, was like a brother to liberal Anthony J. Celebrezze. They looked out for each other in a number of ways. Chief Judge Edwards, appointed by President Johnson, worked hand in hand with Nixon-appointed Judge Pierce Lively. Reagan-appointed Judge Robert Krupansky of Cleveland, who seemingly never saw a civil rights case he could uphold, was a close friend of Judge Keith, who had a sterling civil rights record as a judge. Judge Leroy J. Contie, also a Reagan appointee, and I often shared lunch and many conversations. Though we had different views on civil rights cases, we talked through our differences and occasionally views were changed.

Upon joining the court I learned of the gaps in the sitting schedule. That prompted me to ask my colleague, the experienced Judge Keith, how we were expected to occupy ourselves between sessions. He smiled and said, "You will find out soon enough." I received a similar answer to my question as to how to remain alert on the bench when told that panels' hearings lasted three hours at a time. However, neither the time between sessions nor the three-hour court sessions proved to be a problem.

As one would expect, there were countless requests from a wide assortment of groups for me to make appearances. I used each appearance as an opportunity to educate the public and to demystify the court. All too often, I sensed that some judges felt that it was important to screen out the public and *not* take them into the inner workings of the court's decision making.

I earlier referred to the very first case I sat on just before the public swearing in and my reaction when I interrupted a lawyer with a question. It was a sobering moment. On occasions I have related to law students, when discussing the awesome power of a federal judge, that experience, as well as another time when Clerk of Courts John Hehman came to me late one afternoon with a motion of the government that sought to enjoin a nationwide railway strike scheduled to take effect at midnight. The sole act that could block a shutdown of the nation's railroads before midnight was the issuance of an injunction by the court. I reviewed the government's legal memorandum, and within the hour, signed the order to block the shutdown. That act cleared the way for the railroads to continue to operate. Shortly thereafter, the television networks' evening news reported that a federal court of appeals judge in Cincinnati had enjoined the railroad strike. I recognized that they were talking about me. That was a sobering realization for this former civil rights lawyer from Youngstown, who began his practice by hanging out a shingle because law firms of the stature of those whose legal documents I perused before acting, would, in the past, never have entertained the thought of hiring me or anyone who looked like me.

A chambers staff usually consisted of three law clerks and two secretaries. I hired three law clerks on a staggered basis each year; as one rotated out another came on board. They were hired a year in advance. Some judges preferred to have a permanent clerk, but my preference was for a total rotation, in order to offer the experience to more young lawyers. During the "open" season, when recruitment at the law schools was permitted, I received hundreds of applications, which required a system of internal screening involving my current clerks and my two secretaries. Maintaining a diverse staff was a goal of mine, and rarely was I not able to sustain that objective.

Shortly after joining the court, I had a friendly confrontation with some lawyers who had served on my NAACP litigation team when they paid their first visit to my chambers. They were upset that my three diverse law clerks were male. They expressed their disappointment that I had not selected at least one woman. As they persisted in expressing their disappointment, I got my back up and challenged them. As they pressed their argument, I finally cut them off by making it clear to them that among the law clerks serving the judges of the Sixth Circuit there were already many women, all of them white. Therefore, my immediate priority, with respect to diversity, was racial. Until the white judges began to bring on more law clerks of color, my priority would continue to be hiring black clerks, which would include women. I suggested that their lobbying efforts should be directed at some of the liberal white and women judges to hire black clerks. We all remained friends and, of course, I shall always be deeply appreciative of the great work they did as NAACP lawyers.

Chief Judge Edwards, who had himself hired black law clerks and a black secretary, was fully cognizant of the absence of diversity among law clerks and other court personnel. He endorsed my efforts and those of Judge Keith to push diversity. His successor as chief judge, Judge Pierce Lively, a remarkable jurist, was also fully supportive of expanding racial diversity in the Sixth Circuit even beyond the ranks of judicial law clerks.

Other aspects of the Sixth Circuit personnel practices that underwent change included the adding of minorities to staffs of the various sections of the Office of the Clerk of Courts. John Hehman, the clerk, was extremely sensitive to the need to diversify the different divisions in his office. With the support of Chief Judge Edwards, Hehman reached out to bring in more minorities. For example, offers were extended to black lawyers and clerical personnel in the Staff Lawyers Section. As Judge Keith and I often remarked, the efforts he and I sparked to bring about change led to modest results and a greater awareness of the need to do more. The fact that he and I had black law clerks placed diversity on the court's radar screen. Because my chambers were in Cincinnati, the seat of the court, the blacks on my staff were a permanent, constant reminder of diversity to other judges, administrators, and staff.

President Jimmy Carter qualifies for special praise for his courage. While other presidents who preceded him between President Kennedy and his four-year term nominated a commendable number of

African American judges, it was Carter who burst through the tokenism of the past. Between 1976 and 1980, he named an astounding twenty-eight blacks to the various Article III District seats and eight to the U.S. Courts of Appeal. All of that was done in four years—a total that exceeded the federal judicial appointments of all presidents since the establishment of the federal judiciary.

As significant as those numbers are, what is more important is what they mean. To understand that one must understand the power that President Carter, by those appointments, placed in the hands of lawyers of color. The exercise of such power by judges of the Old South broke the back of historic institutional discrimination. They came to be joined by other enlightened judges as the federal judiciary became more integrated. This led to the acceleration of crumbling walls of discrimination, which current conservatives and champions of states' rights cleverly seek to resurrect and which President Reagan attributed to "activist judges." Yet it is proponents of discrimination who are doing this by manipulating the judicial nominating process. Simultaneously, those forces are intensifying using their power within the judiciary to lock in the techniques of suppression of the votes of minorities. They do this by reinstating a variety of once-outlawed Jim Crow tactics that disqualified minorities. The result is a rolling back of gains. This, make no mistake about it, has long-term effects on our future as a nation.

The nominating environment has become so toxic that it became almost impossible for President Obama to meet his constitutional obligation to nominate candidates to fill vacancies. That was not a problem that President Carter faced, which undoubtedly was a factor in the smooth sailing that my nomination experienced. One of the differences between then and now is that there was no litmus test of the kind that President Reagan introduced in order to evaluate a judicial nominee's legal approach to remedying social and economic problems.

Once the Republicans gained control of the Senate in 2014, it became unlikely that the president would be able to win approval for any judicial nominee who didn't meet the test laid down by advocates of states' rights. It is unlikely that any with the experience of a Thurgood Marshall, Spottswood Robinson, Robert Carter, Constance Baker Motley, or even a Nathaniel Jones would win favor with the Senate. My pessimism on that score stems from the rough road that even the most meticulous selections by the Obama administration encounter. In contrast to previous appointees, the Alliance for Justice (AFJ) reports that about 85 percent of the nominees have been corporate attorneys, prosecutors, or both.[3] Fewer than 4 percent have worked as lawyers in public-interest organizations, as Marshall, Carter and I did. Also, AFJ found that while 43 percent of Obama nominees to the federal courts were previously state or federal prosecutors, only 15 percent were public defenders. Even more striking, at the appellate level only 4 out of the 56 nominees had ever been public defenders, while 21 were prosecutors. To his credit, President Obama continues to try to strike a better balance with what the AFJ calls "underrepresented backgrounds." But again, there lurks a Senate majority poised to nullify these efforts.

Judicial Conferences

Judge Keith and I thought it would be useful to look for opportunities to increase participation by black lawyers in circuit court activities. Chief judges of each circuit have the authority to recommend judges to serve on the various court committees to the chief justice of the United States. He presides over the Judicial Conference of the United States, the principal policy-making body of the federal courts. The first black who had served on that body was the late Judge Wade H. McCree while on the district court in Michigan.

Judge Keith and I had complained to Judge Edwards about the "systems" then in place within the court that made it difficult to significantly alter the racial makeup of the judicial conferences. The process for selecting delegates to attend the statutorily mandated annual Sixth Circuit Judicial Conference was a good place to begin. The policy permitted each active circuit court judge to designate two delegates. Each district court judge was free to nominate a single delegate to attend each conference. If the same person attended five consecutive years, that person became a life member and, thereafter, could attend without a specific invitation. Black lawyers were seldom chosen as delegates by either circuit or district court judges. The reality was that before President Carter, the paucity of black judges was reflected in the small numbers of black delegates. White judges, with few exceptions, did not designate black lawyers as delegates. The tendency was to choose one's personal or political friends, former law partners, and even relatives.

Thus, when I arrived at my first judicial conference, the number of delegates of color was exceedingly small, barely more than a handful. Seeing such a small number of lawyers of color was bothersome. It should be noted that these gatherings were usually held at plush resorts or conference centers where golf and other recreational amenities could be offered. The conferences lasted for several days and afforded opportunities for lawyers to socially interact with the federal judges.

Not lost on me was the familiarity that existed between some judges and those lawyers who were my adversaries when I was litigating a number of the most contentious civil rights cases in the various courts within the Sixth Circuit. During the course of the trials and other appearances, everything seemed proper. Yet at the conferences, I observed these same lawyers sitting around the cocktail lounges, riding in the same golf carts, and having social conversations with the judges at well-appointed receptions that most minority lawyers did not experience. This did not seem quite right. In my conversations with Chief Judge Edwards he lost no time in agreeing that change was in order. He authorized Judge Keith and me to increase our number of delegates each year until a better ratio was struck.

We took advantage of that opportunity and an increasing number of black lawyers began to attend the judicial conferences. This did not go over too well with some of the white delegates, but the practice continued for a number of years. On one occasion during a conference at Mackinac Island in Michigan, my wife, Lillian, and spouses of two of my delegates were in the ladies' room of the Grand Hotel. Their presence had not been noticed by a cluster of white women who obviously were spouses of some delegates. The increased number of blacks drew the following observation from one of the white women: "Do you notice how many more of *them* there are? It is simply terrible." Moments later, when they noticed Lillian's party, they spoke very sheepishly and departed. The practice of increased minority invitations continued during the chief judgeship of Pierce Lively, George Edwards's successor. Several recent judges, unaware of the history that led to the invocation of the dual system for selecting delegates, and taking note of the fact that some of the white judges had begun to pick black delegates, questioned the chief judge at the time, Gilbert Merritt, about the advisability of continuing the practice. He directed that the multiple delegation selection practice be terminated. That decision, however, coincided with the court adopting an "open conference" policy during alternating years. Under that new policy, any lawyer in good standing could attend and participate in the judicial conferences. By opening the conference, the exclusive aspect of the meetings that was so offensive was eliminated.

Another significant change was having black judges serve on the various committees of the judicial conferences. The existence of the conference and of its various committees was not generally known by lawyers who practice in the federal courts, nor by the public at large whose destinies are often shaped by decisions made by those groups of federal judges. The chief judge of each circuit carries considerable influence with the chief justice of the Supreme Court and the director of the Administrative Office of the U.S. Courts, who would identify persons to be appointed to the various committees. Today, judges of color and women not only serve on the various policy-making committees of the judicial conference but hold significant chairmanships.

My long interest in international law and human rights led me to take part in such matters even before I became a judge. While with the NAACP I attended a World Peace Through Law conference in Côte d'Ivoire, West Africa, in August 1973 that attracted jurists and lawyers from around the world to discuss ways of enhancing peace through expanding respect for the law. That trip to the Ivory Coast and my later sojourns to South Africa after joining the court made it easy for Chief Judge Gilbert Merritt to recommend to Chief Justice Rehnquist that I be appointed to the Committee on International Judicial Relations. The function of that committee was to assist the U.S. government in developing programs within foreign countries. This involved my making international visits and hosting foreign delegations on their visits to the United States. These activities were woven in between my regular court duties.

Another committee to which I was appointed was the Judicial Conference Committee on Judicial Conduct, a position I held for more than five years. That committee was charged with offering guidance and responding to inquiries from judges on a variety of ethical issues. Functioning on those committees made up of judges from other districts and circuits, and dealing with issues that affected federal judges similarly dispersed, made me aware of the vast power of federal judges and why it was crucial that those who are appointed reflect the diversity of culture, class, race, and life experience of citizens whose destinies are affected by officials chosen to enforce federal laws.

The questions surrounding diversity in the ranks of the law clerks spread beyond circuit courts and extended to the U.S. Supreme Court. Without success I was quite vocal on the need for more judges to recruit minorities as Supreme Court law clerks.

In a *USA Today* article dated December 8, 1998, Tony Mauro wrote:

> The Supreme Court for the first time is expressing concern about the small number of minorities and women hired as law clerks . . .
>
> But Rehnquist, who wrote on behalf of the entire court, suggested the situation would not change until the pool from which law clerks are selected becomes more diverse.

The letter, released Monday, is the fullest response yet to a USA TODAY investigation . . . [that] revealed that of 428 law clerks hired by the current court, just seven were African American, or 1.6%. Five were Hispanic (1.2%), and 18 were Asian (4.2%). One-fourth were women.

The Washington Post's December 8, 1998, article by Joan Biskupic stated:

Chief Justice William H. Rehnquist told three black members of Congress the justices have not discriminated in the hiring of law clerks. . . .

Rehnquist also rejected a request by the three House members—Danny K. Davis (D-Ill.), Elijah E. Cummings (D-Md.) and Gregory W. Meeks (D-N.Y.)—to talk to minority bar groups about the selection process. . . .

For months, the National Association for the Advancement of Colored People, the National Bar Association and other minority groups have been pressuring the justices to do something about the low number of blacks and Hispanics who become law clerks. Nearly 1,000 civil rights activists protested at the court's opening day in October, and the NAACP in recent weeks has been asking its members to write letters of protest to the high court.

I joined in activities of the American Bar Association to bring greater diversity to the profession. These were causes for which I felt I could advocate and still remain within the restrictions imposed by the Codes of Conduct and the Canons of Ethics, which are binding on all federal judges except Supreme Court justices. Basic to the limits on judicial activism was the principle of advancing the administration of justice. It was my conviction that it was in the interest of advancing the administration of justice to have diverse chambers staffs. After all, judges were adjudicating cases involving discrimination laws and ordering remedies for transgressions. The role of "elbow" clerks (named for their proximity to the judge) in a judicial chamber can subtly shape outcomes. Although judges deny that this occurs, it is very clear to me that the way issues are researched and presented to the judge in bench memos and discussion can have a bearing on how a judge ultimately handles a case. Under the federal rules of procedure, some cases can be disposed of summarily without ever reaching trial. Such matters as to what constitutes a "genuine issue" or what is a "material fact" can rest on the life experiences of a law clerk or a judge. Yet the subjective nature of those considerations can determine whether a party ever has a day in court. That reality is one of the many that prompted me to argue for more diversity in selection of law clerks.

I had more than one judge ask me how I went about recruiting my law clerks. They stated that their efforts to attract minority candidates met with little or no success. I surmise that had a lot to do with the particular judge and the judicial philosophy reflected in his or her opinions. I pointed out to several of them that law students do as much research on judges as judges do on would-be applicants. I agreed to share with some judges the names of applicants whom I interviewed but was unable to hire.

I was indeed fortunate in my choice of law clerks. The occasion was rare to near nonexistent that I ever regretted my choice of a law clerk. Bonds of respect and friendship were formed that continue to this day. We keep in touch and have periodic reunions. I am extremely proud of the career choices they have made and are pursuing. They hold positions in private firms and in the public sector, including the Justice Department and on the federal bench. One of my clerks, who died much too soon, was Jerome Culp. He came to me from Harvard Law School, where he compiled a remarkable academic record. He also had matriculated at the Massachusetts Institute of Technology, where he majored in statistics. The son of a coal miner who grew up outside Pittsburgh, Jerome, as did his siblings, excelled in all that he did. I found him to be invaluable in helping me work my way through a number of difficult cases. He went on to teach at various law schools, including Rutgers and Duke University. He lost a battle with diabetes.

A super prospect who got away has never let me forget it. He was a protégé of Culp's at Harvard. My version of events differs from his, but given that he became governor of the Commonwealth of Massachusetts, I will go with Deval Patrick's version and offer my profound apologies for dropping the ball. It was a hectic period and I obviously did not properly handle the interviewing process. I knew him, having judged the prestigious Ames Moot Court finals at Harvard Law School on a panel consisting of Judge Patricia Wald of the D.C. Court of Appeals and Judge Henry J. Friendly of the Second Circuit Court of Appeals. Patrick's team won, and we selected him as the outstanding oralist. I was later able to play a modest role in his fantastic professional rise, including a strong recommendation to Vernon Jordan, who was heading up President Clinton's transition team. He needed no nudge from me, because his course had long ago been set by virtue of his demonstrated brilliance. Prior to running for the Massachusetts governorship he was vice president and general counsel of the Coca-Cola Company.

My desire for diversity went beyond race and gender because I knew from my own experience that talent can be found in many places. I sought out law clerks from schools other than the Ivy League. And, of course, I found first-class law clerks from a number of other schools. Together, my clerks provided me with rich perspectives on the law. The heights to which my judicial clerks ascended gave me pride and gave the lie to those judges who for years contended that they could not find competent candidates of color to serve as law clerks. Two of my former clerks, Anthony Foxx and Kathleen O'Malley, received presidential appointments. I was humbled and thrilled to have been asked to administer the oath of office to Foxx upon President Obama appointing him to his cabinet as secretary of transportation. This was after the stellar record he made as mayor of Charlotte, North Carolina. He is the first of my former clerks to become a member of a president's cabinet. Another is Judge O'Malley, who sits on the U.S. Court of Appeals for the Federal Circuit, after service as a U.S. district judge. Appointed to the highly significant position of general counsel of the Treasury Department was George Madison.

Two Special Assignments

A judge does more than decide cases that turn up on the regular docket. Judges are called upon to deal with matters that arise in other venues—some judicial and others that bear upon the administration of the federal courts. I was asked to deal with two unconnected matters that related to the conduct of two federal judges. I knew each of the judges and was generally familiar with the issues that caused their conduct to rise to the level of seriousness that they did. One dealt with efforts to impeach U.S. District Judge Alcee L. Hastings of Florida, and the other involved a complaint by judicial colleagues in the Northern District of Ohio of administrative decisions made by their chief judge, Frank J. Battisti. These were not easy assignments to undertake, but I had no choice but to step forward and lend my best efforts.

The Hastings Impeachment

Judge Alcee L. Hastings (now a U.S. congressman from Florida) was appointed to the federal district court in Florida just prior to my appointment to the Sixth Circuit Court of Appeals. He and I met several times and enjoyed a pleasant relationship. We were both Kappas. An impeachment investigation by his circuit grew out of his handling of a criminal case that had led to his indictment and subsequent acquittal. The indictment resulted from an FBI investigation into allegations of Judge Hastings being bribed in a drug case.

Events erupted on the eve of the annual convention of the National Bar Association when its president, William Borders, was arrested in a sting operation, after which Judge Hastings suddenly departed from his hotel in Washington and returned to Florida, with the FBI in pursuit. Borders and Hastings were separately indicted on a charge of conspiracy and obstruction of justice in the Southern District of Florida. Borders was convicted on March 29, 1982, and sentenced to prison. Judge Hastings, who was tried separately, was acquitted by a jury on February 4, 1983.

As the impeachment attracted increased attention, a member of the Judiciary Committee, Congressman John Conyers Jr. of Michigan, captured the mood of many blacks with a statement in a July 11, 1988, story in the *Detroit Free Press*. He said that he was not sure what to make of Judge Hastings. He said he sees "a profile of two Hastings." He was a bright and capable judge, and very engaging as a person. Yet the charges swirling about him were disquieting. His acquittal by a jury did not quiet the storm.

The Judicial Council of the Eleventh Circuit, not content with the acquittal of Judge Hastings, launched its own investigation, led by former Justice Department civil rights prosecutor John Doar, which it hoped would lead to Hastings's impeachment, conviction, and ouster. Upon completion of the investigation in 1986, the Judicial Council determined that the impeachment of Judge Hastings "may be warranted." A year later, the Judicial Conference of the United States concurred and transmitted its recommendation to the Speaker of the House of Representatives for consideration by the House Judiciary Committee. The chairman of the House Judiciary Committee, Peter Rodino, requested the chief judge of the U.S. District Court for the Southern District of Florida provide access to grand jury materials for use in the House impeachment proceedings. Judge Hastings sought a stay of this order. A district court judge denied Judge Hastings's request. Also denied was the request to disclose to Judge Hastings and the public the grand jury materials that were being made available to the Judiciary Committee. At that point, Judge Hastings filed an appeal.

Since the Eleventh Circuit had launched the investigation following Judge Hastings's acquittal, all active Eleventh Circuit judges stepped aside, thus clearing the way for a panel from the Sixth Circuit to be appointed by Chief Justice Rehnquist to hear the appeal. I, along with two colleagues from the Sixth Circuit, Judge Gilbert Merritt and Judge Ralph Guy, were designated. The question presented on appeal was narrow and raised three issues: (1) whether the district court judge who denied Judge Hastings's efforts to block the turnover of grand jury materials to the House

Judiciary Committee abused his discretion; (2) whether the grand jury materials should be disclosed to the entire 535 members of Congress; and (3) whether the grand jury materials should be disclosed to Judge Hastings. It was Judge Hastings's position that the wholesale turnover of grand jury materials without close scrutiny by the district court judge was error. None of these issues dealt with the merits of the impeachment question. That remained for Congress.

As I reviewed points of authorities set forth in the briefs filed by the Department of Justice and Judge Hastings's counsel, my staff and I engaged in our own independent legal research. At the same time I also searched for subtle signs of racial motivation in the call for impeachment. The case was difficult because of the symbolism involved in a federal judge of color from a Southern state (where there should be many more blacks in the judiciary) having created considerable notoriety with public statements that a number of people felt went beyond the bounds of judicial propriety. Even after trial and acquittal, there were judges in that circuit who wanted to pursue an investigation of Hastings's conduct for possible disciplinary action, up to and including impeachment.

The majority of our panel—Judge Merritt and Judge Guy—held that "after careful consideration of the record and the arguments made on appeal, we conclude that the materials requested should be disclosed to the Committee and affirm."[4] I dissented. I wrote:

> Judge Hastings is a member of the judiciary who has long been acquitted by a jury of his peers of any criminal wrongdoing. Although such facts are not dispositive, they nonetheless emphasize the need for the judicial branch to proceed with great caution with respect to sanctioning the production of secret grand jury testimony in pursuit of a generalized inquiry. Such testimony should be disgorged only upon a specific showing of particularized need and this, in my judgment, has not been shown. For the above reasons, I would deny the Committee's request for the grand jury and electronic surveillance materials.[5]

Judge Hastings was impeached by the House of Representatives and convicted by the Senate. After leaving the bench, he ran for and was elected to the House of Representatives from Southeast Florida that included Broward County and Fort Lauderdale, where he continues to serve with great distinction and draws praise from both sides of the aisle.

The Complaint Against Judge Frank J. Battisti

Frank J. Battisti, a federal judge who, as did I, hailed from Youngstown, Ohio, is one of many people who played a significant role in my life. Of all of the extrajudicial assignments I was called upon to undertake after becoming a judge, one of the most distasteful involved the controversy surrounding Battisti. He was a friend and someone I regarded as a judge of great strength but one who was misunderstood by many. He contributed to that misunderstanding, in a large measure, because of the strength of the certitude with which he exercised the power of his office. He had a swashbuckling style that sometimes violated general notions about how those who wear judicial robes should behave. A controversy arose between the judges of the Northern District of Ohio that caused my chief judge to ask for my assistance in its resolution.

Critics of Judge Battisti thought his management style was somewhere between arbitrary and corrupt. I knew he was being misunderstood. Judge Battisti was merely following what predecessors had done going back as far as three previous chief judges.

He took on the most difficult and controversial cases. He tackled everything from the Justice Department's fair-housing case in Parma to the school desegregation case in Cleveland and the deportation case of Cleveland autoworker John Demjanjuk, a man accused of Nazi war crimes. While he was frequently criticized, he was also often praised for his courage in upholding the claims of civil rights litigants in much the same way that some of the Southern judges did. His strong belief in the independence of federal judges was reflected in many of his rulings, writings, and lectures.

The Justice Department began an investigation into Judge Battisti's handling of a bankruptcy matter, which was said to have benefited his young nephew Gino Battisti, a new lawyer. Judge Battisti temporarily and properly turned over the court's administration to the next most senior judge, Thomas Lambros. Many months later, when the investigation concluded with no finding of wrongdoing by Judge Battisti, he sought to reclaim his powers. During the interim, those powers had been distributed by Judge Lambros to the various committees established by the court. Judge Battisti insisted that judges were exercising powers as committee members that belonged to the chief judge. The judges had come to like the new way of doing things and they resisted relinquishing their newly acquired powers. Battisti continued to insist that the chief judge's powers were derived by statute, were his to exercise, and that the Chief Judge must make the decisions.

Judge Battisti then issued a directive to the chief probation officer on a personnel matter that ran counter to a directive from the committee then overseeing the Probation Department. The chief of the Probation Department was caught in the middle. The nine members of the court retained a law firm to prepare a complaint for filing with the Sixth Circuit Judicial Council. Judge Battisti retained a former attorney general of the United States, Benjamin Civiletti of Baltimore. Sessions of the Judicial Council are public, which meant the meeting would likely receive massive media coverage. Judge Merritt and I were asked to play a role in resolving the difficulty between Judge Battisti and his colleagues, partly because his colleagues knew he had great confidence in me. An impasse had arisen that, unless resolved amicably, would have required drastic action by the Judicial Council of the Sixth Circuit.

At the first meeting each side held firm. We took the lead in settlement efforts. It was after that session with Judge Battisti and his counsel that I began to hold private talks with him. Some of these talks went as late as midnight. Due to the fact that Battisti's health was not good, I urged that it was important for everybody involved to do a little face-saving and spare the court the embarrassment of a prolonged public struggle. Ultimately, Judge Battisti agreed to step down as chief judge but remain as an active judge. Shortly thereafter he took senior judge status. On October 19, 1994, Judge Battisti died of Rocky Mountain spotted fever at the age of seventy-two. In tribute, his law clerks and friends initiated a lecture series in his name at Case Western Reserve Law School that attracts nationally known legal scholars as lecturers.

In handling the Hastings, Battisti, and similar matters, the need to maintain public confidence in the integrity of the process was uppermost in my mind. In each of those situations, I realized that we were dealing with individuals perceived to have engaged in conduct that, for some, went against the grain of acceptability. I knew that feeling from my earliest encounters with the criminal justice system when I was representing unpopular causes or people. Even in instances where individuals may have transgressed rules and procedures, I remain convinced that great care must be taken to ensure that fair treatment is accorded.

Bankruptcy Judges

Much of the story of the progress blacks have made in the legal profession and as judges is found in the willingness of earlier appointees to reach back and take the hand of those coming behind. Many black lawyers can cite examples. For me, it was J. Maynard Dickerson, who embraced me when I was in my early teens. He was appointed by Governor Frank Lausche in 1951 to be the first black member of the Industrial Commission of Ohio. He opened doors for young black lawyers, accountants, and civil servants in Ohio. Judge Robert M. Duncan, who, as a bright young lawyer of color, went on to become the first black Supreme Court Justice in Ohio, was brought into state government by Dickerson. He later was appointed as U.S. District Judge in the Southern District of Ohio by President Nixon. Judge Duncan acted boldly in other ways. One was to break with political tradition and, following the Dickerson example, appoint the first black U.S. bankruptcy judge in Ohio.

Prior to 1984, federal district court judges had the power to appoint bankruptcy judges. However, in the Northern District of Ohio, judges had not appointed any black judges to the bankruptcy court. A small group of lawyers exercised near complete control of court appointments. Blacks were seldom a part of that specialized phase of the law practice. Bankruptcy judges were generally selected from a pool of white lawyers who maintained a type of mysticism over this type of law practice. And from among those lawyers, bankruptcy judgeships were passed around by district court judges as favors to former law clerks, law partners, and friends who specialized in bankruptcy law. Once I broke into this tight circle, I heard judges speak about whose turn it was to make the next appointment. One of the advantages of admitting blacks to the inner sanctum of the judiciary was that it allowed us to see and hear what we had not seen or heard before.

With district court judges having appointing power until 1984, when Congress shifted this responsibility to the Courts of Appeal, we at the Sixth Circuit set about organizing a screening procedure that opened the process.

Ohio had vacancies that would soon need filling. I was one of several judges selected by my chief judge to undertake the screening responsibility. We decided that it was important to broaden the pool of candidates and developed a selection process that began with publicly advertising through media and various professional organizations for candidates who wished to be considered for the various vacancies.

The term of office for a bankruptcy judge was fourteen years and carried a salary of $66,000. I was told more than once that the fact that I, a person of racial minority, was sitting on the screening panels sent a signal of inclusiveness to lawyers beyond the traditional candidates. For instance, in November 1984, twenty-seven candidates from all over the circuit applied for the bankruptcy seat in Youngstown, to replace retired Judge Joseph Molitoris, who had been appointed by Judge Battisti. Others on the initial selection panel were Judge Boyce F. Martin Jr. of Kentucky, Judge Harry Wellford of Tennessee, and Judge Ralph Guy Jr. of Michigan. The panel conducted interviews with a broad array of candidates before recommending five names to the eleven-member Court of Appeals Circuit Council. The council then recommended three names to the court of appeals, who then made the final selection. For this vacancy, it ultimately chose William Bodoh, who was a partner in one of Youngstown's largest firms and served through 2003. This selection process, still in operation, resulted in as many as three lawyers of color serving at the same time on bankruptcy courts in Ohio. The candidates selected were of a quality that met with the enthusiastic approval of the bar.

I have special appreciation for the role that court of appeals judges had in picking bankruptcy court judges. In the past few years the nation has been experiencing the worst economic downturn, indeed recession, in at least three decades. Loss of jobs and home foreclosures hit people who had never previously experienced such hard times. The importance of bankruptcy courts has come to the fore, and the diversity of the judges who sit on those courts has added a needed perspective.

My Two-Ness

My nomination by President Carter to be a judge, and confirmation by the Senate, was the pinnacle of a legal career that began with night law school. I began the practice of law at a time when the profession practiced its own form of racial apartheid. However, on entering the judiciary, I was welcomed by colleagues with a genuineness I treasure to this day. Those members of the profession and the public with whom I associated were also highly respectful. Still I am forever mindful of what Dr. W.E.B. Du Bois wrote in *The Souls of Black Folk* in 1903. He described the "double consciousness" that blacks feel. He said, "One ever feels his two-ness—an American, a Negro; two souls, two thoughts, two unreconciled strivings; two warring ideals in one dark body, whose dogged strength alone keeps it from being torn asunder."[6]

Two friends and colleagues, the late Third Circuit Judge A. Leon Higginbotham Jr. and Judge Damon J. Keith, considered ourselves brothers in the judicial bond, and we often compared notes. We were amused by the similarities of our experiences when we stepped outside the circle of those who knew us as judges. Then we were just black people who were expected to perform service chores that white people had come to expect of blacks. That included parking cars for guests at hotels, retrieving them, being accused of parking in spaces reserved for judges, or being asked to serve up a glass of wine in restaurants, especially if we were attired in black tie. We were aware of how deeply ingrained are the roles that people are expected to play depending on the color of their skin. Rather than reacting in anger, we, at times, tried to use such occasions as a teaching opportunity.

I used these experiences to sensitize my white colleagues to the many forms that racism takes—some subtle and some overt—so that they could better deal with the issues of race that come before them. It is about more than calling people the so-called *N* word. The subtle forms can be just as searing and revealing.

An event that shall ever remain with me involved the chief justice of the United States at the time, Warren E. Burger. I was attending a seminar for appellate judges conducted annually at the New York University School of Law. On the final day of each seminar, the chief justice was scheduled to offer closing remarks. Chief Justice Burger was discussing a case involving a welfare mother who lived in public housing in Washington, D.C. As he explained, a regulation prohibited occupancy by any but a single family. It was a rule more often breached than observed. Chief Justice Burger, with a twist of the wrist and a slight movement of his head, said, after he identified the occupant as a black woman, "It was one of those situations, only too common in public housing . . . you know . . . a man in the house but no man in the house." The justice grinned. I was offended. Sitting amid those mostly white judges, I felt my "two-ness." A few judges let go with a nervous chuckle, but to the credit of most, their muteness was an indication of disapproval, if not embarrassment. At the end of the session, a justice of the Alabama Supreme Court sought me out to report his embarrassment and apologize for the chief justice. At dinner that evening, a number of judges expressed their displeasure at the poor taste shown. After mulling it over for several days, I wrote to Dean Robert McKay and suggested that the law school reconsider inviting the chief justice to future seminars, given the diversity that had now come to the federal courts. There was a time when that type of story would have been a big hit. With the diversity of the federal bench, that was no longer the case—a reality that had not yet caught up with Chief Justice Burger.

10

Continuing the Struggle, on the Bench

Becoming a judge offered opportunities to see judicial decision-making not available to me as a lawyer. In many respects I was truly impressed with the intellectual thoroughness with which some of my colleagues approached this responsibility. Their openness and desire to get it right was in keeping with what I thought was requisite in the search for truth. I wish I could say that those qualities were universal. Because they were not, faith in the integrity of the judiciary was sometimes lacking. That was evident in the way many judges went along with policies, without objection, that they knew were incompatible with the oath they took. Nowhere was this more apparent than in drug-sentencing policies and the way the death penalty was often administered.

Prior to my becoming a judge, when I was working in New York as NAACP general counsel in 1973, I noted Governor Nelson Rockefeller's effort to deal with the street-drug problem by imposing harsh mandatory prison sentences. New York's lead was followed by other states disturbed by the increase in crime rates resulting from the introduction of crack. It was then that Congress followed a few years later by enacting the Anti-Drug Act of 1986, which gave rise to the U.S. Sentencing Commission. One of the commission's functions was to eliminate disparities in sentencing by drafting a set of guidelines. The practical effect of this congressional action was to breach the wall of independence that surrounds the judiciary. This breach undermined the ability of judges to tailor punishment to fit the crime and the criminals, particularly with respect to the 100-to-1 sentencing disparity between powder and crack cocaine.

Crack cocaine was a drug largely used in poorer neighborhoods. Those charged with possession and use of 5 grams faced a five-year mandatory prison term, which contrasted with those charged with possession of powder cocaine being required to have 500 grams before being subjected to that same period of incarceration. That led to gross disparity in imprisonment between blacks and whites. In the late 1980s, after a number of judges and others began to decry this shameful disparity, Congress directed the Sentencing Commission to study the situation and make recommendations. Following that congressional mandate, the absurdity of the crack/powder disparity became demonstrable to the commission. Yet Congress rejected the commission's recommendation to equalize the punishment. It took the U.S. Supreme Court to make clear to wavering judges that the disparity between crack and powder cocaine cases need not be. This partial restoration of the judges' independence was a victory for the few of us in the federal judiciary who kept insisting that Congress had crossed the constitutional line.

I took every opportunity through written dissents and in court conferences to urge my judicial colleagues, Congress, and the Sentencing Commission to abate the negative effects that the "War on Drugs" was having on minorities, particularly blacks.

My dissents on the subject were consistent as well as insistent. I was particularly distressed by judges' refusal to speak what they knew to be the truth—namely that this so-called war was corrupting the criminal justice system. I sought to alert my judicial colleagues that, too often, racism was involved in the charging and sentencing rules though often in seeming disguise. For instance, I wrote in dissent in *U.S. v. Gaines*, "Blind adherence to the rules that have been proven ineffective, meaningless, and unjust serves no purpose. . . . Our current crack cocaine sentencing scheme is unjust."[1]

Attorney General Eric Holder, acting on a cue from President Obama, recently took decisive steps to deal with some of the consequences of the evil that the crack/powder sentencing disparities have wrought. Bipartisan Senate action on the Smarter Sentencing Act seems to bear out Attorney General Holder's predictions that 2014 would "be a groundbreaking year." It would soften the harsh mandatory minimum sentences judges were required to impose, and make the new crack-cocaine provisions apply retroactively. As an inducement for inmates to participate in prison rehabilitation programs, their sentences could be reduced. The Sentencing Project hails these changes as "long overdue."

This has given me a sense of vindication for continuing to condemn the discriminatory policies. At times I felt my continual hammering at the "War on Drugs" was a lone voice. However, truth be known, there was a minority of judges on my court and in the other circuits who shared these views and resolved to keep the issue alive.

The Death Penalty

My early baptism in the criminal justice system exposed me to the callousness with which it can operate. If any component of that system—the police, the prosecutor, the jury, or the judge who imposes the punishment—is off-kilter, injustice will result. That has certainly been our history when the criminal justice system is called upon to deal with capital offenses. It has been clearly demonstrated that the system is flawed, resulting in unconstitutional executions.

When I joined the court in 1979, none of the three states in the Sixth Circuit that have the death penalty—Ohio, Kentucky, and Tennessee—had executed a prisoner since the early 1960s. Michigan does not have the death penalty. During the Supreme Court moratorium on executions, these Sixth Circuit states continued to sentence people to death. Appeals claiming constitutional errors worked their way through the state courts. The backlog of cases mounted, signaling that the time would eventually come when the state convictions would lead to the invocation of the Great Writ—a legal document issued to bring a person before a court or judge in order to release that person from unlawful restraint or detention. A person who claims to be wrongfully detained by authorities and wishes to be released from such wrongful detention, may resort, by seeking to invoke the writ of habeas corpus, often referred to as the Great Writ or the All Writs statute, and seek to have a federal judge review the basis of such detention. If it is found that such detention is in violation of the person's constitutional rights, a judge may order the authorities to show cause why the person should not be freed. As appellate judges we reviewed the manner in which state and/or federal judges exercise the power to either release or continue the detention of a citizen. After a person has been convicted in state court, and has exhausted his or her rights of appeal under state law, resort is made to federal courts under the writ of habeas corpus. When it appeared that the Supreme Court would remove obstacles to the various states resuming executions, the federal court began to prepare for an onslaught of habeas corpus petitions.

John W. Byrd Jr.

The case of John W. Byrd Jr. stands out as the clearest example of a misapplication of the death penalty that came before me.

John W. Byrd Jr. appealed an order of the U.S. District Court for the Southern District of Ohio that denied his petition for a writ of habeas corpus, and for a stay of his scheduled September 12, 2001, execution pending an appeal. I was a member of the three-judge panel to whom the case was assigned. Byrd had been convicted and sentenced to death eighteen years earlier, in 1983, for the fatal stabbing of a convenience store clerk, Monte Tewksbury, in Cincinnati, Ohio. The prosecution opposed the Byrd motion on the grounds that it was barred by a new federal statute—Antiterrorism and Effective Death Penalty Act of 1996 (AEDPA), which blocked a person in state custody from filing a second or successive petition for a writ of habeas corpus. There was a serious question, in my mind, as to whether this was, in fact, a second or successive petition, due to the failure of state courts to have reviewed all of Byrd's constitutional claims. Particularly egregious were the claims of prosecutorial misconduct and perjury by a key witness. Given that this was a death penalty case, I took the position that the least an appellate court should do was to order a remand for a searching hearing into the contested facts.

Though Byrd was not to me a sympathetic figure, he was nevertheless entitled to the protection of the Constitution. The challenge that I posed led one of my colleagues to accuse me of, among other things, "lying" in an effort to delay Byrd's execution. The intemperateness of his language so angered my three black colleagues— Judge Damon J. Keith, Judge R. Guy Cole, and Judge Eric Clay—that they fired off a letter to Chief Judge Boyce Martin Jr. condemning the charges and demanding that he seek an apology from him. Of course, none was forthcoming.

One of the judges who favored execution accused those of us on the court who were urging that the stay of execution be granted of being opposed to the death penalty per se, rather than dealing with the law and facts of this particular case. That charge was red meat to editorial writers of the *Cincinnati Enquirer* and *Cincinnati Post*. The unfortunate reality was that many reporters who wrote about the *Byrd* case were taking what was spoon-fed to them by prosecutors. They paid little or no heed to the trial record that detailed prosecutorial misdeeds and judicial errors. They continued to mislead their readers in this case, for instance, by proclaiming that seventy judges had reviewed the case. A troubling fact was that many of the various reviews, state and federal, were mere rubber stamps that refused to take into account errors in the trial record or what the Constitution required of them. Where an error was blatant, it was minimized by reviewing courts as not being important, and harmless. For that to happen in a death penalty case is reprehensible. I felt it my duty, under oath, to do all I could to point out how constitutional errors that could result in death were *not* harmless.

The *Byrd* case became, as the *Cincinnati Post* wrote, "a lightning rod in Ohio's battle over capital punishment." It presented the type of confrontation that the Sixth Circuit sought to avoid when it decided to establish a death penalty task force in Ohio, Tennessee, and Kentucky—the states in which 175 capital punishment cases were pending.

The *Byrd* case was in the state courts of Ohio and the federal court for nearly twenty years. Many states with the death penalty experienced similar litigation time spans. In the *Byrd* case, some of the delay was caused by the U.S. Supreme Court while it considered various issues involving the constitutionality of the death penalty. Once Byrd sought to invoke the jurisdiction of the federal court by means of a "second" petition for the writ of habeas corpus, issues of prosecutorial misconduct were barred. Unfortunately, the government and the media placed the blame for the delay on the parties seeking relief. The drumbeat from the Hamilton County prosecutors and fires constantly stoked by the local media kept the emotional state of the murder victim's family before the public. Those reports of the desire of the victim's family for closure by executing Byrd obscured portions of the record that Byrd's trial had been unfair and that evidence of his guilt was in question.

Many of my colleagues who so stubbornly resisted the efforts of John Byrd and other death penalty defendants to obtain habeas corpus relief came to the court after passing the Reagan administration litmus test on states' rights. Nowhere was their fealty to states' rights more clearly manifested than in their efforts to diminish the utility of the Great Writ. The panel members I served with on the *Byrd* case gave an unwarranted degree of deference to decisions of the Hamilton County judges, to the extent that the abuses of Byrd's constitutional rights went unexamined, as did the prosecutorial misconduct of the prosecutor's office.

I became a federal appellate judge after a career that included representing pro bono, impecunious defendants, serving as a federal prosecutor, and being a national civil rights lawyer. That body of experience gave me insights into the working of the criminal justice system from different perspectives. Thus, the claims of John Byrd and others about the corner-cutting, prosecutorial misconduct, and judicial errors did not strike me as unusual or far-fetched.

In retrospect, this was a case where judges' life experiences should have come into play. One of the reasons that President Carter created Judicial Selection Commissions was to bring different perspectives to the bench. Those who saw the issues as I was raising them were Carter-Clinton appointees. But many of my judicial colleagues with whom I was having strong differences on this case were appointed through a selection process that replaced President Carter's.

Judge Gilbert Merritt of Nashville, who had served as U.S. attorney in the Middle District of Tennessee, had a keen insight into the problems associated with habeas corpus. He expressed concern over what Congress might do with pending legislation designed to place a limit on the number of times a death-penalty prisoner could seek federal relief through the writ of habeas corpus. As a former U.S. attorney, and constitutional scholar, Merritt had great respect for protections the document provides to our citizens. He had an occasion to weigh in on the *Byrd* case when I circulated a draft of my dissenting opinion to the full or en banc court. In agreement with my dissent, Judge Merritt wrote, "I concur in your dissent. The jury should have known about the informant's motive to lie." Another colleague, Judge R. Guy Cole, wrote, "Well said. I concur." Other concurrences came from Chief Judge Boyce Martin, Judge Eric Clay, and Judge Martha Daugherty. Bearing in mind that there could be such a division of judges in a case involving the death penalty, and one of the issues goes directly to the conduct of the Hamilton County prosecutor, it certainly calls into question whether an execution should take place.

Though Byrd was executed on February 19, 2002, I remain convinced that he was not guilty of the death-qualifying act of stabbing Monte Tewksbury. A majority of my Sixth Circuit colleagues either saw it differently or just grew weary of the case.

That the panel majority was in error was clear to me, and the least that should be done by the Sixth Circuit was to thoroughly review the record in order to test the conduct of the prosecutor and the state. This was not a burglary or armed robbery case that carried a number of years' imprisonment. It was a death penalty case. I was convinced that the risk of executing a person wrongfully must be avoided at all cost.

To forestall an injustice, I requested Chief Judge Boyce Martin Jr. to poll the judges "in active service," an act permitted by court rules and done in countless situations when the court is not in session. The chief judge directed the clerk of court to conduct the poll, which is also customary. Upon receiving the result of the poll, the clerk was directed to enter an order, October 9, 2001, which stated:

> A majority of the judges in regular active service have voted that the court remand this matter for the development of a factual record sufficient to permit sua sponte consideration of a request for leave to file a second petition for a writ of habeas corpus. The jurisdictional basis for a rehearing sua sponte is *Triestman v. United States*, 124 F. 3rd 361 (2nd Cir. 1997); *Krimmel v. Hopkins*, 56 F. 3rd 873, 874 (8th Cir) 1995.[2]

Upset by this stay order, the Ohio attorney general, at the urging of the Hamilton County prosecutors, raced off to the U.S. Supreme Court in search of the justice assigned to the Sixth Circuit, Justice Stevens, seeking to overturn the stay order. That was the fateful day—September 11, 2001—when 2,993 people were killed. Because Washington itself was under siege, all governmental activity was halted, including regular activities of the U.S. Supreme Court. In any event, the U.S. Supreme Court apparently did not regard a court order extending the life of a defendant by a few days to warrant its intervention.

The Sixth Circuit had not reviewed the overbearing behavior of the Hamilton County prosecutor. Prosecutors, through an act of perjury, shielded key evidence from the jury. The informant was key to the prosecution's case and the record clearly established that he had perjured himself.

An array of Hamilton County judges winked at the prosecutor's misconduct, which was reason enough for a federal court in this habeas corpus proceeding to resist blinking. What the Hamilton County prosecutor's office was getting away with in this case was not unusual for them. In fact, Ohio Supreme Court Chief Justice Thomas Moyer, and former Justice Andrew Douglas had asked, in another case, "How do we stop prosecutors from engaging in conduct that we tell them time and time again is improper?" Justice Douglas went on to wonder aloud, as reported in a July 26, 2000, *Cincinnati Enquirer* story by its Columbus Bureau reporter, Spencer Hunt, "whether Hamilton County Prosecutor's office has a different definition of the law prosecutors must follow to argue criminal cases." At issue in the case before the Ohio Supreme Court were statements made by the prosecutor in argument to the Hamilton County jury. That is exactly one of the issues complained of in the *Byrd* case. It should be noted that when that court entertained Byrd's appeal, the vote was 4 to 3. I submit that a vote that close in a death penalty case should give pause to any federal court considering a habeas corpus petition. A sobering fact is that by 2001, of the 202 men on Ohio's death row, 48 were from Hamilton County alone.

As I earlier noted, John Byrd had a sordid record and deserved to be incarcerated, but not executed. This is so because in the oath I took I promised not to be a "respecter of persons" in applying the law. The prosecutors relied upon and continued to shield from judicial scrutiny evidence of an exculpatory nature that could have, as my dissenting colleagues agreed, been persuasive with a jury. Tragically, in my view, a number of Hamilton County judges allowed them to get away with it. When the case reached the federal court under a petition that sought a writ of habeas corpus, the questionable technicality of a second or successive petition provided a shield behind which, ultimately, I fear, the majority of the Sixth Circuit judges hid. That shield was contained in a statute later enacted that dealt with terrorism—thus the name Antiterrorism and Effective Death Penalty Act. It had the effect, as demonstrated by the *Byrd* case and others, of denying death row inmates an opportunity to prove their innocence or that a violation of their constitutional rights occurred.

The prosecution's rush to the U.S. Supreme Court on the ill-fated September 11, 2001, seeking an order overturning the delay of the execution ordered by Chief Judge Boyce Martin Jr. and a majority of the court was nothing short of shameful political hucksterism. Tragically, the stay order entered on September 10, 2001, was lifted on January 7, 2002, and the execution order issued. I salute those colleagues who joined with me in efforts to obtain for Byrd an opportunity to develop the record. I wrote in my revised dissent of February 17, 2002, that a "thorough development of the evidentiary record" is essential "when a defendant faces the death penalty." I condemned the ineffectual way in which the magistrate judge handled the subsequent factual hearing because it did not afford Byrd a fair opportunity to expose the state's errors.

In my conclusion, I wrote:

> As a Federal appellate judge, I have tried, in keeping with my oath, to uphold the Constitution of the United States, to prevent the taking of the life of a not-decent man, but one who, with all of his flaws, was, nevertheless, entitled to all of the rights guaranteed by the Constitution. There was a breakdown in this case. My prediction is that history will look back on the handling of this prosecution by the State of Ohio, and the default of the judiciary, as a travesty of justice.[3]

Those who followed the news reports on the late stages of the *Byrd* case and, in particular, his efforts to activate the habeas corpus powers of the Sixth Circuit Court of Appeals, may wonder why so much passion was sparked among judges of the court. The prosecution kept arguing—and the media picked it up—that more than seventy judges had reviewed the case over a period of eighteen years. In my opinion, the number of judges was not the issue; rather it was the ignoring of constitutional errors.

The various ways in which the judges erred were, among other things, ignoring prosecutorial misconduct at a key stage of the proceeding. The prosecutor did not disclose that a "star witness," described as a "snitch," upon whom the prosecution was relying, was facing a possible fifteen-year prison sentence if his hearing before the parole board was unsuccessful. Knowing that, the prosecutor remained mute when that witness, Ronald Armstead, testified falsely, "I don't have no more cases pending." After the false and misleading testimony, the prosecutor, in a letter to the parole board, dropped his strong objection to Mr. Armstead receiving favorable treatment by the board, with an early parole.

In addition, the prosecutor did what the law does not permit, but which the judge allowed: "vouch" for the truthfulness of a prosecution witness. I argued that such conduct was "egregious, astonishing and inexcusable" and should have been stricken by the judge with instructions that it be disregarded. The judge's failure to do that constituted reversible error.

During a hearing before the appellate panel on which I sat, I cited the inappropriate vouching of the prosecutor. It was picked up by acclaimed *Plain Dealer* reporter Bill Sloat. He wrote in the March 12, 1998, edition:

Judge Nathaniel R. Jones of Youngstown said [John] Byrd . . . in the midst of a final challenge to his death sentence, had an unfair trial in 1983 because of unethical conduct by Hamilton County prosecutors. During an unusually combative session in the 6th Circuit U.S. Court of Appeals, Jones said Byrd's jurors had been told by prosecutors that Byrd was responsible for the crime even though such testimony was supposed to come only from sworn witnesses.

He's testifying, Jones said of one prosecutor as he read from the 1,200 page trial transcript that sat in a binder on the bench in front of him.

"That's error," Jones said. "And that's reversible error." . . .

Judges Alice M. Batchelder of Medina and Richard F. Suhrhein-rich of Michigan did not openly express similar outrage about the conduct of Byrd's trial.

But Jones said plenty and all but accused the State of paroling a convict who agreed to testify against Byrd, named Ronald Armstead.

Unlike Jones, who repeatedly cited problems in the case as he pored over the record, his colleagues serving beside him . . . kept their opinions to themselves.

I am now at the point of conceding the futility of believing that the state is capable of conducting a fair trial when the death penalty is at issue.

And I am not alone.

Three former colleagues, who sit on two different circuit courts, have voiced the same views as I did in the *Byrd* case. Judge William A. Fletcher of the Ninth Circuit Court of Appeals in San Francisco; an Eleventh Circuit colleague, Judge Rosemary Barkett of Florida; and Judge Stephen Reinhardt, also of the Ninth Circuit, have written forceful dissents in death penalty cases.

Judge Fletcher flatly warned, "The State of California may be about to execute an innocent man."[4] In the case of *Cooper v. Brown*, Judge Fletcher accused the police and prosecutors of withholding and tampering with evidence for decades and charged the district court with having sabotaged the case.

Judge Barkett, in April 2009, deplored the "thicket of procedural brambles" that hobble federal judges. She was dissenting from a decision by a majority of her Eleventh Circuit decision in which seven of nine witnesses in the high-profile Georgia murder case of Troy Davis recanted their trial testimony. As I was complaining in my dissent in the *Byrd* case, there were recantations and affidavits, which led Judge Barkett to argue that it would be "unconscionable and unconstitutional" to execute him without considering the new evidence. Davis, whose case was stayed by the Supreme Court, was executed on September 21, 2011.

Judge Reinhardt, also a Carter appointee, challenged the constitutionality of Andrew C. Crater's conviction of a robbery and shooting in Sacramento, California. In a 2007 opinion, Judge Reinhardt called the majority opinion a "mockery of the careful boundaries between Congress and the courts that our Constitution's framers believed so essential to the prevention of tyranny."[5]

The reluctance of the public to seriously face the fact that if it is going to insist upon the death penalty being one of its sanctions, as is the case in Ohio, then it has to insist that judges be true to their constitutional oath and also insist that trials be fair. Legislators have to desist from enacting rules and procedures that hobble the search for truth and provide defendants with resources that will permit them to prepare adequate defenses. I do not think that is going to happen. An example to bolster this disbelief was the case of a man named Cameron Todd Willingham being executed for the arson deaths of his children in Texas only to have it revealed in the *New Yorker* five years after his death that he was innocent of the crime.[6]

How much longer our legal system will try to reconcile what has become increasingly impossible to reconcile, only time will tell. A legal system that boasts of guarantees of due process of law to those who are brought within it while blinking at blatant contradictions in order to gain or affirm convictions in death penalty cases does violence to our Constitution. If our Constitution cannot withstand the stresses applied to it by gross and obnoxious social misbehavior, it will not long survive, nor will it deserve to.

Reducing Error in Death Cases; The Road Not Taken

One of the foremost leaders in the effort to improve the skills of lawyers to handle death-penalty cases at both the trial and habeas corpus stages was Henry A. Martin of Nashville, Tennessee. When he saw events unfolding in the *Byrd* case, Martin set out his lament in an April 11, 2000, personal letter to me. He wrote:

I saw the order in *Byrd v. Collins*, and read the dissent. The first two paragraphs renewed my hope that someday a majority of judges, state as well as federal, will find in our Constitution the strength and enduring grace of your eloquent words. . . .

P.S. I have made a copy of the first page of your dissent to keep handy for moments of despair.

The U.S. Judicial Conference eventually established task forces to meet the reintroduction of the death penalty. The aim was to minimize those things that were aggravating the naked abuses that gave rise to more and more people resorting to the Great Writ. I eagerly grasped the challenge presented to me as a federal appellate judge who would eventually be called upon to deal with the constitutional failures common in the states' prosecution of death-penalty cases, particularly by elected prosecutors who had a tendency to play to the gallery. The more grievous the act, the greater the likelihood there was of ambitious prosecutors seeking the notoriety that would enhance their chances of reelection and a later move up the ladder to judgeships or higher elective office. With enthusiasm I accepted the invitation of Chief Judge Pierce Lively to chair the Sixth Circuit's efforts to implement the innovative approach. Even after this effort foundered when Congress defunded it, I point out that Chief Judge Lively's successor urged me to monitor the steps that were being taken in Congress on the habeas corpus front. The ebbing and flowing that occurred in Congress resulted in a horrendous piece of legislation that so hobbled the use of the Great Writ that the recriminations that ensued in the Byrd case were, in my judgment, inevitable, but from which I would not shrink.

The Death Penalty Task Forces

The U.S. Judicial Conference, made up of the chief judges from each of the circuit courts, presided over by then Chief Justice of the United States William Rehnquist, urged Congress to enact the Criminal Justice Act. The aim was to ensure proper representation for each person accused of a death penalty crime. This request emanated from the Supreme Court's concern over the high number of constitutional errors found in death penalty cases. Under the act, Congress and the various states were to set up programs to reduce mistakes in death penalty cases.

Funds were appropriated to ensure that courts in each state and federal circuit could train a sufficient number of lawyers to become proficient in handling the constitutional issues that arise in capital punishment cases. As chair, my responsibility was to coordinate Sixth Circuit efforts to establish task forces and resource centers in the three Sixth Circuit states that had the death penalty. Judges, prosecutors, defense lawyers, the bar association, and civil rights representatives would all be involved. The task forces were charged with identifying and recommending judges and lawyers to take the lead in establishing death penalty resource centers.

Two realities added considerable urgency to these efforts. The first was that the number of people on death row in Ohio, Kentucky, and Tennessee was continuing to grow. The second reality was what was happening on the congressional front, sparked by forces upset by the number of times the habeas corpus relief was sought. The anticipated surge of habeas corpus petitions in the federal courts was set to coincide with the expansion of victim impact testimony—offered to a judge or jury by relatives of the victims of crimes that describe the pain and suffering resulting from the conduct of the accused—at sentencing as a factor in political campaigns of judges and prosecutors. Such highly emotional impact testimony influenced prosecutors to oppose habeas petitions and led elected judges to often overlook prosecutorial misconduct and constitutional errors. Surviving family members of capital-crimes victims seek closure—which to them often means enforcing the death penalty—once a conviction is obtained, with little regard for constitutional niceties. Pending in the Congress were proposals to limit the number of habeas corpus petitions a state prisoner could file. A study had earlier been launched by the American Bar Association. It was a task force on death penalty habeas corpus that included federal judges, state court judges, and practicing lawyers. Its report had not yet been issued. While the all-powerful Judge

Powell Committee held no hearings and took no testimony before completing its report, the ABA task force held public hearings in three cities over a period of six days, and heard from eighty-two witnesses before preparing its four-hundred-page report.

Unfortunately, though efforts were made to have Chief Justice Rehnquist delay the submission of the Powell report to Congress until the ABA report was completed, he sent it to Congress anyway in September 1989. Some suggest that Rehnquist may have harbored deep reservations over the multiple use of the writ. The Powell report was added to legislation introduced by Senator Strom Thurmond, virtually verbatim. A bill introduced by Senator Joseph Biden was more nuanced, though both drastically reduced the opportunities available to condemned prisoners to seek relief from their convictions because of constitutional errors.

The Powell report and legislation Joe Biden introduced both invited the states to set up systems for providing competent counsel to capital defendants in some or all state court proceedings. In return, they set strict time limits for commencing a federal habeas corpus proceeding. The justification for this restriction was the expectation that by virtue of the resource centers, a cadre of well-trained defense counsel and trial judges would be better prepared to handle death penalty cases. This being so, the trials would present fewer constitutional errors and it would be much easier for these better-trained lawyers to package the errors into a single habeas corpus petition. In addition, the resource centers would assist the accused and their lawyers in discovery of facts, and investigate cases more thoroughly. As the theory went, requiring defendants to present all of their constitutional claims in a single petition would speed up the process and ensure that each case was handled with greater fairness. The *Byrd* case is a tragic example of the failure of this system and the fallacy of those assumptions. It was clear that without proper funding, the expectations of the proponents of limited habeas corpus petitions would never be realized and the abuses would continue. It was foreseeable that the funding for the resource centers would be snatched by Congress at the first high-profile controversial case. And that is exactly what happened.

In an effort to alert the public to the problem of the impending avalanche of habeas corpus petitions in 1987 and the efforts of the federal courts to address that problem, I met with a reporter for the Associated Press. In the December 11, 1998, interview I said, "That hysterical demand for the death penalty cannot be allowed to penetrate the threshold of a courtroom door. We are going to have to start facing these death penalties in the very near future. The question of the death penalty stands alone, for death is a finality. There is no appeal from death. In other cases, there is an appeal and compensation for legal wrongs, but not from death."

11

Beyond the United States

The cumulative experience of my participation in the domestic struggle for civil rights apparently had the effect of preparing me in countless unanticipated ways to engage in the international activities in which I found myself. Being a black lawyer and judge gave me a degree of acceptability in various countries I visited. Dr. Du Bois wrote about the color line in Asia, Africa, and the islands of the seas populated by people struggling for their independence and freedom. I sought to carry messages of hope to people in these areas as well. This was particularly true of South Africa.

The legacy of the apartheid system continues to haunt me, as does the legacy of our American slavery. In 1985 when I enlisted in the campaign to end apartheid, I shared with South Africans lessons I learned as I attempted to answer the Call at home.

My first international sojourn was in the early 1960s, when I joined a tour sponsored by the Ohio Bar Association to Spain, the island of Majorca, and North Africa. That was an eye-opening experience, particularly North Africa because of the strategic role it had played in World War II. Later, during my years as NAACP general counsel, I made several law-related foreign trips. The first, in August 1973, took me to the World Peace Through Law conference in Côte d'Ivoire, West Africa. Lawyers and jurists from a wide-ranging group of nations participated. I was particularly thrilled to find myself in the company of recently retired Chief Justice Earl Warren and Justice Thurgood Marshall. Chief judges from various African countries were there in great numbers, accompanied by memorable pomp and circumstance. A close friend from Columbus, Ohio—the trailblazing Robert M. Duncan—was on hand. At the time he was a judge of the U.S. Court of Military Appeals, having recently been appointed by Secretary of Defense Melvin Laird, following service as the first Negro to serve as a justice of the Supreme Court of Ohio. Shortly thereafter, he was named to the U.S. District Court for the Southern District of Ohio by President Richard M. Nixon. Judge Duncan and I teamed up with three other lawyers, Hayward Burns of New York, Timothy Jenkins of Washington, and Richard Austin of Dayton, to travel to a number of villages in the country.

While still general counsel, I visited West Germany, Japan, the Philippines, and Thailand in connection with my investigation into complaints being made by black servicemen about the military justice system. The trip to Thailand took me very close to the fighting in Vietnam. One trip to West Germany was at the direction of the NAACP. Later trips were as co-chair of a Department of Defense task force that Secretary of Defense Laird organized to get a truer picture of the way the military justice system was operating.

After becoming a federal judge, I was privileged to visit such African countries as Nigeria, Egypt, Uganda, Tanzania, South Africa, and Namibia. Those trips were efforts to expand the rule of law and to assist those nations in upgrading their legal systems—a different role from the part I played while an NAACP lawyer. Each time I returned from overseas, my appreciation for the American legal system, with all of its flaws, and for America itself, was enhanced.

There was much about Namibia that I found unforgettable, but the camps that housed South African refugees were most upsetting. These UN camps were far from having the worst of the conditions under which refugees lived. I met with the UN high commissioner in charge of the refugee program, Martti Ahtisaari, a most impressive and compassionate Finn. He won the Nobel Peace Prize in 2008, and I can readily understand why. Yet I must reemphasize that all of this was extremely unnerving. The blue helmets of the UN personnel and the presence of the blue UN trucks were a welcome sight to the thousands of dispossessed human beings longing to return to their homes. Commissioner Ahtisaari brought a modest level of hope and reassurance to the refugees and observers such as me in seeing the United Nations at work on the ground, dealing with the basic human needs such as food, water, medicine, and shelter.

Yet over and above those basic needs, whether in Nigeria or Tanzania or Egypt, an effective, functioning legal system was the cry of people with whom I spoke. Such a system, however, seemed near impossible even to many who had the responsibility for operating it.

Some countries were more open and welcoming than others. In one country, the chief justice embraced my colleagues and me because he hoped we could lend the political support he needed to gain additional resources to beef up the administrative capacity of the courts. As a sitting judge, my views were received with considerable enthusiasm. This chief justice, to demonstrate the chaotic state of court administration, led me to an area where records were kept. He opened a closet door, inside of which files, from floor to ceiling, were each secured only with twine. These were files of active as well as inactive cases. I asked him why they were not in file cabinets and indexed for ready retrieval. He said that the court lacked clerical resources.

When we discussed the ability of courts to review proceedings of trials, he explained that there were no court stenographers. Trial judges kept their own notes. When parties sought to appeal a trial judge's ruling, both counselors had to prepare a joint recollection of the rulings, evidence, and claims of error, which were then submitted to the trial judges for "correction." Thus, the judge whose rulings were the subject of appeal controlled the issues that reached the reviewing court. Many of the judges were interested in exploring ways to cure what all agreed was an inherently unfair system.

My Introduction to South Africa

Two events caused me to begin to take serious note of South Africa. The first was in the early 1980s when I joined a group of American federal judges to attend a conference at Wingspread, Wisconsin, sponsored by the Johnson Foundation, the purpose of which was to discuss international human rights with judges from around the world. Several of the attendees were from the High Court of South Africa. I was particularly impressed, as we all were, with the chief judge of the South Africa High Court of Durban, the Honorable John Milne. But soon after it was over, the events of that conference receded into deeper recesses of my mind because South Africa was so far away, and we had matters to attend to in the United States.

My next awakening to South African apartheid was in 1983, when my wife, Lillian, and I accepted an invitation to attend an international human rights conference at Aspen, Colorado. A special guest presenter was a young black South African lawyer named Ernest Dikgang Moseneke. His concluding message on our final night at Aspen reached the core of everyone there. It was his discussion of what life was like under apartheid and what he personally underwent that drew tears and had everyone frozen in place.

Moseneke was born in a township near Pretoria in 1947. His father was an educator. Because of his hatred of apartheid, young Moseneke spoke out against the system and was subsequently arrested, tried, and convicted for being a threat to the government. He was fifteen years old at the time of his conviction and sentenced to Robben Island. During this same period thousands of people were arrested and sentenced, including Nelson Mandela, whose trial and conviction at Rivonia has become one of the classic cases studied by human rights scholars. Eighteen people were tried along with Moseneke, for whom counsel was denied when five different advocates, also known as trial lawyers, refused to take his case, much the same way Southern white lawyers in the United States refused to represent black civil rights activists. That made it necessary for fifteen-year-old Moseneke to provide his own defense, including conducting his own cross-examination. The trial took three months. The fact that this youngster did such an outstanding job of cross-examining drew a negative conclusion from the judge, who stated: "It shows you knew clearly what you were doing. I must attribute full mens rea [criminal intent] to you. I find you guilty of having conspired to try and overthrow the state by violence. Ten years' imprisonment."[1]

While serving his sentence, Moseneke finished high school and then began working on his college credits from the University of South Africa. Our Aspen meeting was the beginning of a long and special friendship.

South Africa

I readily accepted when the Lawyers' Committee for Civil Rights Under Law (LCCR), asked me, in 1985, to go to South Africa as a trial observer. The LCCR had been founded to provide counsel for civil rights workers jailed in the South. The challenges confronting the NAACP as I took over the responsibilities of general counsel taxed the small staff of lawyers I was able to assemble. The Lawyers' Committee never failed to answer a call for help. (Led by former Justice Department lawyers Robert Murphy, J. Harold Flannery, and David Tatel, the LCCR provided a powerful resource of legal talent. Later, William Robinson, formerly of the NAACP Legal Defense Fund, became the executive director. In him I found a first-rate civil rights lawyer who was always ready to link the resources of the LCCR with those of the NAACP. An instance of the cooperative relationship between the LCCR and the NAACP was when the former came to the aid of the NAACP in the Mississippi boycott case *NAACP v. Claiborne Hardware Co.* In fact, it was the legal prowess of David Tatel before a federal judge in Oxford, Mississippi, that virtually pulled NAACP back from near extinction after a court had imposed a judgment of more than a million dollars against us.) The LCCR had a South African unit devoted to the issues of apartheid that was headed by the Yale-educated Gay McDougall. She led efforts to mobilize resources to support lawyers within South Africa who were challenging the apartheid system, as well as groups applying pressure on the government through economic boycotts.

When Bill Robinson called to see if I would be willing to go to South Africa and serve as an international observer at a trial of seventeen blacks charged with treason and terrorism, he said former Supreme Court Justice Arthur Goldberg would be a fellow observer. After learning more about the role of international trial observers, I satisfied myself that my participation in such an undertaking would not conflict with my judicial obligations. After advising Bill Robinson of my acceptance, and learning more about the time commitment involved, I was provided with copies of the indictment, which included the statement of overt acts each of the defendants was alleged to have committed. On reviewing these papers, any remaining elements of doubt about the propriety of my participation evaporated.

As I'd earlier pondered whether to agree to participate, my thinking was formed, to some extent, by my American stereotypes of what a terrorist was, and what constituted treason. These stereotypes included mental images of marauders who, with bombs and weapons, under cover of darkness, inflicted violence on innocent women and children. Upon reading the indictment and the acts of so-called terrorism described in the document, my eyes were opened to how the repressive regime of apartheid was operating. The overt acts with which these defendants were criminally charged found protection in the First and Fourth Amendment of the U.S. Constitution. Free speech, the right to peaceable assembly, protection from warrantless search, and the right to be free of torture and self-incrimination were being violated and repressed by the South

African government. The "crime" committed by these defendants was protesting against those incursions into their civil and human rights.

In preparing for the trip, my attention became more acutely focused on news accounts of the escalating violence in South Africa. The economic boycott campaign found more companies, churches, colleges, and universities divesting their portfolios of South African stocks. And South Africa felt the economic squeeze from abroad. The tighter the squeeze, the more repressive the government's response with violence—police actions that used sjamboks or whips against the black population, detainment of the more vocal and active protesters, disappearances, and killings. Parliament continued to pass repressive measures in the interest of "national security." Often when lawyers, funded in part by the LCCR and various other international human rights organizations, succeeded with their emerging appeals in the High Court of South Africa, the result of which was government action being declared "ultra vires," parliament would amend the law to cure the defect.

With that background, and in particular his experience at the United Nations, Justice Goldberg was accustomed to traveling with the full portfolio of a U.S. ambassador. It so happened that, in this instance, having the portfolio of an ambassador of the U.S. government would have detracted from the credibility necessary to ensure the success of the trial observance mission. The Reagan administration had created and advanced the policy of "constructive engagement," which was rejected outright by opponents of apartheid, and viewed with suspicion by others as a life preserver to the South African government's apartheid system. For Justice Goldberg to travel throughout South Africa and sit in the international observer's box with the blanket of "constructive engagement" gathered around him would have tainted his conclusions as to the fairness or unfairness of the trial. When he was advised that it would be counterproductive to travel with the imprimatur of the U.S. government—State Department support, limousines, courtesy calls on the governmental officials—he withdrew. I had none of the entanglements that would affect my ability to assess and report on the conduct of the trial—free of the State Department's trappings.

Before I flew to South Africa, I went to Washington for a briefing by Gay McDougall and her staff of the LCCR's Southern Africa Project. Before I left my home for the airport, I saw on the early-morning news that a member of the defense team, Victoria Mxenge, had been murdered outside her Johannesburg home. That news was startling. My first question to McDougall when I arrived in Washington was, "Is the trial going forward on Monday?" She assured me that it was, saying, "I just talked with the team earlier this morning and they are set to proceed." When told that the slain lawyer had been scheduled to meet me upon my arrival in Durban, the unease I felt deepened.

The briefing continued, with a break for lunch that was attended by the chairman of the LCCR board, James Robertson. At lunch he expressed the gratitude of the Lawyers' Committee that I had agreed to undertake the assignment. He added words that caused me some angst: "Judge, be assured, we'll never forget you." I considered as ominous those words, along with a message that Theodore Berry, the distinguished civil rights lawyer of Cincinnati, as well as a special friend, left with my secretary when he called my court chambers earlier that morning. He had called to "wish me well." I wondered what these people knew that was eluding me.

The following day, passing through the international lounge at Kennedy Airport, an attendant with a thick accent checked my ticket and my credentials. He looked at them, and then at me, as he said, "Ah, yes, my good man. You're going to that very troubled country. Godspeed." That comment, added to those of Jim Robertson and Ted Berry, increased my paranoia.

My arrival in Johannesburg brought me in contact with immigration and security officials who appeared stern and unwelcoming. Gun-wielding officials were everywhere. My stay at the airport was brief, in that I was connecting onto a flight to Durban. A number of other nonwhite passengers boarded with me in Johannesburg for the relatively short flight to Durban. They were well dressed and carried briefcases. I took them to be professionals or academics. Upon landing in Durban I was met by a young black lawyer, Mzo Mlhladbla, and his wife. They helped me collect my luggage and upon departing the airport grounds, I noticed billboards and other signs one ordinarily sees at airports. I also noticed what once peppered the South—signs with racial designations. En route to the hotel that would house me for the duration of my stay, Mzo and his wife took me for a brief tour of Durban. I was impressed with the city's cleanliness and the beautiful beaches. Upon arrival at the Marihana Hotel I was ushered inside and checked in by hotel personnel who appeared to be Indian. It was a modern hotel, situated on Durban's beachfront, and reminded me of Miami Beach, with its high-rises.

Mzo and his wife accompanied me to my room with a beautiful view out over the beach. This was more than what I had expected. We had been engaging in spirited conversation since they picked me up at the airport. I was interested in learning as much as I could from my South African hosts. Since he was filling in for Victoria Mxenge in picking me up at the airport, I asked about her death. Mzo explained that it was the work of Inkatha, the political arm of Mangosuthu Buthelezi, whose group was a rival to the United Democratic Front. A year before, Mxenge's husband, Griffith, also a lawyer, had been killed in similar fashion, with machetes, by people believed to have been connected with Inkatha. Inkatha was considered to be a tool of the government.

At the conclusion of our visit in my eleventh-floor room, I accompanied Mzo and his wife to the elevator. When the door opened, a heavyset black man stepped off, bowed as he spoke to us, and moved toward a room. For some reason my eyes followed him as we said our good-byes. I noticed that the man feigned a knock on a door. Mzo departed, and I began the walk down the hall to my room when the man at the door called to me. I stopped. He asked, "What was the name of that chap?" I replied, as I resumed my walk, "Oh, he's a lawyer friend of mine." I was unpacking my bag when I heard a knock on my door. Not expecting any visitors at that hour of the night in Durban, and not knowing a soul in Durban, I froze, saying nothing. The knocking persisted. I then approached the door and asked who it was. "Mzo," came the response.

He asked if I was all right. Upon being assured that I was, he explained that his concern was aroused by the man who got off the elevator as they were leaving. "He's Inkatha," Mzo explained. He added, "I wondered why he was on this floor in this hotel at this hour of the night." He cautioned me to not venture out until morning. I assured him that I had no intention of doing so.

The next morning I met the legal team in the hotel dining room for breakfast prior to departing for Pietermaritzburg. The U.S. consul general, Martin Cheshes, appeared, and would escort me to the courthouse, where I would meet up with international trial observers from a number of other countries.

The defense team was interracial, and led by the brilliant senior advocate Ismael Mohamed, one of the few nonwhite senior advocates in South Africa. At breakfast, the lawyers expressed their appreciation that I, an American federal judge, would come such a distance to serve as a trial observer. It was during that initial visit with the legal team that I got a serious feel for the courage they brought to their mission. Taking on the entire apartheid government required a brand of courage I had not seen since American lawyers went south to challenge Jim Crow laws. In many respects, this was worse because they could not, as the lawyers in America did, retreat to sanctuaries in the North, or avail themselves of the protection of federal civil rights laws or a First Amendment and Sixth Amendment. Granted, in the United States, these guarantees were often ignored under states' rights; nevertheless, the wholesale detention of blacks and the absolute degradation of human rights I witnessed left me numb.

After posing for pictures with the defense team, we drove the forty miles to Pietermaritzburg, where the trial was to be held. When we drew within ten miles of the city, I began to notice armed police officers and military personnel with dogs standing along the highway. The closer we got, the more concentrated the police presence. I asked Cheshes whether this police presence was connected to the trial. He assured me that it was, which prompted him to pull over to the side and stop, go into the trunk of his car, and retrieve two American flags, which he placed on the front fenders in order to identify to one and all that we were Americans. During the trip he mentioned the difficulty the American embassy had getting my visa cleared. It was not until the previous Friday when I was being briefed in Washington, after the intervention with high South African officials in Pretoria by the trial judge, that the government relaxed its opposition to my entering the country.

The consul general mentioned, almost in passing, that his instructions were to deliver me to the judge's chambers in order that he could "renew our acquaintance." I assumed that Cheshes had misspoken, so I did not bother to correct him.

The crowds along the highway and the streets leading to the courthouse thickened. Rather than conduct the trial at the regular courthouse in the center of town, the trial was held in a courthouse used for special native trials, located within a compound, surrounded by high fencing and tight security. Outside the gate, the vice consul general, Leslie Bassett, and several hundred blacks had gathered, held at bay by a phalanx of armed police officers with dogs. As our car approached the gate, the American flags and the consul's ID signaled that we were to be admitted to the grounds of the courthouse. Outside the courthouse door were a large number of spectators waiting to enter the building. The judge's secretary escorted me through the catacombs of this seemingly ancient, one-courtroom building to the judge's chambers' reception room. In a moment, the door to his chambers opened and there he stood in a crimson-and-cream-colored judicial robe. And I recognized him: John Milne. We had met before at the seminar on international human rights at Wingspread, Wisconsin.

We greeted each other warmly and he explained that it was customary in South Africa to invite a visiting judge to share the bench. Given the nature of the trial and my mission, I respectfully declined, noting that there was a place for me in the observers' section of the courtroom. He said, "You are probably correct." However, he invited me to take "tea breaks" with him in his chambers. On only one or two occasions did I avail myself of his kind invitation, preferring to mingle with the other lawyers, the defendants, and the public to get their reactions as to what was transpiring in the courtroom. I did, however, accept Judge Milne's invitation to dinner at his home, where I met a number of the members of the bar and other judges. A friendship developed that led to Judge Milne and his lovely wife, Shirley, being guests in our home on one of their visits to the United States. Sadly, years later, in 1993, Judge Milne suffered a fatal heart attack while vacationing in London.

The objects of my mission as observer of the proceeding of *State v. Mawalal Ramgobin and 15 Others* of South Africa (Natal Provincial Division) were: to represent to those in authority and to the general public in South Africa the international interest in and concern about the trial; to encourage the conduct of a fair trial; to learn about the nature of the case against the accused, the conduct of the trial, and the legislation under which the accused would be tried; and to collect information more generally about the context in which the case arose. I was further to learn as much as possible about the effects on human rights of the imposition of state-of-emergency regulations, and to learn of the circumstances surrounding the allegations of "disappearances" and the operation of "death squads" or vigilante groups.

The trial proceedings began on August 5, 1985, with a hearing on the defendant's motion to quash the indictment. After three days of argument by the defense, the government asked for a recess to consult and reconsider its position in light of the defendant's arguments. Judge Milne granted the motion for recess.

Judge Milne, after hearing testimony in the treason case against these black defendants, ultimately dismissed it. I refer to them as "black" even though some were classified under South African apartheid law as "colored" and "Indians." They themselves preferred the "black" designation. Judge Milne dismissed the case relying upon a decision by my colleague, Judge Damon Keith that was affirmed by the U.S. Supreme Court. Judge Keith heard the case against the group known as the White Panthers. They were opposed to the Vietnam War—a war during which Attorney General

John Mitchell and President Richard Nixon maintained that they could conduct warrantless searches in matters involving national security. Judge Keith concluded that the policy of the Nixon administration that permitted warrantless searches in the name of national security ran afoul of the Fourth Amendment and could not stand. His ruling was appealed to the Sixth Circuit Court of Appeals, where it was affirmed. And when the government challenged it in the U.S. Supreme Court, Chief Justice Warren Burger, writing for the Supreme Court majority, upheld Judge Keith.

Judge Milne faced a similar issue in the treason trial, where agents of the state had secretly wiretapped defendants and in other ways gathered evidence without revealing their methods and means. The relentless defense lawyers argued that their ability to cross-examine witnesses and to test the evidence was impaired. The U.S. precedent with which Judge Milne was familiar required that the sources be revealed. His view was that unless the source of the evidence was revealed, it would not be admissible. The last thing the South African government was prepared to do was to identify the surreptitious means and agents employed to suppress antiapartheid activity. Without the use of that evidence, which included pictures, wiretaps, and informants, the government's case would collapse. As the judge stayed firm, the government dropped the case rather than reveal its sources.

Judge Milne's ability to rely upon international human rights law, to which South Africa became signatory, proved to be a powerful method for testing the various security measures that South Africa was enacting and the government, through regulation, was enforcing, at times with such brutal force.

During the recess in the trial, I was able to respond to a request from Gay McDougall that I represent LCCR at the funeral of Victoria Mxenge. It was being held in King William's Town on the Eastern Cape, a considerable distance from Pietermaritzburg and Durban. Driving me there were leaders of the Black Sash Party—Molly Blackburn; Diane Bishop; her husband, Brian; and Sithile Zondani of the East Cape Council of Churches. Black Sash was an organization of white women that was an avowed enemy of apartheid and had been targeted by the government and the Security Branch. Molly Blackburn, a mother of seven, was married to a Port Elizabeth physician. Diane's husband was a businessman who divested himself of those interests so that he could devote all of his time to antiapartheid activities.

Our trip began with an evening dinner at the spacious home of the Blackburns in Port Elizabeth. Upon departing the following morning, we drove along the Eastern Cape with Molly Blackburn making periodic stops at black townships to check on people with whom she was working. For the first time I became fully aware of the size of the black townships and realized that those located outside Durban were not an exception. Townships, as it became clear, were virtual plantations that housed blacks who were barred by law from living in the cities. They would work in the cities by day but were forced by law to return to the township at night. The most famous township I had heard about before arriving in South Africa was located outside Johannesburg—Soweto.

Fort Beaufort

En route to King William's Town to attend the funeral services scheduled on Sunday for Victoria Mxenge we stopped at Fort Beaufort. I had expressed a desire to visit a black township in a rural section of the Eastern Cape area. Unaware that this particular township, within the past day or two, had been included in the state-of-emergency order, we entered the area. While we were there, a hippo carrying armed personnel made several appearances. We were approached by the officer in charge. Surrounding our five-person party were about twenty to thirty heavily armed riot policemen. We were informed that a permit was required to enter the area and were escorted by armed officers in two police vehicles to the police station.

An officer arrived and proceeded to question each of the people in our party. Curiously, without our previously having identified ourselves in any way, the officer addressed Mrs. Blackburn and Mrs. Bishop, by name. We were fingerprinted, photographed, and charged with a violation of the emergency order. Summonses to appear in court the following Monday morning were issued. I protested because the treason trial was resuming on Monday. The officers were unimpressed. They informed me that the charge carried a fine of 10,000 Rand and ten years in prison.

On leaving Fort Beaufort en route to King William's Town we heard an announcement of our arrests on the car radio. Shortly after checking into the hotel and going to my room, I received a phone call from Judge Milne, who expressed his outrage. He urged me to stay near my phone, that he was attempting to protest to "the top person" and that I may be getting a call. In the meantime, I attempted unsuccessfully to call my wife, who was traveling in Georgia. A call did come from the Natal attorney general Michael Ember and the provincial attorney general, Edward Heller. Following the prompt intervention of the U.S. Consul General's Office, Justice Milne, Natal Attorney General Ember and Cape Provincial Attorney General Heller, the charge against me was dismissed. The U.S. State Department responded to a request of the Lawyers' Committee and urged that the charges pending against the four South Africans also be dismissed. This was done. The whole episode provided an invaluable education on the arbitrariness of South Africa's legal system. One need not exert much effort in order to get tangled up in the web of apartheid laws.

I managed to speak with my daughter, told her what had happened, and requested that she and my brother discreetly advise my eighty-four-year old mother that I had called them from South Africa but make no mention of the arrest. This was because I had gone to South Africa over her strong objection. Apparently the word they passed along did not arouse any concern on her part about my well-being. That changed within twelve hours when NBC and ABC broke the news of my arrest.

While I was attending the funeral of Victoria Mxenge the following day on a soccer field, attended by twenty thousand people, an American television reporter spotted me and asked for an interview. The story of my arrest thus became news worldwide—including in my Cincinnati hometown media. When they could not reach anyone by phone, reporters went scurrying to my home. They went up and down my street, knocking on doors and awakening neighbors in an effort to learn my family's whereabouts and obtain their reaction to what had befallen me in South Africa. The global interest in my arrest by the South African authorities for being without a pass showed how far removed the South African security officials were from common sense.

When I returned to the trial I had a chance to observe Justice Milne in action. The judicial proceedings themselves, held in connection with the effort by defendants to test the competence of the indictment, were conducted with the utmost fairness. As a jurist with sensitivity to human rights Milne was without peer in South Africa and deservedly enjoyed his extremely high reputation among those who handle human rights and political cases.

He was patient and unhurried, courteous, incisive in his questioning, and well informed on the papers in the case and the relevant law. The defendants were treated with dignity in the courtroom. Trial observers, whether representing governments or, as in my case, representing private organizations, were courteously accommodated. This was in marked contrast to what civil rights lawyers sometimes experienced in American courts. The high degree of national and international media interest evident outside and inside the courtroom bespoke the crucial importance of the issues implicated in the case. Media representatives also were extended courtesies by the court and court personnel. This was not at all pleasing to the apartheid government of South Africa.

An observer at a trial in a foreign country must be mindful of the laws under which the case is being tried and that frame the dispute. It is wise to measure the actual proceedings against the legal standards the particular nation has established for the conduct of its legal and political affairs. My observations of the courtroom proceedings, the fairness and demeanor of the judge, the opportunities to be represented by counsel, and the demonstrated skill of those counsel, in this instance, do not provide a full answer with respect to whether justice was going to prevail. This is so because the underlying laws themselves were fundamentally flawed.

Through the courtesy of Michael Ember, the attorney general of the Province of Natal, I was hosted at a luncheon with judges of the supreme court and other judicial officers. There I had an opportunity to educate the guests on American constitutional history. The South African jurists readily conceded the limitations on their power. With no Bill of Rights or other constitutional provisions that protect one's right of speech, peaceable assembly, and to counsel, and with the express prohibition on judicial intervention in cases involving sections of the Internal Security Act, their courts were under a serious handicap.

Laws and regulations promulgated by a racial minority that holds a monopoly on political power administered by or at the direction of that same minority, and enforced against a majority of people possessed of no political or legal status, raised serious questions around the world about their moral, legal, and political legitimacy. The questions surrounding the legitimacy of the Internal Security Act and other laws under which the sixteen UDF defendants were indicted and were facing trial were what prompted me to visit the countryside to observe these apartheid laws in operation and to see the way in which the Internal Security Act was used to enforce those laws. I was dismayed by what I saw. The regulations promulgated under the state of emergency extended to provisions of the Security Act to place its enforcers beyond sanctions for abusive conduct, and to insulate from judicial scrutiny those agents of the state charged with law enforcement. Even more distressing were the indications of the extent of the extralegal means of repression.

There were endless complaints about the state of emergency, which the government declared on July 21, 1985. People protested that this declaration by the government was unnecessary, given the scope of provisions of the Internal Security Act. Jailings based on the preexisting Security Act continued in the areas not covered by the emergency regulations. As of August 26, 1985, approximately five hundred people were detained in such nonemergency areas as Durban and Cape Town. The large number of detentions in the Eastern Cape communities suggests that the state-of-emergency regulations provided a convenient method for the government to suppress dissent on a wholesale basis. As of September 13, 1985, official police figures showed that a total of 4,074 people had been detained since July 21.

As I reflect on the mission I undertook, my mind returns repeatedly to the sixteen defendants in the courtroom in Pietermaritzburg who were on trial for treason and terrorism. Their acts and deeds consisted of nothing more than acts and deeds that are protected by our U.S. Constitution. My mind also returns frequently to the numerous people with whom I spoke in the various townships. The actions of their government toward them would not be permitted by the U.S. Constitution, nor are they sanctioned by the Universal Declaration of Human Rights.

The Universal Declaration of Human Rights, along with the International Covenant on Civil and Political Rights, are preeminent in defining what international human rights are. They hold that people have a right to be free from arbitrary arrest or torture, and to have an entitlement to the security of person and privacy. The detentions and disappearances, beatings, and torture carried out by the government of South Africa and its agents clearly ran afoul of those standards. Laws that render racial groups legally and politically impotent and then criminalize protest activities do not square with the norms of international justice.

In my final reflection on that mission I return not only to the defendants in the dock but also to the more than four thousand people detained and to the hundreds of individuals killed and wounded. With each of these numbers I continue to see a face and hear a voice. I also saw a wife, a husband, a father, a mother, a son, a daughter.

Somalia

Of the opportunities presented for me to engage in international legal activities related to expanding and strengthening the rule of law, none (with the exception of my experience in South Africa) was more exciting or had the potential for such a far-reaching and fundamental change than my invitation to become UN adviser for the Somalia Court System in 1993.

Early in September of that year, the UN Security Council adopted a resolution to rebuild Somalia's police, court, and jail system that had been destroyed following the overthrow of its president, Mohamed Siad Barre. The fifteen-member UN council called for a program to recruit and train police and to restore the court system and bring about economic and political reconciliation. I was asked to consider playing a role in this effort.

Admiral Jonathan Howe was the UN envoy in Somalia, whose initial mission had the goal of feeding starving people. These efforts by UN forces were met with bloody resistance from Somali men and women in Mogadishu, its capital city, led by militia leader Mohamed Farrah Aidid, the chosen head of the Habr Gidr clan that numbered in the tens of thousands. That resistance, and others, intensified measures to capture and even kill Aidid. At the same time, the United Nations wanted to pursue measures to restore governmental structures. It was desirous of rebuilding and restoring the police and court system in Somalia that had been shredded by the civil war between various clans and warlords.

In a September 20, 1993, letter to me, UN ambassador Richard Schifter wrote:

> The UN effort has restored all of Somalia except the capital, Mogadishu, to relative tranquility. Farmers are back on their land again and there was a good crop this year. However, there is no governmental infrastructure as yet which could assure domestic peace in case the UN withdraws.
>
> [But] The area outside Mogadishu, containing over six million people (about 85% of the country's population) is ready for the return of organized government. Negotiations are taking place for the establishment of district governments. In the meantime, the UN is also seeking to build an appropriate infrastructure, focusing on the police, the penal system, and the courts. Other countries are taking

responsibility for the police and the penal system. The United States, however, has undertaken to build the court system. Our AID program is now making $6,000,000 available to get the program started and funded for the first year of its operation.

Admiral Howe has agreed to the creation of the post of UN Coordinator for the Somalia Court System, a person who would report directly to the Admiral and would stay in touch with the UN Security Council, the UN Secretary General, AID, the interested US Bench and Bar, and the Congress, and who would seek to keep the US public informed.

Ambassador Schifter went on to point out that my duties would commence with a ten-day visit to Somalia, and for the next sixty days I would be expected to devote at least half of my time to building a staff. Needless to say, I was most excited to serve in this capacity. In considering the invitation I, in a letter of September 23, 1993, first sought the approval of my chief judge, the Honorable Gilbert Merritt. In my letter to him I outlined the nature of the responsibilities I was expected to assume. This was crucial for me, a sitting member of the U.S. appellate court. His response was prompt and enthusiastic. He wrote in a letter of September 24, 1993:

I see no objection to your service in this capacity. It is obviously a great opportunity to sponsor and help put in place the rule of law in Somalia. You are to be commended for your many services in the past in helping to strengthen the rule of law in other countries in Africa. I fully understand why the Secretary and Secretary General of the United Nations would want you to serve in that capacity. I can think of no one who could offer them better advice and counsel.

After advising Ambassador Schifter that I had obtained clearance from the court to free up the time needed to devote to the mission, I consulted with experts familiar with developments in Somalia. Professor Bert Lockwood of the University of Cincinnati Law School, who directs the Urban Morgan Institute on International Human Rights, put me in touch with Professor Tom Farer, the director of American University's joint degree program in law and international relations, who had recently served as a consultant to the United Nations in Somalia.

In a letter to me Farer put me on notice that the mission I had agreed to undertake would be no stroll in the park. He began with considerable flattery:

> Your reputation long preceded your call. UNOSOM II [United Nations Operation in Somalia II], is badly in need of a person with your qualities who can help it negotiate among the Somali shoals. . . .
>
> Although you have been asked to help only with respect to the judiciary, once you are inside, you will no doubt exercise a much wider influence and thus could add your very considerable weight to the counsels of prudence. In doing so, however, you will have to resist the apparently rigid determination of top US and UN policy makers to move forward without any course adjustment. Indeed, one reason for their calling on a person of your stature might be to strengthen public support for extant policy.

The mission, however, was short-circuited as a result of an October 3, 1993, firefight in which eighteen American Army Rangers were killed and seventy-five wounded in Mogadishu. The TV images of dead American soldiers in Somalia's capital city created such a political reaction that President Clinton ordered the withdrawal of all American troops from Somalia over the next six months. Moreover, the Clinton administration decided to reexamine and eventually scrap plans to use American troops as UN peacekeepers and nation builders. Events continued to remain unsettled in Somalia and other nations in that region. What the outcome would have been if the United States had been able to go forward in Somalia with a strategy for reconstituting the court system, along with efforts to restore the police and aid the problems of hunger and related issues, one can only surmise.

International Criminal Tribunal for the
Former Yugoslavia (ICTY)

A telephone call from a friend of long standing, Judge Gabrielle McDonald, in The Hague, set in motion another flurry of activities involving a possible international responsibility for me. Judge McDonald, who like me had been appointed to the federal bench by President Carter, was serving as a judge of the International Criminal Tribunal for the former Yugoslavia in The Hague. She called to tell me that she was planning to step down and desired to recommend me as her successor.

Judge McDonald had served in the staff of the NAACP Legal Defense Fund, specializing in employment discrimination law. She developed a national reputation that propelled her to the presidency of the National Bar Association, a preeminent organization of black lawyers. Her work as a federal trial judge in Houston brought her to the attention of President Clinton, who nominated her as the U.S. member of the multi-judge international court to try those charged with war crimes in Bosnia and the former Yugoslavia.

As a judge with senior status on the Sixth Circuit Court of Appeals, my docket was such that I could, without resigning from the court, waive sessions for a period of two years in order to undertake the new assignment.

In my conversations with Judge McDonald, I raised a number of questions. I had considerable uncertainty, but she was most reassuring. The court's functioning was explained. I wondered about staffing and language. Though there is court staff, I would be free to bring one or two assistants, if I chose. As for language, she said there were translators to deal with that concern. Also easing my initial ambivalence and uncertainty were conversations I had with longtime human rights lawyers, and recalling my numerous visits to South Africa and other foreign countries dating back to my attendance at the World Peace Through Law conference in 1973. In addition, letters of endorsement were sent to President Clinton, including a personal endorsement from my longtime friend and Clinton confidant, Vernon Jordan.

Judge McDonald advised the State Department that I would favorably consider being her successor if all the administrative hurdles could be surmounted. Within twenty-four hours, materials from the State Department were in my hands. After completing the appropriate paperwork, I was informed that the next step was for the president to send my name to the secretary general of the United Nations for approval by the General Assembly.

My wife and our entire family had become excited about the possibility of living in Europe for two years while serving on that court. The thought of traveling across Europe and visiting the various countries was enticing. As I waited for the clearance, I received a call from Vernon Jordan, who was in Scotland. He said he was calling at the request of the president, who was very upset. Without his realizing it, the matter of filling the vacancy had been routed by the chief of staff, John Podesta, to Secretary of State Madeleine Albright for a sign-off. She had selected Judge Patricia Wald of the U.S. Court of Appeals for the District of Columbia, a kindred spirit of mine within the judiciary.

Needless to say, I was disappointed but readily accepted the apology that Chief of Staff Podesta, also a friend, extended to me and to my daughter, Stephanie Jones, who was by then a part of the Clinton administration. Jordan told me that President Clinton was prepared to "turn it around," which I discouraged.

12

Beyond the Bench

The selection and confirmation processes I underwent prior to becoming a judge were intensive examinations of my ability and willingness to serve as an impartial arbiter of the law. The judicial oath I took committed me to decide cases and administer justice without regard to personal preferences. No matter how I personally felt about an issue, I had to limit my consideration to the facts and the applicable law. I strove to be true to my oath. Once a case was over, however, I reserved the right to discuss the legal principles involved. In particular, I felt free to do so with lawyers and students whom I taught at various law schools. I sought to facilitate a better understanding of and respect for the administration of justice. Increasing the public's understanding is not a prohibited form of advocacy, nor is it destructive of building respect for the legal system. It is just the opposite.

I felt a special obligation to ensure that blacks, who as members of the nation's discrete minority, and victims of historic discrimination, understood the limits of what the law can do with respect to providing remedies for legal wrongs. In that regard I sought out and identified ways and means by which, for instance, victims of the nation's racial desecrations could, and should prepare themselves to take advantage of the opportunities the law was providing.

My extrajudicial activities included mentoring through the Cincinnati Youth Collaborative, taking a leadership role in bringing into being the National Underground Railroad Freedom Center and sustaining it, and continuing my involvement with the American Bar Association's and the Cincinnati Bar Association's programs to bring about greater racial, ethnic, and gender diversity in the legal profession. I felt that the legal profession to which the administering of laws is entrusted had to be free of racial and gender bias if it was to be credible. Thus, I worked with the nation's leading black legal organizations to bring about greater opportunities for minorities in the profession. I continued to accept invitations to address social, civic, and professional groups to speak on topics related to the law and civic governance. As varied as my activities were, I remained frustrated with problems that were crying out for public dialogue but which the canons of legal ethics and the Code of Judicial Conduct did not permit me to address.

Those off-limits issues related to political and some potentially controversial civil rights and political matters. With regard to judicial nominations, too many senators would give a pass to nominees with questionable racial attitudes. Yet some of those senators would parade before black audiences in search of support. Minorities, too often, left senators off the hook when it came to judicial appointments, but would later regret it when those nominees, as judges, voted to resurrect states' rights.

Another matter I was disqualified from addressing while a judge had to do with what I witnessed with respect to redistricting and reapportionment. Until voters begin to pay sufficient attention to developments regarding voter repression in the various states, state legislatures and the Congress will remain lopsided and conservative. The price paid is the choking of progressive legislation and progressive nominations. This grieves me deeply.

The Cincinnati Youth Collaborative

The truth of the indictment Roy Wilkins delivered in 1960 in his famous Cleveland City Club address has troubled me over the years: "The state instituted and wove into a smothering pattern a thousand different personal humiliations, both public and private, based upon color, through legal and extralegal machinery, through unchallenged political power and economic sanctions, a code of demeaning conduct was enforced with a cast, down on children before they could dream, and eroded . . . after they came of age."

He went on to describe the ravages inflicted upon black children by states' rights, much of which I saw myself and personally experienced. For this reason, the mission of the Cincinnati Youth Collaborative (CYC) appealed to me. It was an undertaking that went beyond court-imposed remedial obligations, but appealed to the goodwill of decent people. By engaging them in the mission of the CYC, which was to supplement the activities of school officials, children would be better prepared to receive formal educational offerings. In fact, a part of the mission was to condition the children to participate positively in the competitive, desegregated educational environment with diverse students that school systems were required to provide.

The educational reforms sponsored by school systems, however, have limited reach. Effective education relies on the partnerships being formed with groups like the CYC. The controversies and national nature of the issues I was associated with as NAACP general counsel gave me a different profile from many judicial colleagues with whom I came to be associated. Following my Senate confirmation and swearing in, I moved to Cincinnati, where I received a wonderfully warm reception. There was a spotlight placed on much of my activity in the community. The Cincinnati Youth Collaborative afforded an excellent outlet for me to give expression to my commitment to educational enhancement.

In between the bimonthly sessions of the court, I was able to accept invitations to attend activities that helped me measure the tenor of the community on education and other matters. Occasionally, I found myself in the inner sanctum of decision-making to which, as a civil rights lawyer, I had not previously been accustomed. It began for me when John Pepper, the president of Procter & Gamble, invited me to lunch in his private dining room. His interest and insights into educational issues in urban America struck a chord with me. Another invitation from corporate America came to me from Bradford Butler, a retired vice president of that same company. He invited me to a meeting in 1981 that he was hosting to discuss educational issues of great concern to him.

Earlier in my life in Youngstown, I viewed most corporate leaders as members of the power structure, generally unsympathetic to the cause of social justice. Butler surprised and impressed me with his grasp of the issues of education and the social and economic consequences of not meaningfully confronting them. That meeting, held in the world headquarters of P&G, awakened me to a way that I could participate in an effort to effect change that would not conflict with my judicial obligation of impartiality. This meeting also introduced me to people in the private and public sectors, in a nonadversarial setting, who were prepared to commit resources to the Cincinnati Youth Collaborative. Chad Wick, who was CEO of a nationally respected educational foundation, KnowledgeWorks, as well as a former banker, also teamed up with the various volunteers in developing strategies and generating resources for dealing with the educational deficits that had led to disproportionate numbers of black youth dropping out of school. Early in the life of the CYC, its first top executive was Sister Jean Patrice Harrington, retired president of the College of Mount St. Joseph. Another volunteer member of the leadership team was John Pepper's wife, Francie Pepper, who agreed to maintain the books and records until the organization was up and running with a formal staff. At the urging of Pepper; the new CYC executive director, Dr. John Bryant; and Miriam West, I agreed to become a mentor. That experience proved to be one of the most positive activities I participated in during this period of my life. Being a mentor brought me face-to-face, in a deeply emotional way, with a reminder of the way my own life had benefited from mentoring.

My experience with my own mentor, J. Maynard Dickerson, sparked a powerful, emotional series of experiences with my first mentee, Raymon Mack, a student at Taft High School. I invited Raymon to accompany me to the University of Dayton Law School's hooding ceremony, where I was to deliver the commencement speech. When I picked him up for the event, he emerged handsomely dressed in a new suit, with tie in hand. He said, "Judge, would you help me with my tie? I don't know how." I readily agreed and there on the street corner moved behind him in order to begin the process. As I began to perfect the knot, my mind went back over fifty years to the moment when Dickerson, this distinguished lawyer, performed the same act for me, a teenager. In order for me to attend a high school prom, my mentor loaned me his tuxedo to wear. I dressed for the prom at his home. In assisting me, he and I stood in front of a mirror as he demonstrated the technique of tying the black tie. That this lawyer and civic leader would take the time to help me by tying my tie gave me a special sense of worth. Dickerson's personal interest in me reinforced in me his sense of caring. I was doing for Raymon what had been done for me and I was gripped with emotion.

In 2001, several years after my early morning street corner tie experience with my mentee, I was presented with the Lincoln Award by Northern Kentucky University. In acknowledging the award, I began to relate the story. To my surprise, I discovered that even the mere telling of the story stirred an emotion within me so powerful that I had considerable difficulty completing my speech. Adding to the emotion of the moment was the reaction of the audience as they rose, virtually as one, and extended what could only be described as a giant embrace. This experience has cemented my determination to support mentoring and other programs by the CYC and similar organizations. One need not look far for opportunities to find young people who desire mentors. My college fraternity, Kappa Alpha Psi, has as a part of its commitment a program called Guide Right, designed to provide educational and occupational guidance for youth. Another fraternity of which I am a member, Sigma Pi Phi, aka "The Boulé," has created a foundation with the objective of mentoring black youth. While on the Toyota Diversity Advisory Board, I found good use for many of the lessons I had learned about mentoring from my own experiences and the activities of the CYC.

I was in attendance when Bill Cosby confronted the issue at the fiftieth-anniversary celebration of the *Brown v. Board of Education* decision at Washington's Constitution Hall, which precipitated a national controversy. During most of the evening my mind was occupied with the history of Constitution Hall and the Daughters of the American Revolution's policy that excluded blacks from performing on its stage. For a few minutes, Cosby refused to accept the award and instead exchanged some comic one-liners with Dick Gregory, the presenter. But then it became clear that Cosby was serious as he launched into a biting condemnation of what he perceived as the failure of black parenting. That debate continues to rage. In language that spared no feelings, Cosby charged too many black parents with being absent without leave when it came to giving direction to their offspring and demanding that they adhere to society's standards. He cited slovenliness in public behavior, dress, and speech and being totally indifferent until their sons, in particular, were caught up in the criminal justice system and standing before a judge who was about to impose a prison sentence. At that moment, he said, the parent who appears offers a tearful plea for mercy and just one more chance. Cosby asked, rhetorically and sarcastically, "Where were you when Johnny was acting up in school? Or skipping school altogether?" He went on to challenge parents to be parents.

At the end of the evening, clusters of guests collected to continue what Cosby had started. I moved among a number of the groups to get a sense of their reactions. Some were openly critical of Cosby for using a celebratory occasion to address such a controversial subject. Others agreed with him and urged that the debate continue. It took several days for the national media to pick up on the controversy. Once they did, they ran with it. My view has always been that African Americans can never fully benefit from the gains realized from the civil rights struggle when such a disproportionately large number of young black men are caught up in the criminal justice system. The shamefully high dropout rate among blacks continues to ensure that the pipeline into the criminal justice system remains full. Professor Michelle Alexander, in her thought-provoking book *The New Jim Crow*, documents this very phenomenon and its long-term consequences. Unfortunately later reports of Cosby's own personal moral failures have weakened, if not destroyed, the impact of his counsel.

Every community has the potential to establish and support groups like the Cincinnati Youth Collaborative that can intervene in the lives of young people to slow and even stop the dropout rate, and thereby reduce the high rate of incarcerations. That a national debate ensued from Cosby's indictment of delinquent parents was, from my standpoint, all to the good.

Desegregating the Bar

When I entered the legal profession in 1957, it was very segregated. Law schools and other components of the legal community reflected what was happening in society as a whole. When I joined the court in 1979 there had been measurable change in many legal communities across the country. However, Cincinnati still lagged behind.

On the national level Dennis Archer, who had served in various capacities in Michigan, including as justice on the Michigan Supreme Court, took advantage of his connections in the American Bar Association to awaken that organization to the obligation it had to make a difference. He was appointed by the ABA president at the time, Chesterfield Smith, to head up a commission. Archer's pioneering efforts set the ABA on a course from which it has not varied. An unsung hero in bringing about this redirection was Rachel Patrick of the ABA. Her skills led to a major transformation of the national legal community. Under her tutelage, I became deeply involved in learning the "ins and outs" of the ABA's diversity programs. She took the lead in developing commissions and committees dedicated to enhancing opportunities for minorities in the legal profession. It was my pleasure to serve on the ABA's Commission on Racial and Ethnic Diversity in the Profession. Rachel had a talent for enlisting volunteers such as Paulette Brown, a distinguished lawyer from New Jersey and former president of the National Bar Association who recently became the first black

female president of the ABA; Kurt Schmoke, former mayor of
Baltimore; and Dr. Gregory Prince, president of Hampshire
College, among others who stimulated participation in the ABA's
diversity goals. Patrick and Archer were instrumental in coordinating diversity efforts of the ABA and the venerable black legal
organization, the National Bar Association.

Archer went on to make history by becoming the first black
president of the American Bar Association, to be followed by another distinguished African American, Robert Gray of Richmond,
Virginia.

The rippling effect of the leadership of Dennis Archer and Rachel Patrick has been felt in state and local bar associations all
across the country, and has resulted in a change of policies by major
law firms. My exposure to the ABA initiatives gave me needed answers when Bea Larson, the newly elected first woman president of
the Cincinnati Bar Association, called on me in 1986 to assist with
the troubling racial divisions within her association. She, together
with Inyeai Ororakuma, the president of the Black Lawyers' Association of Cincinnati, visited me in my chambers to discuss the troubling problem of racial division within the legal community.

I spoke with U.S. District Judge Arthur Spiegel, who suggested
that we include his tennis partner, retired Ohio appellate judge
Robert Black, in our discussions. A meeting was held with the
heads of the two bar groups and the judges, during which we discussed ways of making the legal community aware of the racial
division.

Judge Black and I signed a letter to the heads of law firms, corporate legal departments, deans of area law schools, and judges, as
well as leading black and white lawyers, inviting them to a Saturday morning meeting. Thomas Cody, then senior vice president
for law and public affairs for Federated Department Stores (now
Macy's), offered the use of the company facilities for the meeting.
Our unanimous choice for keynote speaker was retired federal
Judge Robert M. Duncan of Columbus, Ohio.

I felt we could illustrate with great effect the problems facing the
legal community through a presentation of Judge Duncan's life

story—and have him do it. This he did, most effectively. It came as quite a jolt to the white lawyers assembled to learn that someone as eminent as Judge Duncan, in effect, had doors of opportunity slammed in his face, requiring him, at one point, to take a bellhop job in a Chicago hotel.

After Judge Duncan told of the racism and door slamming he experienced throughout his life, my co-convener, Judge Black, invited the leaders of the bar to describe the problems that alarmed them. Then Judge Black and I opened the floor for discussion. That was when the "fat hit the fire," as spokespersons from several major firms denied there was any discrimination involved in the dearth of black lawyers in the major law firms. Explanations were offered for there being only two black lawyers at the major law firms. They outlined unsuccessful recruiting efforts they made at Ivy League law schools. However, Peter Randolph, a black lawyer, had a spirited retort to their excuse that "we just refuse to lower our standards." With that, a debate was engaged.

As the debate became more intense, the time approached for adjournment. Judge Black and I had a whispered conference as to whether to adjourn. We polled the attendees on their willingness to return for another session the following week. There was a unanimous vote by the group to return. And return they did, by that time realizing that a problem did exist. At that meeting a decision was made to establish a structure that could deal comprehensively with the issues under discussion. That was the beginning of the Round Table, which has now been in existence for more than twenty years.

The Round Table has sparked a fundamental change in the relations between the diverse members of our local legal community. The Cincinnati Bar Association became a thoroughly transformed organization. The election of John Burlew, now deceased, as the first African American president of the CBA was a result of the change. During his administration, the CBA took dramatic steps and separated itself from its history of excluding black lawyers from membership.

One of the lawyers denied membership was Theodore M. Berry, who had mentored virtually every lawyer of color who practiced in

Cincinnati in the 1930s and '40s. He was involved in many of the major fights to end discrimination in the city, the state, and the nation, along with serving on the national board of the NAACP and co-counseling with Thurgood Marshall in defending black servicemen during World War II. The treatment accorded this esteemed attorney by the bar in Cincinnati was a stain that interfered with efforts to bring racial solidarity to the legal community. Directly addressing Berry's exclusion, Burlew recommended to his fellow officers of the CBA that they acknowledge the error of their ways by publicly apologizing to Berry and recognizing his distinguished legal career. That was done by conferring upon him the organization's Lifetime Achievement Award.

When he accepted the award, Berry explained that he was legally blind and, therefore, had not prepared a formal speech. However, in extemporaneous remarks that lasted more than thirty minutes, the verbally gifted Berry took his audience back to what the climate was like in the 1930s when he applied for membership. The audience listened with rapt attention and obvious embarrassment. When Berry drew to his conclusion, he paused, extended his arms, and declared, "For all of that, I forgive you." Following a moment of silence, a smattering of applause issued from the audience, slowly increasing to a thunderous ovation as the lawyers rose to their feet. From my seat on the dais I looked out over the audience and saw tears in the eyes of lawyers who had known nothing of that history. With their tears and applause, these new and more enlightened lawyers gratefully embraced the absolution Berry granted to them.

As a result of the transformation of the legal community—including the fine work of the Round Table, law firms, and corporate legal departments—area law schools now work closely in mentoring young people and in drawing them to the expanding opportunities afforded by the law.

A problem that still gnawed at the black community and particularly lawyers of color was the legislative "fix" that hobbled chances of having a diverse municipal court. The makeup of the local courts, and the pathway to those judgeships were politically structured in such a way as to sharply limit the access of blacks. Back in 1965, the Ohio legislature passed legislation urged by Cincinnati Republicans to expand the geographical jurisdiction of the municipal court to include the county, which was overwhelmingly white—and Republican. That ensured that even when blacks were appointed by governors, there would be certain defeat at the next election. The joy and excitement that Cincinnati blacks experienced when a governor appointed a lawyer of color to fill a judicial vacancy was invariably dashed at the next countywide election.

To make it possible for blacks to be elected to the municipal and common pleas courts, the old system was attacked and broken through litigation. One of the by-products of diversifying the federal court was that it placed lawyers of color in a position to exercise real power. My presence on the Sixth Circuit Court of Appeals prevented a lawsuit challenging the system from being thrown out. In 1995 Representative William Mallory, assistant majority leader in the State House of Representatives, brought litigation under the Voting Rights Act of 1965 to overturn the system of electing municipal court judges in Cincinnati. The case was about to be dismissed by federal judge Carl Rubin when Mallory's lawyer sought an emergency stay order from the court of appeals late on a Friday afternoon. The matter was presented to me, in that I was the only judge in the courthouse on that afternoon. Upon reviewing the papers, I issued a stay to preserve the status quo, and directed the parties to submit briefs on the following Tuesday. On the basis of those submissions, I continued the stay, and referred the matter to the chief judge for assignment to a panel of court of appeals judges to address the merits of the appeal. Had the status quo not been preserved, thereby permitting my Sixth Circuit colleagues to consider the case on its merits, it would have been dismissed by Judge Rubin. Instead, the final disposition of the case by a panel of judges resulted in a new system of electing judges in Hamilton County on a basis that ensures diversity on that court.

Stretching the Efficacy of Law as a Remedy

In April 2001, at a social event, I was approached by John Cranley, councilman at the time, who asked me if I was aware of a recent police shooting. I had heard the news report about a nineteen-year-old black youth, Timothy Thomas, being killed by police. I asked Councilman Cranley for details. All he would say was, "It is very bad, very bad." It was the latest of a series of deaths of black males at the hands of Cincinnati police. As people were seeking answers, I was once again reminded of the lessons of the Kerner Report and feared they had been forgotten.

Relations between the police and blacks in Cincinnati were already so tense that Mayor Charles Luken had earlier invited the U.S. Department of Justice to conduct a comprehensive review of police practices, including racial profiling. The Thomas incident occurred during the middle of the Justice Department's review, and just as a lawsuit based on racial profiling complaints was about to be tried in federal court by Judge Susan Dlott, who took an innovative approach to resolving the issues.

I was concerned that the latest police shooting would galvanize those who were protesting the police use of force and racial profiling in a way that would drive out rationality. Calls for calm were drowned out by demands for direct action. There did not seem to be anything I could publicly say or do to ameliorate the crisis.

Controversy over Boycott: From Hero to Target

Also festering in the community was frustration over the disproportionately low rate at which construction contracts were awarded to minorities. As anger rose over the use of force by police and racial profiling combined with these affirmative action grievances, calls for a downtown boycott went from sporadic to constant, producing some behavior I considered to be irresponsible.

Since I was tiptoeing toward retirement I decided to speak out against that behavior by reminding the boycotters that as a result of earlier efforts, a set of remedies existed that could be used to redress grievances. I was among the federal judges who enforced those remedies. I decided to speak because I feared the recklessness of the boycotters was giving aid and comfort to opponents of legal remedies. This was dramatically demonstrated in the arena of affirmative action.

The reasoning employed by the new federal court majorities in the employment discrimination cases broadcasted the fact that the courts were on the verge of tightening up requirements requiring proof of specific acts of discrimination before approving racial remedies. Recent cases reaching my court subsequent to the *Steelworkers* and *Bakke* decisions that permitted the consideration of race in hiring and education made it increasingly clear to me that great care must be taken in implementing remedies that were not grounded in actual findings of racial discrimination. Lawsuits that relied on statistics on racial disparities and claims of racial injustices were inviting challenges by conservative legal groups. Limitations on racial claims in affirmative action and employment discrimination cases were morphing into other litigation with racial claims, including, for instance, claims of discriminatory police conduct. It therefore became increasingly necessary that care be taken in crafting legal challenges against improper police behavior. Such claims were at the heart of the case that was pending in federal court before Judge Dlott.

Though the case was proceeding in court, less responsible elements in the black community became more vocal and aggressive. They hijacked the issue from those who first raised it and sought legal redress, and demanded a boycott of the city. As the temperature rose on these issues, particularly with regard to police matters, a young man who had moved to the forefront, Nathaniel Livingston Jr., became more vocal. He began sending emails to national figures, including Bill Cosby, Whoopi Goldberg, and officers of the Progressive Baptist Convention and the National Urban League—all of whom were scheduled to come to Cincinnati for events. Whenever the boycotters learned of a group planning to come to the city, they contacted them with misinformation and tried to dissuade them from making an appearance. In one notable instance they were unsuccessful.

The musical group Sweet Honey in the Rock ignored their demands. As they took the stage at the Aronoff Center, Bernice Johnson Reagon, a founder of the group, chastised the boycotters over their methods and called for racial unity, not division. This was the beginning of a pushback against the misinformation campaign. The Internet provided a tool not available to protesters during earlier confrontations. It was potent in that factually inaccurate statements went out across the country that could evoke reactions before factual responses could correct the misstatements. Some community leaders tried to chase down lies in an effort to head off cancellations. Invariably, the responses came too late.

A black radio station known as "The Buzz" featured a host, Jay Love, who devoted much of his programming to the boycott issues—more designed to arouse than inform. A white conservative (some might say racist) radio talk-show host, Bill Cunningham, whose program aired daily on the most powerful station in the area, WLW, played off the views aired on the Buzz. I ceased listening to either station.

I was disgusted with the early antics of the boycotters because those who had seized the leadership were more concerned with self-promotion than resolving issues. The Kerner Commission report took note of the sense of political and economic powerlessness of the black community in 1967. I was convinced that the boycotters knew little of the time when the black community was truly without political power, and was therefore incapable of measuring the changes that had taken place. By 2001 many blacks had their hands on the levers of power and were significantly involved in much of the decision-making in the community. From my sideline perch I noted the changes that had occurred since my investigation for the Kerner Commission, and privately urged friends to step forward and use that newly gained power in positive strategic ways. To my mind, cries for boycott were shrill and unpromising. I felt that strategies should change as conditions changed. This was not being done.

It was while I was still an assistant U.S. attorney that the nation was hit with a wave of riots and civil disorders. In 1966, in an effort to get ahead of such an event hitting my hometown, I had taken the lead in organizing a group of local leaders in Youngstown to meet each Friday morning for breakfast for a discussion of and strategizing about local problems, known as the Youngstown Leadership Conference. We launched a series of studies into the pathologies that gripped the black community. A report emerged entitled "Past Neglects, Future Demands—Youngstown in Crisis," of which I was one of the principal authors. That report served as a warning and blueprint for Youngstown's business and political leaders. Though controversial, its urgency was not lost upon city fathers. The Youngstown Council of Churches responded through its executive secretary, Dr. Paul W. Gauss, calling the report imperative and practical, said that if it were not acted upon, "we'll pay an awful price in the future." A cooperative spirit soon emerged between black and white citizens. While Youngstown did not remove many of its problems, it made modest progress and averted the violent fate that befell many other cities.

In 2002 an invitation to be the speaker at the Dr. Martin Luther King dinner of the Cincinnati Sentinels (African American police and firefighters) offered a platform to express some concerns. It was then that I decided to speak out against the boycott. My intent was to point out the way that the contributions of the martyred civil rights leader, Dr. King, had combined with the legal strategy of Thurgood Marshall to bring about significant societal change. I cited the statistics in Cincinnati that showed that since the entering of the consent decrees, and in particular since 1986, the numbers of blacks in the police division had risen from 11 percent to 25 percent. These numbers included an assistant police chief, a captain, six lieutenants, thirty-four sergeants, twenty-five specialists, and twenty-two officers. The fire department was headed by a chief who was black. Thus, by no stretch of the imagination was the Cincinnati of 2002 like the Alabama of 1995, or the Mississippi of the 1960s when boycotts were launched, even then as a last resort. Nor was it the Cincinnati I saw when investigating the 1967 riot for the Kerner Commission.

These numbers showed blacks taking advantage of the civil rights laws to change the makeup of the Cincinnati Police and Fire Departments. This was not the only example of changes brought about through the use of legal remedies provided by civil rights laws. I could not help but note the history-making action of Mayor Charles Luken's appointment of the city's first black female city manager, Valerie Lemmie. Given what I knew about the history of Cincinnati, these developments signaled a dramatic change in the willingness of the city to respond to petitions for further advances. As my prepared after-dinner remarks ended, I asked the master of ceremonies, Officer Scotty Johnson, head of the Sentinels, if he minded if I addressed the boycott question directly. He agreed and the audience roared its approval. Since I was swimming against the tide, I thought it best if I laid out my bona fides on the issue of boycotts. The audience applauded my statements that I had long favored boycotts and had litigated the major NAACP case on boycotts that arose in Port Gibson, Mississippi, which resulted in the U.S. Supreme Court upholding the right of organizations like the NAACP to engage in secondary boycotts. More applause. The rest of the story was an explanation of what could have happened to the NAACP if we had not fought so hard in support of boycotts, but how employing it had to be a last resort, not the first. By forgoing other solutions and employing a boycott, they were actually going against the victories we had fought so hard to achieve.

At the completion of my speech, the audience reaction was mixed. The applause was tepid. As I took my seat, Lincoln Ware of the Buzz reminded me, "A lot of the boycotters are out there." However, as I exited the hall that evening, I was pleased that a number of people expressed their appreciation at my remarks. Negative reaction set in on the airwaves the following day.

Prior to joining the Court in 1979 my allies on the national scene, as well as the local leaders with whom I partnered, were stand-up people who did not run from principle. I believed that those calling for a shutdown of Cincinnati were abandoning principle because they wrongly thought that nothing was being done to effect change, even though a variety of tools existed to bring about additional change. It was also true that many challengers were those who had benefited from the changes that had already been made over the years. Others, in what they claimed was in the interest of "not dividing the black community," remained silent.

The rationale that black community members gave for not asserting leadership at the time of the boycott was a false one. The idea of not dividing the black community was bogus, partly because it represents the black community as a monolith. The boycott strategy undercut the economic progress made by a significant number of blacks who had advanced under various affirmative action, educational, and employment programs to an economic level unknown to previous generations. Blacks held positions in the major hotels, Fortune 500 companies, and other downtown businesses that would suffer from the adverse economic effects of a downturn in conventions, concerts, and purchasing power.

To the extent that racial barriers continue to exist, and they do, the best approach, I argued, was to use the legal remedies that have been fashioned to strike remaining barriers down. My call was to not undercut the progress already made, but to use successes of the past to lift anyone still languishing in the educational and economic backwaters. Abdicating one's responsibility to lead by correcting an ill-advised course of action was cowardice in my view, not leadership.

I had grown accustomed in my pre-judge life to displays of courage by Roy Wilkins, Clarence Mitchell, and other civil rights leaders, who, for example, dared to condemn the National Black Political Convention in Gary, Indiana, in 1972. And Gloster Current, who as director of NAACP branches in the 1950s, organized a resistance to the efforts of the Communists and Trotskyites to take over the NAACP. I watched Mitchell fight against such black-power advocates as Stokely Carmichael. I heard Judge William H. Hastie, who upon retirement from the Third Circuit Court of

Appeals, addressed the legal session of the NAACP Convention in 1971, speaking out against black separatism, which Wilkins had condemned as "black death."

In 1973, when it appeared that leaders of the United Church of Christ were giving a sympathetic ear to advocates of black power, and abandoning the integrationist cause, Wilkins and AME Zion Bishop Stephen Gill Spottswood, who chaired the NAACP National Board of Directors, went to Boston's Beacon Hall to urge that the church group rethink its position. Wilkins's exhortations to that highly significant religious denomination were powerful and continue to be relevant even to this day. He pleaded, in part:

> I am here at this convention of churchmen to signal for help, to cry aloud for help, to ask of this body, a body well acquainted with struggle and strain and with the healing effect of the spirit and of the faith, for aid at this juncture. My cry is the well-known one of the Bible: "Come over into Macedonia and help us!" . . .
>
> We Americans are in trouble, bad trouble. We are sick and uneasy as a nation. Did we not have our faith, the way would be dark indeed. But Paul has reassured us as he did the Corinthians, with these rallying words, beginning at the eighth verse:
>
> 8. "We are troubled on every side, yet not distressed; we are perplexed but not in despair;
>
> 9. "Persecuted, but not forsaken; cast down, but not destroyed . . .
>
> 13. "We having the same spirit of faith, according as it is written . . .
>
> 18. "While we look not at the things which are seen, but at the things which are not seen: for the things which are seen are temporal; but the things which are not seen are eternal."

This plea resonated with the United Church of Christ. It sustains me in my belief that regardless of the political winds, there is much we can do to ward off what was whipped up by advocates of black separatism in the 1970s and Tea Party followers of today who seem unable to accept the fact that Barack Obama is indeed, our president.

Having come out of an environment influenced by local and national individuals of force and courage, I was perplexed when I returned to private life to see many Cincinnatians display timidity when courage was obviously called for. Such timidity came at a cost to civic pride and the city's national reputation. This brought on a wave of cancellations by entertainment stars and national conventions. I sought to counter the misinformation about the dispute that boycott leaders had spread to Bill Cosby, who was scheduled to make an appearance, as well as to various national conventions in attempts to block them from coming to the city. It was having its intended effect. This prompted my letter to Cosby of January 28, 2002, in which I tried to counter the barrage of misinformation and show him the real consequences of supporting the boycott.

The only response I received from Cosby was from his agent, Norman Brokaw, of the William Morris Agency in Beverly Hills, California. It said, "Mr. Cosby appreciated very much your taking the time to write, however, I did want to let you know that he will not be making the scheduled appearance and this is Mr. Cosby's final decision. He still feels very uneasy about performing in Cincinnati at this time. I trust you will understand."

The fact is, I did not—and still do not—understand. For a person of Cosby's perceived concern for healing communities to cancel as he did, in the face of the many steps the community of Cincinnati had taken to deal with its problems was, to me, a failure of leadership. The character flaws recently exposed provide some insight into his disappointing decision. The ripple effect of Cosby's cancellation was devastating. It triggered a wave of cancellations by others who knew little or nothing about the issues or of the broad range of remedial steps under way to address the ills common to urban life in most American cities. In particular, when the National Urban League moved its convention to Pittsburgh, it went to a city confronting so many problems with its police department that was at that time operating under a court decree. The Progressive Baptist Convention ran into two embarrassments. One was the fact that St. Louis, the city to which it shifted its convention, had a serious school problem. The other problem was legal, stemming from the contracts it breached with the Cincinnati hotels. The hotels issued demands for payment in the hundreds of thousands of dollars. So serious was the matter that the leadership of the Progressive Baptist Convention called upon me to assist in mediating a resolution of the legal dispute.

Harry Belafonte was to receive an award at the Progressive Baptist Convention in Cincinnati. After the convention's decision to move, he asked me to join him in St. Louis for a meeting on the evening of the award in his hotel suite with a few boycott leaders. I had known Belafonte for a long time. He and Lorenz Graham, brother of my late wife, Jeanne, began their musical careers in New York's Greenwich Village nightclubs. His former wife, Marguerite, came to Youngstown, Ohio, to campaign for me in 1960 during my unsuccessful campaign for the Ohio State House of Representatives. (Launching a political campaign was a way of advertising oneself as a lawyer at a time when the canons of ethics prohibited lawyers advertising themselves.) My infant daughter, Stephanie, was a special object of Marguerite's affection and attention. When the National Underground Railroad Freedom Center chose Archbishop Desmond Tutu to receive its coveted International Freedom Conductor Award, Belafonte accepted my invitation to come to Cincinnati and make the presentation.

Belafonte was on friendly terms with Reverend Damon Lynch III, a leader of the Black United Front, one of the boycott groups. Since Reverend Lynch, too, was planning to attend the Progressive Baptist Church Convention, Belafonte asked him to join in the meeting in his suite, which would also be attended by the leaders of the convention. We discussed matters into the wee hours of the morning, during which time I laid out many of the initiatives being undertaken to address Cincinnati's social and economic problems. The church officers conceded that they had been told nothing about these efforts. Neither had Belafonte, who asked Reverend Lynch whether he would call off the boycott if he promised to continue working with his group. Reverend Lynch replied that it was not within his power to do so, adding, "It is out of my hands."

The highly respected Procter & Gamble CEO, John Pepper, minced no words in a letter to Hugh Price, president of the National Urban League, over that organization's decision to move its convention from Cincinnati. He declared:

I can't tell you how disappointed I am at the announcement of your decision to not bring your Annual Conference to Cincinnati.

I've read the quotations in your press release of July 15th that explained the reasons for this decision. Frankly, I find them perplexing and troubling. . . .

Most troubling to me were your comments that "Local groups calling for boycott of the City don't want any kind of Urban League Conference coming to the City, even if it's focused on an agenda of opportunity, equality and justice for African Americans in Cincinnati." What kind of an attitude is this? This type of attitude stands for an obstruction of progress. I am sorry you give it any weight. . . .

What I personally find so sad about this is that I've never seen a group of community people—business and otherwise—working on so many fronts to improve job opportunities, economic conditions, education, and housing for African Americans and disadvantaged people of all races. I personally am spending at least half of my time, and have been for the last six months, on such projects. Joe Pichler, the CEO of Kroger; Jim Zimmerman, the CEO of Federated and countless others are doing the same thing. Believe me, these efforts are impeded and discouraged by the kind of activity that the boycotters present. Your coming to this City, with a clear focus on monitoring improvement was a positive. It is a positive you have now withdrawn.

You need to make the decisions you feel are right for your organization. I know that. And we will continue on. But as a person who knows and respects you, I trust you don't mind my conveying to you my deep disappointment in your decision. I simply don't think it was the right one.

That letter was a blow to the entire National Urban League family, given the support it and its affiliates all around the country received from Procter & Gamble.

A major disappointment to me, given the tradition of national NAACP officials over the years building on its successes, was to see its national president at the time, Kweisi Mfume, come to Cincinnati and act on incomplete information. It was obvious to me that Mfume was committing the same error as others who were opting for a return to the protest strategy that was in vogue before the refinement of the newer remedies that resulted from the successes of the 1960s and '70s. Moreover, those who were reverting to the boycott strategy viewed marches and demonstrations as easy and sensational solutions to issues that would have been amenable to other approaches.

Those demonstrations soon descended into disgraceful acts of rudeness. Among the most disgraceful occurred at events related to the groundbreaking for the National Underground Railroad Freedom Center, when followers of Nathaniel Livingston and so-called General Kabaka Oba hid in the shadows screaming epithets at thousands of people entering the event celebrating the founding of the Freedom Center. Similar behavior occurred earlier, when combined choirs singing spirituals and carrying lighted candles marched over the Roebling Suspension Bridge from Kentucky into Ohio to join with an assembled crowd led by, among others, Muhammad Ali, Ambassador Andrew Young, and First Lady Laura Bush. When the opening of the Freedom Center was celebrated in August 2004, some of the group mocked the bravery of escaping slaves by being attired in tattered clothing shouting profanities at guests, including Oprah Winfrey, as they exited the affair.

I continued to register my disapproval of the boycott through letters to various individuals and organizations in efforts to offset the negative and misleading information being disseminated. On one occasion, University of Cincinnati College of Law School Dean Joseph P. Tomain and I coauthored an op-ed piece for the *Cincinnati Enquirer*, in which we pointed to Dr. Martin Luther King's "Letter from a Birmingham Jail."[1] In that letter, Dr. King condemned premature use of boycotts aimed at shutting down a city before undertaking negotiation steps.

I sent another appeal to Reverend John H. Thomas, general manager and president of the United Church of Christ. His organization, obviously acting on the basis of false and misleading information, announced that Cincinnati would be excluded as a site of future conferences. In my letter, I registered my "profound disappointment" with that decision. I felt particularly sad about the action of the United Church of Christ because it was before that body's national convention on Boston's Beacon Hill that the late Roy Wilkins made his famous "Come over into Macedonia" speech when the siren song of black separatists were seeking to lure it from its racial inclusive tradition.

13

Life After the Bench

When I passed the bar examination in the mid-1950s and was licensed to practice law, the opportunities for lawyers of color were extremely limited. The notion of being recruited by or joining a major law firm was never considered. In those days, the best that black lawyers could expect to do was to hang out a shingle or be invited to share space in the office of an established black practicing lawyer. Later, one would hope to land a public appointment as an assistant prosecutor, law director, or possibly a position in some other governmental office at the federal, state or local level. I knew a few who were appointed, and then ran for municipal judgeships in major cities such as Cleveland, Columbus, Chicago, Detroit, and elsewhere.

At that time J. Maynard Dickerson had recently been appointed vice chairman of the Industrial Commission of Ohio—a first. We all were extremely proud of William Brooks when he became a judge of the Columbus Municipal Court, to be followed by Robert Duncan. Dickerson was influential in urging Governor Frank Lausche to appoint Arthur Fisher of Dayton to the Dayton Municipal Court and later a distinguished Cleveland lawyer, Charles White, who had served as assistant law director, to the Cuyahoga County Common Pleas Court. But those were rare cases. Even rarer—in fact nonexistent when I became a lawyer—were instances when major law firms hired black lawyers. I recall that when Paul White of Cleveland joined the firm of Baker & Hostetler it was like a shot heard around the world.

I have detailed my activities with the American Bar Association in its efforts to bring diversity to the legal profession. Those activities have borne fruit. Never did I, when I first entered the profession, ever think that I would find myself performing the functions I do for the firm of Blank Rome LLP that I joined upon retiring from the court. It says a great deal about the distance society and the legal profession have traveled during the past quarter century. In particular, I can see the differences in the legal profession at the time I left the bench in 2002 from what it had been when I became a judge in 1979. Even with those changes, the legal profession has lagged behind other segments of society.

In my own experience, a measure of the change was captured by the way in which I was embraced when I prepared to step down. Allowing for the fact that I had undergone a rare experience of serving as a judge on the second highest court in the land, I nevertheless was struck by the interest shown by the professional offers that came my way.

Sharon Zealey, a bright young lawyer who proclaims me as one of her mentors, served as U.S. attorney for the Southern District of Ohio. She and my daughter, Stephanie, were both graduates of the University of Cincinnati College of Law. They had carved out outstanding legal careers for themselves. After Sharon stepped down, she accepted an offer to join the Cincinnati office of one of her former law school professors, Michael Cioffi, who managed the local office of a large Philadelphia-based firm, Blank Rome LLP. Upon hearing that I was planning to leave the bench, she urged that I withhold committing to a firm until I first talked to Cioffi. Without promising to do so, I "cheated" a bit by lending an ear to a few other bidders who wished to engage my services. I did ultimately meet with Cioffi and other senior partners of Blank Rome.

It was good that I had placed my toe in the water before meeting with Blank Rome, because that prior exposure helped to inform my ultimate decision. It did not take long for me to realize that I could be very happy and fulfilled with that firm. Unfamiliar with the workings of a law firm, I retained a trusted friend and experienced Washington, D.C., lawyer, William Coleman, to negotiate on my behalf with Blank Rome. As he was about to wrap up the negotiations, he phoned to ask me "one more question": "Do you want them to provide you with a car and a driver?" After gulping, I chuckled and replied, "No, Bill, that won't go over well in Cincinnati. I'll be satisfied with a parking spot in the building's garage." He said, "OK. I just wanted to be sure that I don't miss anything."

Shortly thereafter, I began my "new" career as a practicing lawyer. My duties were not clearly defined, but I was available to assist the nearly five hundred other lawyers in the firm, located in such cities as Philadelphia, Washington, New York, and other locations where Blank Rome was doing business. There now are many more. Mediation and counseling appeared to be my mainstay, though I occasionally dipped into trial and appellate litigation.

It did not take long for the chairman of the firm, David Girard-diCarlo, and the newly designated managing partner of the firm, Carl Buchholz, to make a trip to Cincinnati to hold a dinner meeting with Michael Cioffi and me. The purpose was to invite me to assume a major responsibility with the firm—that of chief diversity and inclusion officer.

In my post-judicial position at Blank Rome LLP, I was supported in my efforts to broaden public understanding of the obligations of law and courts to be relevant to the lives of individuals currently or once victimized by racism. In my role as chief diversity and inclusion officer I was able to help reshape a large law firm's approach to improving its commitment to diversity. Additionally, I enjoy the freedom to lecture and teach at law schools, as well as to speak candidly to lawyers and judges. For these and other reasons, I welcomed the opportunity to pursue goals by means not permitted of a sitting judge.

Do I Miss the Court?

On June 28, 1991, the media gathered to interview eighty-three-year-old Justice Thurgood Marshall as he arrived at his McLean, Virginia, home, after announcing his retirement as a Supreme Court justice. One of the reporters asked him why he was leaving the court. The justice paused, and with a look of incredulity on his creased face, and with wind blowing through his thinned gray hair, said, "I am old. I am sick." My reaction was one of disgust at the insensitivity evidenced by the question put to this longtime civil rights warrior and legal icon whose work changed the nation. In my view readers and viewers would like to have learned many other things from the great Justice other than "Why?"

Years later, interest in my reason for retiring from the Sixth Circuit drew a similar question from reporters, but my circumstances, as I have explained on many occasions, were entirely different from those of Marshall. Departing from a lifetime appointment, when my health remained good, I believed that my retirement did warrant an explanation to the public. With the passage of time since my retirement from the bench, the most frequent question I seem to get is whether I miss the court. The frequency of the question and my quick response has caused me to pause and reflect on the accuracy of the answer I was giving. The reasons can be attributed to the ability now afforded me in my new role to vindicate the values that have been near and dear to me in my efforts to answer the Call. As I've mentioned previously, there are restrictions imposed on sitting judges from engaging in public dialogue on issues that influence the political climate of the nation. The code of judicial conduct and the canons of ethics require judges to avoid the perception of bias on matters likely to come before the court. My early experience in seeking to eliminate segregated institutions distorted by racial caste alerted me to an oncoming collision I saw with the jurisprudence that was shaped by Charles Hamilton Houston, Thurgood Marshall, and the NAACP in what became the U.S. Supreme Court precedents in such cases as *Brown v. Board of Education* and its progeny. I wanted to do something to avoid the collision. Or at least try.

Unleashed

My decision to move from the court and return to private life would, in the process, allow me to engage in those activities that would help me to answer the Call. Impediments to the full realization of what was laid out in *The Call* in 1909 had begun gaining political and legal traction. My ability to do little more than merely identify those impediments contributed to my decision to retire and be freed of the restraints necessarily imposed on Article III judges. To become an activist once again and to do so in a strategic way held much appeal.

The role I envisioned for myself was that of being a Paul Revere with respect to the impending danger I was seeing to Houstonian jurisprudence. Birth had been given to a subtle but deadly pincer strategy aimed at returning the nation to the era of states' rights. That pincer movement—consisting of attacks on voting rights, and the imposition of standards of scrutiny by the courts designed to inhibit race-based remedies, has been gaining strength and unless it is halted and reversed, separate-but-equal will reign again. Since leaving the court I have tried to sound an alarm.

My determination to reengage in affirmative efforts to answer the Call was significantly driven by reminders left to us by President Lincoln and the philosopher George Santayana. It was in his address to the Congress on December 1, 1862, in the midst of the Civil War, that the following warning came from President Lincoln: "Fellow citizens, we cannot escape history." The amnesia that appears to have overcome contemporary Americans calls to mind Santayana's words "Those who cannot remember history are condemned to repeat it."

Public protests over violent confrontations that resulted in the death of black people demonstrated to me that Lincoln's and Santayana's counsel had been forgotten, and even more regrettable, the lessons of the Kerner Report of 1968 were either never learned or were being ignored. The soiling of our social fabric by these eruptions is too high a price for our society to pay.

Even more destructive is the harm done to the faith of historic victims of discrimination by hobbling the ability of America's courts that so actively had protected their constitutional rights. Recent examples include the Supreme Court's striking down, in the case of *Shelby v. Holder*, a key section of the 1965 Voting Rights Act that required states with a history of voting-rights discrimination to obtain clearance from the Department of Justice before making changes in their voting laws. Another example of a serious setback to the voting rights of minorities that requires the calling forth of Lincoln's and Santayana's warnings can be seen in the U.S. Supreme Court's decision in *Northwest Austin Municipal Utility District No. 1 v. Holder*. In that case the Supreme Court acknowledged the success of the preclearance requirement of Section 5 of the Voting Rights Act. Yet the majority turned around and characterized its success "as impos[ing] current burdens."[1] The burdens could be nothing else but that blacks were free of the inhibitions of race.

The logic employed by the Supreme Court's majority suggests that once the rain stops, it makes sense to outlaw umbrellas, or when accidents are reduced at intersections, it infringes on the rights of drivers to obey traffic signals. How else can the striking of Section 5 of the Voting Rights Act be justified?

In 2012 at a small luncheon meeting with Vice President Joseph Biden, the discussion turned to the issues that should be addressed during President Obama's campaign for reelection. Noting that mention had not been made of the various voter-suppression initiatives launched in several states, including Ohio, I suggested that issues would mean little to voters of color and other minorities if access to the ballot were suppressed. After summarizing testimony I gave before an Ohio legislative committee in which I, to the dismay of the legislators, equated the voter-suppression efforts with the poll tax and White Primaries of the South, the vice president instructed an aide to add voter suppression to their list of concerns to be addressed during the campaign. I cite this as an example of the advantage of being "at the table" when decisions are made.

National Underground Railroad Freedom Center

Officers of the National Underground Railroad Freedom Center honored me in 2005 for my nine years as co-chair of its board by electing me an honorary co-chair and a member of the board of directors. One only needs to visit the Center to understand its potential for shaping the attitudes of individuals. Its extended learning and related creative programs alone transmit valuable information to millions of people in America and abroad. Had such an institution and vehicle for the transmission of knowledge existed at the time I was attending the West Federal Street YMCA forums in the late 1930s and early '40s, many of the deep-seated racial issues that still adhere to the minds of contemporary individuals might have been avoided. A comment frequently heard by visitors to the center is how much parents and others wish that the educational systems—public and private—across the nation would offer the lessons being taught at the Freedom Center.

Without question, the public most certainly is duty-bound to underwrite the costs of those lessons previously unavailable to students. The failure to teach the truth about our history with regard to slavery, abolition, and the consequences of that past, and how that deficit complicates solutions to today's problems, is a reality that school systems have been slow to correct. When this kind of public education does not take place, a strong vacuum is created that is often filled by zealots, an example of which is the Tea Party groups who seek to cripple the functioning of our federal government.

There is not the slightest doubt in my mind about what motivates most of the people behind the nearly all-white Tea Party movement. These actions stem only in part from the ignorance of groups of people about the obligation the Constitution imposes on federal, state, and local government. The protest messages on the signs carried by Tea Partiers tell the other story. Stripped to its essence, the Tea Party grows from its members' unhappiness at having Barack Obama as president, though many, to avoid the label of "racist," advance nonracial reasons. Why else would their protest signs condemn the loss of country, demand a "take-back of our government," and call the programs advocated by President Obama "socialism," even though whites have been or would be beneficiaries? *The Call* described the state of race relations in 1909, as the authors decried the lynchings that took place in Springfield, Illinois, and other manifestations of race hate across the country. The Tea Party movement has the same shrillness and spews the same hate that surrounded the lynch-mob mentality and scenes of that day in 1909 when the NAACP was founded. There are those who would challenge the relevance of references to lynching, as occurred when President Obama equated that chapter of America's history with terrorism. My defense of its relevance is based on the documented acts of violence and terrorism by those who witnessed lynchings or investigated them, such as the NAACP. My hope is that the National Underground Railroad Freedom Center's founding, and a revitalization of America's education and teaching networks, will provide additional powerful responses to the Call.

But the Freedom Center also deals with issues that were not covered by *The Call*. With the end of chattel slavery in this country, the subjugation of human beings continues in a variety of forms.

An awareness of this new form of slavery was created by the exhibit at the Freedom Center called "Invisible: Slavery Today." I was reminded that I had played a direct role in dealing with modern-day aspects of this invisible slavery. This took place during the early and mid-1960s when I was serving as an assistant U.S. attorney in the Northern District of Ohio under the Kennedy and Johnson administrations.

A part of the docket assigned to me by my boss, Merle M. McCurdy, was the prosecution of what were called Mann Act cases. That law prohibited the interstate transportation of women for purposes of prostitution. The Northern District of Ohio was a place where women and girls were readily brought from other states for purposes of prostitution. It was the crossing of state lines into Ohio that gave the federal government jurisdiction to prosecute.

Whether it is called human trafficking, bonded labor, forced labor, or sex trafficking, it is present worldwide, including within the United States. My intent in writing this memoir is to illuminate practices usually relegated to the shadows by sharing the experiences of my life with contemporary people. I hope the phase of my career that involved prosecuting what were called "white slavery" cases will shed some light on a form of human bondage that survives principally because it is supported by so-called good people. Were it not for the profit motive, it could not survive.

14

Justice Clarence Thomas and the Supreme Double Cross

I attended Yale Law School, Yale had opened its doors, its hearts, its conscience to recruit and admit minority students. I benefited from this effort . . . But for affirmative action, where would I be today? These laws and their proper application are all that stand before the first 17 years of my life and the second 17 years.

—Clarence Thomas, 1983[1]

[Affirmative action programs] have given *no substantial benefits* to blacks. That term has thus become a mere political buzz word.

—Clarence Thomas, 1988[2]

The Constitution abhors classifications based on race, not only because those classifications can harm favored races or are based on illegitimate motives, but also because every time the government places citizens on racial registers and makes race relevant to the provision of burdens or benefits, it demeans us all.

—Clarence Thomas, 2003

I am among the countless individuals who struggle to reconcile these statements of Clarence Thomas—a black man who supped at a table spread by his forebears of color, many of whom gave their lives in the process of bending evil segregation laws toward equal justice, only to have the doors leading to the dining room slammed shut in their faces by legal opinions he is now writing.

For many years and for many reasons, personal and professional, I kept my opinion of Clarence Thomas mostly to myself, sharing my thoughts only with my closest judicial colleagues and law clerks. But now that I have retired from the court I feel free to express my opinion. I do so robustly because Justice Clarence Thomas is one of American history's most colossal double-crossers. And if he has his way, the federal courts may become powerless to protect the civil rights of racial and ethnic minorities, women, the poor, the aged, the disabled, and other victims of discrimination.

It both pains and outrages me to see a black man who benefited from the work and sacrifice of Charles Houston, Thurgood Marshall, and other courageous men and women who made his way possible, sneer at their legacy and seize every opportunity to return this nation to the condition from which they helped him escape.

I grew up recognizing how law and the courts incorporated racism into the sinews of the institutions and systems that shaped and distorted the minds and lives of all people, black and white. In my youth, I sat at the feet of men and women who believed in the Constitution and in its capacity to be the instrument of social change. I saw and experienced firsthand how their sacrifices redirected this nation away from its reckless, racist course. Thoughtful Americans should give thanks to them, for they struggled to save our nation's soul. I have spent my life doing all in my power to continue their mission, which has become my own.

This mission compels me to speak up in defense of those courageous heroes who sacrificed and laid the groundwork that Clarence Thomas benefited from and which he seeks to destroy. I am compelled to reveal how my ability to discharge my judicial oath was seriously obstructed by Thomas's jurisprudential double cross. And I am compelled to warn, in the strongest possible terms, of the disaster that looms should Clarence Thomas's twisted view of the law—particularly the strict scrutiny standard in matters of race—be adopted by a majority of the Supreme Court. To justify such a severe indictment, this writer owes the reader a historical context.

History and Context

Context is all-important when discussing race-sensitive remedies. Without an understanding of context, many arguments against civil rights remedies can seem reasonable. Those arguments have political appeal and are useful for demagogues and misled majorities, however at their core they perpetuate a historic racial wrong. In attempting to mute black support for those remedies the proponents of the status quo issue appeals to race pride. They also attack the use of remedies even though, as I have often noted, a constitutional right without a means of enforcing it is no right at all.

When the nation added the Thirteenth, Fourteenth, and Fifteenth Amendments to the Constitution, it included a provision that authorized Congress to enact legislation, when appropriate, to give meaning to those amendments.[3] These various civil rights acts were both comprehensive and targeted to bring about the Reconstruction era. However, Reconstruction ended with the Hayes-Tilden Compromise of 1877, when federal troops were withdrawn from the South, followed by the Supreme Court striking down the Civil Rights Act of 1875. These developments effectively removed federal protection for former slaves, exposing them to the South's campaign of retrenchment. What followed were campaigns, legal and extralegal, that led to the pernicious 1896 Supreme Court "separate but equal" decision of *Plessy v. Ferguson*.

In that decision the U.S. Supreme Court placed the imprimatur of constitutionality on racial segregation. *Plessy v. Ferguson* and the fifty-eight year reign of "separate but equal" allowed the law, the courts, the Congress, and the states to infect, contort, and configure virtually all of our institutions—social as well as governmental—so

322 ANSWERING THE CALL

as to reflect the precepts of white entitlement. These institutions were not remote ivory towers; they actually controlled lives of human beings. For instance, the records of a number of Northern school desegregation cases make clear that neighborhoods did not become segregated by chance. Banks and savings-and-loan institutions were involved. Restrictive covenants, enforced by the courts, brought about the configuration and the demographics of our cities. Through 1961, the Federal Housing Authority determined where people lived through its lending practices. When lenders, real estate brokers, and insurance brokers did not establish or enforce such policies, the government did it instead.

The U.S. Supreme Court overturned *Plessy* in 1954 in *Brown v. Board of Education*. *Plessy* is far more than a name. *Plessy* represented nullification of the constitutional rights won through the Emancipation Proclamation, the Civil War, the ratification of the Thirteenth, Fourteenth, and Fifteenth Amendments, and the enactment of an assortment of civil rights statutes.

I was a law student at the time Thurgood Marshall and his team of NAACP lawyers overturned *Plessy* in 1954 with their victory in *Brown*. I sought to inform my classmates about the *Brown* decision and its constitutional significance, with little success. Many law students believed that the *Brown* decision would have little, if any, effect. I tried to impress upon them that *Plessy* had been affecting them virtually all of their lives. The segregation we were subjected to in the city's theaters, restaurants, swimming pools, and skating rinks all stemmed from *Plessy*. The lack of black teachers and the discriminatory practices of realtors and banks, including racially restricted covenants in deeds, were legacies of *Plessy*. As a result of the 1954 *Brown* decision, a constitutional platform was provided by the Supreme Court for launching attacks on a broad range of discrimination beyond public schools, not only in the South but in the North as well.

After 1954, in response to ongoing attempts of Southern governors, senators, school boards, and other elected officials to defy the mandate of *Brown v. Board of Education*, the U.S. Supreme Court repeatedly reaffirmed *Brown I* and *Brown II* and principles laid down in an assortment of decisions in cases involving findings by federal judges.

The Civil Rights Act of 1964 was a key piece of remedial legislation enacted to correct intractable problems of discrimination and abuse that the constitutional amendments and *Brown* outlawed. When Title VII of the 1964 Act was amended in 1972, the public sector was brought under its prohibition against discrimination in employment. This provided protection for people who worked in the public sector. Without that protection, the segregation and discrimination previously practiced by public agencies at the state and local levels would have continued. Prior to the 1964 Civil Rights Act, there were various executive orders issued by presidents going back to Franklin Roosevelt that relieved courts of an exclusive burden of attempting to deal with these complex problems. It became increasingly evident, however, that additional legislation would be needed to eliminate the residual aspects of discrimination. The reason was simple: since discrimination had the force of law, corrective efforts needed legally based remedies.

The Southern Strategy

Throughout the 1960s, the U.S. Justice Department supported desegregation and enforced federal court orders implementing it. However, in his 1968 presidential campaign, Richard Nixon employed his "Southern Strategy," exploiting white anger and fear with a promise to restore states' rights and rein in federal power to enforce desegregation. The Southern Strategy and the votes it brought helped Nixon squeak past Hubert Humphrey, and he immediately set about making good on his promises and tried to enlist the Supreme Court in its effort to bring an end to school desegregation efforts.

In 1969, the Nixon Justice Department aligned itself with the state of Mississippi in an effort to have the Supreme Court "stay" the various orders relating to school desegregation and affirmative action. As the new general counsel of the NAACP, I was in the packed Supreme Court chamber to hear the argument in *Alexander v. Holmes County Board of Education*. The government took the position that it was acting with "all deliberate speed"—a concept that *Brown II* had blessed in 1955. It was clear from the questions put to the government lawyers—including Jerris Leonard, assistant attorney general for civil rights—by the justices, that the air was fast going out of the government's argument. The justices were simply fed up with the transparent efforts to delay compliance with desegregation orders. Within twenty-four hours of the hearing, the court overturned its "all deliberate speed" timetable of 1955 and instituted an "immediacy" standard.

A significant element of the Nixon anti-desegregation strategy was an all-out attack on the crucial desegregation remedy of transportation—busing. In a nationally televised address on March 16, 1972, Nixon announced the introduction of legislation to call an immediate halt to all new busing orders by Federal Courts.

Fortunately, Nixon's Southern Strategy was stalled by a Congress that challenged much of what he sought to do, and federal judges who would not be politicized. President Ford, Nixon's successor, followed the Nixonian approach in pushing anti-busing amendments, albeit with less vigor.

The 1976 election of President Carter provided the resumption of affirmative civil rights activity. Under President Carter—with the selection of Drew Days III to be assistant attorney for civil rights, and the appointment of a number of minorities and women to cabinet and sub-Cabinet positions—a halt to the Southern Strategy allowed for considerable forward movement. Race remedies were very real in the Carter administration. Carter made history during his four-year presidency when he nominated thirty-nine blacks to be Article III federal judges, more than all previous administrations dating back to the Judiciary Act of 1789. Along with them were judicial nominees from nontraditional backgrounds whose approach to civil rights and other progressive issues brought change. I am proud that I was one of eleven lawyers of color appointed to the U.S. Courts of Appeal.

Enhanced racial diversity became the new face of the federal courts at the time Ronald Reagan went to infamous Philadelphia, Mississippi, to launch his presidential campaign. It was there that he vowed to rid the court of "activist judges"—a derisive euphemism for jurists who, true to their oaths, respected and enforced constitutional protections of women and minorities. He promised to stack the courts with "strict constructionists" who passed a litmus test ensuring their commitment to reconstruing the Fourteenth Amendment and subordinating it to the Eleventh Amendment and the doctrine of states' rights. It is well to be reminded of *New York Times* reporter Claude Sitton, who covered the South during the desegregation struggles of the 1950s and '60s. He told Jack Bass in an interview for the book *Unlikely Heroes*, "Those who think Martin Luther King, Jr. desegregated the South don't know Elbert Tuttle and the record of the Fifth Circuit Court of Appeals."[4] Well, I knew Judge Tuttle and his colleagues, John Minor Wisdom, John Robert Brown, and Richard Rives. They indeed played key roles in desegregating the South.

I learned early in my career on the bench the power that judges wield with their pens. For that awesome power to return to judges dedicated to states' rights is most unsettling, particularly when, as in the case of Justice Thomas, the words they write on civil rights are laced with historical inaccuracies.

As I have noted throughout this memoir, beginning with my attendance as a youth at the Sunday afternoon forum meetings at the YMCA in my home city of Youngstown, I have been privileged to become acquainted with the major actors of the day. It was no less true when I became a federal judge and had the honor of sharing the bench with Judge Tuttle and other judges of the Old Fifth Circuit, including John Minor Wisdom of New Orleans, and Frank Johnson and John Goldbold of Alabama. It was a long road from my days in Youngstown to joining the ranks of such towering judicial figures. As Sitton noted, they effected significant social change.

One of the highlights of my judicial career, and indeed my life, was to participate in a reunion when the lawyers and judges gathered at Ole Miss to reminisce about the Southern desegregation struggles. I was able to add to those remarkable stories by describing how their great work served as precedents as the desegregation campaign moved north. They were fascinated to learn, but not surprised to hear, of what Judge Stephen Roth and Judge Damon Keith faced in Michigan, and of the threats visited upon Judge Frank Battisti in Ohio and Judge W. Arthur Garrity Jr. in Boston. One of these judges whom I had the honor to salute while I was in active service was a white Mississippian, William Colbert Keady, who sat as a district court judge when the law in Mississippi was being transformed from an instrument of the dominant racist groups into a mechanism of orderly change for victims of historic discrimination. He did not allow the pejoration of "activist judge" into a derisive term or deter him from doing his duty with regard to desegregating the schools of Mississippi and reforming the prison system of that state.

The thanks that these and other courageous judges received from Ronald Reagan, and more recently Chief Justice John Roberts and other devotees of states' rights, was to be called "activists." The implicit and explicit signal sent by Ronald Reagan's speech in Philadelphia, Mississippi, was not lost upon blacks and others familiar with the racial violence that led to the deaths of Michael Schwerner, James Chaney, and Andrew Goodman outside that town in 1964, nor was it lost on white Southerners.

There can be little doubt of a design on the part of Southern Strategists to move full tilt into the Reagan states' rights restoration movement and minimize the continued use of federal power to effect change exactly as was done in the post-Reconstruction era. Capturing the courts was necessary to curtail the federal role in, among other things, the court's enforcement of court-decreed and voluntary efforts at bringing about further change. With his election in 1980, Ronald Reagan set about to do just that. No amount of historical rewrite or adoration can alter this fact.

I had seen signs of the Reagan promise being kept with the litmus test applied to his judicial appointees to the Sixth Circuit as well as to the District judgeships within the Sixth Circuit early in the Reagan years. The impact of these appointments became very clear in cases involving long-standing school desegregation orders and consent decrees in employment cases previously entered into in such cities as Detroit, Memphis, and Cleveland. When wave after wave of appeals seeking to overturn various desegregation and affirmative action decrees that had already become firm precedents reached my court, I knew that troubled times were ahead. For a time, we were able to withstand those waves. But as more Reagan-appointed judges were added to the court, it became increasingly difficult to withstand the assaults.

However, as the Supreme Court was to consistently state—until the arrival of the post-1980 Reagan "armada"—the test of any civil rights remedy was its effectiveness. Given this history and the amnesia that appears to have infected later generations, it is necessary to better understand the history of federal civil rights remedies. I saw signs that many of the Reagan-appointed judges had little or no understanding of the role that law played in perpetuating American racism. As a result, they were vulnerable to the efforts to dismantle the progress made.

The appointment of William French Smith as U.S. attorney general brought to the Justice Department a young lawyer named John Roberts who was fashioning ways of reducing the remedial power of federal courts by stripping them of jurisdiction over a whole range of activities. Years later I learned that that person, who is now chief justice of the United States, had a creative and decisive hand in formulating the strategy of resistance to school desegregation and other civil rights consent decrees.

My First Encounter

I first met Clarence Thomas on August 10, 1983, when he was serving as chair of the Equal Employment Opportunity Commission (EEOC). I was serving on the Sixth Circuit Court of Appeals at the time. He and I shared a program at an EEOC opportunity seminar at Vanderbilt University. The event was a training seminar for the staff of the EEOC, which I had been asked to keynote. In his remarks, Thomas reviewed the role of law and of the responsibility of each EEOC employee to bring the reality of the law to those who look to the government for protection. He insisted that this must be done with consistency, promptness, and fairness for all victims of discrimination. As chairman of the EEOC, Thomas brought a special message of inspiration to those who had the responsibility of enforcing the equal-employment policies of EEOC and Title VII. I was impressed with the force and sincerity of his expressed resolve in inspiring his staff to enforce the law with vigor.

To hear those words from the chair of the EEOC was most reassuring because I had seen efforts initiated and speeches emanating from people high in the Reagan administration suggesting a relaxed enforcement, if not an outright reversal, of various civil rights laws. However, my optimism soon came crashing down.

Justice Thurgood Marshall gave a moving speech in Maui, Hawaii, in 1987, on the occasion of the Bicentennial of the U.S. Constitution. It rang with historical truths about what the original drafters of the Constitution meant in 1787 with regard to their treatment of slavery and blacks. He declared:

I do not believe that the meaning of the Constitution was forever "fixed" at the Philadelphia Convention. Nor do I find the wisdom, foresight and sense of justice exhibited by the Framers particularly profound. To the contrary, the government they devised was defective from the start, requiring several amendments, a civil war and momentous social transformation to attain a system of constitutional government, and its respect for the individual freedoms and human rights we hold as fundamental today.

In this bicentennial year, we may not all participate in the festivities with flag waving fervor. Some may more quietly commemorate the suffering, struggle and sacrifice that has triumphed over much of what was wrong with the document, and observe the anniversary with hopes not realized and promis[e] not fulfilled.

I was stunned with incredulity when I read what Clarence Thomas, a direct beneficiary of Justice Marshall's courage, said of that great man. In celebration of Constitution Day on September 17, 1987, he wrote of Marshall in the *San Diego Union Tribune*:

> Hence, I find exasperating and incomprehensible the assault on the Bicentennial, the Founding, and the Constitution itself by Justice Thurgood Marshall, in a speech last May and most recently in a television interview. . . .
>
> His indictment of the Founders alienates all Americans and not just black Americans, from their high and noble intention. Thus quite to the contrary of Martin Luther King, Justice Marshall pits blacks, along with women and all Americans other than defenders of the Confederacy, against the Founders.
>
> As we have seen, Justice Marshall's understanding of blacks and the Constitution stands in stark contrast to that of notable Americans, from Frederick Douglass and Abraham Lincoln to Martin Luther King.[5]

It is now clear that these were the words of one "auditioning" before those Reagan had charged with returning states' rights to its once-dominant place—a place where powerful majorities would again hold sway over minorities—but only if judges with the views of Justice Marshall were cleared from the bench.

The Nomination of Clarence Thomas

Black people of all political persuasions feared that with George Herbert Walker Bush's election as president, it would be during his term that a curtain was likely to close on Justice Thurgood Marshall's remarkable judicial career. Justice Marshall's retirement represented an opportune time for those seeking to regain control of governmental power to make a strategic move. Marshall himself foresaw this and laced his last dissenting opinion with warnings.

For his successor, President Bush reached down, instead of out and up, and chose a person similar in color but far different in kind for Marshall's replacement. It was disappointing to see a president so cynically cater to the right wing not only by stacking the courts with adherents of states' rights, but also by appointing to the Supreme Court someone whose views were so completely at odds with those of Justice Marshall.

Given the political landscape at the time, an outright attack on the Supreme Court was unfeasible. Instead, the right needed a Trojan horse through whom it could slip its agenda through the gates under a seemingly benign cover. A black nominee would be an ideal choice as Marshall's replacement since many people would never believe he would go against black aspirations. Yet the political, moral and constitutional zigzag that brought Thomas to the Supreme Court was apparent for many of us to see.

Initial Reactions

When he announced the nomination, President Bush described Clarence Thomas as "the best person for the position." Many legal scholars and court observers shook their heads in disbelief.

I note the reaction of legal scholars and court observers because they were in the best position to evaluate President Bush's judgment of Thomas's relative fitness to become a Supreme Court justice. I could easily add the startled reaction of a vast number of judges with whom I was in regular contact by virtue of me being a sitting judge. A number of federal judges hesitated to openly render a critical opinion on Judge Thomas's questionable qualifications out of fear that doing so would inject them into a political debate. Thus, their reactions were more guarded. There were others, however, who resented the president's patronizing praise and registered their disagreement based on knowledge of Judge Thomas's record. His record at the EEOC was scrutinized during his confirmation for the D.C. Circuit Court of Appeals seat. It was as unimpressive and at variance from his then hopeful Vanderbilt pledge as were the decisions he rendered during his eighteen months as an appellate judge.

The morally and intellectually impeccable Dr. John Hope Franklin wrote in a *New York Times* op-ed entitled "Booker T. Washington Revisited" that Thomas "has placed himself in the unseemly position of denying to others the very opportunities and the kind of assistance from public and private quarters that have placed him where he is today."[6]

Haywood Burns, a former NAACP LDF lawyer who founded the National Conference of Black Lawyers, himself a graduate of the Yale Law School who served as dean of the CUNY Law School, described Justice Thomas as "a counterfeit hero."[7]

Jeffrey Toobin, writing in the *New Yorker*, commented on Justice Thomas's qualifications: "Before he became a federal judge, he had never argued a single case in federal court. Indeed, before he joined the D.C. Circuit, his career as a litigator consisted of serving his first two and a half years out of law school as an entry-level lawyer on the staff of the Missouri Attorney General."[8] The Missouri Attorney General on whose staff he worked, John Danforth, went on to become Missouri's U.S. Senator who carried the ball during Thomas's controversial confirmation hearings.

There were people who sincerely believed that "once he gets what he wants, he'll change." Thus, the refrain "Cut the Brother some slack, he will come back home." I was not in this camp. Thomas's eagerness to trample on such an icon as Marshall, to advance the right wing's states' rights strategy, eliminated any right I felt he may have had to a benefit of the doubt. I felt that a heavy burden rested on Thomas to demonstrate that he had changed his views.

During the confirmation hearing, Thomas's primary sponsor, Senator John Danforth, and the nominee himself went to great lengths to project an image of Thomas as a caring, racially sensitive person. They traced the history of the civil rights struggle and acknowledged its critical role in Thomas's success. In stark contrast to his other pre-nomination statements he said, among other things:

> But for the efforts of so many who have gone before me, I would not be here today. It would be unimaginable. Only by standing on their shoulders could I be here. At each turn in my life, each obstacle confronted, each fork in the road, someone came along to help. . . .
>
> Justice Marshall, whose seat I've been nominated to fill, is one of those who had the courage and the intellect. He's one of the great architects of the legal battles to open doors that seemed so insurmountable to those of us in the Pin Point, Georgias of the world. . . .
>
> The civil rights movement—Reverend Martin Luther King, and the SCLC, Roy Wilkins and the NAACP, Whitney Young and the Urban League, Fannie Lou Hamer, Rosa Parks and Dorothy Height. They changed society and made it reach affirmatively to help. I have benefited greatly from their efforts. But for them, there would have been no road to travel.[9]

I was not fooled. The remarks Thomas made at his confirmation hearing came from the lips of the same man who said he "can't think of any" good the NAACP ever did and claimed that civil-rights leaders, in general, just "bitch, bitch, bitch, moan and moan, whine and whine."[10]

Clarence Thomas's testimony took many twists and turns, depending on which senator was doing the questioning. An unforgettable moment occurred when Thomas lashed out at the committee for subjecting him to a "high tech" lynching. The real target of the so-called lynching by Senator Arlen Specter and the committee turned out to be a witness, Professor Anita Hill. Senator Specter, who once served as a Philadelphia district attorney, jumped at the chance to show what he once did for a living, oblivious to the fact that Professor Hill was neither a criminal defendant nor an accuser, proved to be a villain. Professor Hill was a fact witness subpoenaed by the committee to relate her recollection of events involving

Thomas's behavior toward her. For Clarence Thomas to protest about a high-tech lynching given the tough treatment Professor Hill was subjected to by members of the committee seemed, to me, to be grossly misplaced.

Clarence Thomas's testimony, while insufficient to settle doubts of many of us, obviously succeeded in convincing enough committee members to ensure confirmation, if only by a narrow margin. Justice Thomas then proceeded to do exactly what I feared he would do. In subsequent opinions he damned civil rights remedies and insisted that there is no difference between invidious discrimination and the benign impact flowing from remedies. I feel that the right wing's Trojan horse had once again splashed through the shrinking river of black aspiration.

I condemn the deception Clarence Thomas employed as he made his way to the Supreme Court, as well as the use he currently makes of his power. I also reserve condemnation for those, such as columnist Armstrong Williams, who partnered with Thomas and continue to defend him. One can wonder how Senator Danforth, Armstrong Williams, and other principal defenders feel about having been so used by Clarence Thomas.

Unlike Williams, some of Thomas's defenders came to regret their support for his confirmation. George Curry, editor of the now-defunct *Emerge* magazine, wrote an editorial in its November 1993 issue that set out the sense of pride and pain that Margaret Bush Wilson, the former chair of the NAACP board, had come to feel about the man she called her "second son":

> It was that kind of rumination, as well as a long friendship, that motivated Margaret Bush Wilson to write a newspaper column in 1991 saying the NAACP, of which she was Chair of the Board from 1975 to 1984, was wrong to oppose the man "I think of fondly as a second son." Instead of seeing Thomas in that way now, the St. Louis attorney is expressing second thoughts about having supported him. As she told Trevor W. Coleman in an interview . . . "I am waiting for him to show some independence."

When death came to Mrs. Wilson on August 11, 2009, this grand and committed woman was no longer waiting for Clarence Thomas to change. She went to her grave feeling deeply betrayed. Although Mrs. Wilson could not bring herself to verbally spank her "second son," others were not so restrained in their criticism of the man a *New York Times* editorial labeled "the youngest, cruelest justice."[11]

Retired Third Circuit Court of Appeals Judge A. Leon Higginbotham Jr. wrote in the *University of Pennsylvania Law Review* "An Open Letter to Justice Clarence Thomas from a Federal Judicial Colleague" dated November 29, 1991, shortly after Thomas donned his Supreme Court robes.[12] Judge Higginbotham consulted with several federal judges as he prepared his letter. I was one of them. He was fully aware that some of Justice Thomas's defenders might be inclined to dismiss his critique as resulting from jealousy, however, anyone familiar with the credibility and scholarship of Judge Higginbotham would not be so inclined. An indication of the interest in Judge Higginbotham's treatise was the fact that the demand for reprints of the article set a record for the University of Pennsylvania Law School.

Washington Post columnist William Raspberry administered as personal a journalistic scolding as was ever given to a Supreme Court Justice. He wrote in his column in response to the horrid decision Clarence Thomas authored in a case of a prisoner being severely beaten by guards:

> Clarence:
> I know I'm supposed to call you Justice Thomas, but I don't want to be quite that formal. I want to talk straight to a guy I thought I knew a little.
> You know what I want to talk about. It's that dissent of yours in the matter of Hudson v. McMillan. Come on, Clarence. Conservative is one thing; bizarre is another. . . .
> What was truly bizarre is that when the conservative-dominated U.S. Supreme Court reversed the appellate decision this week, yours was one of only two dissenting voices.

To tell you the truth, Clarence, I'm personally embarrassed. You know you weren't my choice to succeed Thurgood Marshall on the nation's highest court. You were too conservative for my taste and more significant, I thought you lacked the requisite judicial experience. But I thought I understood your conservatism as a sort of harsh pragmatism that most of us harbor to some degree. I cautioned Black America not to let your conservatism blind them to your intellectual honesty. Conservatism, I insisted, is not the same as stupidity—even in a black man.[13]

Praise and "Whining"

Justice Thomas's dissenting opinion in the affirmative-action case of *Adarand Constructors, Inc. v. Peña* in 1995 gave painful credence to Higginbotham's "Open Letter to a Judicial Colleague" law review article. In his opinion that involved affirmative action for a women's company, Justice Thomas equated effects of a remedy with acts of invidious discrimination. He rejected the notion that there was a difference between the two. As a judge on an intermediate court, I found Justice Thomas's language to be totally incompatible with precedents dating back to the *Brown* decision and beyond, and completely contrary to the promise he made at his confirmation to uphold the Constitution and respect precedents. It certainly does not square with the question he posed during his Associated Press interview on September 7, 1991: "But for affirmative action, where would I be today?"

I lament the way the Fourteenth Amendment and the various remedies that have been fashioned under it are being turned into a barrier for the redress of wrongs. It cannot be credibly contended that the effects of slavery and "separate but equal" have been eliminated. There are those who maintain that the nation is in a postracial period, obviating the need for race-sensitive remedies. They are joined by Supreme Court Justice Thomas, who argues that the remedies are a form of stigmatization. They use Booker T. Washington's pre–*Brown v. Board of Education* arguments and Frederick

Douglass's out-of-context, pre–Thirteenth, Fourteenth, and Fifteenth Amendment utterances to buttress their position that governmental help stigmatizes those who seek and receive it. Those combined arguments of Thomas and the right-wingers directly clash with the Houstonian school of jurisprudence, which is based largely on the Fourteenth Amendment. Significantly, the incorporation doctrine, through which the individual guarantees of the Bill of Rights were made applicable to the states, provided an additional check on state misdeeds. This was a long-sought-after layer of federal protection previously denied to blacks as members of a discrete minority, and others as well.

Until the guarantees in the Bill of Rights were made applicable to the states, all kinds of abuses were inflicted on blacks and the poor. An example of Justice Thomas clinging to the states' rights concept was his opinion in the *Hudson* case that William Raspberry cited in his journalistic scolding. The rationale that Justice Thomas relied upon for not applying the Eighth Amendment protection against cruel and unusual punishment was that the prisoner was *only* beaten and not killed.

In the Marx Lecture at the University of Cincinnati College of Law in 2000, I attempted to address this history and the implications of the current attempt of the Supreme Court, enabled by Justice Thomas and now Chief Justice Roberts, to curtail racial remedies. That lecture was entitled "The Sisyphean Impact on Houstonian Jurisprudence" for a good reason.

I noted the following in my lecture:

Many commentators at the time failed to appreciate that the court's curtailment of remedies in the area of desegregation would begin a long slide down the path of curtailing remedies in other important areas. The venom infecting public discourse on transportation or "busing" would soon spill over into such affirmative action matters as employment, college admissions, and contract set asides, often mischievously labeled as quotas, and voting rights, including legislative reapportionment. This spill over illustrates the seamlessness of racial remedies and the resultant harm when the unraveling begins. As civil rights advocates strenuously argued at the time, backing away from the strong federal enforcement of the constitutional mandate of *Brown*, would ultimately threaten the gains that had been achieved in these other areas. A review of the current and evolving Supreme Court precedents bear out their concerns.[14]

Justice Marshall's opinions were always loaded with history. An example of his wisdom was found in his opinion that challenged the majority in the *City of Richmond v. J. A. Croson Company* case. It dealt with the court majority striking down a set-aside program it said fell into a suspect classification because it involved race. In the opinion of the majority of the court, this constituted invidious discrimination that triggered strict scrutiny, rather than applying the traditional "intermediate" scrutiny for benign discrimination. Justice Marshall dissented, saying:

A profound difference separates governmental actions that themselves are racist, and governmental actions that seek to remedy the effects of prior racism. . . .

The fact is that Congress' concern in passing Reconstruction Amendments . . . was that States would not adequately respond to racial violence or discrimination against newly freed slaves. To interpret any aspect of these [Reconstruction] Amendments as proscribing state remedial responses to these very problems turns the Amendments on their heads.[15]

Such reasoning constitutes a resurrection of the long-rejected *Plessy* doctrine. Yet it is this resurrected jurisprudence by the conservative Supreme Court majority that is being pushed by Chief Justice Roberts and Justice Thomas, who, in spite of the warmth and understanding of some of their confirmation statements, are on the verge of repealing the hard-won *Brown v. Board of Education*, and thus nullifying the Fourteenth Amendment's equal protection clause. In wrenching the teaching of Frederick Douglass from its rightful context and applying it to a different one, Justice Thomas has committed a most egregious wrong. In his concurring/

dissenting opinion in *Grutter v. Bollinger*, the University of Michigan affirmative action case, Justice Thomas, in voting to strike down affirmative action, unforgivably misapplied the words of Frederick Douglass: "What I ask for the Negro is not benevolence, not pity, not sympathy, but simply justice . . . and if a Negro cannot stand on his own legs, let him fall also. All I ask is 'give him a chance to stand on his own legs. Let him alone! . . . Your interference is doing him positive injury."[16] In fact, Douglass had been addressing a group of abolitionists in April 1865, before the Thirteenth, Fourteenth, and Fifteenth Amendments became a part of the Constitution. What Thomas omitted from the Douglass speech were words that conveyed just the opposite argument than the one he now makes. Douglass's actual argument in the speech entitled "What the Black Man Wants" was this:

> I am for the "immediate, unconditional, and universal enfranchisement" of the black man, in every State of the Union. Without this, his liberty is a mockery; without this, you might as well almost retain the old name of slavery for his condition, for in fact, if he is not the slave of the individual master, he is the slave of society; and holds his liberty as a privilege, not as a right. He is at the mercy of the mob, and has no means of protecting himself.

Some license may be granted to Thomas for distorting Douglass's point when engaged in political discourse, but it is intolerable for him to do it in a judicial opinion. One must ask why this Supreme Court Justice, who during his confirmation hearing cited the racial hardship of his own family, would consistently in his opinions choose to misquote this historical abolitionist figure, Frederick Douglass. I feel an obligation to condemn it because it negatively affects the ability of those still waging the struggle for justice.

Education today, as even Justice Sandra Day O'Connor wrote in the *Grutter* case before retiring, remains central to social advancement, especially for a discrete minority group. Yet the position of Justice Thomas in three significant education cases clashes with Charles Houston and Thurgood Marshall, who gave us the ratio-

nale for *Brown*. Thomas, contrary to what he said in his confirmation testimony, acts with reckless disregard for the historical fact
that for many generations, education was completely and intentionally withheld from black slaves. As Douglass and Houston pointed
out, the national policy and practice was to keep the entire black
race in intellectual and legal peonage.

It is disingenuous for Justice Thomas and his conservative Supreme
Court colleagues to heap praise on *Brown* as an admirable precedent
that cleansed the effects of American apartheid from the country's
schools and then hobble all attempts to meaningfully deal with the
vestiges of segregation. This they do by imposing the standard of
"strict scrutiny." Future progress for school desegregation and affirmative action plans are choked off by the strict scrutiny standard,
which limits the exercise of judicial remedial power in cases involving racial discrimination. This places litigation in a straitjacket and
freezes into place the wicked past. Justice Thomas's insistence that
there is no difference between the benign effects of a remedy and the
intentional and invidious discrimination practiced against blacks, is
itself invidious. The formula for accommodating both was approved
by the Supreme Court in the cases *Weber v. Steelworkers* and *Bakke*.
Justice Thomas appears hell-bent on going backward and destroying
these advances, even though he stated, under oath, that he would
follow the precedents so painfully and carefully constructed.

In my testimony at the confirmation hearing for Justice Roberts,
I linked him with Justice Thomas in their shared abhorrence of
racial remedies. In doing so I relied upon Justice Thomas's opinion
in the *Adarand* case and Chief Justice Roberts's role in advising the
White House on ways of challenging consent decrees. I stated,
"Given Judge Roberts' history of challenging the use of federal
power to address the harmful vestiges of racist governmental policies, it should come as no surprise that Black Americans, and those
who worked with us to effect change, are alarmed and wary that
his elevation to the Supreme Court could result in an unraveling of
the gains won at such a high price."[17]

Judge Pierce Lively of the Sixth Circuit, a Kentuckian, who reli-
giously applied the Supreme Court precedents to craft a remedy

for discrimination, wrote in *Detroit Police Officers' Association v. Young*, "One analysis is required when those for whose benefit the Constitution was amended or a statute enacted claim discrimination. A different analysis must be made when the claimants are not members of a class historically subjected to discrimination. When claims are brought by members of a group formerly subjected to discrimination the case moves with the grain of the Constitution and national policy."[18]

Judge Lively's analysis was true to Supreme Court precedents. Now, unfortunately, the Supreme Court's majority opinions have virtually embraced Justice Thomas's views in *Adarand Constructors, Inc. v. Peña*. That view rejects *Brown* and the gains it brought, including such remedies as affirmative action irrespective of our racial history. As Thomas wrote in his opinion in this case:

> I believe that there is a moral [and] constitutional equivalence between laws designed to subjugate a race and those that distribute benefits on the basis of race in order to foster some current notion of equality.

Removing remaining doubt as to his intentions, Thomas wrote:

> As far as the Constitution is concerned, it is irrelevant whether a government's racial classifications are drawn by those who wish to oppress a race or by those who have a sincere desire to help those thought to be disadvantaged.

In case doubt remains, Justice Thomas more clearly rephrased his views:

> In my mind, government-sponsored racial discrimination based on benign prejudice is just as noxious as discrimination inspired by malicious prejudice.[19]

As if this were not bad enough, his opinions in the *Grutter*, Louisville, and Seattle cases compound the damage, which included his misuse of Frederick Douglass's words.

This kind of thinking and reasoning are at the heart of my profound disagreement with Justice Thomas. It undoes the successful campaign waged by Houston, Marshall, Carter, Hastie, and the cadre of lawyers who fought to overturn *Plessy v. Ferguson* and in whose shoes I am honored to stand. Thomas's thinking is the very antithesis of Houstonian jurisprudence and the spirit of *Brown*. It defies understanding as to how one could laud Houstonian jurisprudence on one hand, with all of the suffering that went into building and filling out its framework, and then assert in the next breath that race cannot be taken into account to obtain redress for still-lingering violations of the Fourteenth Amendment.

The intellectually dishonest contentions of Justice Thomas and his new conservative colleagues, particularly Chief Justice Roberts, Justice Antonin Scalia, and Justice Samuel Alito, add up to a massive double cross of the American people, particularly minorities and women. Thomas faked his way through much of the Judiciary Committee hearings by speaking with considerable gratitude about affirmative action and those who made it possible for him to advance. Then, once comfortably ensconced in his seat, he reverted to his pre-confirmation stance on those issues, provoking the following response by a distinguished black judge, U.W. Clemon of Birmingham, Alabama, who fought many a civil rights battle as a lawyer for the NAACP Legal Defense Fund. Judge Clemon, now retired, was quoted as follows in a June 18, 1998, *Washington Post* story: "He is no hero to us. On issues affecting black people, Mr. Justice Thomas has provided the crucial vote against what many of us consider the interests of black people."

Contrary to the Roberts-Thomas-Scalia contentions and those who join them, there remains to this day strong and continuing justifications for race-conscious remedies.

Few can seriously doubt that Clarence Thomas was picked for the Supreme Court because of his skin color; there was color *consciousness* involved. A review of his life story and confirmation hearing demonstrates that any hint of color *blindness* that some seek to claim is downright bogus. For Justice Thomas to deny an awareness of this is to deny his life experience. I refuse to accord to him the excuse that some of his white colleagues can claim. For instance that flippant remark by Chief Justice Roberts reveals an embarrassing lack of understanding about the deep roots of racial, ethnic and gender bias, and stands in stark contrast to the remarkable, intelligent and thoughtful insight revealed by Justice Blackmun in the *Bakke* case, when he wrote, "I suspect that it would be impossible to arrange an affirmative action program in a racially neutral way and have it successful. To ask that this be so is to demand the impossible. In order to get beyond racism, we must first take account of race. There is no other way. And in order to treat some persons equally, we must treat them differently. We cannot—we dare not—let the Equal Protection clause perpetuate racial Supremacy."[20]

And where the current chief justice is concerned, his early role in quarterbacking the Reagan administration's drive to bring about a "sea change" in the makeup of federal courts was designed to deconstruct the body of civil rights precedents developed under *Brown*. To those aware of his involvement in choking off remedies while a lawyer in the Justice Department and the White House, Chief Justice Robert's quip in the Louisville and Seattle school desegregation cases was consistent with his past: "The way to stop discrimination on the basis of race is to stop discriminating on the basis of race."[21] Such a simplistic dismissal displayed gross ignorance of the sacrifices involved in making the Constitution relevant to historic victims of discrimination. To it, I offered the following rebuttal in my testimony before the Senate Judiciary Committee:

> When Charles Houston launched his strategy to overturn the *Plessy v. Ferguson* decision, American law was firmly supportive of racial segregation. Houston and his colleagues, Thurgood Marshall and William Hastie, went from courtroom to courtroom challenging what they firmly believed to have been a hijacking of the Fourteenth Amendment. Race was at the heart of these efforts because it was race that drove the Supreme Court to inject racism into the tributaries of this nation.
>
> These giants had a profound belief in the Constitution's promise to establish justice, ensure domestic tranquility and secure the blessings

of liberty. Through the careful building of precedents, with much sacrifice and struggle, the Houston strategy resulted in the 1954 *Brown v. Board of Education* decision. That decision proved to be the launching pad for widespread attacks on racial discrimination.[22]

Had the Judiciary Committee members done their job as required under the oath they themselves took, Roberts would have done one of two things: first, he would have reexamined his own past and in a straightforward manner told the Committee his views; second, he would have set about educating himself on the nation's racial history to have a better understanding of the issues that would come before him. Moreover, Roberts would have concluded that coming up with clever, simpleminded phrases as he did in *Grutter*, was an inappropriate way for the chief justice to address an issue sufficiently laden with history as to warrant the kind of thoughtful response that Justice Blackmun offered in the *Bakke* case.

Chief Justice Roberts is too bright a lawyer to project such an appalling degree of ignorance about segregation's history. It was under the Fourteenth and Fifteenth Amendments and the statutes enacted pursuant to them that the nation made dramatic, if at times halting, progress against the effects of slavery and *Plessy v. Ferguson*.

At an earlier time, writing for the Supreme Court in *Swann v. Charlotte-Mecklenburg Board of Education*, a major Southern school desegregation case in 1971, Chief Justice Warren Burger provided considerable enlightenment on this point when he wrote:

Absent a constitutional violation there would be no basis for judicially ordering assignment of students on a racial basis. All things being equal, with no history of discrimination, it might well be desirable to assign pupils to schools nearest their homes. But all things are not equal in a system that has been deliberately constructed and maintained to enforce racial segregation. The remedy for such segregation may be administratively awkward, inconvenient, and even bizarre in some situations and may impose burdens on some; but all awkwardness and inconvenience cannot be avoided in the interim period when remedial adjustments are being made to eliminate the dual school systems.[23]

The current Supreme Court's majority view of "race neutral" equal protection in its consideration of Northern segregation detours widely from settled precedents. When blacks, in frustration, took to the streets, there was no shortage of people, including President Lyndon B. Johnson, urging that protesters should take their grievances to the courts. This they did. Sadly, in the face of what the Supreme Court is now doing, such advice is proving to be unrealistic.

It is now apparent that to insist that the Fourteenth Amendment, which was added to the Constitution for the explicit purpose of helping the newly freed slaves and their descendants to look to the legal system for relief, is ringing hollow. Chief Justice Roberts, along with Justices Thomas, Scalia, and Alito, who contend with the use of race-sensitive remedies aimed at redressing clearly identified discrimination, don't seem to understand that they are at war with history, with reality, and with the Constitution itself. To demand that America become color-blind now is to freeze into place the clear and present vestiges of those despicable past racial practices. Those who question whether these abuses continue to exist need only look to the findings of fact by courts—at every level and from all over the country—by fact finders who have the responsibility of examining claims of discrimination in schools, in hiring, in housing, and in criminal justice, to say nothing of voting rights abuses.

The controversies that were stirred by the selection of Judge Thomas for a seat on the Supreme Court continue to simmer. His reactionary states' rights position on a range of issues, notably civil rights, is clear. His opinions on a full range of civil rights, most recently voting rights, threaten to end reliance on federal judicial power to enforce the racial remedies without which the long struggle to excise the vestiges of slavery from the nation's institutions will come to an ignominious end.

15

Obama: Election Reflections

It was an electrifying moment at the Pepsi Center in Denver when delegates to the Democratic National Convention nominated Barack Obama for the office of the president of the United States.

Thousands robustly cheered. I stood silent and virtually motionless as tears welled up in my eyes. On either side of me were my wife, Lillian, and my daughter, Stephanie, who were, through sobs, expressing their joy along with the thousands of others whose voices ricocheted off the walls of that cavernous arena.

When I returned to my hotel room and viewed the television replay of what had occurred inside the arena, my most immediate thoughts were of the previous Monday night, when a cancer-stricken Senator Ted Kennedy had left his hospital bed in Boston to deliver his last political speech. Having known the senator since 1959 and shared the speaking platform with him on several occasions, the realization that this was perhaps his final political plea was painful. Despite his grave condition, he came to sound a clarion call to the delegates to nominate an African American to be the party's standard-bearer for the office of president of the United States.

The Kennedys

In his convention speech Senator Kennedy invoked the names of his two martyred brothers, President John F. Kennedy and Senator Robert F. Kennedy. I first met the three Kennedy brothers in Youngstown, Ohio, in 1959, as the 1960 presidential campaign was getting under way. Ted Kennedy was the youngest of the three, and his role was that of a personal aide to Senator John F. Kennedy. He brushed off his brother's pinstripe suit jacket and carried the folder containing his speech. He made notes on a clipboard as the senator moved through the crowd meeting people. Robert Kennedy, also very young, whose hair length drew comments from bystanders, was tense, unsmiling, and appeared to be his older brother's gatekeeper. Matters of substance seemed to pass through Robert before reaching the senator.

A year later I attended the 1960 Democratic Convention in Los Angeles, where John F. Kennedy was nominated and went on to campaign against Vice President Richard Nixon. I chaired several rallies featuring surrogates sent to the Youngstown area by national campaign figures, including such notables as Chicago congressman William L. Dawson and Harlem congressman Adam Clayton Powell.

The Kennedy campaign struggled to "sell" its candidate to the black voters, many of whom were kindly disposed to Richard Nixon because of his work under President Eisenhower in championing affirmative action in the awarding of government contracts. The Kennedy campaign decided to convene a conference of black leaders at the Roosevelt Hotel in New York to reemphasize their intention of addressing matters of concern to the black community. I attended that two-day meeting, which concluded with an outdoor rally in Harlem at the Theresa Hotel on 125th Street. In his speech John Kennedy promised to appoint blacks as federal judges, U.S. attorneys, and U.S. marshals.

After his election, I became a part of that campaign promise, for in October 1962, Attorney General Robert Kennedy signed the commission appointing me as an assistant U.S. attorney for the Northern

District of Ohio. While such appointments are now unexceptional, it was a "first" for Ohio, and highly newsworthy. It certainly redirected my professional life. I was holding that position in the Kennedy administration's Justice Department when on August 28, 1963, I joined 250,000 other Americans in the March on Washington. That historic event preceded Senator Ted Kennedy's dramatic speech in support of Barack Obama by forty-eight years. My memory went back to the first time I saw him in my hometown. In his role as chairman of the Senate Judiciary Committee, he presided over the hearing that led to my confirmation as a federal judge.

Whose March on Washington?

Recalling that 1963 event reminded me of the historical revisionism that has occurred over time and how troubled I have been by news commentators who continue to inaccurately characterize the March on Washington. I am saddened seeing those who made the event a success being written out of that remarkable history. They include such leaders as A. Philip Randolph, head of the Brotherhood of Sleeping Car Porters, and his principal aide, Bayard Rustin; Roy Wilkins, executive director of the NAACP; Whitney Young, president of the National Urban League; John Lewis, head of the Student Non-Violent Coordinating Committee; Joseph Rauh of the Leadership Conference on Civil Rights; and labor leader Walter Reuther, president of the United Automobile Workers Union. The planning of the march was touch and go. It was the financial backing from Reuther's UAW and Wilkins's NAACP that virtually saved the event.

The powerful "I Have a Dream" speech has prompted the public to identify Dr. Martin Luther King as the principal organizer of the march. The notion took on added force after Congress established King's birthday as a national legal holiday. King's birthday is always heralded with celebrants quoting famous lines from his speech. Included among those are people who were not so embracing of Dr. King or his message during his lifetime.

Though most whites were hearing about the "dream" for the first time, many blacks, including me, had heard many speeches in which Dr. King spoke of it. It stirred us at each hearing. As he stood at the Lincoln Memorial podium warming into his speech, it being one of the dozen or so speeches that day, the famous gospel singer Mahalia Jackson, sitting nearby, murmured very audibly what many of us wanted to hear, "Tell 'em 'bout your dream, Martin." And he did. In the cadence of the response to sermons in the black church, the microphones caught and amplified the famous gospel singer's words.

From then on, the shapers of public opinion took every opportunity to describe the March on Washington as Dr. King's march. Virtually every reference to the March on Washington would bear the prefatory words, "Dr. King's March on Washington" or "Dr. Martin Luther King, who launched the modern civil rights movement." During the planning of the event his role was important but not dominant. None of this distortion was the doing of Dr. King. It resulted from those who lacked a sense of history and failed to exert the effort to learn the facts.

If they had done their homework—the obligation of responsible journalists and commentators—many would have discovered the facts about the origin and execution of the March on Washington. It was not until after Wilkins, Randolph, and Reuther freed up their staffs and financial resources that the march planning came together. Not until they, along with Clarence Mitchell, the NAACP's chief lobbyist; the Leadership Conference on Civil Rights; Arnold Aaronson; and Gloster B. Current, director of the widespread NAACP branch network, swung into action operating on several levels did planning coalesce. Mitchell was particularly active trying to muster support from congressional leadership. Opposition from members of Congress and some in the Kennedy state administration required constant rebuttals. President Kennedy, shortly before the march, tried to persuade leaders to call it off. Fear of violence was not the only motivation for some of this opposition. Entering into the equation were political fears at having tens of thousands of blacks descending on the nation's capital. Leaders of the march, however, convinced the president and his advisers that they had everything under control and that there would be no violence. And there wasn't.

I arrived in the nation's capital early on the morning of August 28, after an overnight bus ride with members of the Youngstown NAACP branch. Ours was one of the first of the endless line of buses to arrive on the Washington Mall. After a briefing we sought out a restaurant for breakfast before locating the starting place for the march. A large number of people had already gathered in front of the Lincoln Memorial, and our Youngstown contingent staked out an area as near the front as we could. Before long the crowd began to swell.

The historical significance of more than 250,000 people rallying in the nation's capital was clear. The message of cooperation and nonviolence permeated the assembled crowd and remained all day. In a democracy, numbers matter. Memories of that day over fifty years ago remain at the surface of my consciousness.

Brief Encounters

When I met Mark Whitaker, then the new Washington, D.C., bureau chief of NBC News, I raised with him the Urban League study of Sunday morning talk shows that my daughter, Stephanie Jones, conducted. Whitaker was aware of the study and credited it with sensitizing NBC News about the need to improve. The study reported that "the exclusion of African-American voices is not unique to Sunday morning talk shows; with few exceptions, the television news outlets regularly fail to adequately include African-Americans, other minorities and women in the vast majority of their news programming."[1]

This brings to my mind Ronald Reagan's words spoken in Neshoba County, Mississippi, as he launched his presidential campaign. One thing he was not lacking was an understanding of the power and meaning of words—and of symbolism. Choosing Neshoba County, Mississippi—the site of the murder of civil-rights workers

Michael Schwerner, Andrew Goodman, and James Chaney—for his campaign kickoff and talking about states' rights was a signal to the South that the "good old days" were about to return. To be sure that there would be no mistake, Reagan backed up the symbolism of the site of his rally with a pledge to end the appointment of "activist judges." This would be accomplished by a "sea change" in the makeup of the federal courts.

In addition to those judges in the South who were slandered were some of their Northern brethren who issued sweeping rulings in school desegregation and other civil rights cases. Many of these judges became targets of threats, making it necessary for the U.S. marshals to be assigned to them and their families. For Reagan to label these judges as he did made them a target for terrorism—American-style. The rush to deify Reagan has been a rush to rewrite history.

He pushed a policy to nullify the effect of court decrees that attempted to reverse the IRS prohibition of tax exemptions for segregated schools. His attempt to justify this was provided in remarks to a group of black schoolchildren in Chicago. He said, "I was under the impression that the problem of segregated schools had been settled, and maybe I was wrong. I didn't know there were any court cases pending." Ignorance absolves neither President Reagan nor the media for the pass it gave him in the tributes at his death.

During my twenty-three years as a judge and the preceding ten years as NAACP general counsel, I was prohibited from participation in partisan politics. Thus, to be able to openly express my views as Obama was being nominated was a freedom I welcomed, especially with journalists.

From 1960 to 2008: The Emergence of Black Journalists

The number of black journalists at the 2008 Convention was another contrast to the 1960 Los Angeles Convention when John

Kennedy was nominated. Black print and television journalists were very visible in 2008. Former Tennessee congressman Harold Ford Jr., Michelle Bernard, and Eugene Robinson were doing commentary for MSNBC; Suzanne Malveaux, Rowan Martin, and Joe Johns were reporting and commenting for CNN. Juan Williams, a mainstay of the conservative Fox channel, did his usual bit.

It was not a bit unusual in Denver in 2008 to see columnists Eugene Robinson of the *Washington Post*; Clarence Page of the *Chicago Sun-Times*; Cynthia Tucker, editorial page editor of the *Atlanta Journal-Constitution*; and hosts of other black journalists—a major change from the 1948 convention.

On the political side, the number of blacks had also increased. The top blacks in the Kennedy camp had been Frank Reeves and Marjorie McKenzie Lawson, both Washington lawyers. While they were part of his entourage, their influence was minimal. At the Democratic National Committee, there were only a few black players of influence, including Congressman William Dawson and his deputy, Louie Martin, among others. But in 2008, the racial diversity was most impressive, with blacks chairing such powerful posts as the Credentials Committee, presided over by Alexis Herman; and the Resolutions Committee, headed by Massachusetts governor Deval Patrick. Another major player was Virginia's former governor, Douglas Wilder. The third-ranking member of the House of Representatives, James Clyburn of South Carolina, and the forty-three-member Congressional Black Caucus added heft that had been nonexistent in 1960.

The contemporary demonstrations of the power of diversity grew from the swirl of activities that gave rise to the 1963 March on Washington. After President Kennedy's assassination in November 1963, President Lyndon B. Johnson picked up the civil rights legislative baton. With the support of civil rights leadership, President Johnson took the lead in pushing through Congress the 1964 Civil Rights Act and the 1965 Voting Rights Act. Those laws became the vehicle on which blacks rode to greater political power to bring about the transformation of politics between the 1960s and 2008. In modern reporting, however, the role played by black leaders in mobilizing their constituencies and expanding opportunities for minorities in the media is grossly underreported.

I wondered how many of those delegates at the 2008 National Convention were having flashbacks and how they were reacting to the dramatic changes. I recall watching the 1948 convention in Philadelphia and the national excitement over a black minister, Reverend Marshall Shepard, giving the opening prayer. The press, especially black newspapers, heralded the event. Reverend Shepard became a national celebrity who was much sought after as a speaker. What we were witnessing in 2008 was a far cry from selecting a black preacher to offer an invocation; racial and gender diversity abounded in every phase of the 2008 convention, with the presidential candidate himself being an African American, placed there by a political constituency made up of multiple races, ethnicities, and genders. As I sat there, my mind did a backflip in time to the beginning of my awareness of race. This was during a period when separate-but-equal was still the law of the land and the virus of racism had infected the various institutions that governed the destiny of black and white people. Conventional attitudes about white superiority and black inferiority were reinforced by law and custom. The Supreme Court in its 1857 *Dred Scott* decision held that blacks were not *persons* within the meaning of the Constitution. I have noted that Chief Justice Roger Taney made twenty-one references to blacks as a subhuman species in his decision. I wondered what he would say now.

Roy Wilkins often said blacks were exposed to a "smothering pattern of a thousand different personal humiliations." These humiliations were the legacy of that *Dred Scott* Supreme Court opinion and did serious damage to the hopes and aspirations of black Americans.

Clearly, the events of 2008 showed the distance we had come. The issue is not simply the distance traveled, which I acknowledge, but the sustainability of those gains. The jurisprudence being woven into the social fabric of the nation by Chief Justice John Roberts, who while serving as President Reagan's legal counsel shaped the strategy for the "sea change" in the makeup of the federal judiciary with the reinforcements of Justices Thomas and Scalia, gives me concern.

Ohio

The outcome of the 2004 presidential race between President George W. Bush and Senator John Kerry had turned on events in Ohio, and this remained fresh in the minds of delegates from all across the nation in the 2008 campaign. As the campaign un-folded, it became clear that in 2008 Ohio would very likely decide the winner. And it did.

Ohio has long been a bellwether state, standing at the center of presidential politics and the development of national policies. Black voters were pivotal to the destiny of the candidates in 1948 when Harry Truman eked out a win over Thomas Dewey. That presiden-tial campaign was my first, when I had just been discharged from the Army Air Corps and was entering Youngstown College under the GI Bill. My hometown of Youngstown, together with the totals rung up in Toledo, Cincinnati, Dayton, and Cleveland, pulled Truman through, winning the state by 7,017 votes. I like to think my efforts and those of my classmates who organized college students and other young voters in our area contributed to the win. The Truman victory yielded the appointment of the first black federal judge, William H. Hastie, to the Third Circuit Court of Appeals in Phil-adelphia and later the executive orders ending segregation in the Armed Forces. Fast-forwarding to 1960, the Kennedy rallies blacks held in my hometown of Youngstown and throughout the state, without question, brought Kennedy close to carrying Ohio and in fact did give him wins in other industrial states.

The political pundits and pollsters in the 2008 campaign in their reporting and predictions were falling over themselves trying to put Ohio into the McCain column by repeatedly elevating the significance of the blue-collar white voters while virtually ignoring the fact that many blacks are also blue-collar workers. It appeared that views of the latter were deemed not to warrant polling. Perhaps November 4 changed that type of reasoning.

The Election

After the polls closed on November 4, 2008, my wife and I were at home awaiting the return of our daughter and niece. Both lawyers, they had come to Cincinnati from their homes in Washington, D.C., and Seattle, Washington, to lend their legal expertise to untangling whatever snarls might arise in connection with the voting process. Though they were tired from toiling at the precincts for more than twelve hours on Election Day, we urged that they join us for dinner at the home of my law partner Michael Cioffi, where a number of friends were gathering to view the election results.

The early returns were fragmentary. As they seesawed back and forth, spirited conversation drowned out the television. But once the announcement flashed across the screen that Ohio returns were about to be reported, voices were stilled. And then it happened. Ohio was in the Obama column. With that, shrieks, tears, hugs, and dancing took over. That was the moment when I, for the very first time, dared to concede that my closely held belief was about to become a reality: this man of color was going to be elected president of my country.

I had earlier, discreetly, separated myself from the merriment by searching out a chair near the television set to await the next round of returns, which I knew would put Senator Barack Obama well beyond the magic number of 270 electoral votes. And moments later, when California's 55 electoral votes were placed alongside Ohio's 20, it was done. What so many in that room and in America never thought would happen had, indeed, just happened.

The exuberant comments I continued to receive from white friends, while flattering, caused me to wonder how many others knew what rocky roads blacks had traveled to reach this moment.

Few of them, I was sure, understood the decades of struggle that paved the way for Obama's election. As early as ten years of age at the YMCA forums, I became aware of the continuous and unyielding barriers that confronted people of color. Yet the campaign to overcome these obstacles was unrelenting. That's where my mind was.

Eventually, the time arrived for the partygoers to depart, which they did with spirits high. As did we. When we arrived home after midnight, the television channels were still crackling with stories about the amazing feat of Barack Obama becoming the first black president of the United States. Scenes from abroad demonstrated that the euphoria was worldwide. While I was caught up in the excitement, I recognized the historical significance of President-Elect Obama's victory and understood that this euphoria must not be allowed to evaporate. During the dark days of separate-but-equal, there were always voices—such as those remarkable speakers at the YMCA forums—that kept recharging the faith batteries of blacks. Once this historic event had occurred, I knew care would have to be taken to avoid being lulled into a belief that the struggle was over, that we are in a post-racial period in which vigilance would no longer be required.

For the twenty-three years I was on the court, I had to remain on the sidelines of presidential politics, unable to do anything but cast a vote. Yet during that period I saw the devastating effects of racist politics and litmus tests and the Reagan-type attacks on courageous federal judges, eating away at the constitutional protections and civil rights remedies I thought had been permanently enshrined in our jurisprudence.

Even as I nurtured the hope that the election of Barack Obama not only would arrest the backward slide resulting from the attack on racial remedies engineered by the Reagan administration but that there would be a reversal of the disastrous policies that have affected racial minorities and the poor, I found myself returning to those events in my own life that had long ago threatened my faith in the legal system. Thanks to the early messages of hope I received, and my refusal to allow racial stereotypes to define me, I pushed ahead to protect the instruments needed to personally fight for equality—education and the vote.

I recalled the feeling I had when I stepped into the shoes once worn by the legal icons who were chief legal officers of the NAACP: a series of circumstances had combined to position me to lead the fight against school segregation by bringing lawsuits in the North to implement the 1954 *Brown v. Board of Education* decision. I thereupon grasped, as part of my answer to the Call, the Houston/Marshall/Carter baton that was thrust into my hands to continue to lead the race toward the finish line of equality.

I wondered how many of those who had gathered to celebrate Obama's historic election were aware of the sacrifices of individuals who had propelled America to this point. The question I was continually asked on Election Night was, "Did you ever think you would live to see this?" The same question was asked on countless television programs by interviewers too young to know the history. The inquiries were a stark reminder to me—once again—of how little people really know of the strategy employed to eliminate racial discrimination. This was a teaching moment I could not allow to pass.

No better example of a missed opportunity to turn an event of high import into a teaching moment exists than Dr. Martin Luther King Day in January. Without question the heroism and inspired leadership of Dr. King is worthy of national note. My problem is with those who have turned it into a day of recitations of his speeches rather than focusing on his nobility of spirit or seeking a better understanding of the implications his life holds for addressing today's issues. The media feed into this superficiality by providing politicians and self-promoters a platform for scoring points and seeking absolution for their own hypocrisy. Too many people who hold views antithetical to King's get a pass by singing "We Shall Overcome" or quoting "I Have a Dream." One of the most distressing instances to me was when President George W. Bush praised Dr. King at a Capitol Hill tribute while, almost in the same breath, announcing the nomination of justices to the U.S.

Supreme Court who were committed to the very states' rights philosophy that Dr. King gave his life to eliminate.

Knocking Down the Barriers to Education and the Vote

Hovering around me in the glow of this remarkable, newly elected African American as president was an unease that it would be misread as an end to historic racism and a reason to terminate programs designed to narrow—and end—economic and educational disparities. Only if there is an understanding that the road of remedies contained an assortment of legal and political potholes, I thought, would there be permanence to this election's significance. There must be no relaxation in the effort to smooth out the road leading to education, economic and social justice.

The litigation strategy for overcoming racism's hold on the institutions that run our lives was devised by Houston and his protégé, Thurgood Marshall. At the core of the justification for institutional racism was the notion that blacks were stained with a badge of inferiority, a thesis powerfully and shamefully argued by Chief Justice Roger Taney in the 1857 *Dred Scott* decision. Thus, Houston's two early targets for undoing the Taney thesis were to knock out barriers to equal education and voting. They were the pathways to undercutting the rationale for denying constitutional rights to blacks.

Along with success in the voting-rights case, Houston's litigation strategy led eventually to the unanimous 1954 decision of *Brown v. Board of Education*, which held that separate-but-equal was inherently unconstitutional, thus violating the Fourteenth Amendment to the U.S. Constitution. In *Brown*, the Supreme Court finally recognized that segregation, in and of itself, deprived minority children of equal educational opportunities. *Brown* ushered in a new era in American history. Although the litigation was about schools and educational opportunities, *Brown* provided the framework for desegregating all aspects of American life.

The infamous Hayes-Tilden Deal of 1876 that led to President Hayes's withdrawal of the federal troops from the South reopened doors to the restoration of states' rights and stripping voting rights from blacks. Such groups as the Ku Klux Klan and the Knights of the White Camellia, along with others, were able to accomplish this by intimidation and violence. Lynchings soared during the 1880s and '90s with the result that former slaves were disfranchised once again. As *The Call* complained, exclusion of blacks from the polls was deemed crucial to a restoration of whites to their former position of political dominance. In addition to outright violence, the grandfather clause, literacy tests, poll tax laws, all-white primaries, and property requirements were legal proxies for outright racial exclusion of blacks from the voting booths. My predecessor NAACP chief legal counsels—Charles Houston, Thurgood Marshall, Robert Carter—and the cadre of local lawyers they recruited who so bravely, and usually without compensation, filed lawsuit after lawsuit seeking to restore the proper meaning of the Thirteenth, Fourteenth, and Fifteenth Amendments for Negroes clearly understood that the litigation path, as opposed to violence, was the inescapable route to the achievement of their legal rights.

Advise and Consent

The election of Barack Obama as president was providential, coming just in time to save the federal judiciary and the Constitution from total annihilation as instruments of social change. While thrilled at the exuberance with which the nomination and election of Barack Obama was being received, I was nevertheless restrained by sharp pangs that kept interrupting my joy. In particular, there were periodic reminders of how little was known or apparently understood by many U.S. senators, whom the Constitution charges with the duty to "advise and consent" to the appointment of persons to the federal courts, particularly the U.S. Courts of Appeal and the U.S. Supreme Court. If they knew more, I am convinced that the indifference displayed by many of them, Democrats and Republicans, would not have ruled the day when it came to approving the nomination of Judge John Roberts to be chief justice of the United States and Judge Samuel Alito to be an associate justice. Senators would have probed more deeply into their views on the role of race in shaping educational and social institutions. Similarly, I am distressed by the fact that there does not appear to be "buyer's remorse" from senators who voted to confirm Justice Clarence Thomas for the seat he occupies on the Supreme Court in light of his consistent opinions and votes against the interests of black people, women, minorities, and the poor.

I find it difficult to believe that if some past presidents who nominated federal judges and U.S. Supreme Court justices seriously drilled down and knew what black people underwent to exercise the franchise, they would not have taken their constitutional obligation so lightly. That would include considering their sensitivity on race as a qualification factor. With the election of President Obama, the nation now has one who knows history and understands fully the respective constitutional roles of a nominator, and that of the Senate to advise and consent. The country can be confident that the nominees to the federal court made by President Obama, if properly respected, will attempt to restore a jurisprudence that will respect the four hundred years of history during which color had placed Negroes in a discrete and secular classification warranting the need for meaningful remedies for the harm they suffered.

It was not so long ago, in the 1960s, when I was a U.S. attorney, that I found myself and my children trapped in the middle of a Klan demonstration on a back road between Cleveland and Akron. The sight of the huge cross ablaze in the night, with hooded Klansmen circling it, was frightening. But states had moved past that public display of intimidation and bestiality to adopt more subtle forms of legal obstacles. Civil rights lawyers used the legal system to shape remedies that stripped the masks of hypocrisy from the schemes—the literacy tests, the grandfather clause, the poll tax, the white primaries, and other devices—all designed to keep blacks locked in the status that existed during slavery. Enfranchisement was key to advancement. Once the Supreme Court responded to the persistent knock of civil rights lawyers—Charles Hamilton Houston, Thurgood Marshall, William Hastie, W.J. Durham, Andrew Ransome, and others—the foot soldiers accelerated their marches to win the right to register to vote. Even then, those brave enough to try were often confronted by mobs, gunmen hiding in bushes, bombers placing dynamite under homes, and other forms of force and intimidation.

In the face of these acts, the tempo increased on the legislative front. This assault led, ultimately, to the enactment of the 1965 Voting Rights Act. No case more dramatically demonstrates the concerted resistance of those opposed to blacks having the right to vote than what happened to Julian Bond, the former chairman of the national board of the NAACP. Bond's story is not ancient history, yet modern-day newspaper and cable television political pundits have scrubbed it from their memories and from their sense of the relevant.

At the age of twenty-five, Bond was elected to the Georgia House of Representatives in 1965 along with eight other blacks. Stunned, the other representatives voted by 184 to 10 to deny him his seat on January 10, 1966. Later that year, by a 9–0 vote, the U.S. Supreme Court overturned a 2–1 decision by a three-judge federal court holding that the action of the Georgia House of Representatives did not violate any federal constitutional rights. The Supreme Court struck swiftly to reverse the lower court. The case of *Bond v. Floyd* is hardly ever mentioned when there is a discussion of the tack-strewn road that blacks have had to traverse in order to get to where we are today. It should be noted that the 1965 vote was 2,320 to 487 in Bond's favor, yet that Georgia House flagrantly denied him his seat. This is one of those tragedies that prompts me to wonder whether the current Supreme Court's strong tilt toward states' rights would have found a way to uphold what Georgia tried to do.

Enforcing the Fourteenth and Fifteenth Amendments

In the various undergraduate courses I took in college, and later in law school, I continually raised the Constitution and, in particular, instances when civil rights subjects were being featured in the news. The 1947 Truman report, "To Secure These Rights," was my "bible." It helped me to point out inconsistencies between what governmental officials were doing and what the Constitution required. Voting rights was a subject I harped on constantly. My "sermons" hammered on the power of the ballot. In a democratic society, access to the ballot is one of the most fundamental rights that a citizen can possess. The power to select leaders is also the power to influence public policy. As long as citizens possess the right to vote, they have the ability to actively affect the manner in which they are governed. Take away that right, and citizens' influence on their government is seriously diminished. But for blacks, the right to vote as guaranteed by the Fifteenth Amendment was more an illusion than a reality during a significant period of our nation's history. At every stage of my adult life, in whatever situation I found myself, I spoke out in support of the need to respect constitutional rights. In the courses I taught at the University of Cincinnati Law School I found it necessary to discuss aspects of our voting-rights history in order for students to understand why racial remedies were necessary. The Supreme Court and others who today insist that we are in a post-racial period could benefit from a dip in a reality bath in order to understand what Justice Felix Frankfurter meant when he wrote in the *Lane v. Wilson* case that sophisticated as well as simpleminded schemes violate the Fifteenth Amendment.

Here is some history of a variety of the schemes contrived to affect the right to vote that I constantly brought to the attention of classmates and law students. The 1910 statute that Oklahoma enacted had provided that: "No person could be registered unless he could read and write." There was an exemption, however, for an illiterate who lived in a foreign country prior to 1866 or had been eligible to register prior to that date, or if his ancestor was eligible as of that date.

Clearly this excluded former slaves.

Today there are still those who act as though the Fourteenth and Fifteenth Amendments were self-enforcing and that the story ended with their ratification. With justices occupying seats on the U.S. Supreme Court in the post-Obama election period publicly proclaiming their "distaste" for race-based remedies, they call for an end to court enforcement of civil rights remedies. Even politicians have the audacity to assert that discrimination automatically ends with the mere enactment of civil rights law.

Those justices, it could be said, have signaled to the white majority that they can reassume their dominant role because the courts will no longer be there for racial minorities as they were for the past thirty or more years. This effort to wipe out the history of struggle blacks underwent to win the right to vote makes it all the more imperative that a spotlight be refocused on the need for remedies. We must revisit history to educate everyone about the links between the past and the present.

Whites in Texas, Oklahoma, and other Southern states came up with black-exclusionary devices as a way to circumvent the Fourteenth and Fifteenth Amendments. These schemes were actively and creatively challenged by litigants, and lawyers.

Oklahoma's Story

Soon after it was admitted to the Union, Oklahoma amended the Constitution that gave it "passage" to be admitted and added a "literacy test" requirement. White voters were excluded from having to take the test because of a "grandfather clause." The grandfather clause, however, was struck down by the Supreme Court as being in violation of the Fifteenth Amendment on June 21, 1915. In the face of the Supreme Court's 1915 decision, the Oklahoma legislation, using typical racist ingenuity, concocted a new scheme as a prerequisite for voting. It required only "new" registrants to take the test—blacks—and exempted those on the rolls who had voted in the general election of 1914—whites.

White Primaries

The aftermath of *Guinn v. United States*, decided in 1916 by the U.S. Supreme Court that struck down Oklahoma's "grandfather clause" demonstrates that those determined to preserve white supremacy never give up. Their next refuge was in the scheme known as the white primaries. In light of that tack, the state of Texas took a different approach in preventing blacks from voting.

Texas law provided that "in no event, shall a Negro be eligible to participate in a Democratic Party election." In 1927 the NAACP, representing Dr. L.A. Nixon, sued the judges of elections, claiming his constitutional rights were being violated and that he was seeking damages. The Supreme Court, in an opinion by Justice Oliver Wendell Holmes, held, on Fourteenth Amendment grounds, that the white primary was invalid and a violation of the equal protection clause. He noted, "We find it unnecessary to consider the Fifteenth Amendment, because it seems to us hard to imagine a more direct and obvious infringement of the Fourteenth Amendment."[2]

One would have thought that in the face of a judicial slap-down by the highest court in the land, authored by one as eminent as Justice Holmes, that the law was clear. But no, on the heels of the *Nixon v. Herndon* decision in 1927, Texas convened a special session of the legislature and circumvented the Supreme Court's ban on enacting legislation that barred blacks from voting by delegating to the State Democratic Party the authority to determine the eligibility of persons to vote in its party primary. The Democratic Party's Executive Committee then decided that only "white" persons could vote.

That decision prompted Nixon to bring another suit—*Nixon v. Condon*. NAACP lawyers, on behalf of Dr. Nixon, attacked that statute and in a 5–4 ruling handed down on May 2, 1932, once again prevailed. The Supreme Court ruled that the Texas maneuver was an unconstitutional delegation of state power and that the party's policy and practice was a de facto state action violative of the Fourteenth Amendment's guarantee of "equal protection." In the face of these pronouncements Justice Frankfurter declared in his 1939 *Lane v. Wilson* opinion that the Constitution rejects and nullifies "sophisticated as well as simple-minded modes of discrimination. It hits onerous procedural requirements which effectively handicaps exercise of the franchise by the colored race, although the abstract right to vote may remain unrestricted as to race."[3]

In the next major constitutional challenge to Texas's attempts to block the franchise for blacks, the Texas Supreme Court held that the Democratic Party of that state was a "voluntary association," thereby clearing the way for the Democratic Party to determine its policies and membership. On May 24, 1932, the party, in convention, adopted a resolution that said, "Be it resolved that all white citizens of the State of Texas who are qualified to vote under the Constitution and laws of the State shall be eligible to membership in the Democratic Party and participate in its deliberations."[4]

That resolution was challenged directly in 1944 when NAACP attorneys Thurgood Marshall, William H. Hastie, and Andrew Ransome, representing Lonnie E. Smith, sued S.E. Allwright and other election judges of Harris County, Texas, for their refusal to permit Smith to cast a ballot for the nomination of Democratic candidates. There was much rejoicing when the Supreme Court issued its decision in April 1944. This was in the middle of World War II, as many of Texas's black sons were on the battlefields of Europe and fighting on the islands of the Pacific while at home state officials were challenging their right to vote. The Supreme Court virtually adopted language from the penetrating brief drafted by those uncompromising NAACP lawyers—Marshall, Hastie, and Ransome. The court declared:

> The United States is a constitutional democracy. Its organic law grants to all citizens a right to participate in the choice of elected officials without restriction by any state because of race. This grant to the people the opportunity for choice is not to be nullified by a state through casting its electoral process in the form which permits

a private organization to practice racial discrimination in the election. Constitutional rights would be of little value if they could be this indirectly denied.[5]

When people in Texas sought to cast their votes, the lessons of *Smith v. Allwright* fell on deaf ears. Many of the courageous "foot soldiers"—those Negroes who defied the mobs and threats to go to the polls and to assist others in voting—became martyrs. The people in control of the election machinery marched in lockstep with the merchants of violence. Because of this, efforts to win passage of legislation to give real meaning to those judicial pronouncements increased. Walter White and Lester Perry, and later Clarence Mitchell, head of the Washington bureau of the NAACP, under the direction of Roy Wilkins and the newly founded Leadership Conference on Civil Rights, mobilized a massive lobbying campaign. Mitchell's initial efforts under Wilkins and the LCCR took the form of hand-to-hand combat through buttonholing members of Congress, and were instrumental in bringing about the first civil rights bill since Reconstruction—the 1957 Civil Rights Act. The role of Clarence Mitchell is a remarkable story of brilliance, bravery, and persistence.

Clarence Mitchell

Clarence Mitchell proceeded to perfect the lobbying capacity of the NAACP with the LCCR to update laws to end discrimination that would thereby provide effective remedies so that civil rights laws would have real meaning for black people. It was Mitchell's mastery of the legislative process, his skill at mobilizing other organizations, and his ability to energize the NAACP branch network that brought energy to the drive for civil rights. His unrelenting and skillful efforts to influence presidents, senators, and congresspersons to overthrow the stifling and arcane rules that choked civil rights legislation bore fruit.

Congressional leaders came to acknowledge Mitchell's superior knowledge of the legislative process and his brilliance as a strategist. He refined the art of vote counting and used the 1,700-plus branches of the NAACP to stimulate demands on lawmakers when key legislation was under consideration.

Clarence Mitchell did not regard the 1964 Civil Rights Act or Title VII, which prohibited employers and unions from discriminating in hiring, promotions, and layoffs, as new laws; rather, he understood that they enforced the imperatives embodied in the Thirteenth, Fourteenth, and Fifteenth Amendments.

Each of these Civil War–era amendments include the following language: "The Congress shall have the power to enforce, by appropriate legislation, the provisions of this Article." When Congress enacted civil rights laws in the 1950s, '60s, and '70s, under the provisions of those Amendments, it was largely due to the efforts of Clarence Mitchell and his lobbying colleagues.

Mitchell's leadership of the NAACP team, in concert with the LCCR, played the major role in winning the enactment of the 1965 Voting Rights Act. Mitchell understood the NAACP's long struggle to remove the barriers that blocked access of black Americans to the ballot. He also understood that meaningful institutional change would not be realized, nor would Negro citizens be personally empowered, without the right to vote. He knew that the policies shaped by public officials would never take into account the aspirations and well-being of black people until they had the vote. But the spirit of the roadblocks that Mitchell removed still lurks such that even in 2008, we experienced the latest version: voter repression through ID requirements.

America's history is replete with instances of those determined to deny access to the ballot to blacks, who after losing in court, resort to violence and intimidation. On Christmas night in 1951, NAACP's Florida executive director, Harry T. Moore, and his wife were blown up because of their voter-registration activities as they slept in their Mims, Florida, home. On June 23, 1940, the body of Elbert Williams, a local NAACP leader who had bravely worked on advocating for black citizens' right to vote, was found floating in a river in Brownsville, Haywood County, Tennessee. Reverend George W. Lee's voter advocacy for people of color led, on May 7, 1955, to his being shot down on Belzoni, Mississippi's main street. Two months later, another leader, Lamar Smith, who had urged people to ask for absentee ballots, was assassinated on the lawn of the courthouse in Brookhaven, Mississippi, in broad daylight.

These and similar tragedies inspired Clarence Mitchell and the leadership and members of the NAACP to press harder for federal protection for blacks who sought to exercise their right to vote. But it was the brazen, cold-blooded murder of Mississippi's state field director, Medgar Evers, on June 12, 1963, and the kidnapping and murders of three young civil rights workers—Andrew Goodman, James Chaney, and Michael Schwerner—in June 1964, in Philadelphia, Mississippi, that awakened the nation to the brutal and savage extent to which racists would go to deny ballot power to black citizens. Evers was killed late at night as he alighted from his car in the carport of his home in Jackson, Mississippi, before the eyes of his young wife, Myrlie, and their little children. Schwerner, Goodman, and Chaney were snatched from their car in Philadelphia, Neshoba County, Mississippi, by local law enforcement officers—never to be seen alive again. Their bodies were found a few months later by the FBI in a local lake. They, too, had been murdered.

It was not until Congress enacted the 1965 Voting Rights Act that voting rolls began to dramatically swell. At the time of the law's passage, the total number of black Americans registered to vote was between 2 million and 3 million; by 1990 that number was in excess of 12 million. Likewise, the number of black elected officials multiplied fourteen-fold between 1965 and 1989, from approximately 500 to 7,200, two-thirds of whom were in the South. The courage that it took for Fannie Lou Hamer to lead the fight in Mississippi against the Democratic Party to win seats for black delegates at the 1968 Democratic Convention clearly places her in the pantheon of America's greatest women.

Frank Parker, in charge of the Mississippi voting rights project of the Lawyers' Committee for Civil Rights, with whom I co-counseled in the Claiborne Hardware boycott case, worked closely with the NAACP in implementing the provisions of the voting-rights law throughout the South. He described the 1965 Voting Rights Act in this way: "The Voting Rights Act swept away the primary legal barriers to black registration and voting in the South, eliminating the literacy tests and poll taxes and allowing the Justice Department to dispatch federal registrars and poll watchers to ensure the integrity of the voting process."[6]

This is important history and relevant to understanding the dramatic victory of Barack Obama in the 2008 election. In the interest of historical accuracy, the connection between the efforts to gain the right to vote and the 2008 election must be understood.

Forming Coalitions

It was clear to blacks from the beginning of the struggle against segregation with the founding of the NAACP in 1909 that they were a numerical minority. Since, in a democratic society, numbers are important, Negroes knew that while they had to become politically active, it was essential to enlist support of whites and to form interracial coalitions. The NAACP itself was just such a coalition— with whites among its founders. One of the most reliable allies from the beginning was the Jewish community. While some Protestant denominations adhered to segregationist positions, others spoke out boldly on behalf of rights of Negroes. One of the strongest voices was Eugene Carson Blake of the National Council of Churches. As the years rolled on, many groups joined in at the local level through their local affiliates. Though craft unions had racial exclusionary policies, the industrial unions were much more liberal on racial issues and became allies. A. Philip Randolph, the Brotherhood of Sleeping Car Porters, and the NAACP led the fight within the trade union movement. The policy of the YMCA okayed segregation, but the YWCA took a more forward-looking position on integration. These and other groups combined with the NAACP, the black churches, and other progressive organizations to fight against segregation and discrimination.

During the 1970s, the slow pace in implementing *Brown v. Board of Education*, the 1964 Civil Rights Act, and the 1965 Voting Rights Act became a point of significant frustration. A number of blacks began to respond to the siren song of black power and black racial separatism. Such adherents drove from the coalition white allies who had been toiling in the vineyard for decades. Particular targets were some Jewish organizations. The prominent role played at the national level by Jews, and in the various local and regional units of the NAACP, prompted some with a Black Nationalist bent to contend that the destiny of blacks was being directed by whites, most notably Jews.

As I mentioned earlier, there is a long history of individual Jewish support for the black struggle. Individual Jews were very prominent in the founding of the NAACP and in its continuing activity over the ensuing years. Allowing for a patronizing judgment by today's standards, Jewish philanthropy contributed mightily to the educational advance of numerous blacks. Whether in Meridian, Mississippi, or Cincinnati, Ohio, Jews were prominent among those who offered their bodies and lives in the civil rights battle. Although it was never true that all—or even most—Jews were directly involved in the civil rights struggle, it is beyond question that proportionately *more* of them than other whites had such involvement. Furthermore, their general liberal and enlightened inclinations have seen them, most of the time, in support of measures such as civil rights laws, aimed at guaranteeing black Americans their fair and equal share of this nation's largesse. The subject of affirmative action fractured this united front. Some of the division resulted from a fundamental misunderstanding and unjustified apprehension by Jews about using race as an element in remedies designed to correct historic wrongs.

Sadly, but necessarily, I note an erosion of the mutual goodwill that has characterized the formal—and much of the informal—interrelation between Negroes and Jews. I hope the strength of the working relationship built over the years will provide the energy needed to put things back together as we approach future problems.

The campaign of Barack Obama brought together and solidified, once again, the fractured coalitions and old allies. It was this reunification, which I had observed emerging over the years, coming together during the 2008 political campaign that led me to believe that Senator Obama's election as president was a distinct possibility. Bricks that formed the foundation on which the Obama coalition first came together many decades ago—indeed as far back as *The Call* in 1909.

My "yes" answer to the question "Did you ever think you would live to see an African American elected President of the United States?" appeared to take some people by surprise. It was an answer informed, in part, by decades of observation and involvement in the struggle to change attitudes, build coalitions, and effect change in relations and attitudes. Having grown up with white playmates, and in an environment that saw whites combine with minorities in tackling problems, often at great risk, I believed in a cooperative approach. It was a combination of those life experiences about which I have written that made me a believer when I heard then Senator Obama explain to delegates to the National Urban League at its 2007 annual meeting in St. Louis his strategy for capturing the White House.

As his strategy unfolded, in particular his victories in the Iowa and South Carolina primaries, I recalled what he laid out to the delegates, and later to me in a personal chat; how he proposed to activate more young people and dispirited and long-disenfranchised blacks, particularly in the so-called red states. Combining that game plan with the changes I observed in human and political relationships, it seemed to me that Senator Obama had properly measured the extent of change that had occurred by virtue of improved relationships, at the workplace, in neighborhoods, on campuses, in schools, and in recreational activities. He was poised to seize upon these profound and historic realignments.

There can be no disputing the fact that institutional changes in the workforce; in housing and public accommodations; in education, and in scholastic, collegiate, and professional sports significantly influenced the precepts that people have of one another. The civil rights litigation strategy drove most of these changes. How permanent those advances will be depends upon the success supporters of *The Call* have in warding off the attempts at reviving states' rights.

Blacks in the White House

The conversations to which I was privy in the late 1930s and '40s when my mentor, J. Maynard Dickerson, and his wife hosted many of the national black leadership in their home following their speeches continue to vibrate within me. I observed the exchanges and heard countless personal insights during these informal meetings with thought leaders of the day. Blacks had virtually no direct access to most presidents of the United States prior to President Roosevelt. The conversations of Walter White were fascinating and laced with comments on the way that he used Eleanor Roosevelt as a conduit for messages to President Roosevelt. For instance, when it appeared that Roosevelt was not sufficiently responsive to their demand for an executive order ending discrimination in employment in defense industries, Walter White, A. Philip Randolph, and other leaders sent word to the president, through Mrs. Roosevelt, that they were preparing a fifty-thousand-person march on Washington. For such a demonstration to occur during wartime would have been a serious embarrassment to the United States. That possibility led to an invitation for a face-to-face Oval Office meeting to discuss the matter. The upshot was that the president issued Executive Order 8802, establishing the first FEPC on June 25, 1941.

I was fascinated when Roy Wilkins, Walter White, Thurgood Marshall, and others, during the informal social sessions at the Dickerson home and elsewhere, shared versions of the behind-the-scenes efforts to get President Roosevelt to issue the FEPC order, as well as one that ended segregation in the armed services. Fighting for the "right to fight" was a paradox those leaders continued to press upon Presidents Roosevelt and Truman. So serious was the matter that William H. Hastie, as I have noted, resigned as special assistant to Secretary of War Henry L. Stimson to protest President Roosevelt's refusal to end segregation of and the mistreatment of blacks in the army.

Throughout this period the black leadership persistently fought for access to the White House to "educate" its occupants. They expressed their frustrations over presidents being surrounded by individuals not fully sympathetic to civil rights issues. In their attempts to shield the president, blacks were generally shunted away to low-level aides who lacked real policy-making power. It was not until Harry Truman became president that lines to the Oval Office meaningfully opened. That led to the issuance of the executive order integrating the military and his bold action appointing William H. Hastie as the first black Article III federal judge, as well as establishing the first presidential committee to study race relations, which produced the monumental 1947 report, "To Secure These Rights." The adoption of that report as the civil rights plank of the Democratic Party in 1948 led to a walkout at the national convention and the formation of the Dixiecrat Party. Those measures triggered a national debate on civil rights that has been raging intermittently since then.

President Dwight Eisenhower set off much discussion among the black leadership when he appointed E. Frederic Morrow, a black, as his administrative officer for special projects, a "first." He also made history by appointing J. Ernest Wilkins of Chicago to the sub-cabinet position of assistant secretary of labor, only to stand by silently as he was undercut and removed by the secretary of labor, James P. Mitchell, and placed in the Civil Rights Commission. President Kennedy named a black, Andrew Hatcher, as his assistant press secretary. That appointment was noteworthy for the visibility given to a black Kennedy spokesperson.

President Nixon made appointments of blacks to sub-cabinet positions, such as Sam Jackson and Arthur Fletcher at the Labor

Department, but the White House power center remained lily-white. Nixon's senior staff sometimes conferred with the Urban League's Vernon Jordan, who was known to play tennis with presidential counselor John Ehrlichman. They often conferred with the NAACP's Clarence Mitchell on legislation, but there were no blacks in serious policy-making positions until John Kennedy and Lyndon Johnson occupied the White House.

In more recent years, particularly since the attacks on civil rights mounted by Richard Nixon and Ronald Reagan, civil rights proponents were dismissed by political opponents and much of the media as "special interest" groups seeking "preferential" treatment. History belies that.

By pressing their claims, blacks were in reality acting in the national interest. One need only look at the strength and diversity of America's workforce today produced by the laws prohibiting discrimination in education, public accommodations, travel, and the workplace; the distance we have come in providing quality education for diverse Americans, though unacceptable gaps still exist; the vitality of the military since its integration; and the strength of the American political system by virtue of the expansion of voting rights. These changes have proved to benefit the entire nation.

The amazing election of President Barack Obama was the culmination of the strategy and struggle pursued by civil rights leaders going back to the time of *The Call*. Obama had the vision to see that the time was ripe for what he had to offer the nation.

When President-Elect Barack Obama took the stage before thousands in Grant Park on the night of November 4, 2008, it was, to me, an answer to *The Call*. Moreover, I saw the America described by Langston Hughes in his moving poem "I, Too":

> I am the darker brother.
> They send me to eat in the kitchen
> When company comes,
> But I laugh,
> And eat well,
> And grow strong.

Tomorrow,
I'll sit at the table
When company comes,
Nobody'll dare
Say to me,
"Eat in the kitchen,"
Then.
Besides,
They'll see how beautiful I am
And be ashamed—

I, too, am America.[7]

    This is the face of America that Michelle Obama was refer-
ring to when she spoke of her sense of pride in our country. Truth
be told, the other ugly faces of America, to which black persons
have been subjected, we hope now, and we pray for all time, have
been buried.

Acknowledgments

After persistent prodding from Chad Wick, former CEO of KnowledgeWorks Foundation; the foundation's former chair Dean Joe Tomain; and retired Procter & Gamble chairman John Pepper, and after seeking the advice of Professor Roger Wilkins of Washington, D.C., I agreed to write this book.

I turned to Roger because of my deep admiration for him. He is the nephew of Roy Wilkins, who had hired me as NAACP general counsel. I first met Roger when he was an assistant attorney general during Lyndon B. Johnson's administration. He later became an officer of the Ford Foundation before joining the editorial boards of the *Washington Post* and the *New York Times*. Roger came to Cincinnati in 1997 to deliver the principal remarks on the occasion of my portrait being presented to the Sixth Circuit U.S. Court of Appeals. In addition to his journalism, he has written several books. I thought it important to know what was involved in writing a book. Chad Wick and Dean Tomain joined me for lunch with Roger in Washington. Roger was most helpful and indeed candid. His bottom line, which I shall never forget, was "It has got to be in your voice." That resonated with me in light of the number of "as told to" books that are published.

Allowing for the technical assistance necessary to put my lengthy story together in readable form, I adhered to Roger Wilkins's advice to do so in my voice. This is my story.

This memoir, with additional guidance from the experienced editorial hand of Howard Wells; the inspiration of my law partner Michael L. Cioffi; and my daughter, Stephanie J. Jones; the constant encouragement of KnowledgeWorks Foundation; and the unfailingly skilled hands and keen eyes of my assistant, Rebecca Bomkamp—without whom this book would not be—documents the extent to which I sought, in myriad ways, to be worthy of their faith in me.

The invaluable encouragement of Tara Grove of The New Press and of Marc Favreau, the Press's executive editor, kept me buoyed at moments when I badly needed it. Access to NAACP files at the Library of Congress was eased by my former colleague Mildred Bond Roxborough. This, together with the cooperation of the staff of the Reuben McMillan Public Library of Youngstown and Mahoning County and Denton Watson, former NAACP colleague and Clarence Mitchell scholar, helped me tell this story. I am also indebted to James Hardiman, Paul Dimond, Honorable David Tatel, Gay McDougall, and Professor Joyce A. Baugh for confirming my recollection of many details of my sojourn.

My additional gratitude goes to the Honorable Alexis Herman and colleagues on the Toyota Diversity Advisory Board for allowing me to help chart a course for a major corporation seeking to change. Certainly my long-held faith in our legal system here was strengthened by the steady hand with which Rachel Patrick and her colleagues serve a redirected American Bar Association and its leadership.

Appendix

M E M O R A N D U M

TO: Mr. Roy Wilkins

FROM: Nathaniel R. Jones

RE: Analysis of Administration Legislative Thrust
       On School Desegregation

DATE: June 10, 1976

As background for the conference with the President on Monday, June 14, 1976, I have prepared the following memorandum:

As you know, the Attorney General had previously considered using the Boston school case as a vehicle for seeking Supreme Court review of the extent to which transportation may be used in a desegregation plan and whether court ordered remedies should be cut back from system-wide to a school-by-school approach. In our May 18th conference with the Attorney General we made the point that these matters have already been reviewed by the Supreme Court in the Swann (Charlotte) and Keyes (Denver) cases, and their application by Judge Garrity in Boston had been affirmed by the United States Court of Appeals for the First Circuit.

Following the decision by the Attorney General to forego using Boston, the President announced that he had directed that the search for an appropriate case   continue and, in addition, he indicated an intention to seek action through the Congress.

Cases Being Considered for Intervention

Information now reaching us through the media and other sources suggest that three new cases are now under active

Mr. Roy Wilkins
June 10, 1976
Page 2

consideration: Wilmington, Dayton and Milwaukee. In each
of these cases district courts have found state-caused or
de jure segregation. Therefore, the courts have the authority
to fashion remedies.

In Wilmington, a three-judge court of appeals has also
found that the nature of the constitutional violations forms
a sufficient predicate to justify an inter-district or
metropolitan plan of desegregation. In reaching this conclusion the three-judge court conformed to the Supreme Court
directions handed down in the 1974 Milliken (Detroit-school)
and 1976 Gautreaux (Chicago-housing) cases.

In the Dayton case, the 6th Circuit Court of Appeals
twice reversed the trial court for its failure to approve a
system-wide plan of desegregation. A new plan has now been
approved that will desegregate nearly every school in the
Dayton system in September. The school board is now appealing
this plan and has sought a stay of the implementation of it.
At the same time the school board lawyers have requested the
Justice Department to intervene asserting that the remedy is
more extensive than the violations found by the court.

The Milwaukee case was decided in January, 1976, and
the court is now in the process of shaping a desegregation plan.

It is unclear whether the appeal in the Wilmington case
would be taken to the Supreme Court or to the 3rd Circuit
Court of Appeals.

The Dayton case is in the 6th Circuit. The Milwaukee
case is still in the District Court.

Mr. Roy Wilkins
June 10, 1976
Page 3

Our position with respect to the government even considering
intervention must be consistent with that we took in the Boston
case. In each instance a court has found that constitutional
rights have been violated. The precedents relied upon by
the trial courts included those cases in which the government
has already asserted a position on busing – and lost. In
Swann and Keyes the constitutional and remedial principles
enunciated by the Supreme Court are clear and settled.
Intervention only serves to keep alive defiance and resistance
to court orders.

Legislative Objectives

The objectives of the legislation which the President is
reportedly seeking appear to include at least the following:

1) Mandatorily terminate the equitable
   jurisdiction of the district courts
   in school desegregation cases after
   three years. If additional time is
   needed jurisdiction may be retained for
   two more years.

2) Limit "government-action" proof to those acts
   committed by school officials, thus
   excluding consideration by the courts
   of housing, zoning and other forms of discriminatory
   government action.

3) Eliminate the Keyes burden-shifting
   presumption that permits a court to
   find system-wide violations on the basis

Mr. Roy Wilkins
June 10, 1976
Page 4

of discrimination proven in a signi-

ficant portion of a single school

district.
                    Discussion

The President's desire to place time limits for the

exercise of a court's equitable power, appears to be absolutely

without precedent. To place it in perspective it is necessary

to have an understanding of what the Supreme Court said in

Brown II about the duty of a district court to effect a

transition from a segregated to a desegregated or unitary

system.

> "[s]chool authorities have the primary
> responsibility for elucidating, assessing,
> and solving these problems; courts will have
> to consider whether the action of school
> authorities constitutes good faith imple-
> mentation of the governing constitutional
> principles. Because of their proximity
> to local conditions and the possible need
> for further hearings, the courts which
> originally heard these cases can best
> perform this judicial appraisal. Accordingly,
> we believe it appropriate to remand the
> cases to those courts.
>
> "In fashioning and effectuating the decrees,
> the courts will be guided by equitable
> principles. Traditionally, equity has been
> characterized by a practical flexibility in
> shaping its remedies and by a facility for
> adjusting and reconciling public and private
> needs. These cases call for the exercise of
> these traditional attributes of equity power.
> At stake is the personal interest of the
> plaintiffs in admission to public schools as
> soon as practicable on a nondiscriminatory
> basis. To effectuate this interest may call
> for elimination of a variety of obstacles in
> making the transition to school systems
> operated in accordance with the constitutional
> principles set forth in our May 17, 1954,
> decision. Courts of equity may properly take
> into account the public interest in the

Mr. Roy Wilkins
June 10, 1976
Page 5

> elimination of such obstacles in a systematic
> and effective manner. But it should go without
> saying that the vitality of these constitutional
> principles cannot be allowed to yield simply
> because of disagreement with them."

This position has been recognized by the Department of Justice
and, indeed, it recently argued (in its brief) that the Court in the
Pasadena case has not only the power but the duty to eliminate
present discrimination and bar it in the future. Here are some quotes
from the Solicitor General's brief:

> "In 1955 this Court recognized that full
> implementation of the constitutional
> commands of Brown v. Board of Education,
> 347 U.S. 483 (Brown I),'may require
> solution of varied local school problems.'
> Brown v. Board of Education, 349 U.S. 294,
> 299 (Brown II). Accordingly, it directed
> the courts to "retain jurisdiction"***
> [d]uring this period of transition (id. at 301).
> Retention of jurisdiction by district courts
> in school desegregation cases has been required
> since Brown II. In Raney v. Board of Education,
> 391 U.S. 443, 449, the Court wrote:
>
>> In light of the complexities
>> inhering in the disestablishment
>> of state-established segregated
>> school systems, Brown II
>> contemplated that the better course
>> would be to retain jurisdiction
>> until it is clear that disestablishment
>> has been achieved.
>
> And in Green, supra, 391 U.S. at 439, the
> Court stated:
>> the [district] court should retain
>> jurisdiction until it is clear that
>> state-imposed segregation has been
>> completely removed.
>
> See also Swann, supra, 402 U.S. at 21, 28.Cf.
> Alexander v. Holmes County Board of Education
> 396 U.S. 19, 21; Carter v. West Feliciana
> Parish School Board, 396 U.S. 290, 292
> (Harlan, J., concurring).

Mr. Roy Wilkins
June 10, 1976
Page 6

The need to retain jurisdiction until the
objectives of the decree have been achieved
is plain. In 'a system that has been
deliberately constructed and maintained to
enforce racial segregation' (Swann, supra,
402 U.S. at 28) it is not enough to undo
that segregation for an instant. The deeply
ingrained nature of state-imposed racial
separation, which has been caused by
deliberate acts of elected officials that
serve to stamp an enduring racial label
on each school, makes it necessary and
proper for the court to supervise the
desegregation process, not only to achieve
desegregation, but also to ensure the
perpetuation of that status (i.e., a status
in which de jure segregation and the effects
of past de jure segregation have been
eliminated).

So far as we are aware, only one school
district ever has been completely released
from the jurisdiction of a district court
upon successfully desegregating its schools.
Other school districts have been released
from the active supervision of the district
court. Because the defendants in school
desegregation cases are public officials,
and because federal courts should not
become permanently involved in the administration of local schools, detailed
"regulatory" injunctions ultimately should
give way to general permanent injunctions
against racial discrimination. In this
latter or "passive" stage the district court
would act only if one of the parties to
the case alleged that the officials were
violating its general injunction against
discrimination.

....Petitioners argue here as they did in the
district court, that the Pasadena schools
became "unitary" the moment the Pasadena
Plan was implemented. Even if this argument
were correct, it would not support petitioners'
claim for termination of the district court's
passive supervision. Continuing supervision
is necessary to deter future acts of segregation by making the contempt power available
and by insuring prompt rectification if such
acts occur. Since the school board has

> demonstrated a proclivity to engage in such
> unconstitutional acts (the injunction
> otherwise would not have been necessary), the
> danger of repetition is present whether or
> not Pasadena is, at this moment, a "unitary"
> school system.

> * * * * *

> The judicial supervision should last until a
> unitary school system has been achieved and
> maintained for a significant period of time
> without the need for additional judicial
> intervention. Whether complete dissolution
> would then be appropriate should rest, as
> do other matters of equity, in the informed
> discretion of the district court."
> * * * *

Thus, it is abundantly clear that the official position

of the government, as reflected in filings and in argument before

the United States Supreme Court on this question, is in favor

of courts retaining their jurisdiction until a school system

is rendered "unitary." The proposed legislation collides

directly with this constitutional imperative.

Discriminatory Housing and Zoning Actions

Once again, we must note that the Supreme Court has clearly

spoken to the issue of the relevance of proof of housing and

zoning policies in school desegregation cases where a causal

nexus can be established. This causal nexus has been established

in all of the major school cases from Swann, down through

cases currently in litigation, such as Boston, Wilmington,

Milwaukee and Cleveland.

In Swann the Supreme Court stated that

> "People gravitate toward school facilities,
> just as schools are located in response to
> the needs of people. The location of schools
> may thus influence the patterns of residential
> development of a metropolitan area and have
> important impact on composition of inner city
> neighborhoods."

Mr. Roy Wilkins
June 10, 1976
Page 8

Combining this, the court said, with "neighborhood zoning"
for school attendance purposes results in a segregated school

The neighborhood assignment policies with discriminatory
pupil transfer features and optional zones impact upon this.
Other factors that interrelate to these practices are
segregation in teacher and administration hiring, assignment
and promotion. The bottom line for all of this is de jure
segregation.

System-wide versus School-by-School Desegregation

This too is a question that the Supreme Court has visited
and resolved. There is no need for "clarification" as the
discussion engaged in by the Supreme Court in the Denver case
makes it absolutely clear that:

   a) De jure segregation in a significant
       portion of a single school district
       may raise a presumption that the entire
       system is similarly segregated.

   b) The duty to rebut the presumption shifts to and
       rests with state and local school
       authorities.

   c) Their failure to rebut it permits the
       presumption to become conclusive.

Limiting a remedy to those schools against which specific
segregation is shown to have operated would have the effect
of repealing the burden-shifting principle approved by the
Supreme Court. The U.S. Court of Appeals for the 1st District,
in the Boston case, ridiculed such a notion, declaringthat

Mr. Roy Wilkins
June 10, 1976
Page 9

unconstitutional segregation is defined not only by percentages
but also by "community and administrative attitudes and
psychological effects."

This teaching has been followed by trial judges in cases
brought by private plaintiffs and in actions initiated by the
United States. In the Omaha case, for instance, the Court of
Appeals for the 8th Circuit, in an appeal filed by the Justice
Department, reversed a district court dismissal of the case.
The opinion reversing the dismissal discusses at length the
appropriateness of proof of housing discrimination and
specifically cites segregation policies of the public housing
authority, the Gautreaux case and racial restrictive covenants,
along with the Code of Ethics of the Board of Realtors.

Going beyond the settled principle that such is proper
proof for consideration, we also find the clear language of
Mr. Justice Potter Stewart in the Detroit case. It was his
concurring opinion that provided the majority vote in that
case. He held that proof of housing and zoning discrimination
by the state could provide a sufficient predicate for ordering
metropolitan desegregation. He reiterated that principle
this year in the Gautreaux housing case.

Housing proof in school cases demonstrates that public housing
tenant assignment practices, restrictive covenants, FHA insuring
policies as reflected in the FHA Underwriting Manual, along
with urban renewal and highway clearance activities have largely
combined to shape the urban housing patterns we now see.

Mr. Roy Wilkins
June 10, 1976
Page 10

This taken together with school construction policies and site
selection forms a nexus of causation for de jure segregation.
Therefore, it is relevant and proper for trial courts to admit
this kind of housing proof in instances where school officials
defend against lawsuits on grounds of neighborhood housing patterns.

National Acceptance of Inevitability of Desegregation

In my view we must be prepared to press the following
argument in the strongest possible terms.

Most candid observers of school desegregation trends now
clearly perceive a growing readiness on the part of the public
to accept the inevitability of school desegregation. This trend
is apparently not understood by the President, the Secretary of
HEW, the Attorney General or the anti-busing elements in the
Congress. Boston's violence is proving to be the spur to a number
of cities across the nation to develop voluntary leadership.
Some examples are Detroit, Denver, Cleveland, Columbus and
Pontiac.

Denver

Judge Doyle, as a part of his order, created a bi-racial
community council, consisting of school representatives, labor,
business, religous and other community-minded persons. This
council regularly reports to the court on its activities in the
area of problem solving, community education and rumor control.
He has stated publicly on many occasions that this council has
been of enormous assistance to the court in obtaining peaceful

Mr. Roy Wilkins
June 10, 1976
Page 11

constructive compliance. So impressed is he that he has

gone to such meetings as the National Institute of Education

to discuss its success.

Detroit

The New Detroit Committee, facing the inevitability of

a school desegregation decree, mobilized that community in a

highly significant way to create a climate of acceptance.

Leaders of business, industry, labor, church, parent organizations

and the like came together and as a result the January desegre-

gation went off smoothly.

Cleveland

In anticipation of a court finding that the Cleveland

schools - where over 90% of all black children are in schools

90 to 100% identifiably black and 90% of white pupils are similarly

isolated, the Cleveland Foundation funded two projects to educate

the community on the subject of desegregation. The two major
                              and
daily newspapers,/television and radio stations have been a part

of the process. The Greater Cleveland Interchurch Council has

been working with neighborhood groups while the Study Group on

Racial Isolation has engaged in extensive research and community

education. A third group, Clearinghouse for Racial Isolation

has recently been formed to supplement the other efforts.

In addition, Bishop Hickey of the Roman Catholic Diocese,

Bishop John Burt of the Episcopal Diocese, Dr. Donal Jacobs of

the Inter-city Church Council, and Rabbi Silver of the Rabbinical

Board, have been meeting together on a regular basis to devise

a joint effort to assist in peaceful constructive acceptance

of the court order.

Mr. Roy Wilkins
June 10, 1976
Page 12

Columbus

The Columbus, Ohio, Chamber of Commerce, for two years, has had an education task force hard at work gathering as much information as possible on desegregation. It has, along with other groups,   taken the leadership role in preparing the community in the event the court rules that the Columbus schools are segregated in violation of the Constitution.

Boston

Contrary to the common impression about Boston, much of a positive nature is going on in that school system as a direct result of the court order. For instance the judge created, along the lines of the Denver approach, a city-wide citizen monitoring counsel as well as district advisory councils, bi-racial and ethnically representative in makeup, involving parents and community representatives. This is a classic and authentic example of true community involvement in the educational system.

Illinois State Board of Education - Supt. Cronin

The actions undertaken by the Illinois State Board of Education, under the leadership of Superintendent Cronin, holds much promise. The state is providing stimulus to the various school districts within Illinois to initiate affirmative action to end racial segregation in the schools. This is a difficult undertaking, but it is proceeding.

Other Examples

Much of what is now being done in these Northern communities is patterned after the successful techniques attempted in the

Mr. Roy Wilkins
June 10, 1976
Page 13

South. The experience of Pontiac, after a traumatic beginning,
shows what can be done when educators and leaders join in
supporting the court orders. In Pontiac, there was a praise-
worthy step taken by Junior High pupils themselves to deal with
problems. Two of these students, Kim Perry and John Bueno,
addressed the January meeting of the Leadership Conference.

Their testimony, along with that from Nan Parate of
Charlotte, Richard Wolf of Prince Georges County and Belinda
Shivers of South Boston.

Vacillation on the part of national leaders, subtle
signals, or even worse, outright support by government officials
of those resisting court orders, seriously undercut the
courageous leadership roles now being played by local citizens.

Notes

Preface: Why This Book?

1. A. Leon Higginbotham Jr., *Shades of Freedom, Racial Politics and Presumptions of the American Legal Process* (New York: Oxford University Press, 1996), 195–96.

Chapter 1: The Call

1. Oswald Garrison Villard, *The Call in NAACP: Triumphs in a Pressure Group, 1909–1980* (Smithtown: Exposition Press, Inc.).
2. Ibid.
3. Ibid.
4. "Lift Every Voice and Sing," poem by James Weldon Johnson (1899), lyrics by John Rosamond Johnson (1900).

Chapter 3: Becoming a Civil Rights Activist

1. Gunnar Myrdal, *An American Dilemma: The Negro Problem of Modern Democracy* (New York: Harper & Brothers, 1944).

Chapter 5: Political Solutions to Racial Tensions

1. Taylor Branch, *Parting the Waters: America in the King Years 1954–63* (New York: Simon & Schuster, 1988), 366.
2. National Advisory Commission on Civil Disorders, *Report of the National Advisory Commission on Civil Disorders* (Washington, D.C., U.S. Government Printing Office, 1968), 265.

3. Marie Smith, "Eartha Kitt Confronts the Johnsons," *Washington Post*, January 19, 1968, A1, A4.

4. National Advisory Commission on Civil Disorders, *Report of the National Advisory Commission on Civil Disorders*, 143.

5. Ibid., 5.

6. Ibid., 11.

Chapter 6: Cutting My Teeth as NAACP General Counsel

1. Lewis Steel, "Nine Men in Black Who Think White," *New York Times Magazine*, October 13, 1968, 56.

2. "The Search for Military Justice, Report of an NAACP Inquiry into the Problems of the Negro Servicemen in West Germany," NAACP Special Contribution Fund, April 22, 1971.

3. Thomas Johnson, "Black Legal Help for GI's Is Urged: Use of Negro Attorneys Urged at Trials of GI's in Germany," *New York Times*, February 15, 1971.

4. Nathaniel R. Jones and C.E. Hutchins Jr., *Report of the Task Force on the Administration of Military Justice in Armed Forces*, report presented to Secretary of Defense Melvin R. Laird, November 30, 1972 (Washington, DC: U.S. Government Printing Office, 1972), 2, 38.

5. Ibid., 48.

6. Dorothy Parker, "Arrangement in Black and White," *New Yorker*, October 8, 1927, 22.

7. Walter White, *A Man Called White* (1948; Athens, GA: University of Georgia Press, 1995), 127.

Chapter 7: Desegregation and the Road to the North: Shifting Legal Strategies—from *Plessy* to *Sweatt* to *Brown*

1. Roy Wilkins, *Standing Fast: The Autobiography of Roy Wilkins* (New York: Viking Press, 1982), 195–96.

2. *Sweatt v. Painter*, 399 U.S. 629 (1950).

3. Genna Rae McNeil, *Groundwork: Charles Hamilton Houston and the Struggle for Civil Rights* (Philadelphia: University of Pennsylvania Press, 1983), 132.

4. *Brown v. Board of Education*, 347 U.S. 483(1954).

5. Warren D. St. James, *NAACP: Triumphs of a Pressure Group, 1909–1980* (Smithtown, NY: Exposition Press, Inc., 1980), 50.

6. NAACP, *Annual Report, 1954*, NAACP Collection, from the Collections of the Manuscript Division, Library of Congress, Washington, D.C.

7. *Swann v. Charlotte-Mecklenburg Board of Education*, 402 U.S. 1, 28 (1971).

8. Jon Nordheimer, "N.A.A.C.P. Shifts in School Fight," *New York Times*, February 25, 1973.

9. Bishop Stephen Gill Spottswood and Roy Wilkins, telegram to Lonnie King, February 28, 1973, NAACP Collection, from the Collections of the Manuscript Division, Library of Congress, Washington, D.C.

10. William Raspberry, "The NAACP: Moving to Defuse the Busing Issue," *Washington Post* February 29, 1973.

11. Nathaniel R. Jones, memorandum to Roy Wilkins, February 26, 1973, NAACP Collection, from the Collections of the Manuscript Division, Library of Congress, Washington, D.C.

12. Nathaniel R. Jones, letter to Lonnie King, February 28, 1973, NAACP Collection, from the Collections of the Manuscript Division, Library of Congress, Washington, D.C.

13. Charles Hamilton Houston, "Segregated Educational System Hit," unidentified clipping, n.d. [c. 1935], Charles Hamilton Houston Family Collection, Houston Residence, Washington, D.C, quoted in McNeil, *Groundwork*, 134.

14. Nathaniel R. Jones, letters to the editors, *Yale Law Journal* 85 (1976), as quoted in Howard I. Kalodner and James J. Fishman, *Limits of Justice* (Cambridge, MA: Ballinger Publishing Company, 1978), 615–16.

15. Derrick A. Bell Jr., response to December 8, 1976, letter by Nathaniel R. Jones, *Yale Law Journal* 85 (1976), as quoted in Kalodner and Fishman, *Limits of Justice*, 620.

Chapter 8: Beyond De Facto/De Jure: The Northern School Desegregation Cases

1. Genna Rae McNeil, *Groundwork: Charles Hamilton Houston and the Struggle for Civil Rights* (Philadelphia: University of Pennsylvania Press, 1983) 134.

2. Bradley v. Milliken, 484 F.2d 215, 242 (6th Cir. 1973) (*en banc*) (*affirming* both the finding of de jure segregation and the propriety of an interdistrict remedy). The Supreme Court granted certiorari and reversed in part. See Milliken v. Bradley, 418 U.S. 717 (1974) (*Milliken I*).

3. Ibid., 249–50.

4. Paul Dimond, *Beyond Busing* (Ann Arbor: The University of Michigan Press, 1985), 108–09.

5. *Milliken I.*

6. Ibid.

7. Bob Woodward and Scott Armstrong, *The Brethren: Inside the Supreme Court* (New York: Simon & Schuster, 1979).

8. *Milliken I*, 717, 759 (Douglas J., dissenting).

9. Ibid., 814–15 (Marshall, J., dissenting).

10. Columbus Board of Education. v. Penick, 443 U.S. 449, 459 (1979); Dayton Board of Education v. Brinkman, 443 U.S. 526 (1979); Oliver v. Kalamazoo Board

of Education, 706 F.2d 757 (6th Cir. 1983); Reed v. Rhodes, 607 F.2d 714 (6th Cir. 1979), *cert. denied*, 445 U.S. 935 (1980).

11. Milliken v. Bradley, 433 U.S. 267, 290, 293 (1977) (*Milliken II*).

12. Notes of the author, who attended the anniversary program and heard Judge Wright's address, in author's personal files.

13. Dayton Board of Education v. Brinkman, 443 U.S. 526 (1979).

14. Swann v. Charlotte-Mecklenburg Board of Education, 402 U.S. 1 (1971).

15. *Milliken I.*

16. James Barron, "Cleveland Ponders 'Petty Politics' After School Chief's Suicide, *New York Times*, January 30, 1985.

17. Morgan v. Hennigan, 379 F. Supp. 410, 172–73 (1972).

18. Nathaniel R. Jones, "Boston and Little Rock: The Issue Is the Same," *Washington Post*, January 3, 1975, A24.

19. Payne v. Tennessee, 501 U.S. 808, 844 (1991).

20. Nathaniel R. Jones, Testimony at Senate Committee on the Judiciary regarding the nomination of John G. Roberts Jr. to the U.S. Supreme Court, September 5, 2005, in author's personal files.

Chapter 9: The Road to the Court

1. Office of the White House Press Secretary, "Remarks of the President at a Reception in Observance of the 25th Anniversary of the Supreme Court's *Brown Versus Board of Education* Decision," May 17, 1979, in author's personal files.

2. Barry Horstman, "Jones' Appointment Symbolic Triumph," *Cincinnati Post*, May 18, 1979, 37.

3. Alliance for Justice, "Broadening the Bench: Professional Diversity and Judicial Nominations," July 10, 2015, 6.

4. In re Grand Jury Proceedings, 841 F.2d 1048 (1988).

5. Ibid.

6. W.E.B. Du Bois, *The Souls of Black Folk* (New York: New American Library, 1969), 17.

Chapter 10: Continuing the Struggle, on the Bench

1. U.S. v. Gaines, 122 F.3d 324, (1997).

2. Order in Re. John Byrd No. 01-3927, October 19, 2001.

3. Byrd v. Bagley, 37 Fed. Appx. 94, 2002 U.S. App. LEXIS 2629 (6th Cir. Ohio 2002).

4. Cooper v. Brown, 565 F.3d 581 (9th Cir. 2007).

5. Crater v. Galaza, 508 F.3d 1261 (9th Cir. 2007).

6. David Grann, "Trial by Fire," *New Yorker*, September 7, 2009.

Chapter 11: Beyond the United States

1. Kenneth S. Broun, *Black Lawyers, White Courts: The Soul of South African Law* (Columbus: Ohio University Press), as quoted in the *American Lawyer*, November 1999, 80–86.

Chapter 12: Beyond the Bench

1. Judge Nathaniel R. Jones and Dean Joseph P. Tomain, "Shut Down Cincinnati? Dr. King Would Say No," *Cincinnati Enquirer*, May 26, 2001.

Chapter 13: Life After the Bench

1. *Northwest Austin Municipal Utility District No. 1 v. Holder*, 557 U.S. 193 (2009).

Chapter 14: Justice Clarence Thomas and the Supreme Double Cross

1. Associated Press, "Text: If Not for Others, 'I Would Not Be Here,'" *Los Angeles Times*, September 11, 1991.

2. Ibid., emphasis mine.

3. The Thirteenth Amendment banned slavery. The Fourteenth Amendment expanded citizenship to former slaves and their descendants, effectively overruling the *Dred Scott* decision, and guaranteed blacks guaranteed due process to the former slaves. The Fifteenth Amendment prohibited the denial of voting rights based on race.

4. Claude Sitton interview with Jack Bass, as quoted in Jack Bass, *Unlikely Heroes* (Tuscaloosa: University of Alabama Press, 1981), 15.

5. Clarence Thomas, "Black Americans Based Claim for Freedom on Constitution," *San Diego Union*, October 6, 1987.

6. Dr. John Hope Franklin, "Booker T. Washington Revisited," *New York Times*, August 1991.

7. Haywood Burns, "Clarence Thomas, a Counterfeit Hero," *New York Times*, July 9, 1991, A15.

8. Jeffrey Toobin, "The Burden of Clarence Thomas," *New Yorker*, September 27, 1993, 38, 46.

9. *Nomination of Judge Clarence Thomas to Be Associate Justice of the Supreme Court of the United States, Hearings Before the Committee on the Judiciary*, 102nd Cong. 115 (September 10, 11, 12, 13, and 16, 1991).

10. Kevin Merida and Michael A. Fletcher, "Supreme Discomfort; More Than a Decade After His Bitter Confirmation Battle, African Americans Are Still

Judging Clarence Thomas Guilty. Is That Justice?," *Washington Post*, August 4, 2002.

11. "The Youngest, Cruelest Justice," editorial, *New York Times*, February 27, 1992.

12. Leon Higginbotham Jr., "An Open Letter to Justice Clarence Thomas from a Federal Judicial Colleague," *University of Pennsylvania Law Review* 1005 (1992): 140.

13. William Raspberry, "Confounding One's Supporters," *Washington Post*, February 28, 1992.

14. Nathaniel R. Jones, "The Sisyphean Impact on Houstonian Jurisprudence," *University of Cincinnati Law Review* 60, no. 2 (Winter 2001): 445–46.

15. City of Richmond v. J. A. Croson Company, 488 U.S. 469, 551–52, 559 (1989,).

16. Grutter v. Bollinger, 539 U.S. 306 (2003).

17. Nathaniel R. Jones, testimony at Senate Judiciary Committee, September 15, 2005, from author's personal files.

18. Detroit Police Officers' Association v. Young, 608 F.2d 671 (6th Cir., 1979).

19. Adarand Constructors, Inc. v. Peña, 515 U.S. 200 (1995).

20. Regents of Univ. of California v. Bakke, 438 U.S. 265, 407 (1978).

21. Parents Involved in Community Schools v. Seattle School District No. 1, et al. and Crystal D. Meredith v. Jefferson County Board of Education, et al., 551 U.S. 701, 40–41 (2007).

22. Jones, testimony at Senate Judiciary Committee, September 15, 2005.

23. Swann v. Charlotte-Mecklenburg Board of Education, 402 U.S. 1, 28 (1971).

Chapter 15: Obama: Election Reflections

1. Stephanie J. Jones, "Sunday Morning Apartheid: A Diversity Study of the Sunday Morning Talk Shows," in *State of Black America 2007* (Silver Spring, MD: Beckham Publications Group, 2007), 11.

2. Nixon v. Herndon, 273 U.S. 536 (1927).

3. Lane v. Wilson, 307 U.S. 268 (1939).

4. Grovey v. Townsend, 295 U.S. 45 (1935).

5. Smith v. Allwright, 321 U.S. 649, 664 (1944).

6. Gilbert Jonas, *Freedom's Sword* (New York: Routledge, 2005), 227.

7. Langston Hughes, "I, Too," in *The Collected Poems of Langston Hughes* (New York, NY: Knopf Doubleday Publishing Group, a division of Penguin Random House LLC, 1994).

Index